EMPTY SKY

EMPTY
SKY

EMPTY SKY

RAF VOICES FROM THE FALL OF FRANCE AND BATTLE OF BRITAIN

Colin Higgs and Bruce Vigar

AIR WORLD

AIR WORLD

EMPTY SKY
RAF Voices from the Fall of France and Battle of Britain

First published in Great Britain in 2020 by
Air World
An imprint of
Pen & Sword Books Ltd
Yorkshire – Philadelphia

ISBN 978 1 52674 771 6

SJmagic DESIGN SERVICES, India.

Printed and bound in the UK by TJ International Ltd.

Pen & Sword Books Limited incorporates the imprints of Atlas, Archaeology, Aviation, Discovery, Family History, Fiction, History, Maritime, Military, Military Classics, Politics, Select, Transport, True Crime, Air World, Frontline Publishing, Leo Cooper, Remember When, Seaforth Publishing, The Praetorian Press, Wharncliffe Local History, Wharncliffe Transport, Wharncliffe True Crime and White Owl.

For a complete list of Pen & Sword titles please contact

PEN & SWORD BOOKS LIMITED
47 Church Street, Barnsley, South Yorkshire, S70 2AS, England
E-mail: enquiries@pen-and-sword.co.uk
Website: www.pen-and-sword.co.uk

Or
PEN AND SWORD BOOKS
1950 Lawrence Rd, Havertown, PA 19083, USA
E-mail: Uspen-and-sword@casematepublishers.com
Website: www.penandswordbooks.com

Contents

This book is dedicated to two pilots who fought in the Battle of Britain
who followed the same education path as the author:

Pilot officer Henry W Moody RAFVR 602 Squadron
20 May 1910 - 7 September 1940
(Shrewsbury House School, Surbiton)

&

Air Commodore James Baird Coward AFC 19 Squadron
18 May 1915 - 25 July 2012
(St. John's Leatherhead)

Introduction

'The sky's very large because you'd see these things going on one minute and twenty seconds later you wouldn't see an aircraft for some reason, only the big black cloud of the bombers, you'd see them going, but the sky would empty very quickly.'

Tony Pickering

This was a common memory of the fighter pilots we met and whose interviews appear in this book. The idea that one minute the sky would be full of aeroplanes weaving and twisting to gain advantage over each other and the next it would be empty.

It seems to sum up the contradictory nature of air combat in 1940, frantic action followed by quiet and calm. It also sums up the difference in nature of the many Battle of Britain veterans we interviewed over the years since 1998.

Our first experience of interviewing a Battle of Britain pilot was with Allan Wright at his farm on the Cornwall/Devon border. Not the easiest baptism of fire as he answered my first question by saying he thought it was 'a bloody silly question'. However he went on to tell us in fascinating detail about his time on 92 Squadron at Biggin Hill including his first combat experiences during the Dunkirk operation. Unlike the men who had created a reputation for the squadron, who were described by Geoffrey Wellum as 'a load of playboys. Ill-disciplined, red linings to our tunics and that sort of thing', Allan was the quiet type who needed sleep rather than alcohol for his analytical brain.

In the early 2000s Bruce and I were lucky enough to go and interview the pugnacious Pete Brothers who was already flying Hurricanes in 32 Squadron at the outbreak of war and continued throughout the battles of 1940. Arriving at his door we were left in no doubt that he did not feel very well and that we could have only an hour before we would have to leave. As Bruce set up the camera and lighting equipment Pete showed me a few of his prized possessions on the mantlepiece, an invitation to the Palace and a picture of his late wife, Annette. As we started the interview Pete lit a cigar, jutted out his jaw and told us it was tough if we didn't like him smoking during the interview.

By lunchtime he was well into it and in need of a trip to the local pub. Generally that means a slow interview wind-down after lunch but for Pete it just moved his memory into overdrive. It was five o'clock before we left him, still with a whisky in one hand and a cigar in the other.

As with Allan Wright and Pete Brothers we were never disappointed by any of the interviews we undertook with Battle of France, Dunkirk and Battle of Britain veterans. They gave freely of their memories and, despite forgetting the odd name or date, it was amazing how much of that momentous summer they could remember. But then for them it was etched forever. Close knit groups of men who lived and died together, drank together and won together.

Having fought their battles in the Summer of 1940 they spread far and wide into all continents and theatres of war. Bob Foster helped defend Australia; Billy Drake fought and flew in West Africa and the Western Desert; two were made prisoners of war, Terence Kane during the battle and David Denchfield in early 1941; many went on to convert to Beaufighters and Mosquitos, or continued with later mark Spitfires and Hurricanes; and virtually all were responsible at one point for passing on their experiences to future pilots as instructors.

I should add that we interviewed the wonderful Hazel Gregory, whose memories appear in this book as well. Her Battle of Britain was spent deep in the plotting room at RAF Uxbridge under the gaze of Keith Park and with an occasional visit from the prime minister, Winston Churchill. Her insight into the day-to-day activities of the WAAFs at Uxbridge adds something extra and special to the story. Her career blossomed as befitted an intelligent woman. She worked extensively at Bletchley Park and then became a trusted assistant in the Air Ministry taking the minutes of the pre-D-Day planning meetings.

We tried to get a cross-section of stories. We were lucky to contact John Gard'ner when he had travelled from New Zealand for the 70th anniversary commemorations in 2010. He was the last of the ill-fated Defiant pilots of 141 Squadron who had been shot down en masse while protecting a convoy in the English Channel. Terry Clark talked about the frustration of flying most nights in a Blenheim and never seeing the enemy until he converted to Beaufighters. William Walker and New Zealander Keith Lawrence talked with great emotion about being shot down over the sea

INTRODUCTION

while David Denchfield, who saw little action, spoke of his fellow pilots in 610 Squadron, their training, their humour and their day-to-day activities.

Together the interviews make a fascinating, poignant and emotional set of personal accounts of the air battles of 1940. This is not a history of the period, far from it. In fact when asked about their memories of certain days, 12 August or perhaps 15 September, they found it hard to remember specifics. What had stayed with them in vivid detail were events such as their first combat, or their first sight of the enemy, and definitely when they were shot down or shot down one of the enemy.

At the time of writing the book just one of the interviewees was still with us. Sadly Terry Clark, who passed the milestone of his 100th birthday in April 2019, passed away on the eve of VE Day commemorations on 7 May 2020. To all the veterans we thank you for your service, your spirit and your inspiration.

Colin Higgs
May 2020

Acknowledgments

The authors would like to thank the many people who made this book possible.

Group Captain Patrick Tootal OBE DL, Honorary Secretary of the Battle of Britain Memorial and Fighter Association, who forwarded letters, advised and was a great supporter of our wish to interview many who were involved with the Battle of Britain.

The Battle of Britain Historical Society, and the many other associations and individuals who provided so much help, enthusiasm and advice.

Colin Hudson and Caroline Fowler from Aces High Gallery in Wendover who introduced us to many of their Battle of Britain friends and assisted with contact with many of the veterans. Their continuing ability to bring the ever dwindling number of World War 2 veterans to meet the public should be supported as much as possible.

Bob Cossey, secretary of the 74 Squadron Association, for his assistance with the John Freeborn chapter.

Mike Jowett and Terry Book, and Aces High, for allowing us to use their photographs of the veterans taken at various events at Aces High.

Of course our single biggest thanks go to the veterans themselves. From 1998 onwards we travelled all over the country to interview these great RAF veterans. They welcomed us into their homes, made copious pots of tea and mugs of coffee, brought out their logbooks and gave of their memories freely.

Author's Preface

Empty Sky is based on interviews with surviving veterans who served with the RAF during the Battle of France, Dunkirk and the Battle of Britain in 1940. All of them went on to talk about the rest of their careers with the service.

Because they are personal accounts rather than cold histories, what and why certain events and details are recalled more vividly than others is dependent on how the individuals regarded them. The accounts are about what mattered to them.

All the accounts have been taken from filmed and recorded interviews. These interviews have then been transcribed and edited. Wherever possible the historical accuracy of the accounts has been checked but it may be that the passage of time means that some names, dates or places are inaccurate. Apart from occasional interlinking sentences the accounts are in their own words.

The rank given at the start of each chapter is the highest rank attained by the interviewee while in the Royal Air Force.

Please note that the views and accounts stated in this book do not in any way reflect the beliefs and personal opinions of the author, publishers or anyone else associated with the compilation of the work.

Air Commodore Peter Brothers
CBE DSO DFC*

30 September 1917-18 December 2008

Peter Malam Brothers, always known as Pete, was born in Prestwich in Lancashire and educated at North Manchester School.

I joined the Royal Air Force because, as a child, a small boy, I played with aeroplanes. I couldn't be doing with toy railways. Fine little aircraft. My father was hoping I'd get over this idea of aviation. In due course I was still at school, rising 16 and he said, 'For your sixteenth birthday present you're going to learn to fly and then you will get bored with the idea,' and so I learned to fly and didn't get bored. Just as soon as I was seventeen and a half, the minimum age, I applied to join the air force and I had my medicals and so on. By then I'd done just over 100 hours flying and into the air force where they took me through training school and in October 1936 I was posted to Biggin Hill.

It was the greatest flying club there was. A lot of competition between us to do aerobatics and that sort of thing and, of course, you were training with the squadron, formation flying and battle flying and tactics and fighter against fighter. It was just a relaxed life. You were on parade at eight o'clock, colour hoisting, prayers and then you went and sat in the pilots' room, waited for your order of the day and usually took off about ten o'clock, flew for an hour, came down, had coffee. If you were lucky you would do another sortie before lunch and then at twelve o'clock over to the mess, have lunch, two o'clock back on the squadron and probably one flight in the afternoon because you packed up for tea at four o'clock. The only grind was in the evening you were in the mess. You were allowed out for sports, sports afternoon was Wednesday, so you only flew in the morning then you packed up and played some sort of sport, whatever your choice was. Wednesday evening you were allowed to dine in dinner jacket. Monday and Tuesday you had to put on the full mess kit and Thursday and Friday you were allowed to dine in dinner jacket or you were allowed to go off for the weekend. So you had a pretty busy time but very amusing.

1

Biggin Hill was a wonderful place. It had the disadvantage of being on the hill so you got a lot of low cloud which meant there was no flying particularly if it was on the ground. You were within easy reach of London so on your Wednesday evening or Friday off you could nip into London, go to a cinema or what have you and it was all great fun.

32 Squadron formed in 1916 and spent the next twenty years, less a short time of disbandment, as a premier fighter squadron. Successively, after their SE5As of 1917 and 18, they flew Sopwith Snipes, the duo of Gloster fighters, the Grebe and Gamecock, the Siskin, Bulldog and eventually the Gloster Gauntlet, the latest fighter and last open cockpit fighter in RAF service.

The aircraft we flew then were pretty old hat now, biplane Gloster Gauntlets which were great fun for aerobatics and so on. Terribly cold when you climbed up to 30,000ft or so because there was no heating so you got pretty jolly frozen despite wearing gloves but a delightful aeroplane.

Air Pageants, Empire Air Day, was the thing and all RAF stations opened to the public and, of course, the only way you could interest the public was by flying and so you laid on air shows, aerobatics. One of our very senior sergeant pilots dressed himself up as a foreigner, rushed out and leaped into an aircraft that was sitting there with the engine running and stole it and then did a crazy flying display pretending he didn't have a clue how to fly it. All that sort of thing and I think we made some money for the benevolent fund. That was a lot of fun. I was doing synchronised aerobatics with a friend of mine. The squadron commander selected us to do this business of opposite loops and rolls and so on and so we had a lot of fun practising this and the OC came and checked it out, decided it was good enough for public display so we were allowed to go ahead. It was camaraderie, confidence in yourself and your aircraft and your chum who was flying with you in opposite directions to make sure you didn't collide with each other. It was a great thing and a lot of interest was shown. A lot of people came to watch the displays.

On a more serious note the pilots of 32 Squadron also had knowledge of the innovative radar system being built in the UK under the auspices of Fighter Command. As early as 1936 the Gauntlets were used for radar interceptions to test the fledgling system.

We had, pre-war, been practising in sections. We were the first and only squadron to start with to operate with radar. We used to intercept incoming airliners from the continent and pretend we just happened to be in the same piece of airspace as they were at that time. We weren't allowed to approach them closely but we had to report when we first sighted them, how far away they were, and what height and so on, which was checking on the radar stations, who were directing us. We knew it was radar, it was called RDF in those days, Radio Direction Finding, and it was backed up by ground transmitters and receivers. One of us to start off with would have to give a transmission for thirty seconds every three minutes and you had a stopwatch. If you were the detailed squeaker, as we called it, when the stopwatch came up, you switched on your transmitter and transmitted for thirty seconds so the ground control stations could get a cross bearing on the plot where you were which was compared with what the radar was saying, how accurate it was and so on. Officially we weren't allowed to talk about it but apparently, and I didn't know this, I learned after the war, we weren't even supposed to mention it even in our flying logbooks, but I used to put it down, RDF exercise.

Without it how were you going to intercept incoming aircraft? You'd have to have standing patrols waiting and then when the raid came in you were probably going to be on the ground refuelling and you hadn't got enough aircraft to keep standing patrols going the whole time so it was vital. In fact we would have been in a very poor situation if we hadn't got radar.

Then of course, in 1938, in the spring we got our first Hurricanes and that was a tremendous advantage because it meant, when the war started, we knew that aeroplane inside out, we knew what it could do and what it couldn't do which I think was the secret of our survival. One interesting thing was, in 1940, that although the chaps in the squadron were shot down, wounded and some burnt, nobody was killed, they all survived 1940 which was quite extraordinary. I put it down to the fact that we had the aeroplane early enough to really know what it could do and so we used it to great advantage.

But Pete's first impression of the new monoplane fighter was not all good.

First views, oh dear, I didn't like being shut in for a start with a closed hood over the top. But you got used to it pretty quickly. It meant it was a bit warmer. It was still jolly cold at altitude and of course the performance, the speed, was so much different from the old biplane that it was a great machine to fly. You each had your own aircraft and if your aircraft was being serviced you didn't fly so you had a bond between yourself and that particular aeroplane. If you had to fly somebody else's for some reason you didn't like it much.

One joy Pete rejoiced in when war came was making his own modifications to his Hurricane.

I thought it was fun. I took the rear view mirror off the outside as it was obviously going to cause drag and bought myself one of those curved car

3

mirrors with a wide angle view and mounted that inside the windscreen at the top and the chaps managed to make a fitting that would hold it. Spitfires were flush riveted on the wings and the Hurricanes were pop riveted so those little bumps used to annoy me. I got cracking with my rigger and we'd sit on the wing and we'd polish off the top of the bumps, not too far or you're going to weaken the whole structure, but you took a bit off, and there were a lot of them, I reckon I got about an extra five miles an hour out of that aircraft by taking the mirror off and filing down the pop rivets.

Pete became a flight commander in 1938 and was ready for war when it came on 3 September 1939.

We knew war was coming and when war was declared as it happened we were out on the airfield; we dispersed our aircraft away from hangars and obvious targets. I made the mistake, when the local civilian air-raid warnings went off, I scrambled with my flight because, of course, I didn't want to be caught on the ground as had been happening in Poland. I got into trouble over that because the station commander said 'I'll tell you when you can fly,' and obviously it had to be kept under some sort of control.

We were indeed the front line. Obviously anything coming in from the continent was going to enter Kent first and, of course, we were close to the channel where there was an awful lot of our shipping which the Germans took exception to. They started to bomb so we had to fly convoy patrols which became exciting when the Germans decided to do the same and bomb it so we had quite a lot of engagements in that respect before they ever started flying over the UK or entering our airspace.

Almost immediately pre-arranged plans were set in action.

On day two after war was declared I was detailed to go to West Malling, a civil airfield, and commandeer it and seize control of all the civil aircraft that were there and tell the private owners who owned them to piss off. I had to write a report on what equipment was there, how many fire extinguishers, how many buckets of sand and all the details of the club house building, was there accommodation in the club house and so on. It became a satellite airfield of Biggin Hill, not that we ever used it because there was no point for us but obviously the thought was if we were bombed out of Biggin Hill it was an alternative airfield we could use.

However the squadron's main base was Biggin Hill, a sector airfield on the borders of south-east London and Kent.

That meant that it had its own operations room and was directly tied up to 11 Group headquarters, the operations room there. We would have our own plotting board and we would get landline information from the radar of incoming aircraft which would be plotted and 11 Group would tell us and the raid would be given a number by group headquarters. Then it would be decided that Biggin Hill would handle that particular raid and so then we'd be scrambled to deal with it. Prior to that, in peacetime, when we were experimenting we had an operations room with a blackboard and those pilots who weren't flying were plotters and finally the station commander was the controller and I would be flying. I remember, the radio would come on, 'Dunbar leader, Dunbar leader. Vector, Vector...how can I see the fucking blackboard with your fat arse in the way?' (laughing) It was some poor pilot who was putting crosses on the blackboard for the raid. Those were the very early and amusing days and it became very pleasurable which was good.

Both the declaration of war and the eventual German attack on France in May 1940 offered a strange kind of relief to Pete and many of the other pilots.

There was a feeling of relief in a way. Before war was declared you were sometimes called to readiness to man your aircraft for no apparent reason and told you had to sleep in the dispersal hut, that sort of thing, and so it was a great relief when war was declared and you could then say right well now we can get organised and we know what we're doing.

Were we expecting it? Difficult to say but of course we hadn't really thought about it and of course then there was the Battle of France going on and our sister squadron from Biggin Hill was moved to France. Late on, after 10 May when the German advance was so rapid, we were sent out to reinforce in France and we would fly out at first light, leave Biggin Hill in the dark, fly to France, land where we'd been told to land at some little airfield, refuel, which we had to do ourselves from tins because we had no ground crew with us, and then we would operate. But it became chaos. We couldn't get any orders or instructions because the headquarters was constantly on the move, retreating, and food, nothing had been arranged. One of our pilots was fluent in French and I remember he managed to beg some bread from a farmhouse near the airfield, which was all we got that day, and we would fly back as it was getting dark, land back at Biggin Hill just about in the dark. By that time, of course, you'd been up since four o'clock in the morning and you got back about ten o'clock to half past ten at night, have a meal, go to bed, be shaken awake again about half past three, get up, get washed and shaved, down to have a quick snack breakfast and off onto the airfield and take off for France. That was very tedious, very tiring and we didn't feel we were making any great contribution because we only had the odd engagement.

We were on a French airfield one day and we were refuelling with tins and a French fighter aircraft was doing aerobatics over the airfield. A German bomber, a Dornier 17, steamed over the airfield at about 2,000 feet and we thought he was going to come back, bomb us and catch us all on the ground. Fortunately he had a plan and he was going somewhere else but we said to the French base commander who was standing nearby, 'Look, a German aircraft and you have an aircraft doing aerobatics. Tell him, he's obviously not seen the German,' and the French base commander said, 'Today he is only authorised for aerobatics and not combat,' and so we thought, 'That's a great help. We look forward to the help of the French Air Force, thank you very much.'

We didn't rearm. We hadn't had a chance to fire at anything and if we had, well that was it because we had no spare ammunition with us and I doubt we had the ability to load the guns ourselves anyway. Also we only had about eight seconds, maybe ten seconds (of ammunition) and that was it. You'd used it all.

On 17 May the Luftwaffe bombed the northern French city of Cambrai. The following day Pete's squadron was patrolling the area when he scored his first aerial victory.

We were jumped by a bunch of 109s; they were going in the opposite direction actually. We saw these little black specks and I thought they were oil specks on the windshield at first and then of course they were growing in size rapidly. I can visualise it now. One of them swept over the top of me, only about twenty feet above and there was this Messerschmitt 109, you could see the oil streaks on the fuselage and so on, he was so close, and you said, 'God where's he going?' You looked over your shoulder and watched and there he was climbing up, turning round and starting to dive on us. He missed me and overshot and I got onto his tail. I was lucky, I was also lucky that I aimed better than he did; and he didn't catch fire, he just went on going down until he hit the ground so that was that. By then the squadron had scattered all over the sky in various different combats and I had fired my guns, I had no ammunition, so I just went back to Biggin Hill on my own, there and then.

It was very tiring indeed and no, I don't think it was particularly effective. The trouble was there was no control in France by then. The squadrons that were based there, they were out of touch but they knew the lay of the land better and they would just go off on patrols having decided they ought to do something and we did the same after the first couple of days. We thought there was no point in hanging around and sitting on the ground so we would fly around looking for enemy activity and of course the first thing we came across was roads crowded with refugees. In fact our first airfield we used was in Belgium and there was a flight of aircraft there, British, who were based there and they were very jumpy when we arrived. The reason they were jumpy was because when they were called to readiness in the morning one of the sergeant pilots didn't appear so they went to roust him out of bed and he was in bed with a knife in his chest, dead. They reckoned this was either a fifth columnist who'd got in and killed him or maybe somebody who was one of the refugees from the road who was hoping to grab something valuable. Anyhow they were walking round looking behind themselves all the time and we were a bit new to that. We only had one day there and by the following day the Germans were getting too close and the resident squadron had already pulled out, I think it pulled out the same time we went back to Biggin Hill.

We didn't learn much about the Germans because we didn't see much of them. Apart from that one engagement when I shot something down you didn't meet them. We didn't see them apart from the German bomber when we were sitting on the French airfield refuelling, that's it. We hadn't started our own aircraft. The Hurricane had two handles which went in each side and our drill was, as flight commander, mine would be started first, I'd get in the cockpit, two of my chums would wind the handles and start it and then I'd get out and leave it running and go and wind the handles on somebody else's aircraft until we'd got them all running. Not a way to run a fighting unit.

At the end of May the squadron got involved in operations covering the troops on the beaches of Dunkirk.

Dunkirk was an absolute eye-opener. A smoking city covered almost in a pall of smoke. It brought home to me that war was not going to be all that funny. There was the Odeon cinema in Calais burning nicely, you thought that could be our local Odeon in Bromley. This is not good enough. I don't like this and it's very serious and then, of course, there were the poor troops not only on the beach but in the water scrambling out, neck deep in the water trying to get on small boats and get away. We didn't hang about over Dunkirk. We tried to get inland a bit to intercept aircraft before they got to Dunkirk. There was no point in sitting over the target and catching the chap just as he was dropping his bombs, that was too late. You wanted to get in before that so you were trying to operate about ten miles further inland from Dunkirk itself but it was quite a shattering experience to see what was taking place.

32 Squadron's war was already becoming relentless.

Well we covered Dunkirk and after Dunkirk we started using Hawkinge. For some reason during the lull that occurred while the Germans were obviously getting reorganised we moved to Hawkinge every day. We then did a 'fly the flag' operation from there, down the French coast to Rouen and back again and apparently the idea was to show the Germans we were still in existence despite having cleared out of France, and it was pointless. In fact it was jolly dangerous and we lost people because the Germans would just have another cup of coffee when they saw us flying out and down the coast and by the time we had turned round for home at Rouen and set off back, of course the sun was behind us which was no way to get mixed up with the enemy. The Germans took off, climbed up into the sun and got behind us where we couldn't see them and then they'd start picking us off. We lost several chaps that way and, in fact, after a few days of this, fortunately the AOC Air Vice Marshal Park arrived in his Hurricane to see how we were getting on. I'm afraid I was a bit short tempered because I was tired and because I was frightened and told him what I thought of this ridiculous operation and the next day we were not called on to do it again which was a great relief.

It was during these days that Pete saw the first signs of battle stress.

We had a chap at Hawkinge when we were doing these silly patrols flag-waving down the coast before the battle and I noticed this chap was covered in perspiration on his forehead and said, 'Are you alright? You look as though you've got flu or something,' and he said, 'No I'm alright.' So I sent him off to the sick quarters to go and see the doctor and that's the last I saw of him. The doctor appeared and said, 'He's cracking up. He thinks everything that's happened to everybody has happened to him. He's been shot down, burned and so on and he can't even fly his aeroplane back to Biggin Hill. You'll have to call somebody else in to do that,' and the chap vanished. It was what in those days was described as lack of moral fibre, LMF. He couldn't take it. However he had a different sort of courage. He couldn't face the enemy but he went testing rebuilt aircraft and he tested a Hurricane, took off but the controls had been reversed. A wing down so he automatically tried to pick it up but it just made it worse and he went into the ground, ghastly crash, smashed himself up, was in hospital for over a year, went back to testing rebuilt aircraft. He had great guts but in a different sort of way. He could face that but he couldn't face the Hun and face the thought of being set on fire and burned.

We then got mixed up with convoy patrols, protecting convoys, and of course Hawkinge was ideal as you'd get to Hawkinge, top up with fuel so that you were absolutely full and ready to go off on patrol. On the odd occasion we got scrambled because a convoy was being attacked and the previous squadron guarding it had obviously had to return and so there was a gap in the cover. That was quite exciting because the Germans were using Stuka dive bombers which were cat's meat if you could get at them but there was usually a heavy patrol of 109 fighters to protect the Stukas so every time you picked on a Stuka, before you got a chance to shoot at it you got a 109 behind you so you had to take great care.

One of the things one found irritating, to quite a degree, was to fly back from a convoy patrol having been jolly busy engaging German aircraft, and sweep over the beaches which were littered with girls in their swimming costumes sunning themselves. It made you want to shout loudly, 'Hey, there's a war on. Get stuck in.' That was quite interesting. The difference, if you like, between us at the time who were busy fighting and people on the ground who were sunbathing and enjoying themselves.

Facilities at Hawkinge were pretty sparse but it almost became a second home for the squadron.

Hawkinge was just a grass airfield. I think it had the odd hangar. All we had was a tent with a telephone and a chap manning the telephone. A few ground crew who did refuelling and were generally helpful but a lot of the time you were looking after your own aircraft. I remember we had to change a tail wheel on one aircraft which we did ourselves and I remember my engine was making funny noises and I took the cowlings off and I was taking the plugs out and putting them back, cleaning them first and that sort of thing. There was an interesting occasion when, to our surprise, there was a great bang, a great explosion and a cloud of earth somewhere far away from us but on the airfield. There were no aircraft and it wasn't a bomb but suddenly we realised we were being shelled from the French coast and the Germans had got a long range gun there so we didn't think much of that. We didn't wait for any instructions. We made our way back to Biggin Hill and said, 'Hey, we've got to do something about that gun. It's interfering with our comfort at Hawkinge.'

Nothing was done about the German guns at that time. Most of the targets for the German guns were ships but only two were ever sunk. During the war these guns fired more than 1,000 rounds. They were finally silenced in 1944.

Hawkinge I remember really vaguely. One day the CO was away and Mike was on leave so I was CO of the squadron. I remember a little airman ground crew with his little blue and red flags and of course the red flag was usually waved outside the tent where the telephone was for the CO to park his aircraft. Well I was CO but the poor little airman didn't know that.

I parked outside the tent and the poor little airman came trotting up out of breath. 'Sir, B flight is supposed to be parked up there,' and I said, 'Go and stick your fucking flight up your backside, I'm CO today,' and having calmed down a bit I got hold of one of the ground crew and said go and get him and bring him here and I apologised for being rude to him. He wasn't to know that B flight was the leading flight that day. It was convenient to us but that was it.

Difficult to describe because one has no special memories of Hawkinge. Some good ones being scrambled with the Huns bombing Dover harbour and Mike wrote in the squadron diary, 'Great dogfight going on. I was on the outside trying to get in and Pete shot down a 109 with a great splash and a great cheer from Pete.' The squadron diary was written in a light-hearted manner as only Mike could write it. Odd memories really. In particular, of convoy patrols. Of course, being so far forward at Hawkinge had its disadvantages. There were occasions when we virtually had to fly inland climbing for height in order to get our height to get at them because if we just headed towards them we would have passed miles underneath.

Despite their experience, and having seen plenty of action, the squadron pilots still had much to learn.

The squadron – well we were all, virtually all, pre-war – a few new boys came to join us and we had to look after them to the best of our abilities. Sadly they were usually the ones who got shot down when the fun began. They lacked the necessary experience and got picked off but otherwise the squadron's performance was first class, except it took us time to learn in a proper battle formation. We were still flying in display type vic formation and quite close to each other, too close, so you were monitoring your leader the whole time and your chaps were; the one next to you, your number two, was monitoring you and number three was monitoring him and nobody was really looking out and we realised after a while we were very slow. The Germans were flying in pairs, usually two pairs, widely spread out so they didn't have to concentrate on following their leader too closely. They could fly along looking round to see where we were and we were very slow in catching up with that wartime battle flying idea. We were using old-fashioned tactics which we had been trained to do of course.

Pete was with the squadron during the Battle of Britain until early September.

There wasn't such a thing as a typical day in the battle. You'd go to readiness at a prescribed time because they tried to rotate squadrons so that two squadrons on the station were not both being up at dawn. We'd usually be up at first light, out to the dispersal and the aircraft would be warmed up by the ground crew and you would sit around awaiting instructions.

You relaxed in the dispersal hut. You read or very often slept because you got very tired and so when I say slept it wasn't a deep sleep. You were really dozing I suppose. Played the gramophone, played chess and other odd games. To start off with we amused ourselves with physical games. We would give one of the chaps a Verey pistol which fired coloured lights, blindfold him and we'd all stand around in a circle and then he had to start turning round and round and round counting up to twenty and then he would fire his Verey pistol. That went on until one of the sergeant pilots got hit in the pants and burned a hole in the back of his trousers. Fortunately he wasn't injured but he had to go and get a new pair of trousers and word got out and that game had to be stopped. Just on the edge of the airfield where we were parking the aircraft there was a little sort of valley that was quite steep and one of the chaps had an old Austin Swallow saloon, a little old and more like a ball than a car. The thing was you had to take a passenger and you had to drive it to the top of the slope then drive it down full throttle and turn the steering wheel quickly and roll it and the winner was the chap who got the most rolls and this went on for a bit until somebody got badly cut by breaking glass, and the car was getting a bit beyond being rolled, so that game had to stop and it was back to chess or reading.

But then the telephone would ring so you'd always be on the alert, grabbing your helmet ready to run and you'd hear the chap answering the phone, 'No, Corporal Smith's gone to breakfast. He's not here I'm afraid,' and he'd put the phone down and we'd all relax. This would happen so frequently we'd say to each other, 'God, when this war's over I'm not going to have a damn telephone in my house.'

It was frustrating in the extreme and then of course you'd get the real call and the chap would suddenly shout, holding the telephone in his hand, '32 Squadron, patrol Ashford, Angels 15,' and you'd all rush out, get into your aircraft and the squadron commander lead off. You'd follow as flight commander with your flight and off you'd go to Ashford and probably before you got anywhere near Ashford you'd run into a German formation. It was quite startling when you first saw them, when you first saw several hundred bombers blackening the sky, and a horde of fighters sitting on top of them. So of course the squadron commander would lead in to attack the bombers. We would follow, by which time the German fighter escort had come down and started getting mixed up with us so you finished up trying to kill them as they tried to kill you. You didn't get much chance at the bombers, not as we were always the number two flight to attack, because A Flight, which the CO led, they'd go in first and B Flight were left to follow so only occasionally did we manage to break through and get a shot at the bomber formation.

The squadron also had to deal with landing back at an airfield that was often attacked.

We were landing between the flags of unexploded bombs on the airfield which were marked by a couple of WAAFs, bless them, who got decorated for their troubles. We were there when the ops room was hit and retired to a commandeered butcher's shop which was down the road. We were there for quite a bit of a pasting.

Of course the plan was for the Hurricanes of 32 Squadron to go after the bombers while a Spitfire squadron dealt with the German fighters.

Oh yes, that was the plan but I'm afraid plans didn't work out like that. For one reason or another the Spitfire squadron that was supposed to be with you wasn't and was already somewhere else and busy so it didn't work out as somebody had thought it might. It was an idea if you like but the difference in performance was so slight that it wasn't going to make much odds. And of course in the battle, I realise there were more Hurricanes than Spitfires in the battle, but one for one they shot down more German aircraft than the Spitfires did. However that's another story and it doesn't matter as long as somebody shot them down.

In fact of the ten aircraft Pete shot down before the end of August, just one, a Dornier 17, was a bomber while all the rest were either Me109s or Me110s.

As part of a squadron the pilots would naturally be dealing with a wide range of other people. Some were happy to stay in the background while others were perhaps more interested in the limelight.

I don't think there was any resentment. Sometimes it was thought the chap was overembroidering what he had done and what he'd achieved, shooting a line in fact, and there were chaps doing that. I insisted on getting camera gun shots of everything you had fired at. Your camera gun would start recording as soon as you opened fire providing you had switched the camera on and there were a number of people who said, 'Oh I've shot down this and that this morning... OK it will be on film... Oh damn I forgot to switch the camera on.' You began to think as his score grew maybe some of it was in his imagination. However you'd no proof and why bother?

Some people looked for cameras. I always went into hiding when someone appeared with cameras. I didn't like having photographs taken.

I was a camera dodger, particularly if it was press. (There was) 'Grubby' Grice, grubby because he was always so immaculate. The photograph is still used. There is a famous photograph of me sitting in the middle, well that's my flight except that Grubby appears in that and he was A flight because we were down to seven people at that time so it wasn't so much the flight rather what was left of the squadron at that time. A lot of them had been wounded.

But perhaps some of Pete's favourite people were the ground crews.

They were absolutely wonderful. I used to... when we were doing the French thing, I know we got back jolly late but before I had a meal I'd get a crate of beer from the bar and take it up to the chaps who were sorting out the aircraft for the next morning and say, 'Take a break, I'll tell you what we've been doing. Come on and have a beer,' which I think boosted their morale a bit. You had to as flight commander, you looked after your chaps. They were splendid.

I met one of them years after the war at Victoria Station and I saw this chap striding through the crowd and for once a) I recognised and b) I remembered his name and I shouted in my parade ground voice, 'Corporal Collier!!' and this chap stopped, saw me and came trotting over. I said how are you and had a chat and asked what he was doing and he coloured and shuffled from one foot to the other and said, 'I'm a captain with British Airways,' and I said, 'Bully for you,' and he was the corporal who had worked on my Hurricane in 1940, bless him, and had obviously got training later on, left the air force and become a British Airways captain. He had survived and progressed.

As with many other squadrons during the battle there were a number of Polish pilots who distinguished themselves in 32 Squadron. Most were a few years older and many had suffered hardship at the hands of invading German forces in 1939 and perhaps had other plans for Luftwaffe pilots who had been shot down.

Splendid bunch. I had three of them: Karol Pniak, who was automatically called 'Cognac', (Boleslaw) Wlasnowolski, who was 'Vodka', and Jan Pfeiffer who was 'Fifi' to make life easier for us pronouncing their names. Karol Pniak was older than most. I believe he had been Polish aerobatic champion in 1928 or something ridiculous but they were first class. You had to keep an eye on them. We shot down a 109 chap who baled out, fell near Biggin Hill, picked up by the police who locked him up in our guardroom with the RAF guard, the RAF police. We heard about this so we bailed him out to come to our dispersal. We were still on duty, we hadn't been stood down and we had the wing of a 109 propped up against our dispersal hut which (Rupert) Smythe had shot down. We went to this kraut and said this is one of your 109s. He spoke fluent English and all he said was, 'Maybe,' so we took him into our dispersal hut and gave him a drink. We had some illicit bottles, but we had to watch our Poles who were sort of fingering their daggers and things and if we had turned our backs I think they would have killed him just like that. I would have done the same in their circumstances so when we were stood down we took him over to the mess and gave him drinks. We had our drinks and he then said, 'May I have a pencil and paper?' and we said, 'What for?' and he said, 'Well tomorrow, when the Luftwaffe blackens the sky and you lose the war I want to write your names down to see that you're well looked after because you have been very kind and courteous to me,' and he couldn't understand why we fell off our chairs laughing. He said, 'What's all this about?' and we said, 'Sorry Chum, you're on the wrong side. We're winning, not you.'

OK he had been shot down but he reckoned we were going into prison camp any moment, which was a degree of arrogance. Some of them, at the end of the war, we collected certain German aces like Dolfo Galland and so on and had them at Central Fighter Establishment for interrogation which was interesting. There was one little fighter pilot, I forget his name, and he was going through the list. He'd been shot down twelve times. He mentioned one particular occasion and Bob Braham laughed. Of course Bob Braham was a great pilot and said, 'Yeah, that was me that got you.' There was one who said, 'I want you to select your two finest pilots, put them over the airfield at 2,000ft, give me a Spitfire and I will take off, shoot them both down and fly home to Germany. If you will do that for me.' Well talk about arrogance. He was on a hiding to nothing but absolutely incredible.

At the end of August 1940, 32 Squadron was withdrawn from the front line and sent north to Acklington in Northumberland for a rest. Pete, however, was only destined to have a very short break.

On 28 August we were moved up to Northumberland to lick our wounds and replace our losses and I thought this is nice, bit of a rest now. I had about four days when I was posted to 257 Squadron at Martlesham because both flight commanders had been killed the same day. I was posted in to replace one and Bob Tuck came to replace the other one.

I started life afresh in 257 where I had my only forced landing in a Hurricane which blew up on a convoy patrol. Somebody was looking after me. I was miles out to sea at 2,000ft and I started worrying about this engine, testing the mag switches, fine, emergency power, fine. Meanwhile I started pointing towards the coast thinking, you are going to get your feet wet one day Brothers, and suddenly there was a great bang and the propeller stopped dead and oil covered the windscreen. I was too low to bail out so thought I could make the beach. No you don't want the beach, the army will have mined it. I managed, with great skill, to stay in the air long enough to just clear the beach and go through a hedge into a farmer's field wheels up. I jumped out, ran away in case it burst into flames, but it didn't, got a sixpence out of my pocket and undid the cowling buttons, took off the side cowling and there was the connecting rod sticking out of the side of the engine. The main bearing had gone.

My Polish number two was circling round above telling Martlesham what had happened and so they got a car organised, local army arrived, bless them, took me to their tented camp, filled me full of brandy and my car arrived and I went back to Martlesham. And that was my own fault. It was a brand new aeroplane and I thought flight commander's perks, I'm having that brand new one and it was a bad choice.

We moved to North Weald. By that time we had got rid of the CO who was rather a strange chap and we wondered why his two flight commanders had been killed. We were told to patrol the Maidstone line at 20,000ft which we did, and then we saw this horde of aircraft approaching, an incoming raid, and we said, 'There they are,' and he said, 'We have been told to patrol the Maidstone line and that's what we shall do until we're told otherwise.' So I departed with my flight and Bob departed with his and we left the CO on his own patrolling the Maidstone line while we went and got stuck in. When this had happened for the third successive occasion we decided that this chap wasn't enthusiastic about firing guns or being shot at and so we got well and truly pissed in the bar and then we rang 11 Group, insisted on talking to the AOC and told him in rather blurry voices, and he was removed the next day. Bob Tuck took over the squadron as he was six months senior to me. That was fine. From then on we had no problems. We had a jolly good squadron. But you can imagine arriving at the squadron, I got there just before Bob, and walked into the pilots' room and there were all these young lads sitting around looking so gloomy and I thought, I know what's going through your minds. 'Both flight commanders, both experienced chaps, both killed. What chance have I got?' So you've got to get them out of the abyss and get some morale into them, and they were alright after that. But I wasn't surprised they were so demoralised with the CO they'd got.

Pete became great friends with Bob Stanford-Tuck. Tuck led one of those almost unbelievable lives during the war. He was in combat almost without a break from France and Dunkirk right through the Battle of Britain and into 1941. He was awarded a DSO and three DFCs but in January 1942 he was shot down by ground fire over France and became a prisoner of war. In early 1945 Tuck escaped from a forced march, fought with the Russians as they advanced, before being repatriated having found his way to the British embassy in Moscow.

Bob Tuck was a super chap. Bob could shoot a line with the best of them and was one of the kindest chaps I've ever met. We were together at the end of the war, and after the war at the Central Fighter Establishment, and lived next door to each other in married quarters. I remember saying to Bob, 'What are you going to do after the war?' and he said, 'Oh I've got a winner of an idea. I'm going to hire some vans and equip them with beds and I shall populate them with appropriate dollies and on the side will be written Tuck's Fucks Ltd.'

One of Pete's more memorable encounters was on 15 September. A formation of Dornier 17s of KG76 crossed the Channel to attack London and was met by RAF Hurricanes including that of Pete Brothers. Pete's target was an aircraft flown by Feldwebel Wilhelm Raab. Soon the aircraft was burning, some of Raab's crew were dead and, losing height, Raab himself baled out, landed in a tree and was captured.

I shot down a Dornier 17 (and a Ju88), and years later a chap came to see me in Devon, the pilot with his 30-year-old daughter, and he rang me up. I said you'll never find me because I'm stuck out in the wilds, but is Cullompton on your map, and he said, 'Ja,' and I said I'll meet you in Cullompton; 'Where in Cullompton?' and I said, 'Where else but the war memorial.' So I went and sat on the war memorial and he came rumbling along in his car, peering round, and I said, 'Are you Wilhelm Raab?' and he said, 'Ja,' and I said, 'Follow me,' and I took him home and we had tea and we had drinks. He said, 'You killed my gunner and my co-pilot and my navigator and you hurt my left engine,' and I said, 'Yes, it was burning nicely, wasn't it?' and he said, 'Ja, I decided to jump out,' and his daughter said, 'Very wise Papa, very wise.' So he became a prisoner-of-war. I've got a photograph of us both arm in arm, and he was great fun, stayed for dinner and about two o'clock in the morning we more or less carried him to his car and his daughter drove back to their hotel.

After months of constant combat Pete was finally rested in January 1941 and posted to 52 OTU, still on Hurricanes, at RAF Debden in Essex as an instructor. Pete admitted he needed the rest.

It seemed to be never stopping and was very frightening some of the time. One minute it was a hilariously funny life and the next minute it was bloody frightening and that was how it went.

You don't worry. You decide early on you're either going to survive or you're not. And if you don't survive you can't worry about it. If you do there's no point so you looked at it that way. There were times where you used to think, 'I've got away with it so far. Probably tomorrow I'll get killed.' That cropped up in your mind now and again but have a drink and forget it. And we drank quite a lot during the war. We even got caught out during the Battle of Britain at Biggin Hill. The cloud was on the ground. The Meteorological chap said it was going to stay there so they told us we were stood down for the day. That was the first mistake. We were very new, it was very early on, and instead of getting the hell off the station and out of the way we stayed in the bar drinking and suddenly at two o'clock, despite the Met forecast, the weather cleared and not only were we brought to readiness we were scrambled in quick time. I remember I was well and truly under the alcohol stimulus, flying along thinking, 'Well what do I do? Yes, turn the gun button on to fire, yes, so that it's ready. Yes, reflector sight, I'd better switch the sight on. Yes.' But it was amazing, as soon as you got in contact with the enemy, the amount of adrenalin, you were stone cold sober in seconds with sheer fright and so it was a normal activity.

During those months Pete got a very good sense for what made a good pilot.

Experience, speed, eyesight, instinct. I think that sort of sense and keeping your eyes open to what's going on. I had the sense one day flying over France, this was in early '40, and suddenly had the sense that I was being looked at. Well you've had the feeling on occasion either on a crowded train, or crowded room, somebody's looking at me. I looked in the mirror and there was the biggest and fattest 109 I had ever seen in my life and as I saw him his whole front end lit up. I think I pushed and pulled everything in sight with no particular plan but I got out of it and he didn't hit me and of course he just zoomed away out of reach. My number two, who was flying in line astern, should have told me but he was brand new and I circled round and I saw he was following and cutting the corner, good lad, catch up and get back in position in no time, and then he lit up shooting at me so I called him up and suggested he didn't do that, that it was unpopular, and when we got back on the ground I said the greatest blow you can deal to a chap's prestige and confidence I think: I said, 'You're off operations for a week and going for intensive gunnery training because you should have cut me up and got closer but you were nowhere near me when you fired.' So he was suitably ashamed; but it had taught him a lesson.

Pete stayed at Debden for almost six months before resuming his operational career. In June 1941 he was posted to 457 Squadron, an Australian unit newly-forming at Baginton in Coventry. This was also Pete's first opportunity to fly Spitfires.

They were a super bunch. They arrived in dribs and drabs and had done their conversion courses on Spitfires and we moved to the Isle of Man to work up and become operational, spent a few months doing that, moved down to Kenley – well we were at Redhill but as part of the Kenley Wing and they were a good bunch of pilots, very keen-eyed. Interesting. They were so used to looking long distances and focusing miles away; they were better than most of us at spotting German aircraft in the distance. We had our fun, and very appropriately, as CO, I was lucky enough to score their first victory, shoot down a 109 and show them how to do it. They were the most wonderful bunch of chaps, a wonderful sense of humour, a lot of fun, full of life and they went back to Australia for the coming battle of Australia. They said they weren't going without me which didn't amuse me at all I'm afraid. I had no wish to go to Aussie, not then, I wanted to settle my quarrel with the Germans before I started on the Japs. However, I was posted to Australia so I went to the AOA Fighter Command, (Air Vice Marshal Hugh) 'Dingbat' Saunders, and said, 'Sir, you've got to get me out of this,' and he said, 'Not a hope. The Australian Minister, Dr Evatt, had lunch with the Prime Minister the day before yesterday and Winston Churchill said, "What a wonderful opportunity for a successful Battle of Britain pilot to lead an Australian squadron in the coming Battle of Australia."' And I thought, 'Oh Christ, I won't even get into Churchill's office once he has decided.' So that was it. We moved the squadron out of the line to pack up and go to Australia and I sent the chaps on leave, and eventually, forty-eight hours before the boat was due to sail, I thought it was time to go home and say goodbye to my wife and kids. So I went home and I was supposed to report at eight o'clock Monday morning to Liverpool docks to get on the boat. Sunday evening I got a phone call from Fighter Command to say you're not to get on the boat, Dr. Evatt has flown out of the country, gone to have talks with President Roosevelt, and now he's out of the way we've got you off the boat. Report to headquarters Fighter Command which I did on Monday but all my kit had gone to Aussie and my clothes were all packed up and on the blinking boat. So that was the end of my Australian story other than the chaps coming to see me after the war, bless them, and making me President of Australia's Spitfire Association.

We were doing sweeps over France in those days. Attacking anything we came across, trains, cars, aeroplanes, you name it. We would fly over

France firstly with the Kenley Wing as we were part of a new squadron. The bottom squadron led by the wing leader and we'd be sandwiched one above with a top squadron to make sure we new-boys didn't get clobbered. They were 602 Squadron on top led by Paddy Finucane, and on one particular sweep we were doing bomber escort. When the bombers dropped their bombs we started escorting them home and I noticed we had lost 602, the top cover was no longer there. A lot of talking broke out over the radio...'Look out Paddy there's one behind you,' and this sort of thing. And I thought, ah, they've got involved in something, so I called him up and said, where are you, and he said he was ten miles in from Calais with a whole bunch of 109s. So I pulled away from the wing which was about half way across the Channel by then and went back to join in. Got up-sun and dived into the melee, lots of glinting wings in the sun and found they were all Spits whirling round. I thought, that's odd, but anyhow went back to Redhill and got a rocket from the wing leader. He said you left the wing without my permission, and I said, well 602 were apparently in trouble from all the shouting that was going on. He said, forget 602, they're always in trouble, come back with a huge score, and they never lose anybody. Thank you very much, and he was one of the original 602 Squadron Auxiliary Air Force chaps so he obviously knew them better than I did.

One of the most regrettable losses while Pete was at Kenley was that of Wing Commander Victor Beamish, the station commander. Beamish had been commander at North Weald during the Battle of Britain but, far from being a 'desk man', he built up a substantial tally of enemy aircraft, flying on many sorties during the battle. He was awarded a DSO in July 1940 (and a bar in September 1941) and then a DFC in November.

We lost the station commander Victor Beamish who was a terrific chap and had been my boss at North Weald, station commander, and then he was boss at Kenley. He was an absolute tiger of a chap. Wouldn't use his car as it was a waste of petrol. He used a bicycle and he'd cycle from the airfield down to the operations room in the morning, about four or five miles, see what was going on, cycle back and then fly with us on the wing as number two to the wing leader. He went at everything like a bull at a gate. He was a wild Irishman and we kept warning him and you'd get the sort of reply when you said, 'There's one behind you,' and he would say, 'I'll fix this one first.' Well that was alright as long as the one behind him couldn't shoot straight and of course he got clobbered which was a great morale blow to the whole wing because he was so jolly good. The wing leader, who was tired anyway, more or less collapsed after that. He went on rest and was succeeded, but that was very sad. We shouldn't have lost Victor in a thing like that.

Despite the apparent enjoyment Pete got from these sweeps across France, they could also be dangerous.

Well it was just for a squadron doing it on its own and those were very early days. We were really a bunch of suckers flying up and down not quite knowing what we were up to. Different story, 1942, '43, and we had a fair degree of air supremacy really and, in fact, when later on at the end of '42 I had the Tangmere Wing as leader we were getting so little reaction from flying over France as a wing looking for trouble that the Germans were just avoiding us. We weren't doing any harm, dropping bombs or anything, so they just ignored us and so we had a bit of a conference and said, there's only one thing we can think of doing and that's putting a bait down. Anybody prepared to volunteer for a bait? And four chaps did, one of whom was an Australian and we said, right, you fly this route round behind Paris and back and we will follow you and sit 5,000ft above you and see what happens. Sure enough they were attractive bait for some 109s who dived in to attack them, and the Aussie in the bait was shouting his head off on the radio saying, 'For God's sake help, I've got four of the so-and-sos shooting at me,' and I was waiting for him to switch off so I could say a few calming words. As soon as he switched off, my number two, who was a fellow Australian, beat me to it and this quiet droll Australian voice came over and said, 'What's the matter Harry Boy, are they picking on you?' which completely restored the situation for people who were getting a bit jumpy and this chap who was so hysterical.

Some sweeps were successful. We had our moments, particularly if it was properly organised with other wings, say a bomber formation with a covering wing to look after it and us as a separate wing to sweep round beforehand to catch any 109s taking off and climbing up to attack this main formation; that type of operation, those were great fun.

In June 1942 Pete was posted as the new CO of 602 Squadron.

Yes, I commanded 602 which was a bit of a shock for them because I told them what I thought of them and their efforts and antics. We were moved up out of the line because they were pretty tired which annoyed me because I wasn't. I'd just had my Aussie squadron on ops for a few months and only then 602 for a week or two before we moved north for a rest. I was then promoted and became wing leader at Tangmere which brought me back onto the scene again.

All through this time Pete was flying Spitfires.

AIR COMMODORE PETER BROTHERS CBE DSO DFC*

I flew Hurricanes until the end of '40 and from '41 onwards I was on Spitfires as the Aussie squadron formed on Spitfires and that was my first squadron. I loved it, liked it. It was a nice aeroplane. It was more manoeuvrable with quicker responses than the Hurricane. Not such a good gun platform but it had other advantages in speed and rate of climb which were very useful.

However, there was a new enemy aircraft as well.

The 190, when we first got mixed up with it in Spit Vs, was more than enough of a match for a Spitfire V, and so the Spitfire IX was developed which was nothing more than a Spitfire V with a bigger engine and a two-stage supercharger to give it extra altitude. That was alright, that was fine. We didn't have those when I had the Tangmere Wing. We were fighting with Vs but we coped with the 190. Perhaps they weren't as good because they were running out of experienced pilots or something but they weren't all that frightening. Then later when I had the Exeter Wing we had Spitfire VIIs and XIVs and they would just make a 190 look as if it was standing still. So the 190 from my point of view had a short-lived life of superiority.

Pete stayed at Tangmere until July 1943 when he initially became an instructor before being given a staff job. However April 1944 saw him back on operations as wing leader at Culmhead near Exeter. His new aircraft was the virtually-experimental Spitfire Mk.VII. Only 140 Mk.VIIs were built and one of the last, MD188, was delivered to 131 Squadron in June 1944 before being adopted by Pete as his own aircraft.

It was designed originally as a high-flying aircraft to attack high-flying reconnaissance aircraft that were normally at 40 to 45,000ft and were a bit too high for most Spitfires so you had a pressurised cockpit and so on. Well, typical of those days, by the time they had produced that aircraft we were using them for ground attack so the first thing I did when I arrived there was say, right, take out all this high-flying equipment, control seals which made the controls stiff passing through rubber seals to maintain pressure and made the aircraft less manoeuvrable, chucked those away, chuck away the pressure cabin equipment to save weight and so on and we virtually stripped them down. They had better range than the average Spitfire because we had fuel in the wings, twelve gallons in each wing, so from where we were at Culmhead near Exeter we could reach the Swiss frontier and back with no problem, which we did. The only trouble was we also got a long range tank underneath which you preferred to get rid of when you got into combat because it was extra weight and extra drag but of course if you were by the Swiss frontier you weren't going to have enough fuel to get home if you got rid of the tank too soon. You needed it to get some of the way home and then you could get rid of it and carry on. We were looking for German fighter aircraft, bombers and anything else. We raided a whole lot of airfields like Le Mans. We did three in succession, one after another, which was good fun because we caught them taking off and that sort of thing which was a salutary lesson for them. We got shot up for our trouble because their flak was pretty jolly good and of course your first attack... (had to count). Ideally you did one sweep across the airfield shooting at everything you could see and then go away. If you stuck around, they got organised with low level anti-aircraft which was pretty well too good for one's health and I made that mistake. Having always told people to get the hell out of the place after your first attack I went back again because there was a chap waiting to take off and he was sitting on the ground in a 190. I didn't want to shoot him on the ground, not fair, I wanted to get him airborne, but he wouldn't take off so I set him on fire on the ground. By then their flak was jolly well organised and they blew bits off my aeroplane which it didn't like much.

D-Day was fascinating. The sea traffic that was pounding along. Everywhere there was something on the water. Naval ships mostly who shot at you anyway. They didn't bother to try and identify whether you were a 109 or Spit, they just opened fire on any aeroplane. They were a bit nervous about aircraft and anyhow it was a fascinating scene. You didn't have much time to hang about and drink it in over the actual beaches because there was a lot of flak and a lot of targets for you to attack. German columns on the move up to join in the front, they provided nice targets. It was a fascinating scene to witness. Not a lot of German aircraft that day. It was incredible. You really had to search them out. You'd suddenly see one launching some sort of attack on the beachhead and if you didn't get after him fast enough somebody else did because they were hopelessly outnumbered, for the first time.

We covered D-Day with three squadrons and this was an occasion where one said, you take the north end of the beach, you take the south end, and we'll take the middle and split your wing up, and patrolled up and down waiting for the Germans to appear. That worked.

Day two was disgusting weather, pouring with rain in low cloud about 100ft over our airfield and my chum who was chief of operations at the local group headquarters, 10 Group, rang up and said, 'What's your weather?' I told him, 'Bolting with rain, cloud base 100ft or so,' and he said, 'Can you get off?' I said, 'Yes we can get off but I doubt we will get back,' and he said, 'That's alright, we're prepared to take 100% loss. You're the only airfield in the UK that can even get off at the moment so get off.' So we went, all three squadrons straight into cloud. We separated and the drill was the leading squadron carried on on its course, the squadron on the right turned five degrees starboard for two minutes then resumed the normal course so that it moved out and was flying parallel so when you got out of the cloud at the top you were all there. We lost one or two in cloud. Whether they had collided or lost control of their aircraft or whatever. Anyhow we got over the beachhead where it was a lovely bright blue sunny day and the Germans played great games, so we got into that lot and then came back. My radio had packed in by then. I could transmit but I couldn't receive anything so I had to get my number two to lead us and told him to get extra control to drop us down to low level over the sea which he did and we broke cloud at about 200 ft and I said, 'Righto, I'll lead now.' Put the whole wing in line astern and led them up the valleys and up to the airfield where we scraped in, refuelled, and one of the squadron commanders said, 'You're not thinking of doing another sweep are you?' I said, 'Yes, if you don't want to I'll lead your squadron,' which did not amuse him one bit and so off we went and did another sortie and so we had a good time on that particular day.

By this time Pete was nearing the end of his operational time in the war. In October 1944 he was awarded the DSO and posted away from the wing. He did a staff course in America and then went to CFE where he stayed until he left the RAF in 1947.

The Second Tactical Air Force chaps had moved into France out of the UK. The battle was getting too far away from Exeter Culmhead. It was a long haul to go and catch up with them so my two squadrons were removed east in England and I was left as Wing Commander social and drinking at Culmhead, but I'd got my Spitfire so I used to go and join chums. Peter Powell was a friend of mine and he had a wing operating from Gravesend so I flew up to Gravesend and said 'May I join you?' and he said 'Welcome,' so I enjoyed flying with him and his wing until there was a great panic, where the hell was I? So I reported back to base and they said you're posted to America so that was a big panic. I packed my gear, borrowed a communications aircraft and pilot, flew up to home just outside Manchester, dumped my gear, said goodbye to my wife and my instructions were to report to the personnel despatch unit at Hendon. I thought, nothing sails to America from Hendon so I'm not going to bother. That caused another panic until they tracked me down at home and said on a Sunday, 'You'd better get to Glasgow quick,' so I got a train to Glasgow, was met by an air force chap, stuffed into a taxi round to a little house in some side street where I met an air force doctor just coming out with his bag of tricks. I joined him in an air force car, into a launch which motored out to the *Queen Mary* which was already on its way and they dropped a rope ladder down and I thought, 'I'm never going to make this. I shall get dizzy.' But they dropped a rope down, hauled our bags up and there were my chums leaning over the rail and jeering. I followed the doctor up the ladder, never taking my eyes off his feet. Somebody's got to check the submarine watch who were ordinary airmen and soldiery going to the States for some reason or other and had been told to stay up all night and look out for submarines. So they gave that job to me on account of the fact that I wasn't there to say no thank you. It had its advantages because I would check the submarine watch at various times during the night and had to report to the captain that I'd done it and he would say, 'Would you like a glass of scotch or sherry?' It was a dry ship as we'd got Americans on board going home and we had no drink so I would go to the cabin I shared with these chums like Billy Drake and breathe on them all and get scragged for my trouble. I had quite a pleasant voyage in that way apart from having to sleep some of the day.

One of the characters Pete had come across early in the war was Douglas Bader.

I shared a room with him back in 1940 when he was first back in the air force and he was a great chap, Douglas, a bully but if you shouted back you became friends. If you didn't he would kick you around all over the place. We got on like a house on fire including after the war when he came back from the bag and joined us at Central Fighter Establishment.

He wasn't the only one with a reputation. He was a great leader and inspirer of confidence amongst all these chaps. He was a remarkable chap. I had great admiration for his abilities in view of his legless nature which I thought was absolutely wonderful but as I say he would bully you if he could and I think he bullied all his chaps who were junior to him. He was one of the great ones. He was a good pilot, yes, but I think he learned his lesson when he crashed that he wasn't all that good.

During the Battle of Britain there had been much debate about the value of what was called the 'Big Wing'. Bader would lead his squadron, together with others based at Duxford in Cambridgeshire, to bring a large number of fighters to attack German formations over London and the south-east. This highlighted the problems found by squadrons right on the front line.

This was Douglas's idea but, of course, he was so far back from the front line he could take off and assemble his squadrons together and then come and join the battle providing it wasn't over by then. We were so far forward it was difficult to even keep a squadron together when you scrambled.

You were all climbing for height like crazy at full throttle, getting strung out and it was a race for height always and, of course, we all used to complain that the controller never launched us early enough. Well, when you thought about it the controller was right. He didn't want to launch you if it was a spoof raid which turned round when it hit the coast and went back home and was merely dragging you into the air to waste fuel. You'd get back on the ground and they'd catch you refuelling with any luck by a following raid coming up behind the spoof one, that sort of thing. So the controller had to make certain that it wasn't a spoof before they launched you. So very often you were launched too late and you were struggling to get to the same height as the enemy and preferably higher of course so we resorted to attacking the bombers head on. That was very often the most you could reach at that time. You certainly couldn't get at the escorting fighters or above them. You had to wait for them to come down and join in.

I used to like head-on because you weren't then exposed to the bomber's gunners shooting at you. I got badly shot up when going for the leader of a formation and closing the range behind him and attracting fire from each side from the aircraft that were formating on him. They had all their guns shooting at me while I was hoping they'd miss me and hit each other.

Bader spent much of the war as a prisoner, ending up at Colditz Castle until his liberation. Pete came across him again when they both flew in the Victory Flypast over London in September 1945.

Led by Douglas, I think it was the most dangerous formation I ever flew in because we were all wing leaders or had been. We all knew we could fly closer than any of the other chaps, so it was a very tight formation, a matter of a foot or two apart wingtip to tailplane which was very dangerous, but nobody collided. We were all obviously quite good at it even though we had spent most of the recent years leading rather than formating. I've no idea how they picked the pilots. I know there was discussion about one chap, whether he really was Battle of Britain, because we were all Battle of Britain pilots. There was some question that one chap wasn't fully Battle of Britain or got in at the tail end or something. Other than that we were all solid and had been in the battle since the time it started. Excitement. Yes, you felt it was your due after all.

Pete joined the Colonial Service and lived and worked in Kenya for the next two years but it was not for him and he became bored. Then, out of the blue, he received a telegram from the RAF.

I was invited back which was a great surprise. I was on safari, came back and my wife was waving a fourteen-page telegram from the verandah when

I arrived. I thought Good Lord, my whole family must have been massacred in Manchester or something. It was from the Air Ministry inviting me back and telling me what my seniority would be and my rank would be and to report to Air Headquarters Nairobi for a medical exam.

When Pete arrived back in England he was not given a job he expected. He was given the rank of squadron leader, having left as a wing commander, posted to Bomber Command and was given command of 57 Squadron, flying Avro Lincolns. In his inimitable style Pete 'kicked' the squadron into shape and offered the squadron's services for a detachment to Singapore. The squadron was the first to take part in the Malayan campaign and flew many sorties in support of ground operations before moving to Egypt. In 1952 he regained his former rank, was made Wing Commander, flying at Marham, and learned to fly the Valiant, the first of the V bombers.

Pete finally retired from the RAF in 1973. He spent many years initially as deputy chairman and then chairman of the Battle of Britain Fighter Association. However, despite his many exploits after 1940, it was still the Battle of Britain that he was best known for.

Group Captain Billy Drake DSO DFC* DFC (USA)

20 December 1917-28 August 2011

Ever since I was about that high I always wanted to fly and I think a lot of people in my generation also had the same feeling. Most of us, I have now since found out, had our first flight ever with Alan Cobham for five shillings.

My parents were dead against my ever wanting to fly. I think like a lot of parents they thought it was an extremely dangerous pastime. But I went on insisting and eventually after I'd come back from school, and I was still wondering what to do, I was about 17 or 18 at that time, I picked up a copy of *The Aeroplane* and in that was an article about a short service commission and the short service commission said that while I was flying for four years I'd be paid a reasonable amount of money and at the end of four years I would be given a gratuity of £400. I read into gratuity as annuity and I went up to my parents and said, 'This is one of the reasons why flying could be up my street. I'd be paid to do for four years what I want to do and at the end I would be given an annuity of £400,' which was a lot of money in those days and they looked at me sideways and said, 'That's not an annuity, that's a gratuity and I think that you're so stupid and so backward with your English you can go for an interview but they wouldn't accept you anyway.' But they were so hard up that they did accept me.

Billy, christened Billy and not William, was a boisterous child and teachers in his early schools found it hard to control him. His parents resorted to sending him to be educated in Switzerland. He gained a love for the country and also for skiing, a pastime he continued enjoying into his nineties, becoming captain of the RAF skiing team for much of his RAF career.

My background to my educational period of three years of going to school in Switzerland was that I came from a mixed marriage of Catholic and Protestant. My father wanted me to go to Uppingham where he'd been and my mother wanted me to go to Downside, and here I was. I'd given them an idea of what I wanted to do and they went on holiday to Switzerland and looked at the cost of education in Switzerland and the exchange was twenty-seven francs to the pound. They said that is where the boy is going because it's going to be much cheaper than sending him to either your school, he said looking at my mother, or mine, looking at himself. And that is why I ended up going first of all to a German-speaking school where most of my colleagues in a special class were Germans or Italians or Nazis in the early thirties and I was the only English boy there. From there I went to a French-speaking school in Geneva where I found that they were all Swiss, but I did have the opportunity of trying to sum up who my opposite numbers were. The Germans, and I found that they were very anti-British, most of them, and I decided in my first couple of years in the German-speaking school that I would show that I could look after myself so I came back after my first holiday with some boxing gloves and spoke to my house master and said, 'I'm having a lot of problems with my colleagues and with your permission if they insult either me or the British Empire I'd like to invite them to a boxing match if you would be kind enough to be the referee, and he looked at me sideways and said, 'Christ, do whatever you like, Drake,' so I had twelve fights and I was knocked down eleven times and the only success was against a little tiny Italian I knocked down but in the end they got so bored with this process they left me alone.

I didn't go straight into the air force. I went home and for about eighteen months I was doing nothing but helping my parents to build their new house and dig their new gardens while I was still trying to decide what to do. Every job that they suggested I did, like banking or being a doctor, I failed all the interviews and the only successful one was after this not understanding the difference between gratuity and annuity. I did pass an interview with the selection board in the Royal Air Force because they literally were hard up for the right type of youngster to join the Royal Air Force as aircrew.

I can't pinpoint it and it does lead to a vexing question later on, the difference between short service people who were being accepted by the air force and the volunteer reservists, and there's no doubt about it there was a definite division of the upper class, shall we say, lads who had been to public school and the working class people who joined as volunteer reservists, and there was quite definitely a feeling, amongst a small number of both sides, who took exception to each other.

Could I see in those days the dividing line? Yes, it was quite definitely a class distinction.

Billy joined the Royal Air Force in July 1936, a time of great change for the service. While the fighter squadrons were still equipped with the Hawker Fury, Bristol Bulldog and Gloster Gauntlet, and the final RAF biplane fighter, the Gloster Gladiator, was still to arrive, brand new aircraft were on the way. The Hurricane flew for the first time in 1935 and the Spitfire in 1936. RAF reorganisation created Fighter, Bomber and Coastal Commands and the brand new RDF, later radar, had its first full-scale trials.

But for Billy, all he wanted to do was fly.

The first thing they did was show me an aeroplane and they didn't really want to find out whether I had a brain or could write or read and as far as I could see they wanted to see as quickly as possible whether I had the right ability to be an aircrew and yes, I couldn't have enjoyed myself to begin with more than I did.

I consider myself good, yes, which brings up an interesting point. That is, when we joined our operational units we were assessed once a year and most of us in No.1 Squadron were assessed as average and I don't think we took much notice of that except that we were average and other people in other units were above average or exceptional, but I realised being average in No.1 Squadron you were up against a very high class of pilots you were assessed against.

Once I had finished my operational training, my flying training, I was asked where I would like to go and I said I wanted to go into Fighter Command, and what unit would you like to be posted into. I realised that at Tangmere 43 Squadron and No.1 Squadron had Furies and I had been trained on Furies and so I therefore think that if I have a choice I would like to be posted into No.1 Squadron at Tangmere which they luckily so did.

When I arrived at my flying training school at Netheravon all the aeroplanes were produced by Hawkers, the Audax, Furies, Harts etc and for a year and a half I flew nothing else. I got used to flying this particular type of aeroplane and it wasn't until two or three years later that we were re-equipped with Hurricanes and thank God, just in time, because this was 1938-39 that we were re-equipped because at the time of the Munich crisis we still had Furies and they were all camouflaged and we were told, and we accepted the fact, that if necessary we would have to go to war. At that particular moment the British air attaché from Berlin came to England to lecture all of the operational units on what we were up against so when we asked what the hell do we do against these 109s in the Furies he looked at us and said 'Ram the buggers' and that was the only pre-war advice we were even given but thank God we got the Hurricanes in time.

When I was posted to Tangmere we all had a feeling that maybe war was imminent but we weren't too worried about that fact and all our information that we had was from the media. There wasn't any intellectual thinking on our part that we were preparing ourselves for an all-out air war. We just accepted the fact that we might go, we might. Nobody had actually told us that we weren't going and therefore – we were still youngsters for heaven's sake, in our 18s and 19s – we just accepted the fact that we had to do what we were told to do.

We were taking part in inter-command exercises before the war. Once a year we took on mock warfare exercises against Bomber Command and we had absolutely no idea what the hell we were doing. We'd read that we had certain exercises to carry out against bomber aeroplanes which meant nothing to us at all but we carried them out. It was all great fun but nothing serious as far as we were concerned and as far as I can remember the only person I came across who gave us any inkling of what warfare was all about was Sir Keith Park who was our station commander at Tangmere. He tried to instill into us the background of his experiences in World War One which didn't really make any sense to us at all but we accepted what he said. I do remember him saying if war does start you will spend long periods sitting on your backsides doing nothing and being frightened for the rest of that period by having to take on the German Air Force.

Were we aware of the threat against us? I think the answer is that in a very vague way we were. The Germans had some extremely good aeroplanes and we had absolutely no doctrine to fall back on as to what we would do if we had to go to war. Our training, and the training of Fighter Command squadrons, during that whole period from the end of World War One to the beginning of World War Two, was non-existent. We had nothing. We didn't even have any senior officers who bothered to come down to talk to us, or if they bothered to come down they were inexperienced and unable to indoctrinate us in anything, and so came 1939 and we all took part in the Phoney War period. We had to work out our own doctrines through personal experiences and it took from that period, beginning of France, through to the Battle of Britain and after the Battle of Britain. We were able to sit down and put on paper what we had learned in those eighteen months and that was the beginning of the strength of Fighter Command and the 2nd Tactical Air Force.

We were dead keen to fly our aeroplanes operationally against our opposite numbers in the German Air Force, but we had nothing, no advice as to what to do. We had to find out for ourselves through trial and error and those eighteen months or two years through France and the Battle of Britain was a learning experience. That is why so many of us were promoted way above our ranks to command fighting units as flight commanders or as squadron commanders or as wing leaders because perhaps we were a little bit quicker or lucky enough to still be alive at the end of the Battle of Britain to train the new pilots that were coming in who had quite a few hours, relatively speaking, on type of aeroplanes but no idea of what they were going into. We were still young enough not to realise ourselves that we in fact knew quite a lot about modern day fighting.

We just flew aeroplanes, we aerobatted aeroplanes, we formated in aeroplanes, and that is about all we ever did. Once a year we went up to an armament practice camp to fire our guns at drogues to see whether we could aim straight and we enjoyed a way of life in those days. The weather was fine and particularly down at Tangmere we had a very nice period where we had the summer routine. We got up very early in the morning, did all our flying in the morning and then had the afternoon off, and obviously when it was dark the evening as well. So it was a gentlemanly existence and our main activity was to fly aeroplanes just for the sake of flying aeroplanes, not to go to war to shoot down this and shoot down that. It was to fly aeroplanes and then to enjoy ourselves with our little cars which we were able to afford. You could then buy a car for five pounds and, if you were very rich, you could go up to about ten pounds and that was our existence. War was not paramount at all.

In 1938 Prime Minister Neville Chamberlain returned from his meeting with Hitler at Munich. He declared that 'it is peace in our time' but many in the country realised that war would come sooner or later.

Well we had, since the Munich crisis, been semi at war ourselves in that one night 43 Squadron would be sleeping down in the hangars waiting for an emergency and then the next day we would be... So for about eight months we had realised maybe that we were earning the money we were paid for in that we were prepared for an attack on Europe and then came September 3rd. Well, again all our information was from the press and so we just accepted the fact that there we were. We were all at readiness down by our aeroplanes and released usually in time for lunches and meals, but we were at war. Of course we had no idea whether the Germans were going to come over en masse to attack Great Britain or not but we were prepared to take them on.

We had all been together at Tangmere, unmarried, living in the mess together, having most of our meals together, having most of our off periods together and so we were rather like a bunch of brothers and we knew each other, we liked or disliked each a certain number of them, but mostly we liked and then when we arrived in France and realised we were at war we got to look at each other a little more closely. We hadn't been frightened at all by the German Air Force at any time so we were still fairly ignorant at our reaction should we ever be required to fly operationally and therefore who did I like and who did I dislike; I liked practically everybody and the people that stuck in my mind were, first of all, my squadron commander (Sqn Ldr P.H. 'Bull' Halahan). We didn't like him particularly because we didn't see much of him and therefore the people that I got to know and respect were the flight commanders, 'Johnnie' Walker was one and Prosser Hanks was the other. They'd been members of the No.1 Squadron aerobatic team led by (later Air Commodore E.M.) Donaldson and therefore we got to know them and respect them but they weren't senior people to us, they were brother officers and brother pilots and therefore it was a family feeling that we all had for each other.

Once again Paul Richey (later author of bestselling book *Fighter Pilot*) and I got on very well because he was a Catholic, he'd been to Downside and had I listened to my mother I would probably have met him there. We were the two French-speaking officers so we got to know a bit more about France than the others who couldn't talk French at all. Killy (Kilmartin) had joined us later on in life. He didn't come out to France to begin with because he was 43 Squadron and he was posted out to us about Christmas time 1939.

We still considered ourselves to be as good as anyone else, as good as any of the 109 pilots we would meet, which we didn't very often, and that we could look after ourselves. I was posted, 1 Squadron, out to France so we lived a different type of life in France to our opposite numbers who stayed back in England and again we had nobody to talk to about war. The French just sat back and had some very good lunches and very good dinners but we very rarely saw them.

My recollection of the 1939 winter was that it was desperately cold. Two factors that were predominantly in our minds were that the beds that we had in the French farmhouse where we were mainly billeted were so cold that we had to heat up bricks to warm our beds, but we were young enough to say, well, not very pleasant but we got through it. As far as the flying was concerned we had quite a lot of ground problems in that it was so cold that the oil used to freeze in the Merlin engines and it took a long time to get our aeroplanes serviceable to start up. As far as flying was concerned the cold meant nothing except to ourselves because the aeroplanes were not heated and, by God, flying at 25,000 feet was a very painful process particularly as most of our patrols were anything up to an hour duration when at that height it was -50 degrees. It was cold.

GROUP CAPTAIN BILLY DRAKE DSO DFC* DFC (USA)

We had no radar and the only operational activities were when we saw contrails above us and we realised, probably, that there would be a German aeroplane going back to Germany and we were scrambled to investigate. Sometimes we did get close enough to do something about it.

We understood that we were there to protect the British Army, or the units of the British Army that were in France. I don't think anybody, including our politicians, realised we were going to sit on our bottoms for about a year doing nothing and, as we now know, that was called the Phoney War period and therefore until April 1940 we didn't realise that we were at war. By that date we came to the conclusion that the war had started and a lot of us were shot down on the first day or the second day. I waited for the second day to be shot down and that was our first taste of warfare. Most of us had dabbled with a few interceptions of these so-called contrails and so we had shot our guns off at the enemy. Some of us were successful others not and so again not until April 1940 did we realise, my God, we are at war and we've got to do something about it and we had nobody to advise us what to do.

We were completely ignorant about radar even when we were in France as the French didn't have any radar and we didn't have any radar except right at the very end. Then we had some mobile organised but we still hadn't been briefed as to what these radar stations were doing and what information they were using to vector us there, to vector us elsewhere, to tell us what height to go to and what to expect and even when April came along we still had no idea so we were fairly ignorant right up to maybe the beginning of the Battle of Britain. We didn't understand that radar was the basis of this defence organisation which was started by Dowding. We didn't even know what these huge towers were. Nobody had briefed us that their whole basis of interception and defence of Great Britain was based upon the information we were getting from radar. No idea whatsoever.

On 19 April 1940 Billy Drake shot down a Messerschmitt Bf109, the first of many successes during the war.

My first meeting with a German aeroplane was with a 109 I intercepted. When he saw me getting fairly close to him he dived to get away from me and I dived with him because that was all I knew how to do. I couldn't get close enough to shoot and eventually we saw a river, must have been the Rhine or something, and the first thing I saw was some high tension cables and he'd flown right underneath these and luckily I was in good formation and right behind him and he made the mistake of pulling up to see where I was and whether I'd hit the cables and that gave me the opportunity of getting close enough to have a go at him.

*This was the first opportunity that Billy, and the rest of the pilots in
1 Squadron, had to find out whether they could match up in skill and tactical
awareness with the German pilots.*

The only doctrine we had was to get as close to the aeroplane as possible,
to shoot and to make certain that we weren't being looked at ourselves.
Make absolutely certain that you kept your eyes wide open everywhere,
behind you and in front of you and to get as close in as possible. We had to
get close in with the machine guns in the wings, we had to get in to about
250 feet, which is very close and fairly bumpy as you have the slipstream,
but that was the only doctrine, get in close and fire as little as possible but
as effectively as possible.

The eight machine guns we had with the Hurricanes, and Spitfires, out
in the wings, they had to be harmonised and there were two harmonisations
that were discussed by ourselves and by the armourers. One was spot
harmonisation to get as many bullets into one small area as possible or
to spread the overall area where one bullet could do as much harm as 200
bullets, and I personally, as a fairly good shot, went in for spot harmonisation.
I wanted to get as many bullets hitting a target as possible as against the
spread harmonisation, rightly or wrongly, but it depended entirely on the
pilot himself as to what he was to choose.

In No.1 Squadron, because we were very experienced pilots and we had
carried out two trips up to these camps to fire, we had an idea what our
ability was for deflection shooting. There were two aspects of shooting.
One was to get right behind and line astern of the target or in dogfights to
go in and to shoot deflection shots. I think in my case and in the case of
certain other pilots some of us had been brought up by our parents to fire at
moving targets (such as) birds so therefore that was our first inkling of what
deflection shooting was all about, that you had to aim well ahead of your
target to make certain your bullets hit. So it was either deflection shooting
or line astern.

Our sights were really only geared up to tell us how close we were to a
particular aeroplane and we were able to say 'that is a 109' or that's a bomber
aeroplane, a Heinkel, and you had to get the wingtips of the aeroplane over
your target within that thing. That was the only aide we had for our ability
to shoot at aeroplanes.

We knew the Hurricane versus the 109, what was the best altitude and
the best altitude was about 10,000 feet as far as we were concerned and that
was the height we flew at, and what we knew with the Hurricane was, if
caught out and if you went round in circles, you could fly out of range and

keep out of range, but you didn't want to go up high, you didn't want to use altitude against the 109 because he would beat you to it.

Most of us had flown formations in vics of three so we didn't know any better until we saw the Germans and we saw they all seemed to be units of four aeroplanes, and then when we looked at the whole thing and thought it over academically we realised that they were safeguarding each other because in line abreast they were looking every way and therefore could operate as two pairs making a four but we only learned that one during the Battle of Britain.

Early on 10 May 1940 the Germans attacked.

It had been very quiet and we weren't given any information at all, any intelligence and we realised something was happening at three o'clock in the morning when we heard aeroplanes flying all over the place. We said, 'Well that can't be the RAF, that must be the Germans,' and then when daylight came up we realised the Germans had started, the Phoney War had come to a shuddering halt and then as a result of that we moved from Vassincourt, where we were, to another base, Berry-au-Bac, closer to Reims.

Well, first of all my experience during that period of the actual war when it started was we were moving from base to base, moving from billet to billet and if we weren't doing that we were standing by and if we weren't standing by we were in the bloody air and being told where to go.

As far as the aircrew were concerned we travelled lightly anyway and any heavy thing had already been earmarked for a certain vehicle when the squadron itself moved so all we did was to pick up our own light holdall with minimum of uniform and take it with us and when we got to the other place there the lorry was with our heavy stuff so we had already organised it between ourselves.

The ground crew had a tough time but the number of vehicles we had in the squadron was sufficient to transport all the ground crew so there was no problem there at all. It was a question of where to go and which unit went first because there was an advanced party and then a rear party.

During the first three days of the shooting war from 10 May Billy shot down three and shared a fourth Dornier 17. However his few days of aggressive action came to an end in a dramatic way.

Luckily, invariably we were being led by somebody so we didn't have to worry too much about what was happening. My first real recollection of actual warfare was my last trip of that period when I went up in a section of four aeroplanes with Prosser Hanks leading and I was not in my own aeroplane but in another one. When I got to 18,000 feet I realised I had no oxygen so

I called up the leader and said, 'I have no oxygen, instructions please,' and in a very curt way he told me to bugger off home, which I was in the process of doing when I saw three Dorniers. I don't think they saw me because I got behind one quite close and was able to inflict enough damage to realise I'd shot something down. I was in the process of getting behind the leader when I found somebody had got behind me and I hadn't seen them. I had broken all the rules I'd been teaching myself over the last four years, not looking behind, and this was a Messerschmitt 110 and he got me good and proper. I was flaming, covered in glycol, covered in everything you could think of and panicking to get out of the aeroplane. I undid everything and then realised as I banged my head that I hadn't released the hood which probably saved my life because the flames were coming up and had I opened the hood, I was covered in petrol anyway, the flames would have got me. So by the time I decided the hood should be released I was upside down and fell out and of course the flames were going up and not against me. I had been hit with bullets in my back and legs and I thought, at one period, that my leg had been shot off. Bits of shrapnel had hit me but when I landed with my parachute I realised that perhaps I had two legs still and then I came across the next nasty shock. That was a lot of French farmers with scythes and all sorts of instruments were coming up towards me and they were absolutely certain I was a German and I found it very difficult to be able to show them my RAF wings but by the time they got close enough to be really lethal I was able to demonstrate and tell them that I was an English pilot. They couldn't have been kinder so they got me to a French medical unit. I was met there by two French orderlies who said in their very best French that they were very sorry but the doctors weren't available because they had gone home for lunch and in any case there was no anesthetic and I was to grit my teeth while they got hold of all the stuff out of my back, which they did so. I appreciated what outlaws and other people in America must have felt when they were being medically looked after without any anesthetic, it was a very unattractive period.

I was just bloody glad to be out of the aeroplane. I was wondering what the hell had hit me. Much more worried about that. I'd never parachuted before. It was just one of those things. Thank Christ we'd got a parachute, and at one period, not this war but World War 1, some very senior officer said don't give them any parachutes. We had the same thing in France – don't give them any armour plating – and he was sacked. We had it just in time because what hit me went through where the Sutton harness went through.

First of all I stayed within the French hospital environment and I went from Rethel (north east of Reims) up in the north all the way down to

Chartres (south west of Paris) into a French hospital and from there I was picked up by my girlfriend who was an American and an ambulance driver. She was in uniform and I wasn't because my uniform had been destroyed and as we were driving through Versailles some French police stopped us and turned round to her, who was in uniform, and said who have you got there and she said a British air force officer. They said, 'Oh yes, has he got any identification?' Not a thing but you can always ring up the embassy and find out whether they've got any records of who I am which they did and they found that the British embassy had left Paris to go down to Brest or somewhere but luckily she had been a girlfriend of an American diplomat so was able to get onto him and he was able to verify who and what I was. Otherwise I might easily have been put up against the wall and shot...but I wasn't so I got back to Paris literally within twenty-four hours before the Germans walked in and she lent me one of her cars. It was a very wealthy American family, car full of petrol and in that car I drove all the way to Le Mans but it took me two days because of all the refugees. The Americans had told me the Germans had won the war and to get the hell out of Paris. I was aware that the battle hadn't gone all that well for us and the sooner I got out of France the better and therefore one accepted these people who were all escaping were a part of war.

It was the most distressing sight I have ever seen including the hundreds of French uniforms who had just thrown everything away and were in this exodus from Paris. But anyway I got to Le Mans and the squadron was still there and I got a lift in an aeroplane that was going back to England, that was how I got out of France.

Billy recuperated fully from his wounds and was posted as a flying instructor to 6OTU at Sutton Bridge, teaching new pilots how to fly the Hurricane.

The majority of the British pilots were volunteer reservists, mainly sergeant pilots and then a lot of Poles came through who had operated in Poland and in France and then had been with the French Air Force and escaped to England and then joined the RAF. They were very experienced people and the head of that bunch was a chap called Skalski who eventually became a general. He had a most extraordinary career when the war came to an end because he decided he would go back to Poland, not to see his contemporaries but to see his parents. When he arrived there he found he was hobnobbing with the Russians and telling the Russians how good the RAF were and the RAF did this and the RAF did that and they took grave exception to this Pole telling them how good the RAF were against others and he was court-martialled by the Russians. He was very nearly put up against the wall but instead he was posted to one of these Gulags where he stayed for two years until they released him. He came back to Warsaw and drank himself to death. The rest were very peculiar people, the Poles that we had. They were dedicated haters of the Germans and any opportunity to slaughter an aeroplane they took full advantage. They didn't destroy the aeroplanes as we did, they destroyed the man who was flying the aeroplane as well.

There's one other story I can tell you about people we had there. At one point we got the Harvard aeroplane and looking at it we couldn't find anywhere to put our hearing aids into, with the Gosport tubing. Eventually we did find some tubing and we could talk and about two weeks after this transformation we had a whole bunch of Canadians arrive and they got into this Harvard and looked at the method of talking to the instructor and said, 'We're not going to fly in this bloody aeroplane,' and we asked why and they said, 'Do you know what you have used to communicate with us? That is our pee tubing because we stay in these aeroplanes for anything up to three hours and we have to have a widdle, that is exactly what you have used. How we communicate in Canada is with a radio.'

We were told to give them twenty hours and teach them the rudiments of formation flying and operational formation flying and that was it. And a little bit of aerobatics and any information that we could give them of our experience of operating this particular aeroplane, which was the Hurricane.

When I got there we had a CO, or chief flying instructor, a man called Edwardes-Jones, who eventually became an Air Marshal, and he had just given up a squadron at Tangmere and I kept on saying, 'Look Sir, this is not my scene at all.' He said, 'No, you've got to do your stint.' So after a few months of this he got so bored with my constantly... he had me posted to Tangmere to his old squadron as a flight commander.

Tangmere was not particularly busy at that time but I was only with them for about a week, did a bit of flying with new pilots to get to know that area which I knew anyway, and the reason I left there was they called for volunteers for this new organisation. I really didn't get to know very much new and Tangmere, to me, was an old friend so I knew it all. All I wanted to do was to get on with the battle.

I was with 213 Squadron for about a week when the CO, (Sqn Ldr D.S.) MacDonald, called me into his office and said, 'Billy, they're calling for experienced pilots to volunteer for this organisation called the Jim Crows, are you the slightest bit interested?' I said, 'What the hell are they?'

He explained what they were and so it sounded as though it was interesting and a rather vital part of the defence of 11 Group and I said, 'Yes, I'd like, if you've got somebody to take over from me, to volunteer for this organisation.' Now the reason I said yes was that this unit, which was only called a flight, had been formed to fill in a gap. The gap was that a part of the German Air Force's attack against Fighter Command was against these huge radar stations and therefore 11 Group was only getting a certain amount of information but not enough to really perform its task. Its task was to intercept any organisation that was definitely coming into England to attack either airfields or industry and the unit that I had volunteered to join was called the Jim Crows. I don't know but I think it's an American expression, some form of scouting organisation.

We started off with Hurricanes first and our job was, as soon as the radar that existed saw activities in France, they called on us to take off to intercept these formations and to give as much information back to 11 Group as to the formation, the numbers, their heights and the directions. That was our job. We were sent off in pairs and it was a hairy one because everyone liked the look of two aeroplanes by themselves both the Royal Air Force and the German Air Force and we were being attacked the whole time by either one or the other and having to verify that we were either friendly or unfriendly to whoever it was that was attacking us. So we had to keep our eyes firmly open. But none of us were ever shot down, we were too experienced for that. So I stayed with this organisation, 421 Flight. It was formed into a squadron in the end called 91 Squadron, and I stayed with them for the next four or five months.

We just shadowed them, kept out of the way and kept talking, and that brings me up to an incident with Keith Park who I'd known before. He rang me up and said, 'Billy, I'd like you to come and have lunch with me,' and I thought, 'By God, I wonder what's cooking here.' And so I arrived at 11 Group and he said, 'Now, before we have lunch I'm going to take you down to the Ops Room,' and on our way down there, as we got closer, you could hear a lot of chatting going on. I thought it was a bit peculiar and as we came into the Operations Room and onto the floor where all the WAAFs were there was the most terrible language going on and I could recognise some of the voices from 421 Flight. We were talking directly onto the table to fill in the gaps the radar and the Observer Corps hadn't covered and while we were doing this we were being attacked at the same time. We were talking in our normal way – 'What the ..... hell's going on?' – and Keith Park didn't say anything apart from 'We'll go and have lunch, Billy, you've got the message haven't you? Tell your boys to moderate their language as the little WAAFs are listening to this and I don't think it's very gentlemanly.' And that was an incident I will never forget.

Having served with him we revered him. He was highly decorated, he flew aeroplanes and he used to wander around in his white uniform and we respected him and not only respected but once again the father and son relationship was very strong there. He used to listen to us and we used to listen to him and we got on very well. It was a healthy relationship at all times and I met him later on in Cairo when he was commander in chief there.

421 Flight operated from three different airfields at one period: Manston, Detling and then Hawkinge eventually, and it was a question of space really. If it was too busy with too many aeroplanes being scrambled there wasn't enough room for us to operate because we had to get up before these people so we ended up basically, during the final phases of the Battle of Britain, at Hawkinge. It meant that we could go from Hawkinge to the French coast and pick up the formations before they left France.

Incidentally what I have forgotten was we started off with Hurricanes but we turned round to Keith Park and said this is a useless bloody aeroplane, it's not fast enough, can you give us any Spitfires; so we were re-equipped with Spitfire IIs. The Spitfire or the Hurricane? My overall answer is how did we operate it because flying operationally is two things, flying an aeroplane and operating it, if you understand the subtlety. You just flew the aeroplane automatically, but operationally it was quite a different thing. How did you operate the aeroplane? Did you go in circles? Did you dive? Did you go up to height? So it's a very difficult choice to make that one.

I suppose in retrospect it was incredible but it was just a job of work. We'd be told to count, within reason, and estimate the height they were flying, but the reason we kept at low level was to look up. At first they had us flying at altitude looking down but that was just not on at all. First of all the time factor to get up there and then find the formation, turn and come with it, was just not on whereas we preferred to climb to 10,000 feet, go there, pick them up and then come home.

I think the job I had to do with the Jim Crows was unusual, not talked about a lot, and is very rarely mentioned as a part of the Battle of Britain success. We were successful and we were only a handful. We only had 12 aeroplanes and 24 pilots to do the whole thing. Having got out of an operational training unit to get into an operational squadron and to do a job of work of importance was, in my mind, a successful part of the Battle of Britain.

Yes we were always given a certain amount of time off, definitely, released for 24 hours and, depending on where we were, decided where we would spend our leisure time. When we were at Biggin Hill then straight up to London. When we were at Hawkinge, down to Folkestone, and all we did was have a drink or two and a meal and if we had any friends then to go and see them. We had a very restricted social life. It was mainly on the station, and if you had time off, (the plan) was to get some sleep in because we used to get very tired. Two or three trips a day for about a week was about the maximum we could take without endangering ourselves or the job we were trying to do.

One of the questions regularly asked of wartime operational pilots was 'were you scared?' As expected Billy Drake had his own personal way of answering.

A lot of people have been asked this, of people who have gone to war. Some say if they weren't scared they were bloody liars. As far as I was concerned we were not worried about being killed. Most of us were worried about being wounded or taken prisoner of war, and I do remember one, this is particularly in the Kittyhawks in the desert, we were worried about being shot in our genitals, and I've got a photograph with my legs firmly closed when I was firing. It's funny, I can only say I was never scared. I was apprehensive but not scared. For example, particularly in the desert, it was a different thing, we were masters of the situation there. What I found was, after a successful bombing raid, for example, with twelve Kittyhawks against a German ground formation, one would land back and get the airman to refuel and rearm the aeroplane and by that time you were half way through a cup of tea and instead of saying 'Tell me when that aeroplane's ready as I want to take off,' by the time I had got to the end of my cup of tea, 'another cup please,' and I had no more wish to get in that bloody aeroplane. I was not personally scared but I was apprehensive.

It was now 1941. Billy undertook a few of the early 'rhubarbs' over France and was awarded the DFC.

By this time I had been one of the many young pilots who had crossed swords with Leigh Mallory who didn't like me at all, but just a few months after the end of the Battle of Britain I was posted as chief flying instructor at a Spitfire operational training unit at Heston so I was not only posted out of Leigh Mallory's but promoted at the same time. So I was at Heston teaching people how to fly Spitfires and I had three extraordinary people as part of the organisation. 'Taffy' Ira Jones was a World War 1 ace and he shot down about twenty-three aeroplanes. He also crashed twenty-three because he had no idea where the ground was when he came into land. His eyesight was completely gone so as many as he shot down he was destroying (his own aircraft) coming into land. Then Johnny Kent, a Canadian, who was with the Poles at Northolt, he was the chief instructor. And then Norman Ryder, and he was chief ground instructor.

In early October 1941 Billy went back to operational flying and for the next few years as his score grew so did the legend. He commanded 128 Squadron in West Africa. He was then posted to the Desert Air Force commanding 112 (Shark) Squadron, succeeding Clive 'Killer' Caldwell and flying with such great pilots as Neville Duke. He was awarded both a bar to his DFC and a DSO while in the desert and led the squadron throughout the El Alamein campaign.

Promoted to wing commander Billy was posted to Malta to command the Krendi wing, swapping his Kittyhawks for Spitfires. Late in 1943 he returned to the UK and commanded 20 Wing flying Typhoons before a trip to the US Command School in Kansas ended his operational wartime flying. He returned to join Eisenhower's staff and his last act of the war was delivering the surrender document to the Quisling government in Norway.

Billy was credited with twenty-four and a half 'kills' during his wartime flying and was known as one of the most colourful, and aggressive, wartime RAF commanders.

He stayed in the Royal Air Force, attaining the rank of Group Captain, until 1963. After living and managing property in the Algarve for twenty years Billy returned to the UK, living in Teignmouth, Devon, until his death.

For a long time Billy was reticent about his RAF career and in particular the war years. Eventually he was persuaded to tell his story to author Christopher Shores but also took the time to be interviewed at length for this project. He was at great pains to tell us why it had taken him so long to tell the story.

You only remember the best bits and the fact that we were at war was neither one thing or the other. It was something we were told to do. We didn't realise it was going to make history. We didn't realise that we were part of history and when we weren't operating whatever it was, in the army, the navy or the air force, we were having fun like any other young people. That more or less sums it up. For most of us it was an enjoyable period, not only enjoyable but also a part of history that one can now look back on and say it was one of our growing pains. One can also say that for some of us it was a time of responsibility that we would never have experienced otherwise at a very, very young age. And then you come to 1945-46 onwards that there was a long period where we all stayed in a sort of vacuum of not experiencing in that long period what we experienced in a very short period. In other words we came back to the normality of growing up, rather the rest of our personalities grew up.

No. I think what most of us, and I'm talking about everyone who took part in World War 2 or World War 1 for that matter, is what our memories can remind us of is a period of our lives which is very personal and that is why very few of us have ever talked to our children about the war. That is why it is you people who are beginning to drag out of our memory cells what was going on. Otherwise who can we talk to about the war except our old friends and most of them are dead or living way out of our respective spheres, and therefore the quicker you get us to talk the more of actual history are you going to get hold of.

It's not to be divulged to other people other than those who were actually a part of that existence and I'm sure that applies to a tremendous number of people like the Land Girls – do they talk about what they did on the farms? Do the factory worker girls, do they talk about it with their husbands and other people, or their children? No they don't. It was a very personal part of their lives at a very young age and it's only years later that people like yourselves have been able to drag us out of our cocoon to talk. You are the people who keep saying you're all fucking heroes. We don't consider ourselves heroes, we just consider that we did a job of work. And I'm talking about everybody whether they were a factory worker, land girl, airman or a sailor. If you start talking to any sailors who were on these convoys, those who were left alive, you can talk to any real bomber pilot and talk about the attrition rate, they won't talk about it. It's so personal and I think most of us think that way. It was so personal. We don't think, or we haven't thought, that there is any interest. I took my two sons eventually, in their forties and just quite recently, to see this hole I had made with this Hurricane in France and they suddenly saw the background of who was taking films. What the fucking hell are they taking films of you for? What the hell did you do? They hadn't a clue. And as a result of that they now see a totally different Drake, a totally different father, who'd like to get more out of me and I am quite willing to do it if they ask reasonable questions, but they also are so used to not asking questions that they still don't ask. They do a bit more. Or they are beginning to realise why they respect me. Why they've always respected me, not as Daddy but as Billy Drake my father.

Wing Commander Peter Ayerst DFC
4 November 1920-15 May 2014

Peter Ayerst was born in Westcliff-on-Sea in Essex and was educated at Westcliff High School for Boys. His early aviation experiences involved helping civilian pilots at his local Romford airfield before he applied for a short service commission with the RAF in June 1938. He flew Miles Magisters at 19 EFTS at Gatwick before advancing to 12FTS at Grantham where he was on the RAF's first ever course on Harvards and the second trainee to fly one.

I finished my advanced training at Grantham in Lincolnshire and I was posted to No. 73 Squadron also in Lincolnshire at a place called Digby. They had Hurricane Is and I arrived there about four or five weeks before war was declared. It was in late July early August and war was declared on 3 September 1939 but it was rather strange. When I went to the flight there was one of the flying officers who was told to take me up in a Miles Magister. They thought I had come through the biplane training scheme and he thought I'd better get used to flying monoplanes. I'd had all my training on monoplanes and with the Harvard, of course, we had to raise the undercarriage, change the pitch of the airscrew and all that sort of thing, so it was quite a good experience. So I went up there and joined the squadron and they said, 'We want old Tommy Tucker – his name was – to take you up in the Magister to show you the sort of things you do in a Hurricane.' Of course I knew all the things he was trying to show me, probably a lot better than he did, but anyway that's beside the point. So I said I'd flown monoplanes and he said there really wasn't much point in having this trip but we had to do it and then I flew a Hurricane. I was briefed on the cockpit and starting procedures and various other things and I did my first solo on a Hurricane which was quite good and I found it a good aeroplane to fly. So this was about a month before war was declared.

The atmosphere was good but we didn't really know war was coming, not until the actual time when the prime minister of the day, Neville

Chamberlain, came back from a talk with Hitler. This was in 1938 just about the time I was going through my training – so when I was with 73 Squadron at Digby. I then flew a few times and we didn't think war was going to be declared but it was getting a bit dicey. The Germans overran Poland and Hitler was really becoming offensive in various other directions as well and then on 3 September 1939 we listened to the prime minister again. It was a Sunday, I always remember it so well, and I was in the mess at Digby, all the pilots were there because we knew the prime minister was going to speak at eleven o'clock, which he did, and then he said, 'Just on a year ago I came back from Germany and I said we would have peace in our time, but I regret to say it hasn't worked out that way. Hitler has not stuck to his word and he's overrun various countries and now we are declaring war on him and so as of now, eleven o'clock on Sunday morning 3 September 1939 we are at war with Germany.' And four days after that they sent our squadron to France.

Peter and the rest of the 73 Squadron personnel went off to France with no real knowledge of their role.

First of all we went to Le Havre because all our ground troops had to go over by boat and they weren't there so we had to wait at Le Havre until the ground forces got there. When we got established in Le Havre together with No.1 Squadron we were doing quite a bit of flying and after about three weeks they moved us up behind the Belgian border to a place called Norrent-Fontes and we were under canvas up there. Also 1 Squadron moved up as well, we were on the same airfield, and also not so far away were the other two Hurricane squadrons, 85 and 87. We were there for about two or three weeks when they decided to move 1 and 73 Squadrons to the south. 1 Squadron went to a place called Bar-le-Duc and 73 Squadron went to Rouvres and that's where we stayed until 10 May 1940 when the Germans overran the Low Countries, but during the time we were there we were very busy.

We used to fly in the old-fashioned vic of three and we used to patrol up and down the French-German border, east of Metz and Thionville, and we used to fly at about 25,000ft up and down for an hour at a time, three of us, and then another three, weather permitting, would come up and we would return to base and the squadron kept this going all day long. On a number of occasions an odd 109 came up to see what it was all about and we got a little mixed up with them. We had the first RAF fighter ace of the war in our squadron, a New Zealander by the name of Cobber Cain, and he was quite a character. He seemed to find 109s where no-one else could see them and was shooting them down in odd places. He didn't build up a massive score but he was doing pretty well. He was my section leader. I was in 'B' Flight and my flight commander was a chap named Ian Scoular and the deputy flight commander and section leader was Cobber Kain. So I got quite a good training into fighter attacks and fighter combat by being with him because he was really quite good.

We used to fly up in wide formation. When we were flying up and down in vics of three we opened up to sixty or seventy yards apart so we weren't trying to do it in close formation. On a number of occasions we got involved and so it was a good grounding for what was to come later in the war. We were the only fighter squadrons in the RAF who had been involved in activity because the UK squadrons, of course, weren't doing anything at all, I mean the fighter squadrons.

On 6 November Peter had his first real contact with the enemy, one that would see him get a new nickname.

We had been down in the area south of Luxembourg for about a month I suppose and we used to do this thing called aerodrome defence. We had a pilot sitting in the cockpit all strapped in and ready to go if a warning came through. Our early warning system was something that is almost difficult to believe. We had some French soldiers in a dugout down one side of the airfield. Rouvres was just a small grass airfield, then with one lane down one side and on the other side of this lane were some French soldiers who dug themselves into trenches. They had a powerful pair of binoculars, they were looking to the east, and if they saw aircraft which they couldn't identify or which they could identify as Germans they used to give us the early warning system which was waving a red flag. So I was sitting there strapped in this day next to our flight office, which was a twelve-foot ridge tent, and someone in the flight said, 'A red flag's waving, the flag's waving.' I started up and it so happened this particular day was a bright clear sky day, a blue sky, and I could see this aircraft coming over our airfield at about 25,000ft I should think and he was obviously doing photographic work trying to photograph our airfield. So I took off, and of course with this two-bladed airscrew it hadn't got a tremendous performance in the climb or anywhere for that matter so I did a full throttle take-off and climbed up. I climbed up as hard and as fast as I could and he saw me coming up and decided he had had enough; he wasn't going to risk it any further and turned round and went back in an easterly direction towards the German-French border. So I thought I'd carry on. I hadn't been airborne very long, I was full throttle all the time so the fuel consumption was quite high, and I was climbing up and gradually getting near him. I got to about 20,000ft and I was still about two miles from him and he'd seen me and decided he was going to go down, and he went down into some cloud at a lower level and I lost him. I didn't get a shot at him at all. So I thought it was time for me to turn round and go home, but unbeknown to me, and I was very inexperienced generally as a pilot, I'd only done less than 200 hours, so I turned round and came back and this particular day No.1 Squadron came over from their base at Bar-le-Duc and it was agreed between the two squadron commanders they were going to put up the first offensive fighter patrol of the war, two squadrons up and down the border. Twenty-four Hurricanes and I was turning round. I'd gone far farther east than I knew about or anticipated and I was way into Germany and I didn't know. I thought I'd gone over the border but not by far. I turned in a westerly heading to get back over the border and I had been going for some time and I saw nine aircraft coming up below me in a line astern formation, one behind the other. And I thought, 'Here come the chaps on patrol with 1 and 73 Squadron, nine of them coming up in sections,' so I thought I hadn't been airborne long so I might as well join up and stay on patrol with them. These nine aircraft were below me and I thought, 'Ah they've seen me, they want me to join on the formation,' because they pulled out in front of me so I tacked in behind and got in close to formate on them and saw these huge great black crosses. I'd never seen a Messerschmitt 109 before and I thought they were Hurricanes so I pulled up, gave a quick squirt at the tail-end Charlie and I went straight down, I was about 18,000ft at the time. I went straight down and unbeknown to me there were another eighteen making a total of twenty-seven 109s. I didn't know it at the time of course, I only learned about it afterwards. So I had twenty-seven of them chasing me and I was flat out, full throttle, and I didn't realise I was over France until I saw a factory where they had sloping glass roofing and in France they always painted this glass with a blue paint, why I don't know but they did. Also, unbeknown to me, as I was crossing the border I led these Germans through a French fighter patrol. They had Morane 406s and Curtiss Hawks, nine of them, and these Messerschmitts were so much concentrating on me they weren't looking at their own backsides and the French people were able to shoot nine of them down. It was the first big air battle of the war and I was dubbed 'Decoy'. By this time I didn't have the faintest idea where I was apart from the fact that I did know I was back over France and I had been flying for some time in a westerly direction before I got into that situation so I thought I was getting a bit low on fuel having been at full throttle for such a long time. I had to find somewhere to land and I just throttled back to save fuel and then I saw some aircraft circling. I thought there must be an airfield there. I went over there and sure enough there was and I landed there and I finished my landing run and turned off and as I turned off my airscrew stopped as I had run out of fuel. It was at Nancy south of Metz and I had to stay there the night because by this time it was about 5.30 and of course being November it was beginning to get a bit dark. I stayed the night there and went back to my base the next day. When I got back the flight sergeant engineer in our squadron said, 'You know Sir you should never have flown this aircraft back.' I said, 'Why not?' He said, 'You've got quite a few holes and damage in the tailplane which might have been dangerous.' And as it happened there was quite a bit of damage to the aircraft. I didn't even know I'd been hit; so there we go, ignorance is bliss.

The Winter of 1939-40 was renowned as a bitterly cold one. From mid-December throughout January and February the temperature in northern France barely rose above freezing and there were heavy snowfalls, severe frosts and thick fog.

We weren't living in tents in that cold period. When we got to Rouvres we were all living in village houses. I was in a house with a very old French couple and I had quite a comfortable bed. My washing facilities were a bowl of water, or rather a bowl with a jug of water, always cold of course, but I had a batman whose name was Ashley who used to bring me a mug of hot water for shaving in and a cup of tea. Unfortunately he lost his life on the boat that went down off the west coast of France during the time we were pulling out. I didn't need much waking up but he did this every morning so I had shaving water but I had to wash in cold water. I did that every morning for months and months but the cold weather, that didn't start until late December into early January of 1940. That's when the snow started and when it did come down it fell very heavily. We had a lot of very deep snow which stopped us from flying. We couldn't get airborne at all but of course it applied to everyone else in the area including the Germans. It was a cold spell of weather which lasted for the best part of two months. We did clear the airfield a bit and as we got on we were able to operate but it was a very bad weather patch.

Throughout this period Peter, along with his fellow 73 Squadron pilots, gained experience flying their Hurricanes.

It was the only fighter that I had any experience of at all so I couldn't compare it to anything else and we always thought it was a good aircraft. The other thing was that in March 1940 they took our two-bladed airscrew jobs away from us and then we got three-bladed and that was much, much better. Better take-off and better performance generally and I think they increased the power of the engine slightly, not by a lot, so it was a better aircraft we got from about March 1940 onwards. Certainly the two-bladed airscrew one was a bit behind the times.

During his time in France Peter had a number of chances to put his training and experience into action.

When I was going up and down on one of these patrols there were three of us and three 109s attacked us. Cobber Kain was leading the section. He got one and we got mixed up with them, and I got one, and he went down and I saw him bale out so I knew the aircraft had crashed. I didn't really see where the aircraft crashed but the pilot had baled out and that was the first 109 that I got. In France I got about two or three. I got two certainly and three probably.

Finally the full force of the German Blitzkrieg hit the allies in May 1940.

10 May was the day the Germans crossed into the Low Countries up north of us. They did bomb our airfield that morning and it was then decided we would pull out straight away because we were the squadron of the RAF that was nearest the German-French border. We pulled out and we moved to Rheims about 100 miles west of where we were and we stayed there for about three weeks. While we were there we were living in trenches but we didn't have any messes or any proper cover. It was a bit tough really because when we needed rest we weren't getting the proper rest we needed. Then after that we moved to a place further south and further west near Troyes, and we were there for a couple of weeks and then they moved us once again and it was there, we hadn't been there long, when they decided that the chaps who had been in France all the time should go home. We had lost one or two and one or two had already gone home and the chaps who were the old timers as I called them, of which I was one, only about five or six of us were left. So they said they were going to relieve us en masse and send some new pilots out and we would go back to UK. Well when it got to the time to go back to the UK we had to go back by train to Paris and wanted to get a train to Cherbourg to get on to a boat. 'Can you please tell us the times?' 'No trains to Cherbourg whatsoever, all cancelled.' So we thought we had to get to Cherbourg somehow so we managed to make our own way. I managed to get there on the back of an old potato lorry and the driver said I couldn't sit in the front with him as he had his dog there so I had to sit in the back amongst a lot of sacks of potatoes and when we got on the road it was incredible. The refugees had started coming away from near the Belgian border and they were clogging the roads up. They were towing cars with horses because they hadn't got any petrol and they were one behind the

other, mile after mile, and they were only narrow these French roads. I was in this lorry and he was trying to pass them. He did most of the time but he wasn't able to keep up a very good speed. Eventually after many hours we got to Cherbourg and I managed to get on a boat to Southampton which was the last but one out because Dunkirk had started further east.

It would not be quite so easy for the ground crew to get away.

In 73 Squadron we had a very good ground crew. We had A Flight and B Flight and our flight headquarters were these twelve-foot ridge tents. We were down in one corner of the airfield and I was in B Flight. A Flight was down in another corner of the airfield and then we also had a dugout with a small control centre, two or three airmen with a couple of phones and they were able to keep in contact with both flights so if the CO went in there and issued some instructions they could pass them on to us fairly well. That worked alright as long as it had to which was until 10 May, the day when we moved out. The ground crew did a good job. They were a very good ground crew. Unfortunately we lost a lot of them in that boat that went down, the *Lancastria*.

I didn't know that we had so many chaps on board until I learned later that a lot of the very good chaps went down on that. I think we lost about sixty 73 Squadron chaps on it. They were all making their way to the west of France, finished up in the French ports down there, and that's where they picked up the *Lancastria*.

Peter's first experience of a German bombing raid was on 10 May at Rouvres. In the ensuing days he managed to see first-hand the abilities of the German fighter pilots.

First of all, the German pilots were quite good as they always had been but what they did have over us was an enormous superiority in numbers. That's where they were on top of us all the time. They had so many more aircraft in the air so as far as their pilots were concerned they were quite good. I would almost put them on a par with ourselves (laughing). The Germans bombed our airfield and it was at that time the CO had been given instructions from the Group – we had a small Group headquarters – and they said we had to get out. So really we just got out. We weren't there for long when raids were going on and they dropped a few bombs on the airfield which we had to take care about so really we weren't there long enough to suffer tremendous attacks. We had the early morning attacks and those were the ones that told the bosses it was time to make a move.

I think it (Me109) was a very good fighting machine. In performance, generally, it was better than the Hurricane but one thing we did have on them was manoeuvrability, we could out-turn them, so although they had speed on us if we saw them coming down we could just wait and suddenly pull round into a tight turn and there was no way they could stay with us, so that was a good asset to the Hurricane when we came across the 109s.

While Peter could not recall much of the detail of his time in France some emotions stayed with him.

I can't remember having been scared much at all. I'd been apprehensive, wondering whether I was going to get through this, sort of thing, but I can't remember being really scared. I always looked at it as, if I was having to fight the Germans I aimed to get him. He would be a dead one before me; and that philosophy I stuck with all the way through the war.

I am very lucky to be sitting here I can tell you. I had many close shaves and I always felt it was never going to be me, it was always going to be you, you bastard.

However Peter did remember his train journey when he returned to the UK.

We landed at Southampton, it was a lovely day, I remember it well. I had to get on the train to get to Waterloo and as we were going through, it was about two o'clock in the afternoon and two or three times we passed cricket grounds and there were these chaps playing cricket, all in their whites, we could hardly believe it. We had been sleeping rough for about three or four weeks and hadn't had much sleep and we were all a bit knackered and there were these chaps having a lovely game of cricket. It was unbelievable.

We got to London and reported to the RTO, the Railway Transport Officer, who was a major in the army and we said, 'Where are we to go to?' and he said, 'I think the best thing for you air force chaps to do is go back to the stations you were at before you went to France,' which we did and three of us returned about that time. We all went up to Digby, and we were in the mess up there and we reported to the station commander. He said, 'Well I don't know what to do with you. I'd better ring up Group,' which was 12 Group who were based not far away. The station commander got onto the AOC of 12 Group, Leigh Mallory, and said he had these chaps here, what did he want him to do with them and he said, 'Tell them to stay in the mess, tell them to stay with you and I'm coming over as I want to see them.' So he came over and we went into the Ladies room in the mess and he wanted to know all about what had been going on in France and how we had coped and so on. He wanted to get as much information as he could from us and then he said, 'I expect you would all like some leave?' We hadn't had any leave for a long time and we said, 'Yes we were thinking of about two weeks leave,' and he said, 'I'll give you four days and then I want you back because we've got some new units we are forming and they are called Operational Training Units. We have two at the moment and we are going to form another one shortly.' The two they had, one was at Sutton Bridge near Kings Lynn and the other one was at Aston Down near Gloucester somewhere, and the three of us were all sent to Sutton Bridge and became instructors. It was the first time we had become instructors; they hadn't had OTUs before, they were all new. We had Hurricanes at Sutton Bridge and they also did at Aston Down. I'd been there for three or four weeks and they said they were setting up a new OTU at a place called Hawarden near Chester and they were going to have Spitfires there so it was becoming a Spitfire OTU and some of our chaps were going to have to go over there of which I was one. I think it was probably in early July when I was posted to Hawarden.

It was while instructing at Hawarden that Peter made his operational mark on the Battle of Britain. It was 14 August 1940.

It was rather strange. In those days we had the extra hour of daylight because they put the clocks forward another hour and we'd finished flying. We were living under canvas at that time and our mess was a marquee tent and our flight offices were tents down the perimeter of the airfield and we parked our aircraft well spaced out. We never parked them close in case of bombing or strafing so they wouldn't present a solid target. We'd had a good day's flying and about half past seven or eight o'clock at night we'd packed up and the ground crews were putting the aircraft to one side and getting them ready for the next day. We went over to the mess to have a beer in the old marquee tent. We hadn't been there more than a few minutes when we heard a lot of bangs, explosions. That's funny, we went outside, looked out and we saw an aircraft flying along and those bangs were bombs it had dropped on RAF Sealand which was only about five or six miles away from us. The ground crew were still out there and we said, 'Get three aircraft ready,' so they started up three aircraft. We all went off and got over Sealand and saw this aircraft. He didn't think he was going to be intercepted by fighters, Spitfires. Up there he thought he was safe. The other two chaps went in and got some shots at it and I went in last. I got him fair and square and he came down. He didn't crash down, he made a forced landing in a field. It was a very good wheels-up crash landing and they all got away with it. It didn't catch fire or anything although they did set fire to it after they got on the ground. That was it, I got a Heinkel 111. The chaps were all taken prisoner and we shot down a He111 on 14 August. I was the last one to attack it and I was the one who saw it crash land. As instructors we used to do patrols over Liverpool and Manchester. We used to do readiness from time to time. And scrambles if they thought any aircraft might be showing up on the radar so we were, in addition to being instructors, semi operational.

Up there we were quite busy. One of our other chaps shot an aircraft down about a month after us but it went into the Welsh mountains somewhere. We kept a fairly good alert on.

At this point in the war, July and August 1940, the squadrons on the front line were under tremendous pressure from enemy bomber formations and their fighter escorts. Aircraft losses could be replaced relatively easily but to find replacement pilots was much more difficult.

The pressure didn't come on us as instructors but it did come on our bosses who were under a great deal of pressure I think. We carried on instructing. We knew the squadrons were short of pilots and they wanted some reinforcements as quickly as possible. On the other hand there's no point in sending chaps down to them who hadn't had sufficient training to make them of some use and help to the squadrons so I suppose the shortest time that some of the chaps were with us was about three weeks, two to three weeks, and by that time they had flown the Spitfire, it was a Spitfire OTU. They'd flown the Spitfire, they knew what it was like to fly in formation. We gave them some opportunity to fire the guns. We had targets in the sea in the River Dee and generally we tried to give them some idea of what was required of them once they joined a squadron. What you can learn in two to three weeks is not a great deal but nevertheless they had flown Spitfires and had some competence on the aircraft.

But perhaps the best advice that the instructors could pass on was the personal flying experience they had gained during the Battle for France.

To look behind you three quarters of the time and in front only a quarter as any attacks always came from the rear, you always looked behind you, hence the reason fighter pilots in the Battle of Britain days wore silk scarves, we started that in France, round our necks because the Sutton harness straps were very hard. They used to come across and fasten and the edge of the strap caught your neck so if you're turning all the time and looking behind you you used to get sore necks and that's why all the chaps on fighters wore silk scarves, or their girlfriend's silk stockings. Of course the bomber boys used to make a bit of a joke about it but there was a reason for it, to stop your neck getting chafed.

To gain the confidence of the chaps you're trying to instruct, giving them a good detailed briefing on the ground before the flight so that they know what to expect and they know what they're expected to do when they get airborne. So you might say you're going to do certain types of attacks or formations, and changing formations. You give them a thorough briefing on what you plan to do with them in the air and then, having completed that airborne sortie, come down and have another debrief on how it went afterwards and go through it carefully. I tried to do that as well as I could and I think it stood the chaps in good stead. A number of them learned things quickly and it probably helped them in their own career later on, possibly saving their lives or whatever.

During Peter's time at Hawarden many of the pilots who came through the training scheme would go on to be aces and senior commanders. Among them was Paddy Finucane, an Irishman who would go on to become an ace, a wing commander by the age of 22, and be awarded a DSO and three DFCs. Perhaps the most famous was Johnnie Johnson who would see the tail end of the Battle of Britain but go on to become the RAF's highest scoring ace of the war.

Jamie Rankin came through, he was only there for about ten days before he went off and became a squadron commander in no time at all. One chap who was a pupil of mine was Johnnie Johnson. Johnnie had completed his advance training at RAF Sealand, which was about five miles away from us, and he came over together with two or three other people from his course who had been selected to go on Spitfires so they came over to Hawarden. He came in through A Flight, which I was a member of, and I taught him the usual stuff one teaches at an OTU. He didn't stay all that long as he came though at a time when the squadrons were crying out for new pilots. Nevertheless he was there long enough to learn a thing or two which stood him in good stead later on.

Of course this was Peter's first posting onto Spitfires, so he had to learn a new aircraft before he could teach others.

The first Spitfire I flew at Hawarden was a Mk.I and it was a good aeroplane but one thing we always remember about the Mk.I was to get the undercarriage up you had to let go of the throttle with your left hand, having made sure that the nut holding it in position was tight, because if you let go of the throttle and it wasn't, sometimes it would vibrate back. Your power was coming off because you had to take your left hand, put it on the control column, take your right hand off the control column and operate the undercarriage. You selected up or down and then there was a pump, quite a long pump with a round knob handle on it. You always knew chaps who were doing their first trips on Spitfires because they would pump, and when the pump got stiff you knew the undercarriage was up and you got a light on in the cockpit, but it was so close to the side of the fuselage they always came away with graunched hands on the back if they weren't wearing gloves as in the summer we weren't wearing gloves very much especially when doing high altitude work. We used to tell the chaps when you change your hands put your hand on top of the pump and you won't get your hand graunched. Everyone did it. The other thing was, of course, on first solos they got into an automatic pump so the aircraft was porpoising. We would say to dig their left elbow into their side and hold it there so you will keep the aircraft steady despite having to pump.

Peter became a very highly regarded instructor and enjoyed his time at Hawarden.

At that time I was pleased to be an instructor at an OTU because we'd had quite a fair old bash at things coming out of France and in France towards the end so a little rest period was very appreciated.

Like all pilots at that time Peter and his friends on the OTU needed some time away from their main task.

We used to have a drink in the evenings and when I was at Hawarden you used to go into Chester once or twice a week. There were two hotels, the Blossoms and the Grosvenor, and we used to start off in those. While I was up at Hawarden we had a well-known World War One ace named Taffy Jones, Ira Jones, who came to our place as an administrative officer. He was a great character who used to love talking to the young pilots so we used to say to him, 'Taffy, we're going into Chester tonight to have a drink, coming in with us?' "Y-y-yes'...he'd stutter a bit, so we drove him in, one of us had a car, and we used to start off in the Blossoms hotel, a nice hotel with a nice bar, and we were in there about six thirty one evening, three or four of us and Taffy Jones, and we decided to have some champagne, and we were pouring it out and Taffy Jones brought out a swizzle stick to take the bubbles out of the champagne. We said, 'Taffy! Why are you doing that? They spend all this time and this money putting the bubbles in and you're taking them out.' He said, 'It's the only f-f-f-form of f-f-f-fucking exercise I get these days.'

In the Summer of 1941 Peter's instructional posting came to an end when he was posted to 145 Squadron near the south coast in West Sussex.

145 Squadron was part of Douglas Bader's wing and he had three Spitfire squadrons. 145 was based at a place called Merston which was south of Chichester and the other two were based at Westhampnett which is still going but known as Goodwood now and they were 610 and 616.

While I was with 145 I had rather a bad car crash, I rolled the car and I got delayed concussion. I was put into hospital so I didn't do much more than about ten hours flying, I can't remember now but not many hours, and then I was in hospital and, having come out of hospital, I had to go down to a recuperation place at the old Imperial Hotel Torquay. I was there for about a month, having medicals all the time, and eventually I recovered but I never went back to 145 again.

Of course this would have been Peter's first opportunity to fly Spitfires in a front-line squadron.

I didn't do much with them. I didn't do any offensive patrols or sweeps because after I came out of the recuperation place they sent me on a navigation course as I still wasn't fit enough to fly Spitfires again yet. They said I could do a navigation course where there was a lot of groundwork, and if I did get airborne it would be in an Anson as a passenger doing navigation of the aircraft, which I did. Then I went back instructing at Grangemouth, No.58 OTU, and I was the navigation instructor.

By this time it was June 1942 and finally Peter was given another operational posting.

I went to 243 to form a new squadron where I was posted as a flight commander. The other flight commander was a chap called Lyons, always called Butch. In fact he was a Jewish chap although you'd never think so to look at him. Fair hair, his family owned the biggest kosher butchers in the country. So he and I went as the two flight commanders in this new squadron, 243, at Ouston just behind Newcastle, and that's where we formed the squadron. They posted in some pilots to us and we had Spitfire Mk.IIs.

They wanted about twenty experienced fighter pilots in North Africa because they had some idea that Montgomery had just been posted out there and he was going to get things in a more offensive situation so we went out there by boat, twenty of us. We picked up this boat in Scotland and went in a huge convoy half way round, almost to the American coast, up round Iceland, coming down and into Freetown on the west coast of Africa to avoid the masses of U-boats that were in the mid-Atlantic at the time. There were a lot of boats in this convoy, heavily escorted by the navy. We got into Freetown and us twenty pilots all got off there and the rest of the chaps were going on down round past Cape Town and up to Suez, mainly army people, to reinforce things in preparation for Montgomery's work. So we then had to get on a coastal boat from Freetown round to Lagos in Nigeria. It took about three days to do that trip round the coast and it was the worst sea journey I have ever had in my life. There was nothing wrong with the sea. It was the fact that the boat was full of animals, fleas, and we didn't even take our clothes off, it was terrible. We were damn pleased to get off that boat. Seawise it was alright, it got us there. Then we had to wait at Lagos for an American Dakota to come and pick us up. They said it would probably be three or four days but in fact it was about ten days so we had ten days in Lagos. There was a transit camp there which wasn't too bad so we used to go and have the odd beer and there were a number of British people out there. There were a couple of bank managers, one from Barclays, and one or two other people trading out there and they were all doing quite well for themselves I think. They were so pleased to see some white English people as opposed to the local people and we used to get invited up to have little drinks parties with them. It was very good. And then the DC-3 arrived to pick us up and took us to Cairo.

Here was a new experience for Peter. He joined 33 Squadron, part of 243 Wing, before moving to 238 Squadron as a flight commander. He was back on Hurricanes after his short period on Spitfires. But it was the first time he had flown over the desert, something that created a new set of disciplines to deal with.

First of all I went back on Hurricanes, the Hurricane IIb, which was a much better Hurricane than the earlier ones I'd been flying, specially modified for desert work and working under hot conditions. It had two cannons and four machine guns instead of eight machine guns, so there were two 20mm cannons, one each side. I'd never flown in the desert before and we did a couple of trips locally just to get used to taking off and landing on the bit of desert. There were no runways or anything like that. It was just a flat bit of sand really so I got used to that and in no time at all I was flying operationally. The idea was we were flying over the British Army in the front line and we were going up and down on patrol. Usually we used to fly at about 10,000 feet, nothing like as high as we used to in the earlier days of the war, and we were trying to protect the troops in the front line from being dive-bombed by the Junkers 87s which always had a fighter escort of 109s, and we did pretty well. We shot down quite a few. I got one or two myself, dive bombers and 109s, and we did this until 23 October which was when the Alamein push started. We were there at dawn on that day and we were over them every day in fact. We had four Hurricane squadrons in our wing and we used to take it in turns to patrol the line so the army had continuous cover all day long. A few of the dive bombers dropped bombs but not many. We managed to keep them away.

As pilots in the wing we didn't liaise with the army. We had a couple of army officers in our wing headquarters and they were liaising. They would sometimes come and talk to us about operations the army were doing and we used to ask them what they thought of the protection and they said well the army are very happy and pleased about the protection you're giving them so we kept in touch that way but we never had army chaps attached to the squadron.

We had four squadrons in the wing, a wing commander in charge, and it so happened the wing commander was a chap I knew, Jackie Darwin, who was a great character. I knew him in UK. He was commanding a squadron at Exeter and I had to fly through there once and I met him two or three times. He was a great chap.

When you were in the air it was fine. Visibility was good. The sand and the dust you got when you were on the ground. You didn't always get it, sometimes it was worse than others depending on the wind direction. It was pretty crude. We were living in tents and we used to dig the tents, we had ridge tents, two officers per tent, and we dug the tents into the ground. We dug a big hole about four feet down so the ridge was just above ground level so if you were being strafed you were below ground level when you were in your camp bed and had reasonable protection from that point of view. It was hot of course but I've never minded hot weather. It's cold weather I don't like.

This was to be the start of the big push. Based at landing grounds LG154 and LG172 Peter saw first-hand the build-up and the attacks for what would be known as the Second Battle of El Alamein.

We had been briefed that an offensive was going to begin. We didn't know when but it was 23 October 1942. The army started the offensive by having a colossal artillery barrage which started as soon as it got dark on the night of the 22nd and then over into the 23rd. We were flying at dawn over the front line, as from then always one of the squadrons was, but not necessarily mine. So between us we carried on giving them fighter cover to try to prevent them from being bombed, trying to shoot down the Junkers 87s which had quite a heavy fighter escort, so what we used to do was put one squadron at lower level going against the dive bombers and the other squadron higher up against the fighters and we used to take it in turns to do that.

In the Middle East the Germans had had to modify their 109s the same as we had had to modify our Hurricanes for the hot weather conditions and they seemed to be pretty well organised. I remember on one day before Alamein started we did a strafing of airfields, all forty-eight Hurricanes, and there were two 109 airfields at El Dhaba. Dhaba was perched on top of an escarpment about 300 to 400 feet above sea level. It was a gradual escarpment from sea level up and then on top were these two separate airfields. They were loaded with 109s and our authorities somehow or other had got the information that they couldn't operate these 109s because they'd had one of these freak torrential downpours of rain which lasted a long time and waterlogged each of those sand airfields. The 109 was something akin to the Spitfire, smallish wheels, narrow undercarriage, and they were sinking in, they couldn't operate, so the powers that be said this was the time to get them on the ground and that's why we did this big strafe. We went in, two squadrons at a time, strung right out across the escarpment and coming across the airfields. Well I was flying next to the wing leader on this day so I was right in the middle and as we came up the escarpment there were some tents located there with the Germans, I shall always remember they were ridge tents, and a chap, a face, came out and I could see the white shaving cream on his face. He was standing there. I had to pull up, get over the top, and right in front of me was a Fieseler Storch, right in front. We couldn't weave, there were too many of us to start weaving. You just had to stick on a straight line and if anything came in front of you you had a go at it. We'd pulled up and we were going down and there was this Fieseler Storch so I got that and I didn't see another aircraft until I got the other side of the airfield where there were some more aircraft lined up and I got into one there. The other chaps were in similar positions, whatever they saw in front of them they could shoot at. If they were unlucky enough to come through and not see anything they had to get away. It was a very successful trip. Forty-eight Hurricanes went in on this. We lost nine. Two were shot down and the pilots went. Two crash landed further south, south of the area known as the Alamein line which was only about thirty miles long. South of there was an area called the Qattara Depression and its very, very soft sand. You can't operate any vehicles or anything there, it's so soft, and that's why the army couldn't go down there, and so two of our chaps landed there and they got away with it but lost their aircraft. There was a lot of ground fire coming up, particularly for the chaps coming in slightly later. We lost nine aircraft but we didn't lose nine pilots. I think we lost two or three and then another two or three were taken prisoner, they didn't lose their lives, and the others got away with it when they force landed in the Qattara Depression.

Strafing was another new art for Peter to learn.

You have to pull up. You can't be low on the ground and strafe otherwise your bullets were just going straight across. You've got to pull up and go down on your target. It was a technique which none of us had really done before but it was very successful. We destroyed many, many aircraft.

Some of the patrols could end up with a multitude of roles and some successes.

That was when we were patrolling over the army and sometimes we had one squadron going for the dive bombers and another squadron would be going in for the fighters and it was on one of those occasions when I managed to get fighters. Sometimes you'd have your go on the fighters and you'd be losing height and as you were coming down you'd see a dive bomber straight in front of you so despite the fact you were supposed to be taking on the fighters, when you had this chap right in front of you you took him. Mainly we stuck to our designated rules.

What seems to have struck many of the veterans who were at Alamein was the intense artillery barrage which began the battle.

That barrage went on all night long and we could hear it and we could see flashes so it was a very intense barrage our Eighth Army put up. I think it was very effective because it surprised the Germans, and the Italians who were also in the front line, and I think it was a very effective barrage to open the offensive with.

I just remember going on patrol quite early in the morning and seeing dive bombers. We were on the lower level and we didn't realise how they were going to operate and it wasn't until a couple of days had gone by we realised they were working with two layers so we patrolled at about 10,000 feet and caught the dive bombers. We got quite a few of them.

Peter had particular memories of the ensuing German retreat and allied advance along the North African coast road.

The part I'm talking about now was just the opening and it lasted for about ten or twelve days maybe before the Germans decided to pull back. In North Africa there's only one road, that's the coast road, so all their vehicles had to go up it. They couldn't take all these hundreds of vehicles across the desert, they would never have made the journey, so they all had to stick to the coast road. They retreated and then they set up another line round about Mersa Matruh and held that for a bit and then gradually went back. After that we went on a special strafing tour. Two squadrons from our wing, mine which was 238 Squadron and the other one was 213 Squadron. We were sent up to a place about 400 miles behind the enemy lines, south of Derna, because we knew the Germans were now making a big retreat, nose to tail, thousands of vehicles all down this coast road and then, when they got to Benghazi, they had to go due south to Ajdabiya round the corner. That road was sixty or seventy miles long and all the German vehicles coming down there were nose to tail so they put us onto a strip of sand, it was a complete airborne operation. The chaps who found the area for us were army chaps, the Long Range Desert Group, and they had found an area which they thought aircraft could operate from. We all went out there and these chaps were waiting for us in their vehicles, they were used to driving round the desert. They used to go in single vehicles, or sometimes they might have a couple, and they got the message back saying where this area was and we went and we all landed there. Our food, our supplies, our fuel, everything went in by air in Bristol Bombays. And when we got there our job was to strafe these vehicles, so from where we were we were going in a due westerly direction and we used to spread right out, say twelve of us, and all attack this road, strafing, once again you couldn't weave, you had to stick with your course, then pull up, go the other side, don't pull up too high, go a couple of miles away, turn port and do the same thing coming back, and then when we got back we would turn starboard, and we did really four attacks, two each way, and we destroyed hundreds of vehicles, I know we did. We could see them all struggling. There was one small airfield there and the Germans had one of their transport aircraft there, the Junkers Ju52, and a couple of other small aircraft. Their chaps used to stop there, they had a big feeding depot, they had vehicles where they were getting food, all the chaps coming off the road and getting food, and we strafed that place, destroyed the vehicles and destroyed the food store and God knows how many men we killed, dozens of them.

We were only there four days. Of course after three days the Germans were wondering where we were coming from. They sent out some reconnaissance aircraft and they found the area where we were. Somehow or other our authorities, the intelligence, got to hear about this so they said they had found out where we were so no doubt it wouldn't be long before they would be attacking this bit of sand with twenty-four Hurricanes on it so they said pull back. On the fourth day we did a strafe and pulled out. It was a highly successful operation and we went back to our usual operating area.

On 4 November 1942 Peter had one of his most memorable experiences.

On one occasion we'd been doing one of our usual patrols and I'd shot down a dive bomber and a 109 and I was on the tail of another 109 when flak got me. I was at about 8 or 9,000 feet. It was heavy flak which knocked a hole in my starboard wing. It also hit me in the tail unit as I could feel from the controls they weren't responsive enough and also in the engine as I got a stream of glycol coming out of the exhaust manifold, glycol being the coolant.

In all I wasn't in very good shape, or at least the aircraft wasn't, I was OK. I thought, I've got to go as far east as I can. I was well over enemy lines and I hadn't got much power left in the engine. I turned in an easterly direction as I was gradually losing height and people on the ground were firing at me with everything they'd got, catapults as well I think, so I started to weave to avoid this ground fire and eventually I saw a track ahead of me and I thought I've got to get down there come what may because I haven't got sufficient power to go any further, in fact I'd lost nearly all engine power, and so I made a wheels-up crash landing on this track and all the time I was coming down I was getting lower over the German troops and they were all firing at me with every damn thing they'd got. It was about five thirty in the afternoon and in November the period of twilight goes from daylight to darkness in the space of about half an hour. I thought it was about half past five, I must get down here. I did a wheels up crash landing, leapt out and lay flat on the ground because the bastards were still firing at me. I didn't move and they thought they'd got me I think. As soon as it got dark I stood up, shook myself down and thought I had better start to walk in an easterly direction as fast as I can. Just about to pick myself up and start to move and I heard a vehicle coming up very fast and I thought, 'Here come the Germans. I shall be a prisoner for the rest of the war.' Instead of which an Australian voice shouted out, 'Anybody there?' and it was a jeep with an Australian major with his driver and I said, 'Yes.' He said, 'Get in quick.' I leapt into this jeep in the back and he went off at a helluva speed. They knew exactly where to go and after about twenty minutes or so we got into a safe area and the major said to me, 'You know that track you crash landed on? You couldn't have landed anywhere else because it was all mined.' I didn't know and of course they were in the front line and they had seen me come down but couldn't come out to get me while it was still light. Then they had done this very rapid jeep drive to pick me up, which I thanked them for very much.

Within a month of the Alamein offensive the Allied Eighth Army had retaken much of Libya. Tobruk and Benghazi were back in Allied control and preparations were in hand for the thrust on the Libyan capital Tripoli which would eventually fall in March 1943. At the same time Operation Torch saw Allied troops come ashore in Morocco and Algeria and rapidly advance into Tunisia. At this point Peter's role changed.

When I was still up forward, in November 1942 the invasion of Algeria had taken place and they hadn't been on the ground for more than about three weeks when they had torrential rain there. They had Spitfires brought in from the UK and they couldn't operate them on these waterlogged airfields.

The Spitfire with its small wheels and narrow undercarriage tended to be nose heavy and they just could not operate the Spitfires at all, totally waterlogged. So the powers that be said they had to have some fighter support somehow and they said if we get some Hurricanes from the UK, by the time they had been crated, put on a boat and sent to Gib and then uncrated and put back together and test flown, the war would be over, so they decided between them they would have twelve Hurricanes sent to them as a matter of immediate urgency from the Desert Air Force. I was selected to lead these twelve Hurricanes. They had come from a maintenance unit somewhere which had a small store of spare Hurricanes and they were taken to Benghazi by ferry pilots I suppose, and that's where we had to pick these aircraft up. They sent a transport aircraft into our airfield to pick up myself and the pilots from the other squadrons, about four pilots from each of three squadrons, not the South Africans, and we were flown to Benghazi. There were these twelve Hurricanes which were just about geared up and ready to go. The next day I briefed the chaps. We couldn't go direct from Benghazi to Algeria because we hadn't got the range even with long range tanks fitted so we had to go via Malta. We took off from Benghazi, decided to keep low, no more than twenty or thirty feet above the water going to Malta and we landed OK at a place called Ta Kali. The funny thing was when we were about two thirds of the way over we saw another big convoy of aircraft going south. They were Germans going to reinforce the troops there in North Africa. We couldn't do anything. We would never have got to Malta if we had tried and in the same way they couldn't touch us because they had to stay escorting their resupply aircraft. The object was to refuel and go off the next morning. We refuelled and the next morning the weather clamped. It didn't happen very often on Malta but the weather clamped completely and we couldn't get off. We were there for two or three days and after the second day the AOC, who was Keith Park, who had been AOC 11 Group during the Battle of Britain and knew me, said, 'Peter, these chaps want these aircraft very badly,' and I said, 'I realise that Sir and just as soon as the weather clears we will go.' 'Yes,' he said, 'I know you will, but I just had to let you know.' We were there for four days including Christmas Day 1942. My Christmas dinner that day was a little bit of bully beef with some hard tack biscuits because all the supplies had been going in by submarine, food, fuel the lot. In the earlier days when they had tried to get them in on convoys all the convoys were sunk and that's why they reinforced Malta with submarines at night. They moved into Valetta at night and went out again the next night.

We got off after four days and we went due south for fifty miles at low level and then turned due west. We had quite a way to go to cross the Tunisian coast between Sousse and Sfax. The reason we were going so low was because the two islands, Lampedusa and Pantelleria, were loaded with German fighters, 190s, Focke Wulf 190s and 109s, and so they didn't pick us up because we were really so low. When we got to the Tunisian coast we had to pull up to get over the hills and then, of course, the range of mountains went up to about 8,000 feet and we had to get over them, and we had no radio aids whatsoever, and I was leading these chaps so I said, 'Right, pull in close formation. We're going to have to go through this cloud.' We got to about 2,000 feet and went into cloud. 'We'll go through this lot,' and we didn't come out of the top until we got to about 10,000 feet and so I said, 'We're going to continue flying on a westerly direction,' which I checked on the compass and I said, 'We'll gradually let down when I think we are clear of the mountain range and hopefully break cloud at a reasonable level,' which we did but of course I had no idea where we were. No radio aids whatsoever, so I said to the chaps, 'Throttle back to save fuel,' because we had been airborne for about two and a half hours I think, quite a long time. I said, 'We've got to find an airfield somewhere and I haven't the faintest idea where we might find one so just go slowly and keep your eyes open. Don't fly in too tight formation so you can keep your eyes open and if you see an airfield give us a shout.' I saw what appeared to be the makings of a new airfield because there were a lot of big heavy digging vehicles there and there was a stretch of mainly mud. But, nevertheless, I said to the chaps that we had to get in there come what may as we were running low on fuel. We went in. I tried to get off to let the chaps come in behind me and I was having to throttle so hard to get through this deep mud because of all the severe rain they'd had that I just went up slowly on my nose and got stuck there. I didn't damage the aircraft at all but luckily the other chaps were able to get in behind me. I didn't realise before I'd made the landing how thick the mud was and how it was going to slow me up so much.

The Americans were there and we managed to contact the British in Constantine and told them we were there and that we couldn't get off because the airfield was such a quagmire. They said leave the aircraft there and we'll arrange for those to be picked up. In the meantime stay overnight and we'll send some transport for you tomorrow, which they did and took us into Constantine. We got twelve aircraft over there and they did the job they wanted. They were able to get them away from this airfield. First of all they were able to refuel them and got them into an airfield and they were able to use them. I think they were quite effective until they were able to get the Spitfires going again. It held things over.

After we got back from that trip, it was in early New Year of 1943, they then decided that our squadron had had a pretty tough time of it and they were going to send us back to Port Said, doing a switch over with 94 Squadron I think it was. So we went back to Port Said and we were doing defence of the Canal. At that time Malta was coming back into its own and they were reinforcing it with supplies coming up through the Suez Canal and into Malta from the east. They couldn't get through if they came from the Gib side so they had quite a few supplies going in convoys from the east and we were doing patrols over these convoys. We never saw enemy aircraft but nevertheless we were giving them patrols. We were doing quite a bit of flying while we were there but we had an easier time of it and we used to go into Port Said in the evenings and have a few drinks and there was rather a nice hotel there called the Eastern Exchange Hotel and they had quite a good cabaret. One of the girls was a Greek dancer named Marina, very attractive girl too, so I was getting to know her and that's what made me put the name Marina on the aircraft.

Peter took on a variety of jobs over the next year. He instructed at Abu Sueir at 73 OTU in Egypt; spent time with No.1 Air Delivery Unit at RAF Takoradi in the Gold Coast, now Ghana; and instructed on Tiger Moths in South Africa before his next posting came through and he returned by sea to the UK where he became a senior flight commander at 124 (Baroda) Squadron. Throughout the lead-up to D-Day and the rest of 1944 the squadron did high-level interceptions, ground strafing and patrols based at various south-east airfields including Detling, Bradwell Bay, Manston and Westhampnett. During this time he was promoted to squadron leader and awarded the DFC. Much of Peter's time was taken up with escorting RAF bomber formations.

In my latter stages of operational flying in the second half of 1944 I was leading the squadron and doing a lot of bomber escorts. Up until mid-1944 the daylight bombing had been done by the Americans in their formations so they had a bomb aimer in the lead aircraft and as they were approaching target he would be directing his pilot and then he would call all the other aircraft in a fairly close formation and he would say, 'Right...five, four, three, two, one, release,' and they would all drop together doing carpet bombing. If the bomb aimer was good it was very effective. Sometimes they weren't always that good, whereas our bomber boys, when they started doing daylight work, they did it in an entirely different way. They flew in a big stream. Supposing they had 500 Halifaxes and Lancasters, they would be between, let's say, 18,000 and 25,000 feet in height and then spread out as a stream over probably about a mile wide, so you had this stream, all spread out, no close formations. I did lots of escorts when they were bombing the Ruhr which is about thirty miles long and about ten miles wide, heavily industrialized in those days. The flak over that area was intense and we used to do close escort for the bomber stream, have some each side and some would do top cover, Spitfires on top of the stream. One day we were doing close escort and I had a Lancaster about sixty or seventy yards away from me on my starboard side and the flak was coming up. When you saw the Ruhr with the flak it looked just like one black carpet of black smoke and this chap on my right got a direct hit before he'd dropped his bombs. Oh what a mess! He went down in bits and pieces. I saw quite a number of our Lancasters or Halifaxes shot down by flak, but during the time we were doing escort to them I didn't see one shot down by a German fighter. I'm not saying it never happened but as far as I'm concerned I never saw one.

No special technique really. Just to stay with them. We used to have one wing which would go in ahead of the bombers to sweep the area, and if there were any fighters around to drag them up, get them airborne so they could be on the ground refuelling by the time the main stream went over. Then of course we had another wing at the back to help the lame chaps home. It was well organised. There was close escort each side, top cover and then advanced and rear. Lots of Spitfire squadrons about in those days. We had long range tanks with us. We had what were called slipper tanks underneath the fuselage. When we first had these tanks fitted we hadn't flown with them before. They had ninety gallons which almost doubled our capacity and when we had used all the fuel in the slipper tank we used to get a little red light on in the cockpit and we used to switch to main supplies and what we used to do was eject the slipper tank. Well Germany must have been covered as everybody was doing this. The Germans must have wondered what all these tanks were coming at them for. So much so that the manufacturer said could you ask your pilots to bring the tanks back if possible because we can't produce them fast enough, so then we had an agreement we would only eject the tank if we got into combat. Very often when we did these things we never got into combat but we were with them all the time so we brought most of them back after that.

It was January 1945 and I'd done the best part of four tours of fighter ops and they said you'll be coming off ops and however long the war goes on now you'll never get back on operational flying again, you've more than done your share. So they asked whether I had anything in mind, so I said 'Not really,' and then I was talking to a chap and he said, 'Test flying's not bad if you can get it,' and I had met Alex Henshaw before so I gave him a ring. I said, 'Alex, are you in need of any test pilots?' He said, 'It's a funny thing. I've got a slot coming up in about two or three weeks time. Would you like to be considered for it?' I said 'Yes I would.' So I told my authorities, I said, 'I've spoken to Alex Henshaw who wants another test pilot and could they let me go and join him.' So they said, 'Yes, as far as we're concerned that's alright.' So I rang Alex back and told him they had said OK, they would let me go and join him if he would have me. He asked me to come up and see him, so I drove up to Castle Bromwich, had a natter with Alex and we agreed that that would be the thing for me so I went to my people and said, 'Yes, Alex is very happy about everything.' So it was all fixed up as an official posting to Vickers as a test pilot.

Castle Bromwich was a Vickers 'shadow' factory which had increased in importance after the Spitfire factory in Southampton was bombed. In the war years Castle Bromwich was responsible for more than half of the Spitfires, more than 10,000. So began Peter's final wartime job. For the next year he would test hundreds of Spitfires that were still coming off the production line. However Peter's first trip with legendary test pilot Alex Henshaw was definitely not what he was expecting.

My first trip at Castle Bromwich. Alex said to me, 'Peter, I'd like you to come up with me in a Lancaster so I can show you the normal procedures we carry out in our testing and then you'll know exactly what to do.' So I said 'Yes, OK.' I sat up front beside him and took off, and climbing up full throttle, climbing speed, engine pressures, yes they were all OK. Keep climbing and we got up to about 15,000 feet continuing to check the climb on the way up and then we did a level run with all engines flat out to see if it would build up to the required speed. Of course these Lancasters were only engines and airframes, they didn't have any gear on board, no guns or radios or anything so it was a lightly loaded Lancaster. We got up to 15,000 feet and he said, 'I'm going to do a level run now. Full throttles on each engine. Yes, pressures, temperatures, yes. OK. Controls OK. We'll just let the speed build up to see if it gets up to what we want,' which it did and he said, 'We've got one more thing to do. We've got to put it into a dive to test what the upflow on the ailerons is.' On the inside edge of each aileron there was a little line painted and if it came up above that it failed the test. So Alex put it into a dive and got up to 390 which was quite a high speed for a Lancaster and he said, 'This one's OK, the upflow on the ailerons is fine. So we'll just pull up now and lose a bit of height and then we'll go back.' So he's pulled up and the next thing is, I was sitting beside him, we went round and we did an upward barrel roll in a Lanc. I thought, 'What the bloody hell's he doing?' as I'd never flown in a Lanc before anyway. We did this upward barrel roll just to gain height but lose a bit of speed and then we eventually returned to Castle Bromwich. I used to tell some of the bomber chaps about this and they could hardly believe it because don't forget the aircraft they were flying were heavily laden with all the equipment they had to carry, all the radio equipment, this that and the other. It was eye-opening for me.

However I never flew one. I didn't test Lancs at all. We had an Australian pilot there who was doing the testing on Lancs and he had been in a Lancaster squadron. The production rate was only thirty a month whereas the rate on Spitfire production, at the maximum rate of production, was 320 a month. We had five of us testing. One chap doing the Lancasters but five of us, including Alex, doing the Spitfire tests.

Alex was wonderful, marvellous, a fantastic pilot. Of all the important people who came to see how things were going in the factory, including Churchill and the King of Norway, they all came up to Castle Bromwich because all the bosses in the Air Ministry knew that Alex was there and he would put up a good performance for them and there was no other test pilot in the country who could touch him. They were good test pilots, but as far as demonstrating the aircraft he was fantastic.

Of course Alex's demonstrations in the Spitfire were something to be seen and to be believed. Marvellous. First of all he went into it at quite a low level. Most people would be much higher and I once saw him do a bunt from about 1500 feet: he just pulled the throttle right back almost to stalling speed and let the nose drop, and as the nose dropped so at only 1500 feet he came right round upside down going the other way. He was only about fifty feet above the ground, maybe a hundred feet but not very much anyway, he wasn't going fast, he was going as slow as he could while he was coming round and once he was inverted he picked up speed and he was able to roll the aircraft round and get it flying in its proper flying position and then he opened the throttle, remarkable. Of course he would pull up, do several upward rolls, all sorts of things. Whatever you could do in a Spitfire he could do.

I think I saw him as a perfectionist really. I think that's good terminology. He went into things in great detail. He ran the flight sheds. The main factory was across the road and then all the aircraft were towed across by tractors and all day long they were bringing aircraft across, as I say the maximum rate of production of 320 a month, about 10 a day coming across and they would come to the flight sheds where they would be gone over, fuelled up, and checked out in every possible way they could on the ground before it was pronounced fit for test flying. Alex Henshaw used to cover all of that which of course covers all the ground crew who were working in the flight sheds, a very big hangar. Alex had his office in the front, I always remember it. He had big round windows so he could see everything that was going on on the airfield and he was very much a perfectionist. I think that is the best description of him.

Peter's experience gave him a great impression of what made a good test pilot.

As a production test pilot, as opposed to an experimental test pilot, whatever mark it is, you have a set procedure and our procedure was to take off, check the engine revs and pressures and things, and raise the undercarriage, make sure that operated correctly, and all the warning lights came on as they should have done and then climb up, set the engine at climbing revs and speed, check everything, and at Castle Bromwich we had no radio. The weather factor there for a large part of the year was very bad but we flew in all these weathers. We had two good landmarks there. The power generators and the coolant towers. There were five of these things and it was a good job they were there because they were only about five miles from the airfield. When there was cloud over them the heat they generated pushed the cloud up so if you were above the cloud, and it wasn't too thick, you could see this bulbous cloud coming up, so you knew without any radio aids. We used to fly set courses for testing, so, take off, climb up, get up to the test flight height, depending on the mark of Spitfire, it varied, but supposing it was 15,000 feet, you would get to 15,000 feet and you would fly on a set course and then do certain tests going out, turn round and come back on an opposite heading continuing tests then perhaps turn round and put it in the dive as every aircraft had to be dived testing uplift on the ailerons. Sometimes of course the cloud was so thick and heavy that you didn't get that help of the bulbous cloud although the heat was still coming from the ground so we had to just use our compass and fly on a time. Five minutes or ten minutes in that direction, come back, five or ten minutes coming back and do the test that way. You got used to it and lots of people wouldn't even bother to fly in the weather as sometimes it was so bad.

As one of the RAF's most experienced fighter pilots Peter was able to assess the many different marks of Spitfire he flew.

I've flown fourteen different marks of Spitfire. The last one was the Mk.22 which was the one with the Griffon engine which was double the weight and had double the power of the Merlin. To take that extra engine with all its power they had to really design a completely new fuselage, mainplanes and everything else. It was a new aeroplane altogether. It was a very powerful cookie, and I have flown more Mk.22s than anyone.

My favourite one, and I have to look at it from the operational point of view, was the Mk.IX. I did a lot of operations on the Mk.IX. The 22, of course, didn't come in until after the war had finished but they were still producing them. While I was testing the 22s my last squadron was 124 (Baroda) Squadron and they were based nearby in Leicester and so I thought I would go and see them one day. They said come and have some lunch so I went over there and talking about old times and they said, 'What type of aircraft did you come in?' and I said, 'a Mk.22.' They said, 'What's that?' having been on the earlier marks, IXs and so on. I said, 'It's a very powerful aircraft, it's very good.' They were up there converting to Meteors and they said, 'After lunch we are taking six up in a formation.' And I said, 'That is about the time I shall be taking off. I'll have a look at you.' 'You won't catch us, you won't get anywhere near us. Meteor? Far faster than a Spitfire.' They didn't appreciate this Mk.22 so I took off after them and they had formed up in their formation buzzing around and I caught them up and was flying up and around the formation and they were absolutely shattered. They didn't think any Spitfire could do that to them as they hadn't seen or heard much about the Mk.22.

Peter left the RAF in 1946, soon after the Spitfire factory closed, and became a publican. He stayed interested by joining the RAFVR but the lure of the RAF was too big so he applied and was accepted back into the service as a flight lieutenant in 1949.

Over the next few years Peter took on a number of non-flying roles until 1952 when he went on a refresher course and converted to jets. Between 1953 and 1956 he flew Vampires with 16 Squadron and then commanded 5 Squadron, both in Germany. Various RAF and NATO roles followed before he became deputy station commander at Wattisham in Suffolk in 1971. At that time Wattisham was a fighter airfield, equipped with the Lightnings of 29, 56 and 111 Squadrons, and in the front line of Britain's Cold War defences. His last Lightning flight was in 1973, just before he retired and went into business.

Wing Commander John Freeborn DFC*

1 December 1919-28 August 2010

Foreword

Readers will find that a recurring theme throughout this chapter is John's 'dissatisfaction' with Sailor Malan. Malan was a South African who had joined the RAF in 1935 when he transferred from the Royal Naval Reserve. By the time John joined 74 Squadron in 1938 Malan, nine years older than John, was a flight commander. At first John's relationship with his immediate superior was excellent, but the aftermath of the 'Battle of Barking Creek' in 1939 saw John's opinion of Malan plummet (see more information below). Readers can see from his comments that the relationship never improved again. John was 88 years old when we undertook this interview and his opinion had not softened with time. However, there is no doubt that Malan was a fine pilot, well respected by many who flew and served with him, so readers should be aware that John's opinion was a personal one based on personal experiences. For more information we can recommend Tiger Cub *written by John Freeborn and Christopher Yeomans,* A Tiger's Tale, *and* Tigers, the story of 74 Squadron, *both by the squadron association secretary, Bob Cossey.*

John Freeborn was a Yorkshireman through and through, educated at Leeds Grammar School. He chose to join the Reserve of Air Force Officers (RAFO) which was one of the organisations that made up the RAF Volunteer Reserve.

Well it was a time when the country was in a very bad state. Financially there was very little work and war was looming and so they brought conscription in and I didn't want to be conscripted. They wouldn't have asked me about it, they would have just said you are going. I was looking in the *Yorkshire Post* as I did every morning, looking for a job, to see if anybody wanted a layabout, and they started advertising for short service commissions as air force officers. So I got the papers and I thought reserve air force officers, that's the one I want because I can learn to fly, I'll be a competent pilot and at the end of a year I would then transfer away from the air force onto the reserve and then I can get a job. I was accepted into the Reserve of Air Force Officers. It seems funny these days as I was taken down to London by my father to an interview at the Civil Service Board, people of different trades and professions, and they fired questions at such a rate. They wanted to know what colour my tie was, another came straight out with what was the name of the engine that brought you down, was it LMS or LNER and things like this. They muck your brain about so much but anyway I answered all their questions as best I could and they seemed very happy with it so I imagined I would have a medical now. I had an appallingly bad cold and I couldn't blow the holograph up, I couldn't blow the mercury up the tube. So they said come back in a fortnight's time, we'll let you know. Anyway they let me know and sent me a first class railway ticket and I thought this was just the job. I held my breath for the minutes prescribed and blew the mercury up for a minute. Then a few days later they told me I had been accepted and had to report to Sywell in Northamptonshire to 6FTS to learn to fly and from there on I had the pleasure of the air force. So I went to Sywell and I must have been by far the youngest one there, I was just 18 or 19 or something like that. I learned to fly and I was the first to go solo from my course.

At this time the flying training on De Havilland Tiger Moths was run by Brooklands Aviation under a contract with the Royal Air Force.

I wasn't frightened and before you could say Jack Robinson I was thrown in it, but they were great with me. I wasn't doing the work the way it should be done and so I was sent for by the commandant I suppose; the place was run by Brooklands Aviation. Anyway he sent for me and said, 'I'm not satisfied with you. You're going to pull your socks up and stop going out drinking.' I was drinking all the money I got. He said, 'You're going to take the end of term exam and you're going to take it this week.' And so I got back and they said, 'What did he want you for? Are they throwing you out?' and I said, 'No. He wants me to take the end of term exam. No chance!' People like Ron Courtney, who was a charming bloke, said 'Can you pass the exam?' so I said, 'I haven't got a clue,' so they said, 'You will have by the time you take it. Sit down and look at these papers,' and every minute I had spare one of them was at me. I passed the exam with no problem at all. So they said, 'We're pleased to tell you you have passed the exam, the right number of points required, and so you won't have to take the exam at the end of the course but you will be able to go flying.' They were so good and friendly, lovely people at training school.

WING COMMANDER JOHN FREEBORN DFC*

Having completed the first part of his training John was posted to 8FTS at Montrose in Scotland.

We had done fifty hours of flying on Tiger Moths. That took three months and we were still civilians and then we had to go to Uxbridge. I went to Uxbridge for a fortnight and all the military tailors turned up; you could pick whoever you wanted and the uniform was made for you. In quick time you had been measured, during the first week, for fitting of your uniform and then in the second week the uniform was put on and if it fit that was good, if it didn't they did the alterations. So everything was where it should be, all in place, and then we got a scroll, a parchment with a stamp on the bottom from George RI. That was it. I was commissioned then in the Reserve of RAF Officers. From Uxbridge we were put on a train to Montrose, what an awful bloody journey that was. You had packs of sandwiches and things like that, but we did have a separate carriage. We were well looked after but it was a long, long journey. Anyway we got to Montrose and we had a room each, everything was a step up from being a pupil to being an officer where you were going to learn to fly proper aeroplanes and I call them proper aeroplanes because that was what they were in those days, the Hart and the Audax and other things of the type. We had instructors who were keen, in fact everything about Montrose I enjoyed except the Sunday morning parades when we had to march into church. We marched down in two courses, and in those days it wasn't in threes, it was in fours, and you had the kids running along, and they could be quite rude, and you'd go into your fours with a clatter, clatter, clatter. But they were the happy days of our career, learning to fly with proper aeroplanes. There was a great bond of friendship formed over the nine months and we were all hoping we would go to the same squadrons and things, but they said it doesn't work like that. I was sent on to fighters so I stayed at Montrose and was put onto Furies. A lovely little aeroplane but we didn't have many of them. They were fast, nice aeroplanes, proper fighters.

The next thing was they told us where we were going from Montrose. I was sent on a fortnight's leave and then you will join such-and-such-a squadron, so I saw my name down for 74 Squadron and I said, 'Where are they?' and they said, 'Hornchurch,' so I said, 'Where's Hornchurch?' 'Near London.' So I said, 'I want to go to Church Fenton' because it was near Leeds, and they said, 'It's not what you want, it's what we want, and you're going to Hornchurch.'

74 Squadron had built a fearsome reputation as a front-line fighter squadron in seven months of fighting during the First World War. Converting from a training squadron to fighters the squadron was equipped with SE5As and boasted aces such as Mick Mannock and Ira 'Taffy' Jones. Reformed in 1935 the squadron was equipped with Hawker Demons and subsequently Gloster Gauntlets. John arrived at Hornchurch on 29 October 1938.

It was a good posting because it was a wonderful squadron. It had some senior pilots but the promotion wasn't there. There were flying officers and that was it. You'd look at them and there they were with First World War medal ribbons on, campaign ribbons. Anyway they quickly disappeared and the squadron was built up with people who had been in the air force a year or two, I mean with a squadron, and so I think I was very lucky getting to 74 in many ways.

We had a sergeant pilot, Ernie Mayne, and he was ex-Navy. His career started as bugle boy in the *Hood* and he was on the *Hood* when it was supposed to do its trials, but it never did its trials. It went to Gibraltar from Portsmouth in twenty-four hours, that was all the trials it got. Apparently it was a very happy ship and he enjoyed it. Of course they had aircraft on the *Hood* which were catapulted off, mainly seaplanes, and he was so interested but he was only a bugle boy. Finally he became a tradesman, he was a fitter, and then they transferred him from the Navy to the RAF and he was a sergeant pilot in the pre-war lot who were picked from volunteers but the volunteer had to be a leading aircraftsman and he had to pass his trade test as a sergeant because he was going to be a sergeant if he learned to fly and that was one of the stipulations of those who wanted to fly. Surprisingly the numbers who failed were not through inability to become a pilot but were colour-blind and things of this nature and so they wouldn't have them which was rather a shame because there would have been many good pilots. However that was how it was. Ernie Mayne carried on as a sergeant fitter but still flying. He'd done his four years of flying and the RAF kept him on flying.

There was a bloke called George Lillywhite and he was a sergeant pilot at another squadron at North Weald. He was standing on the tarmac with other pilots and they were talking. They had Siskins there and the Siskin wasn't the easiest aeroplane to land and a crow landed on the aerodrome just in front of them and he said, 'That Siskin came down well didn't it.' He was so blind he couldn't tell the difference between a Siskin and a crow and so he was taken off flying and sent to Upavon to the instructor's school where he was put in charge of blind flying and instrument rating. So this was the type of sergeant who was kept on, got to the top of the tree but never commissioned.

Ernie Mayne of course was made the squadron training officer and I used to talk to Ernie an awful lot and he would say 'Fly, fly, fly as much as you can. Get in the air as much as you can. When there's an aircraft available see if you can get into it.' If my flight commander allowed me I would fly and Treacy and Malan were both good flight commanders in that respect, particularly Treacy. We were equipped with Gloster Gauntlets in those days and, like the Fury, a lovely aeroplane to fly but more complicated, all the pipes were split and the joints were going, they leaked air and were never serviceable, but they would always get one ready and I was allowed to fly to Yeadon at the weekend. I said to Treacy, 'Why are you allowing me to fly to Yeadon near home?' and he said, 'It's good for you, you're finding your way about,' and this was the type of people I was living with. But when I joined Hornchurch, I turned up on a Sunday night and there was one bloke in the mess, that's all, and he had got something on his sleeve I didn't recognise. He said, 'I'm an orderly officer, you'll learn all about this, don't worry,' and it was marked for 65 Squadron. I never realised there would be three squadrons at Hornchurch. I just thought Hornchurch was 74 Squadron but we shared it with 54 and 65 Squadrons. I enjoyed Hornchurch.

They were such nice blokes. One of the things they did when I was just a kid and arrived at 74 Squadron, I think Sampson decided he was going to train me to be an officer, not a kid who can fly an aeroplane a bit, and so we had a bad boy in the squadron called (Norman) Pooler and Pooler had just come out of hospital. He had been in the RAF hospital at Halton with gonorrhoea and they had made it very uncomfortable for him and he came back to the squadron and he said, 'We're going to be great pals,' and I thought, 'I don't want any part of you.' Anyway a week or two went by and the next thing was, late Sunday evening, there was kicking on my bedroom door and it was Mainwaring and he said, 'Get yourself ready for tomorrow morning.' He said, 'That bloody Pooler, he's in bloody prison, and we're going to get him out and bring him back.' Mainwaring was one of my good friends. He was much older than me but he was kind and helpful and all the time he wanted to make me like himself, worthwhile, and so we all dressed up and off we go into London and people are saying 'What's that uniform you are wearing?' 'RAF, can't you see? RAF.' 'Oh, so what are you then?' 'I'm a pilot.' 'Don't be silly. Of course you're not.' I said, 'What are these?' We had a laugh, and then when we got to the nick and got Pooler out on bail, and bring him back to Hornchurch, there's a sad story here, he was in trouble and I think he was down for kicking out of the air force. He'd got lovely parents and he was just a bad boy and just needed discipline and whatever we were, the air force, we were disciplined. And Pooler went missing again. 'Anybody know where Pooler is? Where did he go? Are the police around?' and nobody could find him and then a bloke came in and said, 'I've just found a dead bloke.' 'Where?' 'Ah,' he said, 'he's in the rose garden.' 'Oh I'm not going out there.' But anyway somebody went out, came back; and it was Pooler, he'd shot himself with a four five. He'd put it in his mouth and pulled the trigger and, of course, again, who was the poor bugger to go to the court of inquiry?

It was a sad time because when I arrived at Hornchurch there had been a murder at the back of the mess and I went in and the only bloke I saw was Robert Tuck and he was orderly officer and he fitted me up with a room and everything and filled me full of beer. I was so young and so naive I had a helluva lot to learn and Robert Tuck was an awfully nice bloke and, despite the fact he wasn't in our squadron, he looked after me. He was one of those that helped me because there was nobody my age in the three squadrons. I found it difficult, difficult to make a chum of anyone. Pooler was quite happy but I wasn't happy with Pooler, I didn't want him. But then people like Mainwaring, these were married men and then of course we had Gordon Heywood who said 'We'll have to look after you,' and so he began showing me how to do all the right things and making me a better person which I was. He was a great help but unfortunately he got posted to the Middle East before the war started so I lost Gordon. I liked everything about him but at this stage I was growing up quickly from being, literally, and not knowing it, a schoolboy to being a man. I found that these people were very, very helpful and made my life quite a pleasure.

Just a few months after John had joined the squadron they were one of the first to get the new Supermarine Spitfires.

We were the second. 19 got theirs first and we got the second lot. Malan was sent up to Duxford to fly one and of course he flew straight to Hornchurch and flew round the aerodrome and I thought 'Good God, the speed of that thing.' It made our Gauntlets and 54 and 65 Squadrons' Gladiators very, very slow. How are we going to deal with one of these? It wasn't very long afterwards when we got the first, the second and the third. By this time I'd been made squadron adjutant. I was fortunate in this respect that our CO was a very hard Australian, George Sampson, well liked by the pilots and other people in the squadron and a very fair-minded man.

So the Spitfire came and I was in my office as adjutant, and Treacy walked in and said 'Get your things together, you're flying a Spitfire.' So I got my things together, put my parachute on, walked out to the Spitfire and, this is a tip for anyone, if you're asking the way or you're asking something don't ever let them face in the opposite direction because they get their lefts and their rights wrong. So Treacy was standing on my wing looking back towards the tail, looking at me, telling me what to do and he told me all the wrong way round because he was looking the wrong way. I got the elevators wrong and the trim wrong and he said, 'Don't be sitting on the ground very long, they boil very very quickly, the oleo legs are in the way. Get it in the air.' So very carefully I taxied out, swinging so you could see where you were going and I got to the end of the grass aerodrome, turned it into wind and opened the throttle. Oh God, I'd never known anything like it, this vast acceleration and power; but it was the day I did everything wrong. I went between the hangars because I had trimmed it wrong way round. Anyway that didn't matter when I got it in the air. I was climbing when I looked at the air speed indicator. I'm looking at all the instruments trying to discern what was this and what was that and the air speed indicator showed 180 mph and I was climbing. I thought 'Ruddy hell, what an aeroplane this is.' I flew it for about an hour and did everything with it, tried all the trims and accustomed myself to it and it literally did everything for you that you wanted to do. It was like it could read your brain and I found it was a pleasant and comfortable aircraft to fly, and then of course the time came when I had better go and land. I thought, 'What did they tell me?' Bring it in at ninety mph, keep it at ninety until you were getting near the boundary of the aerodrome then just ease the throttle and then it would drop down and touch the ground at sixty mph. Well if the wind was blowing at thirty it would toss me round at thirty mph. They were making it sound so easy and I thought I wasn't sure but it did exactly that. I touched down and I was that pleased with myself. Now I've flown the real thing. That was February 1939.

John and the rest of the pilots in 74 Squadron were undoubtedly given an edge by getting and flying their Spitfires for so long before the war started.

Oh absolutely. Both our flight commanders and our CO, Sampson, Barry Treacy and Malan. I was in B Flight with Barry Treacy as flight commander and I used to get sick of his snide remarks, as an Irishman, always on about Yorkshiremen. What Yorkshiremen had done to Treacy I don't know. So I said to Sampson, 'Can I have a transfer to A Flight?' He says 'Have you asked Malan?' I said 'No.' 'Well ask him then.' So I asked him: 'Can I come into A Flight?' and he said 'Of course you can,' and so I went to A Flight. At that stage Malan was very, very friendly and we used to walk and had quite a close relationship, a youngster and a 29-year-old man. He talked all good knowledge, well good for me, and I always used to talk to Ernie

Mayne and he used to tell me what to do. Don't low fly whatever you do; he said that was the best way to get myself killed and maybe killed a lot of other people too. If you want to low fly find a layer of cloud, stratos cloud, at 10,000 feet, and do your aerobatics and everything over that and that would be the ground as far as you were concerned. If you do something and you go into the cloud then you say if that had been the ground you would be dead. It was this clever way of teaching you what you had to do and how to make yourself safe and how to become a good pilot. With Ernie Mayne's tuition and Malan I became a very good Spitfire pilot.

However, flying the aircraft didn't necessarily mean you would be a good fighter pilot in combat. For that you needed some opposition.

Well, we had the home defence exercises and things like that. The French came over to attack London and we took them on, things of this nature, but we did mainly our training with our own flights, with A and B Flights which was as good as anything and then when we got the Spitfires 54 and 65 were still running their Gladiators and it looked like they weren't going to get Spitfires for some time to come and I always remember if I saw a Gladiator I would chase round and if I saw Robert Tuck I'd have a go at him and he used to say 'You young bugger, what do you think you are doing?' I said, 'I'm shooting you down, you can't get anywhere near me. I shot you down' and things like that. There was a lot of banter and fun. It's things like this that make good fighter pilots.

Within a few days of the outbreak of war John was involved in an unfortunate incident, one that would change his relationship with Malan and affect the way he flew from then on. John would not talk much about the 'Battle of Barking Creek' but it is a very important chapter in his RAF career. On 6 September 1939 two Hurricanes of 56 Squadron were identified as enemy aircraft by ground controllers and 74 Squadron was scrambled to intercept. In the ensuing few minutes both Hurricanes were shot down. One, flown by Pilot Officer Montague Hulton-Harrop, was shot down by John and the pilot was killed. The other was shot down by Paddy Byrne but the pilot survived.

Yes, it's had an effect on me all my life. It made me a better fighting pilot. It upset me very much and, of course, Byrne didn't make it any better because he was involved in it as well. Forget about it. It did make me a better pilot. It made me more careful. It made me look round and see what I was doing before I did it and then when the war proper came we had to go and fly over Dunkirk, that's when it did its job. I think my eyesight in those days was so good I could see a speck in the sky and could have told you what it was, whether it was a 109 or 110, I had very, very good eyesight. Years later I got polio and it affected me in the head and my eyesight went. I couldn't drive, I couldn't walk, I used to fall off pavements. They got me glasses and that was even worse. And then it cleared itself as time went by, after about three weeks or a month I was back to normal again. It was the time when they thought polio came from water and my wife took my daughter to go to her sister, who had children, to Whitby. They went there for a month and I think I must have picked up the bug in the swimming pool at Whitby. That's when it started. I wasn't seeing very well. I wasn't seeing clearly, and when you get to the stage where you see two roads, which one do you drive on, that's when you stop driving and find a doctor very quickly. Anyway it was the most peculiar thing because you're feeling quite alright and then you just sit down and you feel very bloody ill, and I couldn't go to work, I had to go to bed. An hour or two later I felt better again, and I'd get up and by the time I got up I had to get back into bed. It was a terrible thing and I think I was very fortunate in many ways but it did effect, eventually, my hearing and my eyesight. When I came out of the air force, the regular air force, I went into the reserve and I had to go to Doncaster to do flying training and have a medical. And the doctor said to me 'You're not going to fly much longer. You can't hear,' and my hearing was going and they still didn't do anything about it until I went to live in Spain and my wife and stepdaughter thought I was deaf and thought I ought to have hearing aids. I said I could hear alright but they knew I couldn't so ultimately I got hearing aids.

Immediately after the squadron landed both pilots were put under close arrest and in John's opinion he took it seriously while Byrne treated it lightly. At the court-martial both pilots were exonerated but what upset John more than anything was that his own flight commander, Sailor Malan, did not support him. In fact he acted as a witness for the prosecution, for which John never forgave him.

I thought he was a very nice man. We used to walk round the aerodrome, in the early morning just after it got light, when the war started and we used to chat about all sorts of things. He would tell me all about his life at sea, his family, and he wanted to know about mine, which I told him, and we were very close and friendly until the third day of the war and A Flight was scrambled. We were given a course to steer and the Observer Corps and the radar, I don't know what they got wrong, but they saw on the radar many aircraft coming in and, in actual fact, it was a Blenheim, these many bandits!

Everybody was sending aeroplanes in the air and there was going to be a great air battle and it was a complete disaster. We landed. Sampson said,

'You are in serious trouble. Go to your room. You are under close arrest,' and he sent Byrne to his room and he was under close arrest too. He said, 'Where's Malan?' and Malan had done a bunk. He lived out. He was married and he lived out and he had gone home. He went to get his story right. And he got it right.

From October 1939 the squadron began using Rochford as a forward base. Twenty-five miles east of Hornchurch, and just north of Southend, Rochford would be closer to the action in the forthcoming Dunkirk operation.

We were off to Rochford. It was not Southend in those days, it was a private flying school. We were sent to Rochford and we were only going to be there for a fortnight and it didn't matter to us because that was what was going to happen. They knew better than we did. So off to Rochford we went and of course the Dunkirk evacuation started. The Germans were advancing at a great rate and our forces were being overtaken very quickly. So our army were told to evacuate and, of course, probably the cleverest general of the war, Alexander, who was the last man off the beach, put it all together, a brilliant soldier. We didn't see the beaches as they were photographed because we were too high. The soldiers on the ground would ask, 'Where is our air force?' Well our air force was right above them but we were at 10, 12, 15,000 feet so they didn't see us. We were there and we shot quite a few aircraft down. I remember the first ones we got after were Ju-88s and I was flying number two to Malan. He got behind this 88 and he knocked one engine straight out of it and it burst into flames and I thought My God, Malan does it, that's marvellous. These eight guns are something and then I got behind an 88 and I thought these guns aren't any bloody good. It hadn't gone like Malan's had. Anyway that was the start of it. Funny things happened, people talk about dogfights, well there wasn't such a thing. If you mix with the enemy, right we'll shoot one down or one is going to shoot you down so you got out of the way and one must remember that the closing speeds were anything up to 800mph. We were doing 400 and they were doing 400 as well and we were coming towards each other. Anyway we did what we could and one day I got into a cloud between the Hook of Holland and Dunkirk. We got into the cloud and when we came out of cloud I couldn't see anybody. The rest of the flight had disappeared and then I saw a 109 knocking hell out of a Spitfire so I chased after it and I shot at the 109. I must have hit him because, as I was getting very close to him, he pushed his stick forward and, with the fuel injection, not carburettors as we had, his engine wouldn't cut out. So he could put his stick forward and he could go straight down. Well I saw this and thought, I know what I'm going to do as well, so I half rolled into the cloud and turned. We came out of the cloud and there he was just in front of me and I'm right behind him. I'd got him in the turn so I shot at him again and then it was getting very low and I must have been wasting bullets on him. I could see my ammunition exploding on the aircraft and he went down and down until he was just above the hedges and then he hit a telegraph pole with his prop boss and I think then he must have been dead. I don't think any pilot could survive that. He bounced off that into a farmhouse and I thought well he is dead now. And then there was a French farmer near the farmhouse shaking his fist at me and I thought, 'You shouldn't do that, buster,' but I didn't have any bullets left or I would have given him some as well.

I came back to Rochford and I never thought in those days. I must have been a bit of a twit because I must have thought the petrol was everlasting, it will always be there, but I found out that was the downfall of Malan. It isn't always there because we were doing an escort of a troopship to Calais from Dover and they loved to do formation aerobatics for the troops and they probably enjoyed seeing it. I could stay with Malan but Hawkins couldn't, he wasn't good enough. We'd been doing aerobatics and we were practically over Dover harbour. We were right on the water, we were so low you could see the slipstream making a wake on the water, on the sea, and we were going round North Foreland, and the petrol came to mind and I wondered how much petrol I had left. I pressed the button on the bottom tank, there were two petrol gauges, one for the top tank and one for the bottom tank; the top tank drained into the bottom tank so the bottom tank was the one to read. The top tank showed empty and the bottom tank showed empty as well so I said to Malan, 'Can we go into Manston? I've no petrol.' 'Rubbish, what would they think of us.' So I thought, 'Can I have some height then?' I looked at the map, and you can see it's a long way from North Foreland to Southend and it's all sea, there's nothing to land on so I said, 'I have no petrol left.' He said, 'No, because you've wasted it.' I thought, 'That's bloody good,' so I asked if we could get some height. He said 'Yes' and we got to 7,000 feet and we were about equidistant between North Foreland and Rochford and my engine stopped, that was all the petrol gone, and so I called up Malan and said, 'I'm out of petrol, my engine's stopped.' 'Well you'd better do the best you can then,' and I thought 'That's bloody charming,' so I trimmed it and held it back. I was literally pulling it up with a stick and I kept it round about 100mph on the air speed indicator and made for Rochford, I could see Rochford no trouble. I glided and glided and I'm losing height and very gently I was sure I was going to make it. Don't put your undercarriage down and don't put your flaps down until you have cleared the railway line because the railway line ran alongside the aerodrome and in those days there were hundreds of telephone cables that the railway companies had; keep your wheels up until you've crossed the line. The railway lines appear under your wing at the back end of the trailing edge then wheels down as fast as you can and flaps down and I touched down rather quickly at Rochford. I ran right across the aerodrome, right to my dispersal point and the fitter was there to greet me. The fitter grabbed my wingtip to swing me round and then pushed it back into the bay and, as he jumped up on the wing helping me out, he said 'What did you stop your engine for?' so I said 'Because I had no bloody petrol otherwise it would still be running.' 'Oh,' he says, 'I thought something had gone wrong,' so I said 'Why?' so he said, 'Malan's in a bunker on the golf course and the poor bloke is upside down.' So I thought, 'Bloody great, that serves him right.' When I saw him he said, 'Lucky bugger.' I thought it was a piece of brilliant flying and the next thing I hear is (Denny Barchose) the CO of 54 Squadron who had just been promoted to station commander at Hornchurch and he said, 'You'd better recommend Freeborn for an AFC for that clever flying.' 'Just what I was thinking about Sir.' He wasn't thinking about it at all, he was hoping I would go in the bloody sea. I never thought about this, that he could be so bloody cruel until well after the war when somebody said 'Didn't it ever dawn on you he was trying to get you killed?' and when I think about it he was. Now I was a 19-year-old pilot officer and he was acting squadron leader at the time, he wasn't a squadron leader, he was still a flight lieutenant, but he was acting as CO with the changeover between Sampson going to 2 Group as group controller.

With George Sampson going off to 2 Group the new squadron commander for 74 was Squadron Leader Frances 'Drogo' White.

Squadron Leader White took over from Sampson. In fact he took over from Malan who was very upset about this because he thought he should be. He was known as Drogo White. His career in the air force was fantastic. He was at school and he was so good there that they sent him to Cranwell where he learned to fly. He was one of these blokes who did so well that he came out of Cranwell as a flight lieutenant. Very few do but, as with the most important part of the RAF, he did remarkably well. Whisky got the better of him but he could shoot anything down. He could put fifty or sixty bullet holes in a drogue while Malan could probably put thirty in and I was lucky if I put fifteen in. He was very good but whisky was his trouble.

Malan just ignored him. A pig of a man was Malan, a pig, a bully. I can't say anything nice about him. I must say this, he was a brilliant shot and he could shoot aeroplanes down and if he had had aircraft like Johnnie Johnson had then Johnson wouldn't have been in the running. He was the top scorer. And if Malan had cannons he would have wiped the German air force out. He was absolutely spot on, and of course Drogo White was as well but he didn't like the war.

As the Dunkirk campaign neared its end 74 Squadron had survived virtually unscathed until one, in John's opinion a silly one, operation.

Malan was a silly ass. He would listen to Byrne, there was a baddie, and he used to say 'Look Sailor, the bloody war's under our feet and we're not seeing it.' Now our instructions were to fly from the Hook of Holland down to Calais and home to refuel, and this at 10 to 15,000 feet. That's why the army never saw us, but Byrne would say 'Let's get down there. Let's get in and see what's going on.' And we did and we lost half the bloody squadron. We went straight into a battering. I actually heard the cannon shells passing over my canopy and going either side of me. I heard them and it was very frightening and of course people like Sammy Hoare were shot down, Byrne was shot down, quite a few were shot down on that silly business of Malan going down to let Byrne see the war. The war was at 15,000 feet not 2,000 feet.

For 74 Squadron Dunkirk was a success. We'd have probably come out almost intact if we hadn't have gone down, and of course we lost good pilots, and when we went up to Leconfield after Dunkirk we were literally re-formed. Fortunately we still had people like Ernie Mayne, but we literally had to re-form the squadron. At that stage, while I was only a pilot officer, I was given a lot of authority by Malan and I used to lead the squadron quite often despite the fact we had Charlie Meares. He commanded C Flight which is the service unit of the squadron and he spent a lot of time in the ops room controlling. He was a clever and a very nice bloke but I would be given preference over people like Charlie Meares. Then we got to the stage where I was like a supernumerary squadron leader and Malan would come into the flight office and say, 'Freeborn'. He always did the first off, early morning, crack of dawn the squadron went off and he always led it. Thereafter, when we landed and got back, he would say, 'Freeborn, take over. And I don't want any nonsense from any of you. He's in charge.' I found it very embarrassing but I used to lead the squadron in his place and Drogo White didn't even have a go. He got shot down at Dunkirk and didn't enjoy it although we got him back.

The court of inquiry after Dunkirk gave John a chance to consider his feelings about the short, but sharp, campaign.

After Dunkirk, and literally a defeat as Dunkirk was, there was a court of inquiry to be held and I was sent to the Air Ministry and, oh God, there was lots of gold braid there and a man from the Treasury asking questions about Dunkirk. How did we get on? What were the aircraft like? All things that were necessary to be known and I told them as best I could. Why I was sent I don't know but I think White didn't like Malan otherwise Malan would have gone so he sent me instead. I told them what I thought. I told them it was very difficult, our radios were so bad, we had an old TR9D, oh it was a bloody awful radio. Some days it was wonderful but the following day we couldn't hear a damn thing and it wasn't until we got the VHF sets that the radios were good but they didn't have them at Dunkirk. So one of the things I told this board was that we needed better radios than the ones we'd got and it would be a big help. A case of how it would have helped: there was Malan and I was flying number two with Malan and number three was Peter Stevenson. Peter's father was director of operations at the Air Ministry, he was an air commodore or air vice marshal or something, and we ran into some Germans so I called in but no-one could hear me. Malan asked Peter Stevenson if he had any ammunition left and he said 'Yes, I haven't used my guns.' Why he hadn't I don't know as we'd been in a right melee. Anyway he bullied Stevenson and said, 'Get after those bloody Dornier 17s then,' and he was flying in formation with them and they shot him down. He got down and got into Dunkirk and the navy commandeered him and put him on a destroyer and gave him a .303 and they said, 'If any officer tries to bully his way onto this ship you shoot him, dead. Don't just shoot him, shoot him dead.' They would take it in turns but all these fellows couldn't swim. Up to their chins in water, trying to get on the ships that were there and they couldn't climb aboard a destroyer very easily. Anyway Peter Stevenson did that job and he got home. Had we had proper radios, radios that worked, he'd have heard exactly what was said to him and got the hell out of it instead of getting himself shot down. It's fine shooting the bloke in front but when you find you've formatted with one at the side it doesn't work that well at all and so poor Peter got shot down and we couldn't afford to lose the aircraft.

This sortie was on 22 May 1940, early in Operation Dynamo. The squadron lost another aircraft, this time after Dunkirk, in what John felt were very strange circumstances.

We lost an aircraft just after Dunkirk and they said, Malan was off, it was one of our pilots. If anybody mentioned Hitler, or what a bastard Hitler

Above: 219 Squadron in front of one of their Mk.1 Bristol Blenheim night fighters. Terry Clark is fourth from right, top row.

Below: A Bristol Blenheim Mk.1 night fighter. This example is K7059 of 90 Squadron. (BAE)

Left: Air Vice Marshal Sir Keith Park taken while commanding RAF squadrons on Malta, September 1942.

Below: Armourers prepare. 303 ammo for a Hurricane Mk I.

Above: Boulton Paul Defiant in flight.

Right: Brian Kingcome and Squadron Leader Geoffrey Wellum of 92 Squadron at Biggin Hill.

Hawker Hurricane MkI of 501 Squadron at Betheniville in France.

Left: Hawker Hurricane being refuelled in 1940.

Below: Hawker Hurricane formation 1 Squadron RAF in flight 1940.

Above left: John Ellacombe holding his damaged trousers.

Above right: John Ellacombe.

Right: John Gard'ner and Dudley Slatter with Defiant 141.

Above: RAF Spitfire Mk I being refuelled early in 1940 (Flight).

Left: Sailor Malan 74 Squadron RAF by Cuthbert Orde, 1940.

Above: Squadron Leader Pete Brothers DFC, CO of 457 Sqn Redhill, 1942.

Below left: Terry Clark later in the war.

Below right: Tony Pickering.

Above: The classic image of a Luftwaffe Heinkel III over Wapping, East London during the Battle of Britain.

Left: Wing Commander Billy Drake in the Middle East c.1943.

was, this Bertie Aubert straight into our faces would say he's not a bad man, he's put Germany on its feet, and we would say 'We're fighting him,' but he wouldn't have it. The next thing we know Bertie Aubert is missing and shortly after that the Germans were flying a Spitfire and Bertie was put in a position where he could escape and get back to England and he did do and he came to the squadron and we lost another aircraft and that was the last we saw of him. I always said to Malan 'That bastard's a spy.' He said 'Do you think so?' I said, 'Well if you look at things the way they are, he came from San Diego, he was living with his mother in San Diego, his father had died, and he had to get into the war so he went to Canada and joined the Canadian air force. They took him on and vetted him and he was alright. I think it is known that the Canadian Intelligence Section are the finest in the world, certainly better than ours, and better than the Americans. They gave him a clean bill of health.' But he went on about Hitler, and of course, we used to wind him up as any squadron would do and it would get him going. He didn't like it at all. The net result was the Germans were flying a Spitfire and we'd lost Bertie and he got back and then later the Germans were flying another Spitfire but Bertie didn't come back this time. I supposed he was very busy polishing his Iron Cross with diamonds.

Once the squadron had re-formed it returned to Rochford but also using Manston as an advanced landing ground.

After Dunkirk it was then they were going to invade us, that was the worst flying I ever had to do because some bright spark at Fighter Command always sent us off at the same bloody time every day, afternoon, evening or morning, it didn't matter. We had to go and fly as far as Lille, or Bethune, looking on the aerodromes for gliders and the build-up of heavy passenger-carrying aircraft, Ju52s and things like that. It was always at the same bloody time and I dreaded this. Two of us would go and the last time I went I was with Don Cobden and we were over Lille. Now Lille is a long way from Manston, we were staged at Manston then and it's a long way from Manston. I saw two 109s, maybe more, and we were flying at about 15,000 feet and I said to Cobden, 'Those two 109s are going to chase us so stick your nose down and go as fast as you can and low fly out of France.' I said, 'I'll climb and draw the other one off,' and I climbed to about 25 or 26,000 feet and this 109 was pretty fast because he was within shooting distance of me and I thought, 'Right, into this cloud.' It was a great big thunderhead and I entered that. It looked, with static electricity, as though my prop was on fire and sparking between the blades of the propeller and then sparks coming back to the wingtips. I thought 'Bloody hell, what's this? It's static electricity, it's harmless,' at least one would think so, and certainly hope so, but I was in this cloud and my instruments were everywhere. The blind flying panel, the instruments were all over the place, the gyros on the artificial horizon and your blind flying panel. The only thing that was working properly was the turn and bank indicator and that wasn't gyros, that just worked by natural movement so everything's gone. The compass is spinning, the multi-compass, what we used most of all, gyros were going with the static electricity, me turning over and trying to get some semblance of getting the aircraft right. Looking at the air speed indicator I was doing 400mph, at least it was indicating 400, and I thought I was climbing. I thought bloody hell so I had my turn and bank indicator and my air speed indicator but then I thought I wasn't climbing, I couldn't be, but I'm going to be. I was in the clouds so I put the stick back and finally got it down to about 200 or 240mph and the turn and bank indicators, the top one's needle was on centre and the bottom one was on centre so I now know I am flying straight and level. Now I've got to get out of this cloud. This thunderhead must have gone all the way to Norway. How the hell I got out I don't know but I saw blue sky and I was thankful for that. I get into the blue sky and all my gyros settled down and everything was back to normal. Now the bomber's blind flying panel, they could stop the gyros by pressing buttons on the instruments but we couldn't, we didn't have that luxury. Anyway I got settled, I made a course back to fly west and then I went up the coast, in cloud, and got back to Rochford where I refuelled and went back to Manston and thought 'I don't want any more of those trips' because the Spitfire didn't steady itself very well. Once you've lost your blind flying instruments due to the gyros toppling they take a long time to settle down again and you don't have to be jerking all over the sky, you want to be going straight and level. If you can't see anything, try; anyway, I saw this blue sky before my gyros were working properly.

During the intense combat of Dunkirk John had learned a lot about air fighting. The lessons would be put to good use during the Battle of Britain.

Well you know how to shoot an aircraft down. Your guns are synchronised, they were synchronised at 200 yards onto a small-sized disc. Then you probably got into a fight with something without a great deal of success. Well then they gave us the De Wilde ammunition and it was like a sparkler hitting the aircraft. That was a help but you've got to have your guns set right so I had my guns set back to 125 yards and then I was having success.

You've got to keep your eyes open and keep looking back. You've got to have a good number two, but if your number two gets adrift it's so easy to lose your leader, and you need him there to be watching because you are watching for him as well as he's watching for you, but its nasty when bullets start hitting your aeroplane. I'll give you an instance. We were sent off about two o'clock one afternoon from Manston, the whole squadron, and as we took off from Manston I said to Malan, 'We're trying to climb up to meet the Germans when they come and they are way ahead of us, up above us and they jump us every time. What we should be doing is, when we take off, take no bloody notice of the course they give us to steer, fly towards Maidstone and at Maidstone you've got 10,000 feet if you want and then come back on a course to steer, that control give you, and by that time you're at 25,000 feet and you're in with a chance then.' It was difficult. The Germans didn't like it. They would duck. Of course one must remember, I never thought about it when those conditions occurred, but the Germans probably didn't have more than fifteen minutes and they had to turn back. They weren't running away, they hadn't the fuel, so then you chased the bombers of course. The German Ju88 was the most difficult thing to shoot down because if he had any height he'd push his nose down and he had a great deal of speed, probably a good 300mph, and you'd think 'Great. I've got him lined up now' and his flaps go down, his diving flaps go down, his undercarriage goes down and he literally comes to a stop. I would shoot past him, waving as I went by, and by the time you'd got round to have another go at him his flaps were up, his undercarriage was up, everything was up and he was going. They were very good aircraft, those 88s, and they had some very good pilots too.

Height was the main thing. It was most important to get as much height as possible and we had normal carburettors whereas the enemy had fuel injection which made a big, big difference. It wasn't until some little WAAF mechanic said 'I know what your trouble is with these Merlin engines, why you can't push your stick forward like the Germans do. I'm telling you now, drill a little hole in the float, in the carburettor,' and they said 'Bloody rubbish' but they tried it and sure enough you could push the stick forward. It took a little WAAF, a flight engineer, to work this out while quite clever engineers hadn't worked it out. They said fuel injection is what we required, but at that time the aircraft weren't being built fast enough although I do believe they were building more aircraft each month than the Germans were but we were building them wrongly. Going on to the old SU carburettor as though it was a Jaguar sports car. If we had had fuel injection it would have made a big difference. Anyway we didn't have it. We could have had more height and when you're at 30,000 feet it's not funny fighting something that is very superior to you, that could climb away or run away. The only way you could do was if he went down you could catch him.

I discussed formations with Malan. I said, 'We've got to have a system where everybody can see everybody and flying in threes is not the way to do it.' He said, 'But we've always flown in threes.' I said, 'Well it's time we flew in fours, a section of two and a section of two but a separate flight. We want to let everybody see each other.' And of course it stops the blokes being jumped. It was very important that we changed this, and of course the Germans used that system.

These dogfights, well there weren't such things. Everything happens so rapidly, and when you think you've got ten miles a minute they are a long way away from you in a minute. On one particular occasion we were being controlled by the Germans at Calais, they were using all our code signs. They were so simple that a kindergarten kid could work it out, but the Germans used them and we got a course to steer and the controller said there were many bandits below us and sure enough there were, and we were to turn to attack. As we were turning I looked back and there were bloody loads of 109s above us so I told Malan and he said 'Go and draw them off then' so Tony Mould and Ricalton were my two and three and we went after them and they were climbing. I climbed and I registered something in the region of 28,000 feet. By this time I had lost both Mould and Ricalton, Ricalton was shot down and Tony Mould was shot down. Ricalton was killed and Tony Mould baled out and he landed with his parachute on a chimney. He was knocked about quite severely and was in hospital on and off for a couple of months and I was left there with all these 109s.

I thought, 'What am I going to do?' but there was one thing I did know, I could turn inside them. The wing loading on a Spitfire was much lower than the German 109s so I thought I could turn inside them but when I'm turning inside them I have to get away and how was I going to do it. One of these Germans was in a position where I could get underneath him and so I was chasing round to get underneath him and I thought they won't shoot at me in case they hit him. I just pressed my button, there was a three second burst and there was a ball of flame in front of me so he'd obviously got empty tanks and he was on his way down to refuel because full tanks don't set on fire, it's the empty ones that do set on fire when incendiary bullets hit them because of the gases.

I got rat-a-tat, oh dear, bullets hitting me everywhere and I'm going down as fast as I could go. I saw the twin piers at Brighton and thought I had better get right down to those as quick as I can and they won't chase me round the piers, that's for sure. By the time I got down I'd burnt the Merlin out. The engine had seized because you'd only so many seconds at 3600 revs, the maximum was a few seconds at high revs on the Merlin engine. Anyway the engine had gone, I was hit all over the place, I was bleeding, my hands were bleeding, blood was soaking into my trousers, the bloody aeroplane wouldn't fly properly, I had no power and I thought 'How am I going to get to Manston?' not thinking there were fields and I could get down anywhere I want. I wanted to get back to Manston and I passed Manston at about 300mph so I must have been going at a great speed when I was over Brighton and I came into land at Manston. I was straight in and as I touched down I got left rudder, the rudder had been hit by cannon shells obviously, the bar on top of the rudder had been knocked into the fin so I couldn't move the rudder at all. So many times it had gone but bloody near everything had gone and as I touched down at Manston it was running and turning and of course I couldn't stop it turning. The wingtip went into the ground and then it shot up onto its nose and by the time it's got onto its nose I'm out the door and I'm on the ground. Fire engines and an ambulance came. It was covered in foam and I was covered in foam and ambulance people wiped me down. I said, 'I think I'm bleeding to death. I don't think I shall live very long after this,' and they said 'Don't be so bloody silly.' They wiped the blood off my hand and do you know? The blood had gone. There were bits of shrapnel, I've still got shrapnel in my nose, and sometimes I can get hold of a piece in my nose and pull it out and it's a bit of glass or a bit of metal. They had me down the sick quarters and said, 'You're alright. Go and get yourself a new uniform, battledress, go straight down to stores and you're alright.' So new battledress, back to dispersal point and Mungo Park checked my helmet and threw a mask at me. He said, 'Perhaps you'll have more luck if you're wearing that. I've got yours and you've got mine on.' And of course the mask was full of blood. I said, 'You'll have to get yourself a new helmet and mask.'

We'd been on the ground perhaps an hour and Malan did a bunk. I can remember so clearly, I was shaking, I was trembling, I was bloody frightened, I really was frightened and the squadron was scrambled so off I went. They said there were many bandits flying west at about 20,000 feet, and we saw them, they were making smoke trails, and so I said 'RT silence' and we got right underneath them and they never saw us at all. I pulled up and I got the leader of the formation, couldn't have got him in my sights better, and pressed the button and I hit him and down he went. I'm chasing him down towards the twin piers and thought, 'I'll get my own back now,' and he goes in the sea and there's a bloody voice, 'Mayday, Mayday,' and it was my number two and he was calling for a lifeboat to pick him up. I said, 'If I had any bullets left there would be no bloody Mayday,' so anyway they got him. We got back and they thought we had done a good job. We had shot four or five of them down, which was a lot because you hear these stories. A classic was where a pilot, I won't mention his name, was shooting a 109 down and as he was shooting this 109 down a 110 goes past him so he stops shooting at the 109 and goes after the 110. He shoots that down and goes back to the 109 and shoots that down. For his story he got a DFC and for that story he deserved one. I've never heard so much bloody rubbish in all my life.

John also found that the fear worked for him although it didn't make him like the air fighting any more.

That's very true. It does work for you because it's no use people saying it, I've heard on the television a veteran saying 'the happiest days of my life'. I have never heard such rubbish because they weren't the happiest days of my life. What I did when we weren't fighting probably were, but they certainly weren't when we were fighting. When we intercepted something the adrenalin pumped very, very hard, you know. At times there were six of us and I was leading a flight, I was flying as yellow leader and Ju88s were low flying and Malan had a go at it and of course bits and lumps were flying off all the time and then he got out the way and let the rest of his section have a go and, of course, all the time I was watching this, it just wasn't nice when this thing stops firing back, you know the rear gunner can't fire back because he's either dead or no bullets, or there's something wrong. Then the next thing is it hit the sea, the rear gunner came out the canopy and he was somersaulting. He went higher and higher and then of course he was down into the sea and the speed of the aircraft forced literally him under the waves and I thought well that's finished, unhappy families. I didn't like it at all. In fact I didn't like the bloody war.

Being in the forefront of the battle meant that Manston was regularly attacked.

Oh it was bloody awful because we used to have to do cockpit readiness. We went taxying out, three aircraft at that time would taxi out and take a trolley ack out to start up and the poor old erks, they would be sitting there under your wings and you're sitting in your cockpit and you can hear these shells coming from Cap Gris Nez. They were shelling Britain and these one ton high explosive shells were coming and hitting the aerodrome and all around and that is very, very frightening. If it was my turn to go I went without arguing but I didn't like it. There were a lot of things I didn't like but the thing I didn't like most of all was Malan and he did the dirtiest jokes on me. Now I think about it, after these things had been said to me, he was trying to get you killed. I was quite convinced he was but I was too good a pilot, I was too good for the Germans although I say it myself. I was probably one of the best Spitfire pilots of all time. I could certainly fly Malan out of the sky. I was very good, and I can say that because I'm 88, so I must have been.

John explained there was one main reason why he became such a good pilot.

By doing what Ernie Maybe told me to do, practise. Get into an aircraft if there was one there and fly it. Do what you like with it but just fly it, which I did, and I became very good.

And whatever they tell you to do, do it, and this was Ernie Mayne again, always on to me: 'Do as you're told not what you think you should be doing.'

Like all of the squadrons at that time 74 had its fair share of overseas visitors.

Don Cobden was a New Zealander and we had two Poles. One was a captain. He was at least 35 if not more and he was a very nice bloke and he said, 'Do you think your father would write to my wife in Warsaw?' So I said, 'I'm sure he would. Tell me how it's done.' And so it was done through Switzerland and my father wrote to somebody in Switzerland and the letter was then sent on to his wife. This went on for quite some time, letters backwards and forwards, and then all of a sudden it stopped. Of course they caught her and it was the gas chamber. I don't know how the Germans, very much like us, Anglo Saxons, how they can be so bloody cruel. What type of people? They can't all have been bad.

All came to fight the war. They all came to fight for Britain. Our two Poles had a long journey to get to us. They'd gone through Egypt and got into France and they then got to England with the help of the Free French, I think. They were very good, both of them. A pleasure to know. The older one, I thought it was very sad when his wife didn't answer the letters, and of course she couldn't have because she was dead. I don't know but this underground business seemed to work very well, but she was gone.

Despite the intensity of the action John and the other pilots did get a chance to get away from the airfield.

We'd probably get to the pub somewhere. We enjoyed ourselves. We went to parties. We were invited out and indeed they did buy us a drink. They were very kind to us, extremely kind, and we had people like Peter Chesters, he had a cracking father, he was as keen as we were and he used to give us booze-ups in his house and I remember one night he said, 'Now which of you lads would like a cigar?' Don Cobden said, 'I'd like one.' Don didn't smoke and there was this big New Zealand rugby player with a cigar in his mouth and I watched his face change colour and up came about three days of food and the end of the cigar. This delighted Peter Chesters' father but they were lovely people and we got invited out to a lot of places. It made life tolerable.

Kent had no-go zones. We could go because I had a sticker on my car windscreen which we were told to stick on. People couldn't go and say let's have a day at Margate. They weren't allowed. They couldn't get into the area at all because it was completely no-go but I think these people wanted to pat us on the back. When the war was at its worst, if I can put it that way, when they were bombing every night, we couldn't live on the aerodrome, we had to sleep out because they were frightened we were going to get bombed. The other thing was the shrapnel from our own guns had to fall somewhere so the guns were put in a position that when they did fire, if they didn't hit the target, it wouldn't explode, of course, and the shrapnel would fall on designated places like an aerodrome where there were no houses to get damaged and things like that. People in command used their brains but I thought my bloody car's going to get damaged, which it did, it smashed the windscreen. But the people in Kent, to us, were very very good, very kind, and very thoughtful. They watched the war with great interest and they saw a lot of it above them.

At the end of the Battle of Britain there was barely a short pause before the pilots were back in action, only this time the fighting was over France.

We did some sweeps to try and bring the Germans up but they weren't going to have this at all. If we were to do sweeps over France then we could do sweeps over France. Get on with it because we're not going to fight you. They would have been at a great disadvantage so eventually people like Malan wanted to go on and go on until blokes were sick and tired of this business.

Paddy Treacy got shot down and they captured him and they took him into an army camp and he did the old trick of going to the toilet where he smashed the window and they shouted, 'He's escaped through the window!' And of course he was at the back of the door, the Germans went and chased outside looking for him. It's the oldest trick in the book, they were doing this in the Boer War. Treacy walked out but he got caught again and he was put in with some prisoners. They marched him to Germany and he found himself walking alongside Basil Embry and so Basil Embry said to Treacy, 'When I give the nod, into the ditch and we'll both get away.' So they were marching on and Treacy looked behind and there was no Embry. He'd gone and apparently he'd seen a sign saying Embry (a small town some twenty miles east of Le Touquet and the Channel coast) so he went. He had quite a journey through France but Treacy thought he had to go and find him and he went but he couldn't find him anywhere. Instead he found a rowing boat and wanted to row back to England across the North Sea. No bloody idea which way to go but the Germans sent a seaplane after him and he got whacked on the head and pulled into a seaplane and brought back. Treacy said, 'This is not good at all, being a prisoner, I'm going to go,' and he did another bunk and he found a bicycle so he was on the bike and thought, 'If I can find a Consul he can help me,' so off he went. He cycled and he kept going, he wore the tyres out and he rode into Marseilles on the rims. At this time it was Vichy France, and the Germans weren't particularly bothered at that time. The Irish Consul said they would get him to Lisbon and from there you'll be on to an aircraft and you'll soon be back in England. So off he went again and they got him to Lisbon, and the aircraft he was going on was a Pan Am, and of course the Americans weren't in the war, and Treacy said, 'Are you going to England?' and they said, 'No, we're going to America, get in.' So they took him to America and he had to come back in a cargo ship. So he gets back to England and they gave him a squadron. He was very happy; he got a squadron and was going back to war again.

Malan took the war to them; he wouldn't let go. I will say that about him, he was very good at having a go at the Germans, but what Malan forgot about, I flew more hours and more sorties than any fighter pilot in the war and I got sick and tired of it. Then, of course, we didn't speak, I hardly spoke to him unless he gave me an order. I don't like the man, I didn't like anything about him. He was a bully and he was going to go over France doing sweeps and that's alright but I didn't want to do sweeps over France. I wanted to get out of the bloody war altogether. I wanted elsewhere and the next thing I know is they had just promoted Mungo-Park to squadron commander, so I thought, you lousy bastard, Mungo wasn't fit. A charming bloke, Mungo-Park, he was good to know, he was a good friend, but he wasn't a good pilot and he wasn't a good leader. Try as he would he just couldn't do it. If they had offered me the job of commanding the squadron I would have said no, I don't want to, I've had enough, and so I was sent to Hawarden, to 57 OTU.

John finally left 74 Squadron on 6 June 1941. That meant he had been at the squadron for more than two and a half years including almost two years of war, the longest time any Battle of Britain pilot spent with a single squadron. During that time he had been awarded two DFCs, one in August 1940 and a bar in February 1941. The 1941 citation read, 'This officer has continuously engaged in operations since the beginning of the war. He has destroyed at least twelve enemy aircraft and damaged many more. He is a keen and courageous leader.'

He instructed until January 1942 when he was sent to America. Initially training pilots at Selma, Alabama, John subsequently tested many types of aircraft at Eglin in Florida.

I'd been out to America for a year. I was test flying. I tested the Thunderbolt and the Mustang and things like that. I was at what they called the proving ground. And they had everything there from German motorcycles, there were Nortons, Triumphs, BSA, cycles of all types and all these things, all being tested and they were picking the best out of everything to make their own. They had a Beaufighter and the Spitfire and Hurricane. They had a Master which I think was one of the best trainers ever and as fast as a Hurricane and you could have a lot of pleasure with it. I know I did.

But even time away did not mean he could forget about old 'enemies'.

I came back from America and I'd been there a year. They asked me if I wanted to stay on or come back. I said no I'd like to go back to England. I said I wanted to go home. I went to the Air Ministry to see somebody. I saw this bloke and he said, 'You'd better have three weeks leave,' so I stayed at the Strand Palace and I went across the road and into the Savoy because there would be somebody there I knew, somebody to talk to and to have a drink with. And who should be there but bloody Malan. He said, 'And where have you been?' so I said, 'I've been in America.' He said, 'What?' I said, 'I've been in America for a year, test flying.' 'You wouldn't have bloody well been there if I'd known.' I thought, 'Lovely.' That's how Malan was. He wasn't straight at all. I loathed and detested him.

On his return he was posted as station commander first at Harrowbeer, Exeter, and then at Bolt Head on the south Devon coast. However, John could not stay away from flying for too long. In February 1943 he joined 602 Squadron as a supernumerary squadron leader leading bomber escort sorties before he was posted as squadron commander in June of the same year to 118 Squadron at Coltishall in Norfolk.

I got command of 118 Squadron. It was without question Malan's doing. It was the worst undisciplined squadron in the air force. You wouldn't believe the bloody rubbish. It was Spitfire Vs and I thought, 'Couldn't I get something better than this?' But I disciplined that squadron to such an extent that it was one of the finest fighter squadrons in the air force when I left it. I got these two, and I got the squadron, I got the flight commanders, and I said, 'What right have you got to be here?' Anyway, later on I sent for them but they never turned up so I said, 'Send for those flight commanders again,' and told an orderly to go find them and they brought them in and I said, 'You were told to come and see me over an hour ago or even longer than that and it was too much trouble.' So they said, 'You know what it's like,' and I said, 'I know what it's like but you don't. Get your gear together and get off this station by Friday.' They said, 'You can't do that,' and I said, 'I've just told you. Get out. Out of 118 Squadron. Out of Coltishall. Whine all you like but don't whine round me as I don't want you.' The next thing is someone from 12 Group rings me and says, 'What's gone wrong?' so I told him and said, 'I don't want them. I want two flight commanders not two idiots,' and they sent me two from Malta. Mike Giddings was one and Tony Drew was the other and they were cracking blokes and they really were flight commanders and I had a lot of pleasure with 118 Squadron.

A large part of 118's role was to escort US bomber formations. Here John yet again made his feelings known.

Fifteen minutes for the Germans over here but we took long-range tanks. We used to take a thirty-five gallon tank. It bolted on under the fuselage and you used the thirty-five gallons first. You took off with your main tanks and as soon as you were off the ground you switched them off and straight on to the thirty-five gallon drop tank and you ran on that until it ran out and then back onto the main tanks again. I did an awful lot of escort flying, escorting the American Eighth Air Force, their Marauders, and it was hell on earth because they were so bloody stupid, flying into cloud in formation, and hitting each other. You've no idea how stupid they were. I can't honestly say I ever saw them hit a target. They would say, 'We've got a big one on this time,' and it was a big one. It was four boxes of American Marauders, there were seventy-two bombers in each box. I was leading the left front seventy-two bombers and they said, 'We're going to bomb the docks at Le Havre and we're going to bomb on the leader of the front section,' and I thought 'This is going to be good.' We got over Le Havre and all their bombs went from all their bombers. They went into the town, not one went into the docks. Oh it was a mess. But it was like an atomic mushroom cloud going up. I thought, 'Why do they bloody do this?' and then on our return there was a 190 attacked them, just one German aircraft attacked them, and we were waiting to go down but no, all the bombers shot at him and he literally disappeared, shot to pieces, and when we landed they said, 'A successful raid, we made a good job of bombing Le Havre and we shot fifty-one 190s down.' Great.

Throughout the war the only aircraft John flew operationally was the Spitfire.

That was the only aircraft I fought in and I flew the Spit I, the II, the V, which should never have been made, the VI, the VIII, and I never flew anything better than that, and a Spitfire IX. The II was my favourite, the Spitfire II. It felt right. It flew right. It had automatic undercarriage and things like that. It was fast, manoeuvrable. The V I couldn't stand. Ugly, potbellied bloody thing, and when I went to Italy I thought I would get real Spitfires there. I got 286 Wing with Spitfire Vs.

John's combat war ended as one of the RAF's youngest wing commanders in charge of 286 Wing in Italy. He finally left the RAF in 1946.

John spent his post-war career as a driving instructor before being asked to join the Yorkshire brewery Tetley Walker. On retirement he moved to Spain for twenty years before returning to England where he finally settled in Birkdale on the beautiful Lancashire coast.

John caused much controversy both during his wartime career and after with his forthright opinions about the service and many of the people in it. He would take a dislike to a pilot, or a commander, and, never lacking in self-confidence, would make his views plain and obvious. To his clear dislike of Sailor Malan can be added Douglas Bader, Al Deere – 'I never liked Al Deere a great deal despite the fact he was a New Zealander. I'd have thought there was one bad New Zealander' – and he even made his views clear about Prime Minister Winston Churchill – 'Churchill wasn't a good man for anybody' – later adding, 'Churchill was, in my book, a bloody idiot.' However at the same time, despite his opinions, when it came to his own wartime service he often skirted round some of his own incidents and successes. He would not talk about crash-landing in France during the Dunkirk operation, evading the enemy and walking back to Calais saying, 'I won't talk about it because it leads onto things that shouldn't be said.' Off limits was 11 August 1940, the day he shot down three enemy aircraft in three sorties, passing it off as nothing special as he had not shot them down in a single sortie rather saying 'Yes but I didn't shoot three at once. I was rearmed and refuelled. Each time I had a full skip of bullets and petrol. It isn't possible otherwise.'

John Freeborn was one of the last of the great wartime characters, always in demand to speak, never short of an opinion and always followed by controversy.

Group Captain Allan Wright
DFC* AFC
12 February 1920-16 September 2015

At the time I joined, which was about March 1938, there wasn't any thought of war, not in people I talked to. Very soon there was, of course, but it didn't affect us very much, not at that time. Later on the thing that most affected me was when we were on holiday in 1939 in July, we were down south near Plymouth and I saw a hoarding which said Germany and Russia Combine, or something like that, and I thought 'God, this is the end,' I mean, we couldn't stand up against both those countries, what the hell's the future? which perhaps is a different answer to the one you'd get from many service people who say I knew we'd win the war from the very beginning, but I can't say that was my thought at all.

Allan Wright was born in Teignmouth in Devon and educated at St Edmund's in Ware, Hertfordshire, the oldest Catholic College in England. He was a deep thinker and carefully considered all options before making a decision, perhaps not the archetypal vision of a Battle of Britain Spitfire ace. Both he and his older brother, Mandeville, joined the Royal Air Force. His father had been in the Royal Flying Corps since 1916 and would not retire until 1943, and so as soon as he reached the age of 18 Allan applied for and was awarded a cadetship at the RAF College at Cranwell. His brother chose bombers and would later, on 16 October 1942, be killed flying a Wellington of 115 Squadron on a minelaying operation off the Bay of Biscay ports. However Allan chose fighters.

Everybody wanted to be a fighter pilot but when I was there and when I left and we did our gunnery training we did it in the Fury. We didn't know anything about Hurricanes and Spitfires, that was early 1939. What we'd also been flying was the Tutor and the Hart, the Audax and those aeroplanes. It was small, it manoeuvred, you could fly along, open the throttle and loop just like that. No diving to get speed and you could twiddle and turn. It was a delight.

It might have been for a peacetime air force but no training we had was suitable for what arose. We had these various number one, two and three attacks which were taught even in March (1939) when we first got our Spitfires. There hadn't been any war since the First World War and the thought was that Spitfires and 109s were so fast you couldn't have dogfights you had in the First World War. Apart from that nobody gave a thought, it seemed to me, that the German fighters and our fighters would come against each other at all because Germany was too far from England for the two to meet. Because of the Maginot line, I suppose, nobody gave a thought before the war that they would just march across, so we had to start from the beginning.

While at Cranwell Allan took his first flights in a Spitfire.

A lovely aeroplane. It was lovely to fly, but it had two disadvantages, well one disadvantage which one could see in two different occasions. One was that if you tried to pull up after you'd landed because you were short of runway or grass many people tipped up on the nose because the centre of gravity was so near the wheels. The other thing was that you couldn't see straight ahead on the ground at all and people happened to collide with other people and in the air. The disadvantage was that you really couldn't, if you had to take a deflection shot of anything like fifteen degrees or more and if you were taking a correct shot, you wouldn't be seeing your target at all because it would be underneath the nose, and then again I think that one reason Hurricane pilots perhaps scored as well as they did compared to Spitfires was that they could see what they were shooting at while the Spitfire pilot couldn't unless he was more or less behind. It could have been a so much better aeroplane if you'd been able to see over the nose. In every other respect it was wonderful.

Allan was posted to 92 Squadron at RAF Tangmere on 29 October 1939.

We were going to be a night fighter squadron and we were given Blenheims. They had no armament, they had no radio, and yet we were sent up every night to fly around the countryside doing what? – we hadn't the faintest idea. And then suddenly, that was in October so through that winter from Tangmere and then from Croydon, suddenly 1 March Blenheims gone. We had to go and get them, we were going to get Spitfires, so we tootled off to somewhere in the middle of the country and were shown a Spitfire and told, 'Take it away.' So that was quite amusing because to get the undercarriage up you had to work; it didn't come up by itself. You had a lever like and you pumped it to and fro so when you took off you started with your right hand on the stick and your left hand on the throttle, you shoved it forward and when you got off the ground you had to change over and hold the stick with your left hand and pump with your right. The result was that when one went forward the other went back so when you saw somebody off on his first solo inevitably once wheels began coming up it would jump up and down.

At the outbreak of war elements of Fighter Command were sent to France. No Spitfires went and so the brunt of the Battle for France, from a fighter perspective, was borne by the Hurricanes.

We weren't ready, we just weren't ready. We were told we were operational I think May 16. We went to Northolt and a few days later we were sent to Duxford and off we went. So France didn't come into it.

In the early months of the war fighter tactics were seldom discussed in squadrons. What they had been trained to do at Cranwell they continued to do during wartime. However, information of their tactical shortcomings, learned at such cost by the Hurricane pilots, did not find its way back to the Spitfire squadrons in Britain.

I don't know whether we could have expected it. I mean how could we unless we met them individually and the channel was in between and my impression of those early days anyway was that there was very little co-operation and discussion of tactics? That came much later. You just piled in and we just discovered that's what happened because you'd be tooling about over Dunkirk, minding your own business and looking around but if you saw any aircraft you immediately had to try and recognise them of course. You'd see where it was and you might be told what to do but after one or two sorties if you waited for that they'd gone so the form usually was you'd see where they were and go straight down. We weren't flying in pairs in those days so we were on our own. Conversely if you were surprised and suddenly something happened, whoever noticed it first would shout 'Break!' and everybody would peel over and curl round and look for themselves to see what happened, so hardly tactics.

In fact Allan's belief was that there were actually some great benefits to using the old ways at that time.

It took a particular way of flying. You came in very slowly. I've always found it very interesting. The form was that you took off and you joined up. There were two flights and each flight had six aircraft so there were four threes so to speak. In the event there would be three threes in line astern and one in the box and two of that last three would be weaving above trying to keep up and a little bit ahead and they would be watching your tail. I think in 92 we continued with that well into the Battle of Britain. It was almost not until we started flying in France (in 1941) that we changed and it was Douglas Bader, I think it was, who brought in the flying in pairs idea, copied from the Germans of course, who had learned how to do this over Spain. People do forget that there was an advantage in this way of flying for the protection of south-east England. The information on the enemy was very scant and we were sent up as soon as we could. Once up they'd still be trying to find out where the enemy was going, how many and in which direction, so we'd constantly be told to vector and fly in a different direction. Well with the aircraft in tight formation like that the leader could change direction in no time at all, but if you were trying to do that in pairs it becomes impossible. If you've got two aeroplanes flying a mile apart and you have to do a 90 degree turn to the right or left, one of them is left out in the cold.

On 23 May 1940 the Spitfires of 92 Squadron were finally called into action. That day Allan flew two sorties over the coast of Northern France. Over Cap Gris Nez he shot down a Me110 and by the evening he had attacked and damaged a further two German aircraft.

I do remember the very first occasion, I don't remember the result. Remember we hadn't met the enemy before. We were sent over Dunkirk, we weren't even told at that time why we were sent over Dunkirk, we were just told to fly up and down not below 10,000 feet, and if we came across the enemy shoot him down. So we got there and we started patrolling and I was interested in the situation in the countryside round Dunkirk. I don't think the massive cloud of black smoke was up on that first occasion so the first thing I was aware of was seeing several silver coloured aeroplanes passing by a little below and thinking what a pretty sight but it was only then that someone said '109s!' and I realised we needed to do something about it. Somehow I hadn't just switched on to a wartime situation. Well I hadn't met the enemy before.

It was during the Dunkirk campaign that Allan learned all about dogfighting.

It just happens. I had an experience at Dunkirk as I suppose there were probably more dogfights then because there were more fighters in a confined space. If it was dogfighting at all it was pretty short with one aeroplane and then either you got that one or another one was threatening you and you'd be into another one. And sometimes there seemed to be lots of aeroplanes about, difficult to choose what was what, and then you'd be concentrated on something for a moment and then you'd look around and they'd all gone. It was because the speed was such that if you happened to be going in the same direction OK, but in the opposite direction, at 500 mph or something, people disappear when they are separating at that speed.

One little short experience, I must have been in some sort of dogfight and everything had gone and I looked around and over there something was going on so I charged over there and there was a milling going round. I went straight in towards the milling and chose a target and as soon as I chose the target it whipped by me more or less head on. So I chose another one and that went by head on and another one underneath. I can't get at anything here. What the hell is going on? Oh, I realised I was in a circus so to speak and I was going the wrong way round so I pulled up in an Immelman turn as they call it and went straight up to lose speed and down again and then I was in the circus and I could pick one up. The idea that these things were happening and collisions were possible and not realising that one's in the circus going the wrong way round. They were 110s mostly and they had rear gunners so it was quite useful for them to go and turn circles to defend their own tails and at the same time they would shoot back but I never thought of adopting a circle with other Spitfires, not a bit.

We only got armour plating half way through Dunkirk and two things came for the Spitfire very quickly. I think they did wonders in those early stages. In those ten days our squadron was fitted with armour plating and instead of having push-pull propellers, or whatever you call them, with either fine or coarse pitch, and were good for going at speed or cruising slow, we had constant speed props which were replaced.

There was some criticism of the RAF over the Dunkirk operation, in particular from the army.

We didn't discover it until afterwards. We went down there on 23 May, it didn't start many days before that and was over by 2 June so it was ten days or something like that, and also we were restricted to this 10,000 feet so unless you happened to be chasing something, in one or two cases in our squadron someone had to crash land on the beach, we didn't really know what was going on down there. The only thing you really saw was this phenomenal plume of black smoke so I don't think we could have done any more than we did. The main thing is that we were so few. When you remember how far we had to fly, because of our endurance, we didn't have long range tanks, we could only have perhaps an hour, perhaps less, over there and to try and keep that up in May which is sunshine from five thirty until ten or eleven at night how could we be there all the time? I also think that Churchill was reserving some aircraft for what he knew was coming ahead. And we took casualties. Some squadrons were shot out of the sky.

Although we shot down many more Germans than casualties on our side, so we think, we were down to nine aircraft on the second day, I think, and those have to be replaced pretty quickly, pilots untrained, so we were given a couple of days off and back in the fray again. It was more intense from my point of view than the Battle of Britain.

One of the biggest issues in that short period of time was bringing new pilots up to scratch.

I felt jolly sorry for them because you couldn't give much time to them. You could only take them up in formation and see if they could fly the aeroplane and talk to them when you got down. Then you could play around trying to get on the other's tail perhaps, but the Spitfire was better, you could always get away, you could tell them these things. If you see him turn inside and you'll always be able to turn inside more quickly than the Hun and get up higher, you must be higher, and preferably in the sun as far as he was concerned. And if you were attacked, once some bullets flew get out of the way.

Dunkirk was the first time Allan had to cope with losing colleagues on the squadron. Among those lost on the first day were squadron commander Roger Bushell and Allan's best friend Pilot Officer Pat Learmond who had been at Cranwell with him.

You couldn't afford to be too bothered. I did attend one funeral during Dunkirk and then it was stopped because quite rightly they reckoned it wouldn't do morale any good and I thoroughly approved of that. I lost my best friend in the very beginning and I was deeply affected that evening, that night, but then the next morning you just carried on. Sometimes people came and went and you hardly knew them. I remember one occasion I was extremely put out. I had two friends later on, this was in 1941 when we'd been at it for a year, well some of us, and these two had been there most of the time and they weren't the sort of narky couldn't-care-less types. They were thoughtful people and I was getting very tired by this time and just before I went these two were posted, each as a flight commander to another squadron, doing the same job, and I thought this is not right. These people have had enough. You can't send them out because they would be the only experienced people in the squadron but also it was an operational squadron so they had their own problems. They were both killed within a month. I was upset at that more than anything else.

I thought about this more after the war than during the war. It didn't occur to me before. I mean there you were, you'd got your chums and you did things together. You depended on each other but you didn't think about it, but after the war, when people got married and started living out, I didn't like it. A squadron is a very close community, and another thing people forget these days, war for us did not end in 1945. Almost immediately Russia became the threat and, in Fighter Command anyway, and probably Bomber Command, we used to have to fly to the limit in dreadful weather. We'd constantly go up and practise dogfights and close formations, but we had to drive ourselves and when you were in a squadron you knew who you could trust and you knew how to get other people to behave and it became a very strong unit. Of course in the mess you drank together and you knew each other but when people started living out it lost that and that was a great pity I thought.

However, despite this intense baptism of fire for Allan and the other pilots, he considered the Dunkirk campaign to be a success.

Excellent, I would say looking back. Well it couldn't have been better really, because although we did suffer the casualties it was a situation where higher command could withdraw if they wanted to whereas if it had been the Battle of Britain, everything, all the stops, had to be pulled out all the time and without our experience of Dunkirk the casualties would have been very much higher. You see the Germans had the experience of Spain, they knew exactly what they were doing. They knew about fighting and we absolutely didn't know a thing, so it was just as well it was short and sharp and gave us that experience.

After their experiences over Dunkirk the squadron was moved to Pembrey in South Wales. During this time of recovery from the casualties sustained, some of the pilots were asked to fly night fighter patrols. One of these resulted in what Allan believed was his most unlikely victory, against a Heinkel He111 of KG27 on 29 August.

Oh that's quite a joke between my wife and myself because a newspaper said 'he followed their flames' or something ridiculous like that. It gives a lovely sort of picture in the mind. It was very much a cat and mouse affair, not what the rest of the squadron was like at all. Anyway, we were sent to a field, two fields locked together, a flarepath made up of six rows of bulbs, that was the flarepath we had, you couldn't see it until you'd found it. We used to have a coloured light and they'd put it five miles from the airfield and you had to remember where the airfield was in relation to it when you got back and then find the flarepath and get down so that was tricky for a start. Then we had no homing device at all in the aeroplane so first of all they had to pick you up when you took off and the way they did that was to tell you to fly left or right and see which blip on their screen was the one that did that. Sometimes they got it right and sometimes they didn't so sometimes you were up there not under control and wondering when you would be under control or even whether you would get back to base or not. On one particular occasion I was sent up and I patrolled. I think they had lights on the ground and if you were told to so you'd do that while they decided if they wanted to control you and I wanted to ask questions so called up and didn't get an answer. I did this several times and then I realised that somebody had left his transmitter on down there and I heard them talking to each other and asking for cups of tea etc while I was sitting out there in the black depending on them for my life apart from anything else. That was very annoying.

Anyhow on this occasion I was told to go after a bogey which was near Bristol at 20,000 feet or so. So I flew in that direction and saw the searchlights obviously looking for something and as I got nearer to it there was this one in the searchlight. As soon as I got up to it the searchlights came back to me and the ack ack came on me instead of them. This was again something that occurred because it was easier to follow something directly than try and get ahead of it. I did what I had to do which was to flash a light I had underneath which tells them to stop firing so they stopped firing. And then the lights went out as well so it was black except for the stars up there, lots of stars, black night and I was looking around wondering 'Where is the bugger?' and flying in the sort of direction I thought it was. I saw a red glow and another red glow next to it and I thought that must be it so I went after these two glows. It was difficult to concentrate on the speeds and not look in the cockpit at all to keep sight of these so eventually I did get into position and I went on firing at this thing and eventually flames came from one of them and that made it easier. I kept going on one then the other and then they both went out as it curled away and then I couldn't find it anymore so I came back, but in fact both engines caught fire and it force landed on the south coast somewhere.

I felt here's one for the book. They've been sending us out here tooling around, two of us had been lost altogether and had to bale out, one over Cornwall and the other over East Anglia, because they had been lost and at last we'd got something, but when I got down, I think it was Brian Kingcome who was flight commander, he wasn't at all pleased. He said, 'Why did you do that? We're not here to prance about in the night, we're day fighters and now they're going to go on sending us up and we won't get any joy.' So that was disappointing, but years later another chap had been writing his biography and he mentioned this thing. He said at last somebody had succeeded, clever chap, and I thought after all these years I'd been vindicated.

On 8 September 92 Squadron was moved into the front line. They would spend the rest of the Battle of Britain based at that most famous of airfields, Biggin Hill.

Masses were coming over and in fact we were replacing 79 Squadron. They had had such a bad time, been hit so badly, they had to go straight away, suddenly, and that's how we came in so suddenly. We knew perfectly well that the country was at stake. I don't know what others thought but I was absolutely aware that this was it. We'd just got to do the best we could. We'd got to get them down.

Well I think several airfields were (bombed). Manston was, Kenley was. In a way we came into it late. We arrived at Biggin on 8 September and when we circled round to land we could see it had taken quite a pasting. At night they had to move us out of the mess fairly soon to some galvanised iron huts at the edge. We were attacked at night, Biggin and everything, but we weren't personally affected. They had already dispersed the squadrons round the edge of the airfield and then they decided that being in these sheds wasn't terribly safe and so they commandeered another house a little way out and that became our mess, so to speak, enjoyed very much by most of us.

There is an old adage about the use of the Spitfires and Hurricanes during the Battle of Britain. Spitfires went for the fighters while the bombers were left for the Hurricanes. Allan had his own opinion over what actually happened.

If the bombers were on their own the policy was to attack the bombers, as they were occasionally. If they were being escorted, if you tried to get the bombers you'd surely get shot down yourself because they would see you and they would have the advantage. You have to slow up for the bombers so you had to get the fighters first so that's how it came about and then during the Battle of Britain it more or less came that the Spitfires went for the 109s and the Hurricanes went for the bombers. Still, we managed to get them both if we were lucky.

(Attacking a bomber is) a bit off-putting. You've got two lots of gunners shooting back at you, or even if it's a large formation and you're on your own you could have a lot of firepower directed at you. Mostly I ignored the single ones. A single bomber, if you were after that you jolly well ought to be able to get it. You had much more firepower than he had. One or two things were developed. I suppose other people thought the same as myself but I was confronted after an effort high up and then looking around and seeing a great stream of bombers going by or coming across me. I could get at them and what was I going to do about it? My first thought was do I go down into that mess or don't I? All the rear firing – but of course I went down. I reckoned the way to do it was to go down at vast speed, pass them at the rear and then with that speed, and at full throttle, get ahead of them underneath and then pull up, again at full throttle of course and turn round and shoot at them from underneath so your first shot with luck would be about thirty degrees deflection, where he wouldn't even see you, and then the rest of the time until obviously you fell out of the sky and had to go down again you would get a pretty good shot at them. And because you were coming up from underneath they would be unlikely to look for you there and even if they did you'd have the ground whizzing between you and them and you would be more difficult to follow and that was a good thing.

All through the battle Allan understood the importance and value of radar and the home defence system.

(It gave us) time and helped with finding the enemy. It was different for the south-east early on but once the enemy began they thought the best way of flying was to get a mass of squadrons of bombers and fighters together and this meant that they had to collect on the other side of the channel. Our radar was sufficiently good to be able to see this going on so we had time to get up but not have to get straight into the fray. Although 11 Group, which I was in, had to get up as soon as possible, 12 Group didn't. They did have the opportunity if they were sent off to fly back and gain height and then get at them either over London or on the way home again. Because there was a difficulty they had what they called a Jim Crow effort at one time and I was chosen, not personally but my squadron happened to be chosen for the first one.

By October a dedicated flight, which later became a squadron, was formed to help fill gaps in the radar coverage caused by German bombing of the coastal radar stations. However in September individual squadrons were selected at various times to provide extra coverage.

I took off from Biggin at the first sight of blips on the radar to fly up and down just off our coast to see if I could see when they began to move and send that back and thereby give some better idea than the radar. I was supposed not to attack anything, my job was to do that. Why not pairs? I don't know. So off I went, scrambled, climbed up to 25,000 feet, tooled up and down. I did see two 109s which I reported, they were about 1,000 or 2,000 feet below. They did see me and started manoeuvring to come up so what could I do about that except to go down and get one of them, so whether that affected the result I don't know. At least I had reported them but I didn't stay up there to report the numbers of bombers. Anyhow nobody complained.

(I remember) events I suppose rather than dates but they do go together. I think 15 September was my Jim Crow day so I rather missed that but 27th was another occasion. I can't remember what effect I had on it. I think you can see from the record. I certainly fired at several and I think I got one and damaged others, that sort of thing, but I remember flying back, when I'd finished my ammunition, at 1,000 feet or so back to Biggin and it was the only occasion I really felt a thrill about the affair. I thought 'I've done it. I've got some bastards,' and that was it. The rest of the fighting wasn't a particular thrill but I really felt I had done something that was worthwhile.

That same day, 27 September, Allan became 'B' flight's commander. There was, however, no respite from the constant aerial battles.

Whenever you were on the station you were operational and as soon as there was an enemy attack to the south-east off we went. Biggin was probably attacked many times when we weren't there because we were in the air. I can remember one occasion when I happened to be coming back from leave and as I approached the dispersal area there were obviously things going on. I looked up and there was a battle and I saw a single-engined aeroplane circling down. It hit the ground with a crump and of course I immediately looked round to see if there was anything I could fly and fortunately there was. Most people were diving into the shelters and it was happening in front of me. I saw an aeroplane there and it had a parachute on the tailplane and nobody was rushing out to it so I thought that's for me. There was a ground crew there, he hadn't dived down the shelter, so got me started and off I went into the battle which was just south of the airfield.

That sortie, on 30 September, would prove to be Allan's final one of the battle. The record shows he shot down two 109s that day but the story behind that sortie shows how dramatic it really was.

Well it was in fact the occasion when I rushed out to the aeroplane at Biggin having come back from a day's leave or whatever we were allowed in those days and this battle was still going on. (There were) fighters just to the south and I was looking around to get into it and I saw a Spitfire ahead of me and a 109 was just curving into it so I shouted, if anybody would listen, 'Spitfire being attacked. Take evasion,' and then I didn't see what happened to this character but he did tell me afterwards. It was (later Air Vice Marshal Robert) Deacon-Elliott (of 72 Squadron), and he hadn't seen him of course.

I was slightly above and the 109 curved up and I was able to get close enough to have a go. I got black smoke out of him and some white smoke and he peeled off. There was plenty going on so I thought I had got him. I should go for something else but by the time I looked round the sky was clear. This sort of thing happened. You'd be in the middle of a gaggle and then everybody would disappear so I climbed up away to the south, quite high, about 25 to 27,000 feet, and slightly above me was a vic, about seven of them, of 109s. They shouldn't have been so close to each other but they were, in formation, obviously going home. Maybe they thought it was all over by then, and I could only creep up because of the difference in height, hoping I wouldn't be seen. Maybe I started firing a little bit further away, about 200 yards instead of 100, so again I got black smoke but nothing more and I ran out of ammunition. He peeled off from the others and started going down, obviously as fast as he could. I thought well, I'll see what happens because I'd like to know whether I got the other one, and flew after him, I could do no good otherwise and just followed him as he went down. He went for longer than I thought. He went on down and the black smoke was still coming out, right down to perhaps 1,000 feet, and there was the south coast and I thought, for goodness sake, and very soon he obviously was slowing up and the black smoke stopped and then very low and then he hit the water, cartwheeled and that was it so I thought. Now I can get at these intelligence officers who never allow you an aeroplane when it's only got black smoke coming out of it and I turned back and looked around and the coast seemed to be clear.

A few moments later there was a crash and a bang and bits were flying all round, and of course I didn't think, I just pulled the stick up and round and the next thing I knew I was looking straight into the sea at about 500 feet. The aeroplane took control, I didn't do anything. It just went down and for a moment I thought 'I won't get out of this,' but hauling on the stick I did get out of it, but the aeroplane was behaving very peculiarly and obviously there was a hole in the wing. It was also obvious I had been hit in the thigh and, strangely enough, as I looked at the instrument panel it was clear in the middle and later on I realised it was the shape of the armour plate behind me, but outside there were bits everywhere. The thermometer for the water was twisted round which is the important instrument I wanted to see because with all those bullets around if he'd got my glycol or oil I'd be in the same position as the other guy. I obviously turned for the coast and nursed this thing, and myself, got to the coast, turned left, and everything I looked at to force land on had motor cars on it as they used to do in those days. I looked at the sea and there was gravel with these joins going up and I thought if it stops I'll just have to go in the water just outside there, but I did get as far as Shoreham which was just ahead. There was nothing on it so I put down there, and like on another occasion I put the wheels down because I thought I could see that there was probably damage there because of the holes in the wings, but I didn't dare put the flaps down. I thought of putting them down and in the end I did decide to put them down. I put the wheels and the flaps down and I got in but as soon as I got down I had great difficulty keeping it straight because one of the tyres had burst. I sat there a moment and my boot was full of stick and I thought 'What have I done?' and nothing happened. I think I was expecting an ambulance to come out, that's the usual thing, but not a bit. Then I saw a little Morris, an open Morris, bumping across the airfield towards me and I got myself out and limped towards it. There were two airmen there who looked like they had been sunbathing or something and they got me into this thing and took me back to the apron where the hangars were and they said 'I think the ambulance must be somewhere' and then I can't remember what they did next but I got out of the Morris and said, 'I'm sorry I made a mess of your seats.' I remember saying that and then two ambulance men came by and said 'We can't start it,' so I said 'You stupid ....' and one of the ancient three tonners came by. It was a Thorneycroft and I remember particularly because the chap helped me in and one of the ambulance men got in as well and I was obviously suffering from loss of blood. I remember getting considerable consternation by holding his hand, of all things, and as I looked at the front it had a sort of square bonnet and it even had the finage round the top as they used to have which indicates how old this thing was. I just wanted to get to hospital and be looked after so I said, 'Get me to the hospital,' so we went off to the east and came across a drawbridge and a river and the drawbridge was the wrong way so one of them got out, opened the drawbridge and I thought, 'When are we going to get there?' We got to Hove and I was getting a bit beyond it. They put me in the reception place and still nobody came so I started shouting and they said, 'You're alright. We'll look after you soon,' and so they did.

That very night Hove was attacked and, lying in bed with an army chap next to me, there were great flashes and bangs going off and I thought, 'Do I stay here or do I get under the bed?' In the end I thought I may as well get under the bed because if all those windows go there will be a lot of glass; but no harm was done.

I think we knew we'd won because I was there from September onwards so the whole of that month was very active. I was shot down and in hospital for about two months and came back in December, early December. By then there were practically no bombers but just 109s coming over with a bomb each, well that was obviously different and what I thought was, well this is winter and I suppose they're getting their people together to have another good go next summer. Meanwhile this is just to annoy us.

While he was in hospital Allan was awarded the DFC for shooting down an enemy bomber in difficult conditions and having 'a keen desire to engage the enemy on all occasions'. By this time he had shot down four enemy aircraft and damaged four more.

At no time did Allan ever think they were losing the battle with the Luftwaffe.

Not lost, no, damn difficult, and how long is this supposed to go on. Do we spend the rest of the war doing this? I didn't know, of course, the effect of casualties on either side. We seemed to have more people coming along. The Germans kept going, how were we to know? But it did cross my mind that I didn't think I'd be able to cope with this for a year or two.

Determination. I'd say nothing else matters at all. It didn't matter what type of person you were. Obviously to be successful you either had to get in so close so that accuracy wasn't terribly important or else you knew how to fly the aeroplane and fire the guns. But when it comes down to it its determination to get something, to get the enemy. I don't know of any successful fighter pilot who hasn't been shot up himself because a fighter plane is a very vulnerable thing from a seeing point of view. If you can imagine a Spitfire, you've got two planks that stick out either side of you and to the front so you can't see anything from the front and nothing much behind. You can't see underneath, you can only see straight behind and if you're lucky you might have a mirror but that's not much good and it's difficult to see straight up. So really you've got a great area of perhaps from vertical to back, except for the sides, and completely underneath apart from a little bit in the corner, where you can't see, so it's not surprising that even people who try hard do get bounced.

Allan however proved to be a very different type of fighter pilot to what many believed was the stereotype.

Probably one in ten or twenty fighter pilots had the sort of make-up I had. They were usually, in my experience anyway, not so serious minded I think. I've often been told I'm very serious minded you see which maybe so, I probably am, so don't take what I say as usual for every fighter pilot.

I do mull over things perhaps more than others, or maybe they don't talk about it. It think it happens a lot. A chap appears to be happy on the surface but really it's an excuse maybe, the drink and all that. Tony Bartley said, 'I don't know how you coped during the Battle of Britain. We had to get drunk every night or else we couldn't have survived.' And I said, 'If I drank every night I wouldn't have survived anyway.'

I used not to like him but we've become great friends. He's just very different.

Allan's quiet and studious approach also meant he never really got to know others on the station very well.

I think some people were better at that than I was. I have to admit I didn't know my crew very well, my ground crew, not to the extent that other people did. They were good lads and they looked after the aeroplane and I expected the best and I got it. No I didn't know them terribly well. As to the others there was very little opportunity. The controllers at Biggin, I think they gave two parties. Their own place was bombed and so they were given a house and had a pool and all that sort of thing for their mess and had a wonderful time. Lucky chaps we thought but we didn't know them well because they were distant. They were five or six miles from us. Most of the lads when they were off would be down the pub. They wouldn't be thinking we ought to go and have a chat with the controllers.

The squadron stayed at Biggin Hill until January 1941 at which time they moved to Manston. From then on the policy was to go on the offensive and take the fight to the enemy. However this meant flying over enemy-occupied France.

We were just putting ourselves in danger, and for what? Because obviously if somebody clobbered your glycol or oil you would have the same trouble as the Germans had when they were fighting the Battle of Britain, so if you were damaged in any way it was not at all certain you could get back. You could bale out over the UK alright, but what were you achieving? It was peanuts as far as we could see and we were just wasting lives because we lost lives alright. Later on I must say I still had the feeling when I was doing it anyway that I had got to get in there, but from reading what people had written afterwards it soon became like a boxing match, if you like. If someone was at you and you could nip out of the way you would, and then you'd come back again. You'd never bother to go for anybody higher than you were. You'd have plenty of time to try and get yourself into position. It was a sort of, I don't want to use the word game because of course it was life and death, but it was a game in the sense that it was concentrated... is it worth doing or isn't it worth doing?... whereas the Battle of Britain, I must say as far as I was concerned, if there was anything to be shot at, get at it come what may, the danger to yourself was secondary.

When we were sent over France in 1941 there may have been some squadrons told to stick with the bombers, but we certainly were never told to because the object of the exercise wasn't the bombs they would drop but to get the 109s up. I had an unusual coincidental conversation with the AOC of our group one day. I thought I'm only a pilot officer so I'm very far away from him and it can't make a difference so I'll ask him why on earth we keep being sent over France to get clobbered. We really should be learning how to shoot better because I was well aware that I should have shot down more aeroplanes than I had, and he said two reasons: One is it's important to keep your hand in and the other one was to keep the Germans in northern France, as many as we could, to keep them away from the Russians. The Russians were complaining we weren't helping them and at the present time it was the only way we could.

Some fairly complicated tactics were used when many fighter squadrons escorted the bombers. This included multi-layer fighter cover across a height of 25,000 feet or more.

One day the squadron was sent and we were going to be the bottom of the pile that stretched up to 30,000 feet. We were to fly at just about 7,000 feet over St Omer to try and get the Germans to come up and join in and we were supposed to be there for five minutes. Well some of us went before others and I think I was at the bottom. I was coming up with my chap and as I was flying out towards the west I looked behind and there was my number two. On another occasion I looked behind and there he was, we had blue spinners in those days, and then I saw tracer going past me and I wondered, 'What's he found that I can't see?' I looked ahead to see what it was and the next thing was they are all over me and I did a quick pull to get out of the way. When I tried to straighten out it wouldn't straighten out. I seemed to be doing a corkscrew round the sky to keep the nose up as best I could. Eventually I got the hang of it, which was to have the stick extremely over to the left and left rudder, and that was the only way I could stop it rolling and rolling. What had happened was that the first pull of the stick to the right had raised the elevator on that side and down on the other side and then a bullet from the enemy made it stick there and whatever I did didn't move it so to keep level the aeroplane had to have both ailerons fully up which meant they were pointing down so in effect only the middle bit of the aeroplane was holding the aeroplane up. It also upset the fore and aft, so having got it there the thing would go straight up or down to the ground. I forgot all about looking behind then to see if I was going to be shot up again. It was all I could do to control the aeroplane. Got back eventually, and I didn't put the flaps down as I had holes in various places and if one flap didn't come down I would have had to go round and round again so I put it on the ground. Of course I knew I hadn't got much lift so I put it on the ground at 150mph on its belly and that was alright. I must add this little bit: it was very early in the morning because we had taken off at six o'clock and it was half past seven as I crash landed on Lympne, the nearest place to the coast, took my stuff off, thought about breakfast and went into the Mess. There was practically nobody there. Big Mess, lovely polished tables. There were three waiters in white shirts looking after four elderly pilot officers and flight lieutenants from the First World War, reading their newspapers which were in front of them on a polished table and I was dying to tell somebody. I must have looked a sight of course, that I'd just got away with it, and I looked and they weren't the slightest bit interested. They didn't even notice I was there and I thought that was very odd.

Of course what I should have said... the thing was that this particular flight of Germans happened to have blue spinners when I thought it was my number two. He was a newcomer to the squadron and of course we talked about this when I got back. It was almost his first flight and he said he saw something down there and he didn't think anything else but to get it and he didn't even think of telling me so he shot off after a Hun and I was, in fact, on my own.

By this time, Spring 1941, the squadron was flying the uprated Mk.V Spitfire. Over the next few years, especially when commanding the Air Fighting Development Unit later in the war, Allan had the opportunity to test and evaluate many of the best Spitfire marks and compare them to the best from other countries.

In 1941 we were doing the sweeps over France and really there were duels all the time with the 109E and various others and eventually the Focke Wulf 190. During the battle itself we took the Spitfire as it was and it was very efficient and we liked it and it was wonderful. That's all there was to it. There wasn't a great thought about it.

(However the Mk.V was) just faster and we had problems. I should have mentioned earlier really, two more things about the Spitfire. One a very good thing on the whole was if you were going to trim her so you could fly hands off, if you go slower than that and you didn't hold anything the nose would come down and you would get faster. If you went faster the nose would come up so it was stable to an extent. I understood that the 109 was opposite of that, I never had a confirmation of that, but it could account for 109s going down more steeply when hitting the ground. One disadvantage, which happened with this character I shot at doing a Jim Crow he dove straight down, funnily enough he dove straight down towards the centre of England on that occasion and not back to Germany. He thought he didn't need to worry as he was faster, I don't know but I had no time to adjust the trim and I was just going at him and pushing and pushing and pushing until, after I had got some result from him I let the pressure off a bit and immediately the nose came up, and so quickly, and without enough reaction myself I just went out altogether, completely. I just don't know, I left at about 7,000 feet, why I remember that I don't know. Anyway the figure of 7,000 does come back because the next thing I knew I was more or less upside down and it said 7,000 feet on the clock, I don't remember much else, but at least I was able to control the aeroplane on that occasion.

On another occasion over France when that occurred and I woke up I just didn't know a thing, I didn't know where I was, and eventually I went, 'I'm in an aeroplane...and a Spitfire.' I looked out and the sun was shining and I thought, 'Is this England?' It seemed it took minutes to get enough brain back to realise where I was and to get back to UK in the right direction. Anyway so that has its advantages and disadvantages.

The other thing was that from the very beginning, although the Spitfire was beautifully manoeuvrable at normal speed, at 350 or anything like that, or in a dive, or going at it or going after a 109 it was very heavy on the ailerons and that does indicate that when you are chasing something at speed it's very difficult to get the sights on. If the sight drifts, because he's going one way and you another, you go a long way away before you can get back to it so it is difficult to keep shooting when you're going at high speed. So they tried to rectify that, they had metal ailerons I think instead of fabric ones for one thing and eventually they improved it, but even by 1944 when I was at AFDU and comparing them, and I flew a 190 then, I was absolutely amazed.

This 190, you could flick it round at any speed and I asked people questions, and I looked round the aeroplane, and I fiddled and I couldn't see anything that enabled the aeroplane to do that. Also, in the Spitfire and Hurricane and Tempest and many of them, you trim it for one speed. If you open the throttle or close the throttle and because of the torque of the propeller it drifts one way or the other and if you get faster or slower you have to adjust the pedals for the same reason. This thing you could open or shut the throttle, fast or slow, and it didn't affect it at all. One thing I did notice was the fins seemed to me to be a little bit offset from the centre and I just wondered whether the propeller, the axis may be offset as well. Now this will make you laugh, because in the old days before I joined the air force, I used to have the usual model aeroplane and elastic. I was in the south of France at one time, on a hillside, and rather stupidly I said I must see if this thing flies and I launched it, of course it would go further if I launched it downhill, and it always came back and I would go and fetch it. I tried various things to make it go straight all the time and one of them was to change the axis of the propeller, which I did, and sent it off and it never came back. It just went into the valley 2,000 feet below and it went on and on. That's what gave me the idea, but I don't know to this day what was done and no-one I have spoken to has given me an answer.

Later on I compared the Mk.IX and the XIV. The XIV was an extraordinary aeroplane. It was so powerful and made such a noise, even in the cockpit, it was like flying a motorbike. That was my feeling about it. You were certainly one with the aeroplane and when you pushed you were really moved. It was great but it had these even worse problems with the effect on the controls. In fact you had to be careful when taking off that it didn't swing, so for amusement I thought I would work out how to get off as quickly as possible. So what I did was, I can't remember which foot it was but let's say it was my left foot, I'd turn into the wind and put my left foot full right round. Then I would open the throttle until it began to move and then I'd keep it there, and as the speed increased so I could get the throttle forward, so having my foot already on the rudder I was having maximum energy to get off the ground. And also when I did that and I opened the throttle the wing would drop as the wheels were fairly close together and there was such torque it was enough to turn the aeroplane in the opposite direction, so for the size of aeroplane it was a very powerful engine.

In February 1942 Allan was appointed chief instructor at the Pilot Gunnery School at Sutton Bridge. This experience, together with his extensive time in combat in 1940, made him the ideal pilot, later that same year, to be one of a team sent to the USA to meet American pilots and discuss gunnery and tactics.

From our point of view it was delightful. I had heard about the Americans but hadn't met many, but I always knew everything was bigger and better in America, and for once, four of us went over there; they just hung on every word we said. They knew because they'd already had a pilot or two over here and they'd got shot to bits, that they'd got to learn and fast. My part was the gunnery side and Jamie Rankin was on tactics and I came across a quite extraordinary situation with one of them. His name was Major Darling and he was the king of gunnery in some squadron in the south-west and his method was, he would come past and fire one shot. Doing this he hit every time and so his score was nearly 100. But of course you can't quite do that in war, you can't just go backwards and forwards against somebody who was flying along straight and level. In fact we had this ring, with a dot in the middle in which you gauge the crossing speed, and fly towards the middle. They had a thing like you had on a sharpshooter, it was like a Christmas tree and you aimed up or down according to how far you were away, but there was nothing to the sides. You just got behind it and you did that, so it wasn't a sight you could use in war; so they had no idea, some of them, at all. They thought we were so wonderful, and it must have been the same with the others. They said, 'Here's a Lightning, show me,' and we'd never seen the aeroplane before. The first flight, I said I must have a flight on my own first to see what it's like, but it seemed to me the first flight I went up with ammunition to fire on a drogue, to get a good score to know what I was doing, and that was a twin, mind you, that was tricky. And the same with the other one, the Thunderbolt. But we weren't used to flying different aeroplanes, the only plane I'd ever flown before was a Spitfire, and I was getting to know the idiosyncrasies and what speeds for landing etc. You just had to ask and remember. But it went off alright.

On his return from the USA Allan was ready for another operational tour but this time he decided that he needed a different challenge.

Many of the well-known names stayed on day fighters and the ones that were successful in the Battle of Britain went on to North Africa etc but I felt that I had shot my bolt actually. I felt that I had got away with so much that if I wanted to last, to last the war to be quite frank, I felt I couldn't just not go on operations. But I felt I was more the calculating kind than the other sort, so when it came to the time I thought I had better try to get back on ops, I decided to go for night fighters, simple as that really.

Allan was posted to 29 Squadron, equipped with Beaufighters and based at West Malling in Kent.

Like all Bristol aeroplanes it was a bloody great thing. Powerful, the Beaufighter, inordinately cold, there was no heating whatever and of course if you patrol at 15 and might operate at 25,000 feet, there was nothing to keep you warm. That's why the greatest thought about the Beaufighter was that it was so cold. But it was effective alright. When I say it was a bloody great thing, it was, but they were good aeroplanes the Bristol aeroplanes.

GROUP CAPTAIN ALLAN WRIGHT DFC* AFC

On 3 April 1943 Allan shot down a Junkers 88 night bomber and damaged a second.

The time I got this one it was too easy really. It was only too easy because I'd just had a go at another, whatever it was, and should have shot it down. I was so furious with myself I was determined to get this other one come what may. Well I won't say that night fighting was fun, it wasn't at all because very often you'd be in this thing and you'd be flying in a black night and you couldn't see anything out. You might just as well be sitting in the office and you had to tell yourself you were going at 300mph and if you were supposed to be going at 1,000 feet, with the hills below you at 500 or 600 feet, you had to be jolly careful you didn't let the wavering instruments take you below where you wanted to be. Well, there's a very good radar, GCI (Ground-controlled Interception) which was low angle, particularly off Manston and that area, and they (the Luftwaffe) used to minelay because ships coming round the corner and into London would come round that way and they would drop their mines at something like 1,000 feet or 800 feet and if you were going to get one you had to be below it to be able to see it. You had to be below that and follow instructions and not fly into the sea and see this damn thing. We also had at the back of our minds a programme that even at night you've got to recognise it as what it is. It's not a Beaufighter, it's a 110, Ju88 or whatever it is, and on a black night it's almost impossible to see.

The Beaufighter, like any other aeroplane, when you close the throttle white flames come out at first. I think they die down after a bit but there's a flash of flame out of the exhaust. This thing was flying slower than me so there became a moment when I had to close the throttle, flames, and of course I was seen by the rear gunner and he started having a go at me. Meanwhile I was trying to get close enough to recognise him and I had this fixed in my mind and he went round and about and all over the place, and I was going around, and George, my chap at the back, shouted, 'Shoot the plane. Why don't you shoot?' and I said 'I can't recognise it. It's so dark.'

In this process I found myself overtaking very fast and I knew I couldn't pull back otherwise I wouldn't be able to see so I put the flaps down and that hauled me back a bit and then we went on, and so I increased the speed and eventually again, as happened in the Spitfire, I found I couldn't keep the thing straight – it kept drifting off to the side – and I looked down at my directional finder and because of the manoeuvring it was going haywire, the artificial horizon, so I just had to break off and settle down. I thought perhaps I had been hit you see and one of the flaps had broken, but in fact one of the flaps had been blown up, I discovered this later, I saw that the flap lever was still down so I put that up and then it settled and it was all OK again.

And then he said, 'I've got another for you,' so I said, 'OK, send me to it,' and by the time he'd got me near this aircraft it was going south-east and began to climb. As it got up, of course it's a bit easier to see, and I could see the French coast down there and I thought, 'I'm going to get this so-and-so.' I was brought up to it and he flew up there and he closed the throttle and I came up behind and I looked and saw it was a Ju88, fired and he went straight into the sea. But was it really a Ju88? Immediately I thought, I was absolutely on tenterhooks, I didn't recognise him. I said recognise but I shouldn't have said that. I didn't recognise him because I was going to get him and so I wasn't going to concentrate on anything else. So for the rest of the night I was worrying about this and by the morning I rang up the control and I said, 'Will you find out what our bombers were doing last night and whether any of them were in our area?' and fortunately there hadn't been. In actual fact if you were going out to a target you wouldn't suddenly pull up. He thought he had done his job. For him the French coast was safety so he just climbed up and motored along and didn't bother to look out any more.

Later in 1943 Allan was posted to take command of AFDU based at Wittering in Cambridgeshire. At this time he was a wing commander and just 23 years old.

It was called the Air Fighting Development unit, which was a vague term but the main task was to compare different types of our own and the enemy, if you could get them, just to advise, for example, who would gain height if you were climbing or who would go faster going down without throttle, and obviously the turning circle and the rate of roll. The turning circle was vital but the rate of roll was perhaps even more important because obviously if you're shooting at something and it moves from one side to the other the only way you can get back is to roll slightly, so if the one in front of you rolls by the time you've been able to get into the same circle you were miles away, so rate of roll was very important. That was the sort of thing we would say in our reports for example.

I should add a little bit to that. That was in 1944 and that was supposed to be our task but as rockets came along and ground attack was more important so we began to assess the best way to approach the target. One of the best ways to demonstrate was how extraordinarily different the angle of dive you say you're at and the angle of dive you think you're at. If you realise, you see an aeroplane coming into land at Heathrow or somewhere like that and you look out and say 'well what's his angle?' Ten or fifteen degrees possibly. Maybe even twenty. In actual fact it's three. The normal approach to an airfield is three degrees, so when you're telling somebody they've got to get over the target and dive at seventy degrees he will attempt it and it will be about thirty-five so he's not experiencing what you've been experiencing at all. We had an artificial horizon, as you know it's common now, and it shows the position of the horizon in relation to the aeroplane, the most valuable instrument there is. I thought I might be able to use this in order to find out myself what the angles really were so I got one of my chums to cut a hole in the side of this thing and to put a disc on it and a pointer – it's run by a gyro inside – and stick it on the side of the cockpit. If you try to use it it disappears at once, it won't give a steep angle at all. So this was how I learned that forty-five degrees was really very difficult and twenty or thirty are what they were so when we advised angles I'd have to say this is the angle you should do it at but it will be a lot more than you'll think you're doing. Otherwise how can you communicate? So we did and one of the interesting ones we did was with a Mosquito. It is a biggish aeroplane and I hadn't much experience of ground attack but a lot of it was obviously designed to get things coming in low down especially in any cloud cover. If you go over the target and then dive down, even if it meant going beyond and coming back because that's the easy way to do it, you get much greater accuracy by coming down at forty or fifty degrees than at a lower level. That was quite interesting because you discovered how much space you had to leave before you had to pull out to avoid hitting the ground. But the advantage of course was getting away quickly.

I don't know why the Tempest disappeared but the Typhoon seemed to go on and on as a ground attack aeroplane. But it was clear that by that time there was a XIX and a 21 but they were for different purposes, with the XIV you couldn't get further than that because the aeroplane's controls, ' the ailerons etc, couldn't cope with the power that was coming out of the thing. And another thing, I flew it at night and, I did it in the semi darkness first, but the flames from the exhaust were completely, it was bad enough trying to get into a night when you can't see ahead, if you get flary exhausts coming at you as well it was almost impossible, so it wasn't very good at flying at night.

The Spitfire was less flexible because it couldn't carry very much. That I suppose was why the Typhoon came in, and quite a lot of squadrons of the Typhoon. I don't know if we ever thought, I certainly never thought, that you could take it for granted that there wouldn't be many enemy fighters around.

But of course they were locked up very much with the American bombers so we weren't affected so much as the Americans were and that's where the Mustang was so useful and so effective. The Mustang was a beauty but I didn't come across that until I was at AFDU when I tried it out against the Spitfire, the IX at the time. It was pretty well as good and its great advantage was that without drop tanks it could go miles. In fact they took the American bombers right into Germany, the Fortresses, eight hour trips, can you imagine. Eight hours having to look over your shoulder all the time. I couldn't cope with that.

But then the beavers realised that something was going on about jet engines, and I don't know how soon we knew the Germans were achieving something, I'm told that we could have been much sooner if Whittle had been paid much more attention to, but that was the next thing, and it was while I was at AFDU that the Meteor became available. I went down to Farnborough and flew it, I was one of the first three or something. It was an experience but I wasn't allowed to do anything with it. Three hundred mph was the maximum I was allowed to fly it at that time, but obviously that was the next step and all the piston engines would go out the window. And one great advantage, there was no torque on a jet engine.

I think the RAF took it in its stride. I mean we were always used to new aeroplanes and some were very different than others and the piston engine did have its drawbacks. In particular it wasn't very good high up, and the enemy, in order to get away from us defenders, would go higher and higher and how (this new) aeroplane performed better up there was magnificent so it was welcomed with open arms. I think at the beginning we were told, and it made people a little bit concerned, that it was much slower to respond when you were coming in to land, engine wise. With a piston engine you close the throttle and then, in a sense, the propellers were stopping the air so it's like brakes whereas a jet engine doesn't have that. And also if you're coming in too low and slow, and you want to pick up a bit, the piston engine will react immediately, but not a jet engine. In fact you mustn't, at least in the early days, move the throttle too quickly or else it won't do anything so you have to move it slowly and slowly it creeps up so coming in to land is a little bit more difficult and night flying is more difficult than day and having got on the ground you don't stop unless the brakes work, while the piston one does stop eventually by itself. That's when they brought in all sorts of things to look after you if you overshot the runway.

I flew the Vampire, apart from this one shot in a Meteor. In the early days in my time at the AFDU the first jet aircraft I flew was a Vampire and

I threw it around a bit and it was an awkward thing. It wasn't easy to start and could be quite surprising because the engine was between the fuselage and the tailplane at the back, and with all the jet engines, more so at the beginning, it was a slow business winding the engine up before it caught. Of course paraffin would be going into the engine while it was warming up, you hadn't any control over that, and sometimes it just didn't catch when it should. The paraffin would pour out of the end and catch fire on the ground. You'd have all parts of the Vampire with a fire in the middle and so you had a chap with a fire extinguisher. Well you can hardly take off in a hurry if you had to wait all that time and the thing's going to catch fire when you do, so there was a time in the early days when they weren't all easy to get going and the speed wasn't great and there were certain limitations. I think we all felt that this was bound to develop. It wouldn't always be like that, as with any aeroplane. So I think that we all looked forward to better and better things.

With any fighter aeroplane that's a single seater, at the beginning, your first solo is your first solo, you don't have any instruction on the aeroplane at all. They did produce two-seater Spitfires and they did produce two-seater Hunters eventually; whether that made much difference I don't know, but if there were these problems (with crashes on the early jets) it probably was due to the fact that you had to be more careful coming in to land and it's got to have good brakes. In fact they tell me that disc brakes were first invented for jets because the other ones wouldn't last because they got too hot.

Allan stayed at AFDU until his final wartime posting in early 1945 to command the fighter wing of the Middle East Advanced Bombing and Gunnery School at RAF El Ballah in Egypt.

Allan remained in the RAF until 1967 and in that time he did his fair share of instructing, lecturing and desk jobs. However two particular commands brought him back to the front line of the RAF.

First, in the 1950s he commanded the fighter station at Waterbeach, north of Cambridge, with up to four squadrons of Hunters and Javelins. Second, and Allan's final RAF posting before retirement, he commanded the giant 'golf balls', the Ballistic Missile Early Warning Station at Fylingdales near the Yorkshire coast.

Allan's reputation as an ace fighter pilot had been confirmed during the intense days over Dunkirk and during the Battle of Britain. He had some firm opinions and memories that stayed with him for the rest of his life.

What was certain were his views on the Spitfire.

While I was flying it, it was the only aeroplane in the world. If you were doing a flight test in the evening after the sun had gone down you'd do your test and then you'd fly around a bit, perhaps do a few aerobatics. One knew that it was just as noisy in the cockpit as it was outside but somehow it felt that everything was quiet in the world and everything was beautiful. It was like a motorbike. When you're driving a motorbike you aren't saying to yourself, I must lean over here and I must do this, it goes where you want it to go, you don't have to do anything so to speak, and the Spitfire was just like that. When you saw anything you didn't say I'm in an aeroplane I must take it over there. You said I'm going over there or I'm going that way.

He also expressed his opinion on the oft-used comment that the later Spitfires lost R.J. Mitchell's original vision.

I don't think he would have minded. I think he was much more concerned, as we fliers are, with performance than with looks. It makes a little difference, but people say if it looks good it will be good, but I'm not an engineer. I fiddle about with that sort of thing and looks really have nothing to do with efficiency. It's in the eye of the beholder.

He also had strong views about being one of 'the Few'

(It was) real life. Undeserved to a degree in the sense one feels that other people are being left out. So many operations in different commands. People had to go through desperate adventures, things that a single seater fighter would never want. I would never want to command a bomber and have people dead and dying around me and have to cope and wondering what was best to do. I went down in a submarine once and I would never want to go down again and the people in the submarine said they would never like to fly a Spitfire, so it depends on your experience.

After all, the Battle of Britain afterwards has become a famous thing just because of the words apart from anything else and looking back it was a very important occasion. Yes it did save us until the Americans came in but at the time everybody was at war and it just happened that we were the people. The air force at the time was in the thick of it, other people weren't but they all knew, I mean people were getting prepared to defend the beaches, they would be just as heroic as we had been if there had been an attack. It wasn't until afterwards that it was realised just how important the situation was and therefore journalists weren't so head-over-heels about us at all, thank goodness.

I think it's true that it was a vital time in the history of this country, and I also believe that the same way as the army has Waterloo and the navy has Trafalgar the air force has the Battle of Britain. The Battle of Britain, to my mind, is just as important as either of those other two, no more no less, and that's a wonderful thing for a young service to have in the public eye and equivalent to the other two services but, as I say, as far as those were of any concern, we were just lucky. I think Shakespeare said something about that. Yes, it was the Battle of Agincourt, wasn't it, how lucky you are to be the people who are going to be remembered for the event, and that's my view too. The Battle of Britain is still relatively close. I think the air force do consider themselves as a vital part of the defence of this country, more so than they might have done. After the First World War I don't suppose the air force was considered greatly in the public eye vis à vis say the navy, but yes I do think the Battle of Britain put us on the map if you like, compared with the other services. We can take our place, we know what we can do, and we know how to do it and I do think, I am surprised, in a way, after all these years of peace and the dedication of the people in the RAF, particularly if they are sent anywhere to do anything, they perform magnificently, there's nothing that takes our mind off what they are doing, that's what I think.

Flight Lieutenant Terry Clark DFM AE
11 April 1919-7 May 2020

I think it all started when I was about 9 or 10 and I used to get the American magazines that were showing the war in the air. There was the air gunner sitting behind the pilot with his silk scarf round his neck and flowing in the wind and I thought I'd like to do that sort of thing.

Terry Clark was born in Croydon and watched the civil aircraft taking off and landing at what was London's main airport throughout the twenties and thirties. He never flew from there, but his first flights were with 615 Squadron Auxiliary Air Force from RAF Kenley just four miles south of Croydon.

Of course eventually I got to the age of about 18 or 19 and I saw they were going to form a new Auxiliary Air Force squadron at Kenley. I went up to Kenley, had an interview with the CO, and he said, 'What do you want to be, Clark?' because it was going to be biplanes with a pilot and air gunner. So I said to him, 'I'd like to be an air gunner, Sir,' and he laughed and said, 'Hmm, I don't think you'd see over the scarf ring,' and I thought what the so and so's a scarf ring? but I said, 'Yes I will Sir, yes I will. I'd see over that,' and it sort of shocked him a bit so he said, 'Alright Clark, you can be an air gunner.' But of course when I started flying in the Hawker Hector I suddenly realised what the scarf ring was. It's a tubular ring round my cockpit to rest your machine gun so you can swing it around. And that's how I joined the air force, as an AC2 under training air gunner.

For a lot of people it was just a way of getting some what you might call cheap flying. At Croydon airport there were some civil aircraft for which they'd charge you ten shillings a time for a five minute trip. I could go up to Kenley and join the Auxiliary Air Force and get lots of flying in for nothing so I think a lot of people did, especially the pilots too, because that was rather like a private flying club. That's my impression. Fair's fair it was good training for any future trouble. I suppose when you think about it no-one ever thought of war when you joined the Auxiliary Air Force. I think it was just fun being involved in flying.

I loved it. That's where I think my passion for the Royal Air Force came into being. It was a place where you made friends with all sorts of people, friends that you remember even now. I think it's a great pity that there's not more of that sort of thing. It gets people together.

The first thing I remember is walking up Whyteleafe Hill. It's a very steep hill and you're just about worn out by the time you get to the guardroom. It was where, too, I was introduced to the NAAFI and when there was a break from work in the hangar we would go outside, the NAAFI was there and we would get a 'wad and a char'. I thought, I have an idea that the char is tea but what the devil's a wad? It turns out to be a penny bun, so one of my favourite thoughts I remember is the NAAFI and a wad and a char.

Terry learned to be an air gunner on the Hawker Hector, an army co-operation aircraft that replaced the Audax. It was the last of the great line of Hawker biplanes. In front line squadrons it would soon be replaced by the Westland Lysander but for those few years before the outbreak of war it was an invaluable asset in training.

The Hawker Hector was only one of a series. There was the Hawker Hart and Hawker Hind and the Hawker Hector. I think they were mainly thought of more at the RAF shows that used to be on at Hendon in those years but I don't think it was a very well known machine really.

In my air gunner days I don't remember wearing anything but our uniform and an Irvine jacket if it was going to be cold. Most of the time would be spent in the armoury where you had to be able to take your Vickers K machine gun to pieces and then put it together blindfold and we used to do that time and time and time again. When I look back I don't think I would have done much damage with it.

I do recall when we were at two weeks' camp at RAF Thorney Island we had two aircraft prepared for air to sea firing. I was nominated as one of those and we had to be at the hangar at two o'clock to get on the aircraft. They told us as we were flying over the sea we would have to have a Mae West. Well I knew what a Mae West was but when I went down to the hangar to find it, and the aircraft was taking off at two and this was about five to two, there were a formation of three but only two of the air gunners found Mae Wests; I was the unlucky one. I could not find one anywhere. I searched room after room and eventually I did find one and of course that delayed the flight going off. We eventually took off and just before going off I was given a little cardboard box. I said to the flight sergeant, 'What's this for?' He said, 'The pilot will tell you what to do when you're airborne.' So we were airborne and we all went up several thousand feet and then the pilot said, 'We're over our area. I am going down to sea level and I want you to throw that little cardboard box into the water,' which I did. When the little box hit the sea it broke open and distributed a heavy lot of aluminium powder which spread and then made quite a big patch of whitish colour on the sea top so that it would form a nice target to shoot at. He then went back to several thousand feet and we were about to start when suddenly he said, 'We're not going to carry on with this exercise.' I said "Why not?' and he said, 'We are close to seaside resorts and it's getting rather full up with tiny boats and we feel that we'd better not take any chances.' So we landed without doing any of the exercise. When we landed I was put on a charge because I had delayed the aircraft from flying off. Had it been wartime that would have been a very serious offence and my punishment was to scrub the flight commander's room with RAF carbolic soap and I've never got the smell out of my nose ever since.

Terry has vivid memories of the last weeks before war started.

My memory takes me back to annual camp at RAF Ford. Then it was a naval station, and we had two weeks each year for training and this was the last two weeks in August 1939. We were in tents and there were signals coming through to the orderly room. People were beginning to talk about war because in the papers it was getting quite serious about the possibility of war and suddenly a signal came through and we had to down canvas immediately. We were taken back by coaches to RAF Kenley, our main station. We were inoculated, given our £5.00 calling up money and told we could go home for a couple of hours, get any extra clothing we wanted and then report back. From there, from Kenley, the squadron moved down to Croydon airport which had then become RAF Croydon and two days later war was declared so I will always remember how that came about.

I shall always remember that date (3 September 1939) because my Mum and Dad came up and I was able to talk to them through the railings that shielded us from the public. I think at that time we were still young and silly and we thought, 'Wonderful, we've now got our machine guns and can put them to the test.' Silly really when you think about it but I think that's how we felt and we didn't realise quite what was going to happen.

In May 1939 the squadron had been re-equipped with Gloster Gladiators.

Of course the Gladiator was a single and I had now finished (training) so the squadron went, about November 1939, to France and I didn't go with them. I was sent back to Kenley and I went into the armoury and just wasted my time there. Several weeks went by and I had an interview with the station adjutant and I said, 'What's happening to me?' and he said, 'Just wait.

126

It will eventually come. Something will happen.' A month or so went by and I had another interview and he said, 'Yes, before long something will be happening,' and eventually, in April 1940, I went to Jurby, RAF Jurby on the Isle of Man, and did a refresher gunnery course. There of course we were involved with the Blenheim and getting used to being in a turret. That course lasted about four weeks and I was then sent back to Kenley and I had nothing to show I had passed, I had no documents, and I had no air gunner's badge, I had nothing. I was just sent as an AC2 back to Kenley. It wasn't until a week later that I was then posted to RAF Catterick in Yorkshire to 219 night fighter Squadron flying the new Blenheims.

219 Squadron had only been formed in October 1939 and was equipped with the Bristol Blenheim 1F, the fighter variant.

So I arrived at RAF Catterick and I had an evening meal in the airmen's mess and then the following morning I reported to the 219 orderly room and saw the corporal there. I remember his name, Corporal Beck. I said, 'I'm AC2 Clark, Corporal,' and he said, 'Ah, you're the new air gunner that's posted to us. Where's your brevet and where are your stripes?' We'd heard rumours that aircrew would be made up to sergeant so I said, 'I don't know, Corporal, I've heard nothing about this.' He said, 'Here's a clothing chit. Go down to the clothing store. Get your sergeant's stripes sewn on, and your brevet. Come back here at two o'clock and then you can see the CO. You can't see him like that.' So I had breakfast in the airmen's mess and lunch in the sergeants' mess and I thought I rather like the air force. So then of course I was involved straight away on night operations in the Blenheim night fighter in my turret.

Our relationship with other NCOs was a little awkward at times because we had become brand new sergeants and they had taken many years to get to that rank. However, gradually the situation eased and we became friends together in the sergeants mess. With officers it was still very much separate but as time went by and you got more used to each other, although you were quite 'Yes Sir, no Sir' with an officer, it was much more friendly. And as far as the NCOs were concerned we were just all mates together.

I felt pride in belonging to an operational night fighter squadron. You felt, in a way, that you were doing something really worthwhile, and I remember my first squadron, 219 Squadron, and I shall never forget that number. It was wonderful, great to be a part of them.

When I joined 219 Squadron and I became what was called operational, in other words that you were then flying at night on operations, I felt a great thrill. I felt this is what I've been trained to do. We were airborne at night and we used to patrol along the coast waiting for enemy action. I was ready with my machine gun to do my job as I had been trained. Night after night we would go up hoping that we would see something that we could engage and destroy.

The squadron was broken into two flights, A Flight and B Flight, and B Flight would be on for two nights and then A Flight would go on for two nights and vice versa and during the time you were off you would do more training and more German aircraft identification and visit searchlight units, just to get to know all the operational parts that went on even when you were in the air. I must admit as we went on month after month, and we were not getting any activity, I was beginning to wonder if I should ever fire my gun. We did then go down to Redhill and change and that's when it all started.

When I think about sitting in my turret with my one machine gun I often wondered as to whether, at night, with probably no moon so everything would be dark, whether I should ever get a chance to fire at the enemy. He would have to be fairly close if I'm going to do any damage and if he saw me first he'd probably wipe me out before I had my chance to do anything so it was rather a case of hit and miss really.

When I think about the Blenheim, the Mark 1 short nose Blenheim, I used to have the feeling that I don't think we're going to get very far here. We really need something faster and with more equipment than just machine guns because we had machine guns in the wings and I had my machine gun but I felt that we were lacking. If we were really going to get down to night fighting we really needed something better.

It was my pilot and myself as an air gunner, there were just two crew. On occasions we would have a third man who might be an LAC. He would have with him a Mk.3 AI. AI meant airborne interception, or more commonly known as we went on as radar when the word came into being, but the Mk.3 equipment was very much in its infancy. We really were reliant on ground control giving us instructions and pointing us in the direction of the enemy. That was about all we had at that time. It wasn't until later that we were equipped with the Beaufighter. It was a far superior machine, plenty of machine guns in the wings, but it didn't have a turret and it had no air gunner. It had four cannons and a radar operator using AI, Airborne Interception equipment Mk.4.

In August 1940 there was a heavy raid in the north and 219 Squadron was scrambled from Catterick and I think about eight or nine of our aircraft went up and intercepted the enemy aircraft. There was an exchange of gunfire but then the Heinkels decided that they had had enough and sped off into the distance. From what I can gather I don't think our Blenheims had the turn of speed which would keep up and overtake them but unfortunately, on that occasion, I was away with one of the flight commanders on air to ground firing so I missed that one little effort I'm sorry to say.

It was not until October 1940 that 219 was sent south to Redhill in Surrey.

When we were told we were converting to the Beaufighter aircraft, and of course we'd never seen a Beaufighter, we didn't see one until we arrived down at Redhill and one or two started trickling in, my first reaction was well where is the turret? There wasn't one, there wasn't going to be one. There wasn't going to be an air gunner. It was an AI operator, airborne interception, once again the word radar came in. So I had to give up my air gunnery, all the air gunners objected and wanted to go to Bomber Command but we were not allowed to go because we knew about this AI so we had to retrain on the squadron and become operational immediately. I first of all thought what a waste of time this is but then when I got into it I could see this was going to be the answer. This was where we were going to get in touch with the enemy aircraft and do some damage because the Beaufighter was equipped with four 20mm cannons and that would certainly make the enemy cough and that was a thrill then. I really felt that at last we were getting something to use that would do the job.

When we had the Beaufighter aircraft of course, I must mention, we were still two crew, but when you had AI on board you had to... you were kept together because, with AI, you had to talk a picture. You had your AI equipment but from what you were looking at you had to talk to your pilot and describe what was going on, where the aircraft was, was it above or below, left or right, and was it getting closer. You had to create a picture of your talking to the pilot so he could more or less know where the enemy aircraft was. That is why once you were teamed up you were kept with the same pilot. I kept the same pilot for three years and we got on like a house on fire. I mean I was still a sergeant and my pilot was a flying officer but as time went on, of course, he became a squadron leader and I eventually became a warrant officer.

Being with the same pilot, it was absolute teamwork together. You would sit in the crew room and discuss ways I would talk to display to him what he felt was better for him to understand. I might say, 'Hard, hard starboard,' and he would like the emphasis in my voice because it would convey to him the urgency and how quick he'd got to respond.

My pilot was then Dudley Hobbis. He was, I didn't know it at the time, a well known amateur tennis player. He was a great chap. Friendly, he'd talk to you, a great one for one or two jokes that he played on me and we just got on extremely well.

Terry's memory of flying with Dudley Hobbis gives us a fantastic eye-witness account of night flying in a Beaufighter.

In the air we kept very much to what was going on. We never used to have any discussions about this, that or the other, or politics, or what was going on anywhere. There would probably be silence. Until I managed to get a contact on my equipment we might just say the odd thing to each other or he might say if things were quiet, 'We'll go cloud chopping,' and we would try and chop little bits off a cloud in the moonlight sky just for something to do while we were on patrol waiting for something to come our way, but there was never much. I know some kept up quite a conversation but we really didn't have an awful lot to say. I was too anxious looking at my equipment waiting for something to appear.

Of course our seating arrangements were not side by side. I was half way back, I had my perspex dome so I could see out into the night sky and he was up in his pilot's cockpit right up in the front. Between us were all the – hanging on the fuselage – drums of ammunition. The four cannon were below my feet and, if he used up the ammunition out of two drums, I had to take the old drums off and put the drums on rather like a powder monkey. Then we eventually got belt-fed cannon so that job ceased. But I was halfway back roughly.

Some people sometimes wonder how on earth we ever made contact with the enemy but, of course, when you were scrambled the moment you were airborne you would eventually be taken over by GCI, Ground Control Interceptor Station. They, like you, had radar that could see all that was going on in that area of the sky, big equipment. I had radar that would only have a limitation of three miles and my little radar equipment would indicate to me whether an enemy aircraft was to my left or my right, above me or below me, and then I would have the moment we got a contact. First of all the GCI would call us up and say we had business in our area and they would give us a course to steer towards the enemy. I would then be watching my radar, and the moment I got a contact, what I would call a blip, which would indicate to me where the enemy aircraft was, the ground control station would then stop talking to us and it was then my conversation with my pilot, giving him instructions that would eventually get him close to the enemy so that he could see it. Once he could see it then it was entirely up to him because he controlled the four cannon.

The way we carried out operations: Normally you would have a dusk patrol and a dawn patrol but otherwise you would sit in the crew room and wait to be scrambled when enemy activity entered your area. You would be scrambled, you would contact GCI ground station and they would see you on their radar. They would give you a course to steer that would head you towards the enemy aircraft and then as soon as they were in the three-mile range I would pick them up on my radar and I would then give my instructions to follow the enemy. He might dive down or climb up or swerve off to the right and I'd got to follow him on my radar until I could get him close so that my pilot could see him.

My pilot liked me to put him just below, dead behind him and just below, so he could tilt his nose and pump 20mm cannon into his belly, that's what he liked. But it wasn't always possible to do. The enemy aircraft might suddenly swerve off, and of course until he actually fires I'm looking at my AI because just as he's about to fire he might suddenly nip off again. I am supposed to, with my pilot, identify the aircraft as to what it is, but I didn't always get that chance. I kept my eyes on the AI.

When I look back at my time at Catterick when we were night flying from there I never realised that what we were flying through, if I can put it that way, was the Battle of Britain. It wasn't until, I think, Winston Churchill made the statement that one realised there was such a thing as the Battle of Britain. We had no idea. We were just going up, doing as we were told, flying as we were told and doing our job. I don't think anybody had any idea how vital that was.

My relationship with the ground crew. I always think to myself my God the ground crew, so whenever I go out and I give a talk I finish up by saying one thing that is very important, not only to me but to everybody, and I just say a few simple words... If it was not for the ground crew we would not be flying because they serviced our aircraft and being on a night fighter squadron they were at it day and night and if it wasn't for the magnificent support the ground crew gave us we would not get airborne. They were just as important as we were.

I think we used to have a little rivalry with Wing Commander Cunningham, 'Cats Eyes' Cunningham's squadron. We'd have to try and do better than them but I think the main rivalry was amongst our own ground crew as to whether their aircraft was getting more downs than the other flight's aircraft. I think that was where the friendly rivalry began but it was all in good fun and of course if we came back having destroyed some enemy aircraft the ground crew were delighted. They would go out and pat their aircraft and say, 'It's our aircraft that did that...jolly good.' It was great fun and specially when we came back having got two in one night. Oh the ground crew thought it was wonderful.

From December 1940 and for the next eighteen months, 219 was based at Tangmere in Sussex. For almost all of that time the squadron was commanded by Wing Commander Tom Pike who would end his RAF career as a Marshal of the Royal Air Force, Chief of the Air Staff and Deputy Supreme Commander Allied Powers Europe before retiring in 1967. However on 16 April 1941 fate intervened to bring Tom Pike and Terry Clark together.

I remember only too well. The night that fortune came my way I had just done two nights on with my own pilot and I was in the sergeants' mess and the telephone rang. It was the flight commander of B Flight and he said, 'You're on duty tonight Clark. You're flying with the CO, Wing Commander Pike,' so I said, 'I've only just done two nights on.' He said, 'Doesn't matter, you're on tonight with Wing Commander Pike, the CO of the squadron.' I thought, 'Oh dear, one mistake and I shall be posted back to a school somewhere.' So I went down to dispersal and that mid-evening we did a night flying test, had a chat to him, and I felt very nervous because I just wondered whether he would be used to my way of producing the picture. Anyway, we were airborne and before long we were put in the direction of an enemy aircraft. We chased him and he was a little so-and-so. Wing Commander Pike said afterwards, 'By God you had a job with that one.' He made three ninety degree turns apart from changing height and swerving about but I was determined that I was not going to lose him. Eventually we caught up with him and the pilot said, 'I can see him,' and I heard the cannons go off. The next minute there were gasps from my pilot and he said, 'Good God, he's blown up!' and the next thing I heard pitter patter pitter patter when bits of their aircraft were hitting our aircraft and I thought, 'For heaven's sake please don't hit the propellers.' That was it. He just blew up in front of us and that was that.

We continued flying and my pilot suddenly said, he called up the GCI ground station, and said, 'There are searchlights some way away on my right. Is there enemy activity there?' and they said, 'Yes,' so he said, 'Right, tell the searchlights to go out and give me a heading on to the activity,' and so off we went and in due course I got a contact and this one was another that thought he was going to get away, went all over the place, and I felt, 'You're not going to get away from me.' It was rather like cat and mouse. Eventually I got him close enough and the cannons went off and we saw him burst into flames and we followed him down and he crashed and that was that, that was number two. And so the pilot said, 'I think that's enough now. We've been up long enough.' We couldn't land back at Tangmere because of fog so we landed back at Ford where Cunningham's squadron was and when we landed Wing Commander Cunningham was out there to greet us so that's the first I saw of Wing Commander Cunningham. The following morning we flew back to Tangmere and we heard afterwards from intelligence that both of them were carrying mines, two mines each, and incendiaries, and they were on their way to Chatham so we saved Chatham a bit of a do. Of course the pilot, Wing Commander Pike, received his DFC for that.

The next thing I did when I was back at my own dispersal was I went over to my pilot and apologised. I said, 'Don't think for one minute that because we got two with Wing Commander Pike that I worked better for him than I did for you because I didn't.' I felt guilty.

About a couple of weeks later I managed to get Dudley one. We made contact with the enemy aircraft, shot him down and he went down in flames. A week or two after that I got another one with Dudley and so that made me four so he got the DFC and I got the DFM.

While we were at Tangmere my pilot suddenly decided that he would go over to a Turbinlite flight we had on the other side of the aerodrome and, of course, where he went I had to go, that was the rule in those days. I went there with some displeasure, I must admit, because I'd heard about these Turbinlites with the great big searchlight in their nose, formating at night with their illuminated strips and carrying a ton of batteries and not even a peashooter and I wasn't very pleased with the idea of doing that, but over to Turbinlites we went.

A Turbinlite was a powerful searchlight. In 1940 an Australian inventor, Sidney Cotton, had the idea of attaching one to the front of aircraft to illuminate enemy aircraft at night. Cotton had been one of the men responsible for the development of photo reconnaissance and he now teamed up with William Helmore, a senior scientific adviser to the Air Ministry. Together they developed the concept and had them fitted to the front of unarmed Douglas Havoc twin-engined night fighters.

The Havoc was a Boston, an American aircraft converted. I would have said it was on the lines of a Blenheim roughly. To be quite honest I hated it so much that I really couldn't be bothered looking at the aircraft. It was somewhat similar to a Blenheim. You had the pilot and the radar operator and illuminated strips at night which didn't please me.

EMPTY SKY

In 1941 the RAF created ten new flights for the new Turbinlite Havocs. These would later be enlarged into squadrons with their accompanying fighters. Terry and his pilot joined 1455 Flight, still based at Tangmere.

The theory was that you would be up at night and you would have a couple of Spits or Hurricanes formating on you by the aid of the illuminated strip on the wings. I would then chase the enemy and get him close and once I'd got the enemy aircraft within searchlight range there would be a codeword sent to the Spit or Hurricane. Then another codeword which would send him out and above you to your left ready for a dive and on the next codeword he would commence his dive forward to get more or less in front of you. As he commenced that dive my pilot would pull a lever and expose the searchlight, expose the enemy aircraft, and the Hurricane which was diving down towards that area would see him and shoot him down – wonderful!

The problem, to start with, was that the Hurricanes and Spitfires did not want to play with us for rehearsals, that was one of the problems, they just did not want to play and I can't recall a time when I was at Tangmere with the Havocs that we ever had two aircraft formating. To the best of my knowledge, I would have to look up my logbook, but I don't recall many night flights at all. The Hurricane pilots just did not like formating with us at night.

The pitfalls too, if the enemy aircraft suddenly dived off to the right I've got to instruct my pilot to follow him and the Hurricane has got to keep there as well and at night that's not the easiest of things. I never thought much of it and six months later they packed it in but to me it was a dead loss and a waste of money and good crews who could have been night fighting and doing a real job.

I had fifteen months while I was on Turbinlites and I would put it down to a life of misery. To me it was a waste of time and that was not what I was meant to be doing. I should have been back with 219 destroying enemy aircraft. I know it was a wonderful idea but in practice, personally, I didn't think it was any good. That's only just my thoughts.

It was Dudley Hobbis, you see, I was still with him but, poor man's gone now, I think to him it was just a job. That's what they wanted him to do as CO of the flight so he did it.

I mean, to me, there was no exciting crew room where you heard someone over the telephone say that they were on their way back home and they had shot one down and you'd say 'That's one up for the squadron again.' There was nothing like that at all. To me it was terrible. I hated every week and month of it, but it wasn't until I got back on to 488 (NZ) Squadron that I got back onto Beaufighters, and then we were in the right trade again.

The same month, July 1941, that Terry was posted to the Turbinlite flight he was also awarded his DFM.

It was a very proud moment, I suppose. It's difficult to describe. Going to Buckingham Palace and being received by your King and him pinning a medal on you was something I'd never thought would happen in my wildest dreams and so I'm very proud of it, but I hesitate to wear my medals because I feel everybody's looking at me. It's like a nice feeling. I know they're only perhaps trying to admire them but I don't mind wearing the small ones, the evening dress ones, I don't mind those, but I'm not a lover of wearing the big ones. And the trouble is I've got so many, in fact six, my small chest they take up all the room so...no, I'm very proud of it.

In May 1942 Terry and Dudley Hobbis were posted to 1451 Flight, later 530 Squadron, at Hunsdon in Hertfordshire. Hobbis was the CO of the flight so Terry became the senior AI operator as a warrant officer.

When I joined 615 Squadron in 1938 as an AC2 I'd always thought wouldn't it be nice to have a commission, you know, it's a much nicer uniform, looks much smarter, and I thought, you can dream those dreams but you don't expect them to come true. I remember, I shall never forget this to my dying day. We were on Turbinlites, my pilot Squadron Leader Hobbis was the commanding officer, and we were at RAF Hunsdon. My pilot said to me one afternoon, 'I want you in my office at nine o'clock tomorrow morning, Terry,' and I thought, 'Hell, what have I done?' I couldn't think of anything I'd done that I shouldn't but anyway at nine o'clock the following morning I went to his office and he said, 'Sit down. See those papers there, fill them in,' and I said, 'What are they?' He said, 'Just sit down and fill the papers in.' So I looked and I said, 'Oh, it's for a commission.' I'd been talking to him about the possibilities and he said 'Yes' he said, 'and when you've filled those papers in I've arranged this afternoon for an aircrew medical for you because you've got to have another one to get a commission and tomorrow morning I've arranged for you to see the station commander and he will interview you. Then you'll eventually be called down to 11 Group and Air Vice Marshal Leigh Mallory will interview you and see what happens then.'

So I had the aircrew medical and we'd had a party the night before and to go and have to blow that tube of mercury up and keep it there for a minute was tough going. I had the interview with the station commander and that went off alright. Then I went down to 11 Group and that's interesting.

I reported there and I met a flight lieutenant who was obviously the aide to the air vice marshal, so he said, 'We'll wait here until we are summoned,' and we were summoned and we went next door to this room. We only stood just inside the door and Air Vice Marshal Leigh Mallory was quite some way away across the room and he said to me, 'Ah Clark, I hear you've had some success with Squadron Leader Hobbis?' and I said, 'That is correct Sir.' He said, 'Thank you,' and the flight lieutenant nudged me and said, 'That's it, you can go home now. You'll hear in week or two.' Two or three weeks passed by and my squadron leader Hobbis rang me up. I was in the sergeants' mess. By that time I had got a warrant officer's uniform which was rather similar to the cloth of an officer and I had warrants on my arm. So he rang me up and said, 'It's through,' and I said, 'What's through?' and he said, 'You clot, it's your commission.' He said, 'Have a quick lunch in the sergeants' mess and I'll get the staff car and we'll go to the pictures in Hertford. After the pictures we'll have tea.' And I thought, 'That's fine.' So off we go. We went to the pictures. I have no idea what we saw and I thought well he's going to take me to some nice restaurant and have a nice cup of tea and we were driving along and I suddenly realised we were going back to camp. I thought, 'Oh, bang goes the nice tea in some nice restaurant, miserable devil,' I thought. We stopped at the civilian tailors and he said, 'Come on, we're going in there,' so I said, 'I don't want to go in there. I've nothing that needs attending to.' He said, 'Get out and come in.' And he'd played another joke on me before so I thought, 'Oh, there's another joke coming.' So we went in and he said, 'Take your coat off.' I thought here we go again, he's the CO so here's my coat. He gave it to the tailor and he said, 'Take those warrants off and in its place sew a thin blue ribbon.' So he gave the coat back to Dudley Hobbis who said, 'Come on, we'll put it on now,' and he said, 'now Pilot Officer Clark, we'll go to the officers mess for tea,' and I thought, 'What a wonderful chap to do it all like that.' I've never forgotten that, ever.

(Being an officer) put me in closer touch with Dudley Hobbis as I would be in the same mess with him now. I could talk to him on more level lines, and I always remember he said 'You can call me Dudley now,' and I said, 'No I shall not do that. Whenever you're in the mess you're always talking to wing commanders and squadron leaders and all this sort of thing, and in the crew room if I went up to you and said "Dudley" and you're a squadron leader you're entitled to Sir.' I said that wouldn't be good and I never called him Dudley. However (the mess) was totally different. For a start I had better quarters. When I woke up I was in a nice bed with white pillowcases and white sheets, something I hadn't been used except when I went home.

FLIGHT LIEUTENANT TERRY CLARK DFM AE

Finally, in October 1942, Terry was posted away from the job he disliked so much to be an instructor for six months before rejoining Dudley Hobbis at a new squadron.

After about fifteen months being on these Havocs I was extremely pleased when at last Squadron Leader Hobbis was posted away to 488 (NZ) Squadron, and of course I went with him and of course I was now a pilot officer. Squadron Leader Hobbis became flight commander of A flight and I became one of the senior navigators. It was a New Zealand squadron and most of them were New Zealanders and they were a grand bunch. The aircraft we were now back on was my good old Beaufighter. We joined 488 up at Ayr but we weren't there very long before we moved down to Bradwell Bay in Essex and we converted onto the Wooden Wonder, the Mosquito. To me (it was) the most beautiful aircraft I've ever flown in, the difference being that the pilot and I more or less sat side by side which was a tremendous help.

488 were equipped initially with the Mosquito NFXII, essentially Mk.II night fighters converted to carry the new Mk.VIII AI radar. These were soon replaced with the brand new NFXIIIs with upgraded Merlin engines which made the aircraft faster.

(The Mosquito and the Beaufighter were like) chalk and cheese. Totally different. For a start you sat side by side. Much better, although you still had your radar, but much better being next door to your pilot. You had under your control a magnificent fast aircraft, it made all the difference. I mean the Beaufighter was good but this was a superb aircraft. All the conditions were better. Beautiful aircraft. I've always said I only loved two women in my life. One was my wife and the other was the Mosquito.

For Terry it made the whole process of finding and stalking an enemy aircraft more real.

You just see the dark image. The pleasure of being in the Mosquito is you sit side-by-side with the pilot and therefore you can see everything that goes on. When you're chasing and then he suddenly says to you 'I can see it,' you can look up and for the first time you can see the outline of the enemy aircraft, it's quite a thing really. I know, if you stood up in the Beaufighter and stuck your head far over the side, you might see a bit of a wing or something, but this was seeing the enemy right in front of you.

I thought it was a beautiful aircraft and I think that's the right word for it. Just a beautiful streamlined aircraft and of course I eventually found out that it was actually faster than the Spit. It had two engines of course but it gave you a sense of, you could call it, superiority. You had not only the machine guns and the cannon but you now had a slim, fast aircraft, and I think my best days, in a way, were spent on the Mosquito, but also my worst day.

Dudley Hobbis had been in before the war, a short service commission, and he was a flight commander in A Flight, and by this time I was a flying officer. He came to me one day and he said, 'Terry, I'm going to be grounded. I've finished flying and they are going to put me on a desk job. You'd better find yourself another pilot.' I found a young New Zealand pilot, and we seemed to get on alright, and the CO approved of the new effort and so I joined B Flight with this Doug Robinson. He was a pilot officer then. Dudley Hobbis, I used to see him in the mess of course, and we were in the mess one day, and I shall never forget this, I was sitting playing cards, we were actually playing bridge, and Dudley Hobbis came in and he said, 'Our flight's on tonight and I'm just going to make one last trip, just as a farewell,' and I thought, 'He'll ask me,' but he said, 'I'm taking the spare navigator. I can't take you because you're B Flight and I must take the A Flight spare navigator.' So I wasn't on that night and I was playing cards when, about an hour and a half or two hours later, a chap came up to me and stood beside me and said, 'Did you know that Dudley has bought it?' and I said, 'What do you mean?' He said, 'Bought it,' and of course I knew exactly what he meant. So I could do no more. I couldn't play cards. I said, 'Sorry, I must go down to dispersal.' So I went down to dispersal and I did something I shouldn't have done. I picked up the phone and got the controller at North Weald and said, 'What is happening?' and they said, 'All we know is that in the Mosquito one engine caught fire' – well, that's not the end of the world at that stage – 'and he's told the navigator to bale out and they're over the North Sea' – so that wasn't too good – 'and that's all we know.'

After the war I still had a friend at the Air Ministry and I said, 'Can you find out? Are there any more details?' and he said, 'No, that's all they know.' Then he said, 'Six months later the navigator's body was washed up but no news of Dudley Hobbis whatsoever.' And they don't know whether he baled out or whether he went down with the Mosquito and I don't know. I feel that he went down with the Mosquito and what disturbs me is I don't know. And it upsets me. And after three years with that man right from the start, and I don't know what's happened to him, it does get to me.

Well a few weeks later, with Doug Robinson, my new pilot, we went up and we got one down. It was Doug Robinson's first and he was absolutely over the moon. And I thought, 'That's for Dudley, that one.'

FLIGHT LIEUTENANT TERRY CLARK DFM AE

Terry's success with Doug Robinson was on 20 December 1943 but by March 1944 his tour was over. He was sent to North Weald Sector Operations and trained to be a controller.

Then they thought it might be a good idea to send me away on rest somewhere and so I went back to North Weald and while I was there, my fiancée and I had been planning, this is 1944, planning to get married so I thought well, North Weald isn't far from Croydon where I lived and so we got married.

I had a week's honeymoon but I only got four days because I was called back to North Weald. I was in the ops room and I shall never forget that because as I walked into the ops room after only four days, and I thought that was a bit much, the moment I got inside there were three words that came up over the tannoy: 'Diver, Diver, Diver,' and of course we'd been briefed on what this was and it was the doodlebugs. They started coming on the plotting board and that was that. And then I, with Cyril Raymond who was the senior controller, I said to him, 'Any chance of a weekend?' The squadron had now gone to Colerne (in Wiltshire) and I said I'd like to go and see the squadron and I think he realised my heart was not in control in the ops room and he said 'Yes,' so I said, 'I've already spoken to Group Captain Pritchard, the station commander.' He was a nice old boy and he had a DH Rapide for use and I said, 'If I can find a pilot, would you loan it to me?' 'Of course.' So I flew down to Colerne, went straight down to the ops room because of course Doug Robinson's flight was on. I was sitting in the crew room talking and suddenly his navigator said he couldn't fly. He felt pretty queer and then said it's no good, I'm not in a position to fly. I don't know quite what it was but he was ill and he was out for six weeks. Doug Robinson had no navigator now, so I jokingly said to him, 'Well if you like I'll take his place,' and he said, 'If the CO agrees will you do it?' and I said, 'Of course I will, I can borrow a helmet and that,' so the CO said, 'If Clark will do it then by all means,' so we were scrambled and went onto a beachhead patrol and while we were there we got a contact, we chased it and we shot it down.

When we got this one over the beachhead, whether he thought he was on safe ground or not I don't know, but he really didn't take much avoiding action. He did chase a bit but nothing as serious as it would have been earlier on, so whether they felt that towards the end of the war there wouldn't be quite so much activity I don't know.

By that stage the Germans must have been getting a bit weak on aircrew and probably didn't have what I would call the same fighting spirit.

I'm pleased for Doug because he got the DFC for that because he'd got one before so my two got him the DFC. I was very good with my three pilots I had, Dudley Hobbis, Doug Robinson and Wing Commander Pike, because I shared it out, I got two each with them, so they can't complain. I like to be fair!

The next morning Doug flew me back in the Mosquito to North Weald and about two weeks after that I suddenly got a posting back to the squadron. I wasn't there very long. I couldn't go with Doug Robinson and I was given another pilot and then a posting came through to group, to 11 Group.

Terry had been a very successful AI operator during his tours.

Oh crumbs. I think what made me good at it was because I liked doing it. I liked going up and finding that we'd shot them down. I was a bit bloodthirsty I suppose. I know we were killing people, but at that moment in time just to get them, that's what drove me. Flying and doing something and I liked flying.

I went down to 11 Group and they said they wanted me to go on a course. They said, 'We don't really know what it is yet, we don't have a name for it.' So they said to have a week's leave and then go down to Detling and waste your time there until they get it sorted out.

Eventually I was posted to Honiley to No.1 GCA Course, Ground Control Approach, and I was the second in command but the squadron leader was never about so I took No.1 unit to Prestwick in 1945 and I was demobbed from there. GCA was the new Ground Control Approach system where you talked them down. You sat in a truck with two WAAFs and two pilots who controlled the talk-down, 'Lower flaps, undercarriage, land,' and in November 1945 I was demobbed.

Terry had had a successful war. He had emerged unscathed from hundreds of hours of night flying and fighting. And it is the squadrons he flew with that stayed with him most and, of course, his unfortunate first pilot.

Thinking of 219 and 488, which are the squadrons I most remember, one with Blenheims and Beaufighters and the other with Mosquitos, being a member of those squadrons, I'm very proud to say I belonged to them. They were two wonderful squadrons. I've never forgotten them and never will. It was just something, and the camaraderie was, well it's difficult to describe, that makes it so awkward because my pilot Dudley Hobbis, unfortunately, didn't survive. That was a tragedy and I get quite upset about what happened to him after being with him for three years.

Wing Commander Terence Kane
9 September 1920-5 August 2016

Terence Kane was born in Maida Vale, north-west London, and educated at various schools, finishing at Varndean in Brighton.

My inspiration to fly was derived from my brother because he had joined the air force in 1934 on a short service commission and he was telling me about flying so I decided that I would too like to fly. That's the basic part of it. The second part is that there was an advertisement in a daily paper, I can't for the life of me remember which, advertising for people to apply for short service commissions in the RAF, minimum age 17½ and I think the maximum age was 30.

I don't know how I expected it to be in the RAF. It was all a new life, a new adventure for me. I was living away from home in the company of a lot of other young men of various ages, only one of them younger than I, and the rest of them were into their mid-20s, so it was a completely different life for me

Terence started his training at 3 Elementary & Reserve Flying Training School at Hamble on 25 July 1938.

Life in the RAF was, to a certain extent during daylight hours, fairly intensive. You were either attending lectures or you were being taught to fly, getting into an aeroplane with an instructor and then later on going solo without an instructor and being taught manoeuvres in the aircraft, the theory of flight and navigation and engines and airframes, that sort of thing, even air force law. All these things you had to learn in order to be able to pass examinations at the end of what we knew as the junior term. There were two terms of about three months each in length, junior term and senior term, and you were slightly more privileged in senior term than you were in junior term. Probably more by virtue of the fact that junior term looked upon you with some respect, which you hadn't had from the instructors of course.

The instructors varied a great deal from sergeant pilots up to the squadron leader although the squadron leader didn't, in fact, do any instruction. He supervised the whole thing and also did flying tests to assess your ability at the end of each term. The other instructors in between varied from flying officer to flight lieutenant, varying amounts of experience, varying degrees of skill. Some of them were outstandingly good, they were all competent but some of them were really very good.

We had fun. Mainly in our off-duty hours we had fun. The usual thing, in those days anyway, of young men in those circumstances, we were still fairly disciplined, we had to dress for dinner every night, four nights a week we had to dress in what is known as mess kit and two of the other nights you wore a dinner jacket and the seventh night you could wear a dark lounge suit. You could walk out for your evening meal on Wednesday, Saturday and Sunday provided you got your CO's permission. Frequently we would go to town and have a drink and something to eat and chat among ourselves, enjoy ourselves. We found the evenings fun. You weren't very highly paid so that you couldn't go mad but on the other hand things were very much cheaper in 1938. You went out for the evening and if you had five shillings in your pocket you reckoned you'd be alright. It was autumn/winter 1938.

We tended to talk of things that were of particular interest to us. About our girlfriends, what was happening at home, what we'd done at the weekend, normal sorts of conversation. As far as the war clouds were concerned we were all well aware of them, you could hardly have been anything else. No-one could be in any doubt about it following Munich and the Austrian Anschluss and the threat to Czechoslovakia. It was obvious that war was coming and that we had to be ready for it; it wasn't the sort of thing that bothered our daily conversations very much. Mainly what I wanted to do was to fly aeroplanes. I didn't, at this point, consider whether I should be a fighter pilot or a bomber pilot or any other sort of pilot.

Terence moved to 5FTS at Sealand in Wales in September 1938 where he was injured and hospitalised after a crash.

I did crash at Sealand which was my Flying Training School, up in Flintshire, and I was flying an Audax which was a solo flying aircraft. You had room for a gunner in the back, but of course as it was a flying training aircraft we didn't carry a gunner. It had been very very wet the week before in December, not long before Christmas 1938, and I came into land. The airfield was very wet and I must have landed on about the muddiest part of it and the wheels got stuck in the ground and the aircraft tipped onto its nose and then onto its back. My flying straps, the safety straps that held me into the cockpit, didn't lock so that when the aircraft touched the ground I was thrown forward and I hit my head against the windscreen. I still have a scar across my brow which rather spoiled my beautiful looks but one has to put up with that. I spent a while at Christmas in hospital having it stitched up and recovering from that.

This accident certainly caused me some concerns. There was the obvious court of inquiry as to how it had happened and I was called on to give evidence but anyway at the end of that it was agreed it was an accident rather than any malfeasance on my part. The station commander interviewed me and asked me whether I thought I could continue, having missed out on three or four weeks of lectures, and I told him I thought not. It was too much to be able to catch up in a short length of time and I thought that I had missed too much. It was about a month of lectures and, even including the Christmas holidays, I felt I was missing too much to be able to make a creditable showing in the exams at the end of term, so it was arranged that I should be transferred to another flying training school at Ternhill.

Ternhill in Shropshire was the base for 10FTS.

To be moved from Sealand to Ternhill must have made a difference because it put me back a month or something like that. I presume that there were postings available if I had passed out from Sealand that were not available when I passed out from Ternhill, but on the other hand it also worked the other way.

Following completion of his training at Ternhill Terence had a number of postings before he became an instructor.

I had a period where I was at a bombing and gunnery school in Dorset at Warmwell. I was flying aircraft towing drogues for gunnery students to fire at so this was really very much an interim period of my life but I went from there to Upavon Central Flying School to learn to be an instructor all of which came as something of a surprise to me. I had always considered that, on the whole, the best students went to become instructors because they were perhaps more capable of passing on their greater skills to pilots and I was not a particularly good pilot. I was certainly not an outstanding student, however I was posted to Upavon to become a flying instructor.

Training before the war meant that Terence had enjoyed plenty of time to get it right. Once the war started the pressure grew to turn out pilots a bit quicker.

We were given something like nine months altogether, including breaks in training. Going from flying training school, I went from September to June but it would have been May if I'd stayed at Sealand. When I was instructing – I was instructing the junior term – I was teaching them the basics of flying. I think junior term lasted four weeks, including night flying of course.

I don't think there's much point in my conjecturing whether the four weeks was enough. It certainly produced more people able to fly aeroplanes, but you have to remember that the end of the junior term was really only the beginning. OK you'd got your wings but you were only really at the beginning of your flying career. Another four weeks of flying more advanced aircraft was perhaps not enough but these desperate times needed desperate measures. We were very short of pilots. I was towards the beginning of the expansion of the RAF and that was only in 1938. I'm not sure when exactly it started, 35, 36 or something like that, and it hadn't been long enough to get all the squadrons fully manned with fully trained pilots, but few of the squadrons were ever manned with fully trained pilots. Everybody has got to start somewhere.

After his instructor's course he was posted initially to 14FTS at Kinloss in Scotland and later at Cranfield. However there was always something niggling with him that he should be operational rather than instructing.

Well I did agitate that I should... I didn't agitate against my posting to CFS, I don't know why I didn't but I quite enjoyed it there, but then having started instructing, and the war was becoming more intense, and even when we were flying around you could find German aircraft about the place, I began to think maybe I'm not doing the right thing here, I should be using my abilities to fight the enemy other than training other people, and I did agitate for it and eventually that paid dividends.

It would be September 1940 before Terence was given his chance. First of all he went to Hawarden, to 7OTU, and converted to Spitfires.

I remember it well. One of the aircraft I had been instructing on was the Miles Master and I had accumulated 200 or 300 hours flying experience, instructing experience, on the Master. When I went to Hawarden they said, well, before we let you into a Spitfire we've got to teach you to fly a Master, so I said well I've got 300 hours on Masters and showed them my logbook, but it didn't make any difference, regulations say you have to go with an instructor in a Master and show you can fly it and then yes, I do remember my first flight in a Spitfire. What happens when you get into a single seater for the first time is that somebody shows you or you get lectures on the layout of the aircraft and what controls there are and how they work and then you go over to the aircraft and you sit in it while an instructor shows you again and then you're on your own. It was a very nice sensation, my first flight in a Spitfire, very nice. I liked it very much.

Well I suppose it was the smoothness, the ease of handling. Landing it was perhaps slightly more difficult than most but not particularly. You have to remember in those days landing was a rather different proposition to what it is now. Now you have a tricycle undercarriage on virtually every aircraft. Only the very small ones, the Tiger Moths or the old aircraft, have a tailwheel or a dragger, but all aircraft had in those days, the Spitfires had what we call three points, the two main wheels and the tailwheel landing simultaneously and you did your best to land it on three points. Most people in the beginning tended to land on the main wheels, but as a flying instructor I wasn't prepared to do this. I had to try and land it on three points from the beginning, I didn't always succeed but eventually I got it.

I felt about the Spitfire that it was a beautiful aeroplane, it flew very nicely, it was quite fast and there was a good chance that, in that, you could shoot down some enemy aircraft. There was also quite a good chance, if you learned to fly it properly, you could avoid being shot down. You felt a sense of joy flying a Spitfire. I think every time I got into a Spitfire I felt a sense of joy because it was a lovely aircraft to fly.

We flew twenty hours on Spitfires, I think it was twenty hours, before we went to a squadron and that doesn't give you very much time to do much more than become accustomed to the aircraft. Even to land you are not fully able to take advantage of all its abilities, and every time you flew it you experimented in a different way so to an extent I suppose we were taught how to evade being shot down. I think mainly, however, you were taught how to, as an interceptor aircraft, intercept and shoot other aircraft down.

It was mainly in lectures and you didn't get very much practical experience in dogfighting or anything like that. You had to wait until you got to the squadron before you were taught that sort of thing. I don't know that we were taught any particular tactics in the classroom. As far as I remember the more advanced part of your learning to fly a Spitfire, or any other fighter aircraft for that matter, was to take place at the squadron with the assistance of more experienced pilots than yourself.

234 Squadron had been in the forefront of the hardest days of the Battle of Britain. Initially based at St Eval it had moved up to Middle Wallop in Hampshire in August. The squadron had a torrid time, as did many in those few weeks, but the worst day was 7 September when the CO, Joe O'Brien, and Australian ace Pat Hughes were both killed. A few days later the squadron returned to St Eval for rest and recuperation and it was there that Terence Kane arrived to take up his posting.

I was posted down to 234 Squadron, which had the additional name of Presidency of Madras Squadron, at St Eval and I arrived there on 9 September 1940 which incidentally was my 20th birthday.

I took the posting as being what it was, an order from higher command. I wasn't particularly pleased or displeased at it. I really had no idea what I was going into. When I got there I found quite a few chaps there I already knew that I had met over previous years and we were changing squadron commander at the time. The squadron had just lost its CO and it was, the day I arrived, being commanded by a flight lieutenant, but the next day, or within the next couple of days, a squadron leader arrived to take over the squadron.

I wasn't landing among total strangers and I was made welcome, and the morale of the squadron, even though they had recently been stood down from a more active role, the morale was good.

Terence remembered his first operational flight with the squadron. It was 22 September.

I went up with a Sergeant Harker, I was his number two, he was the more experienced pilot, and one of the things I do remember at that time is the radio was very faulty. We had great problems with the radio. When you see films about the Battle of Britain and 11 Group particularly, they were able to talk to each other without any trouble; I never was able to talk to anyone without trouble. You get spasms when it wasn't too bad but on the whole it was very unreliable, the radio was very unreliable. Anyway we went off and as the newcomer to the squadron, naturally I didn't get first choice of aeroplane. So he was going off and I was supposed to be number two to him but he was getting further and further ahead of me, I just couldn't stay with him. We were in pursuit of a Junkers 88 and he fired at it and some distance in front of me some smoke came out and shortly after that he turned round and decided to go home and I looked at my fuel supply and decided that I'd got enough to go a bit further. We'd both been catching up with the 88, he'd been doing it faster than I, and I came up within firing range and it was going down by this time. He had smoke coming out of him and he was going down, and I fired at him and I think I hit him, some more smoke came out of him. He took a steeper dive and he went into the sea. I didn't claim anything as Sergeant Harker had shot it down but in fact Intelligence officers decided I should have a share in the victory so that was my first. My first plus mark was a half victory. It is a different thing, getting entangled with enemy aircraft rather than practising dogfighting with your squadron members. One of them is learning and the other one is deadly earnest.

11 Group was very much more intense than 10 Group. I should explain that St. Eval was in the 10 Group area and we were in 10 Group which was defending the South West. It was far more intense in 11 Group which was

defending the South East and London areas. Obviously we awaited enemy aircraft that were coming our way but we didn't get the density of attacks that they did in 11 Group. We had attacks on Plymouth and Bristol, places like that, and some of us went out to try to intercept the bombers with mixed success, I can't remember details of it at all. I had one or two other sorties over the next few days but didn't come into any contact with enemy aircraft.

The next day Terence's brief operational period came to an abrupt end.

23 September. The day I was shot down. I was sent up on patrol as the number two to a chap called Geoffrey Baynham, and again the radio was not particularly good. I lost contact with him on the radio fairly quickly and again he had a far faster aircraft than mine. I couldn't keep up, and looking back on it I often think what I ought to have done was to have gone home but I didn't. We were way above cloud and I really didn't have the slightest idea where we were because I had been following him so I thought I had better come down and see what the situation was and where I was. Incidentally I would have had to do that if I had decided to go home as I needed to know where I was. Anyway I started to go down and just above cloud I came across two 109s. Well I thought then I was above them and I don't think they saw me. I lined up behind one of them and shot him down. It was quite clinical really and I started looking for the other one but he had disappeared and then I had a small explosion inside my engine and my prop stopped. It didn't catch fire or anything like that but it was a useless aeroplane at that point. I had no idea on two points really. I have thought about this quite a lot. No ideas where the other aircraft was. I had no idea whether that shot was fired at me or whether it was just a cannon shell wandering round looking for somewhere to roost. But anyway it did for me. Well the first thing I did, being so close, was to dive into cloud as I thought I had better get out of the way in case he fires at me again. Once in cloud I decided the best thing I could do was, I didn't know where I was, whether I was above hills or what, I'd no idea what the terrain was like underneath me for landing, so I thought I had better bale out. I unfastened my safety strap and started to climb out. I turned the aircraft on its back and I started to climb out and I realised when I was half way out that I was still connected by my oxygen tube and my RT lead, so I had to climb back in again because I couldn't reach the sockets. So I climbed back in again, released these two sockets, and by this time the aircraft was flying on its side rather than its back, so I put it on its back again and I started to climb out. This time I got clear. I'd never used a parachute before but I knew what to do so I started feeling for the ripcord and I couldn't find it. I went further

and further round my body, my fingers looking for the ripcord, and it wasn't there. Of course panic began to set in so I had to fight that down and I went back to the middle and started again and of course I'd gone beyond it and here it was and so I pulled that and the parachute opened very nicely. When it opened I broke cloud and I could judge that I was about 500 feet above water, above the sea.

Thinking back on it the terminal velocity of the human body is 120mph or 176 feet per second and there aren't many 176 feets in 500 feet so if I'd delayed three seconds longer in finding the ripcord I wouldn't be talking to you today. Anyway, I landed in the water and my flying boots began to drag me down so I kicked them off which I regretted years later when I was in prison camp as I could have done with a pair of warm boots. I was in the water for quite a while. Again it was cloud above. No idea which direction was which. No sign of land. No idea of which direction I should swim or whether I should even bother. I didn't really think I should even bother as there seemed no point, but when over the horizon came the hull of a vessel I quite soon realised it was German and flying a German flag. They took me aboard and I was greeted by a junior officer. 'For you the Var is ofer!!' He was quite right, it was. Anyway they took me ashore, dried my clothes for me and gave me some different clothes, took me ashore, put me in a prison cell and then that was that. That was 23 September.

They told me what to do and they had the power so I did what I was told. I did investigate any possibility of breaking out of the prison cell but I found it beyond me so I was in there for two days. Then they came and fetched me, took me by car to an airfield where I was put on board a Ju88 and flown to Germany.

I think it was fairly well known that you were allowed to tell them your name, rank and number and that was it and that's what I did. There was no coercion to do any more. When I got into Dulag Luft I was again put in a cell. Dulag Luft was the transit prison camp that took all aircrew and questioned them again. They tried various methods. They tried shouting and tried the good guy bad guy sort of thing but I'd like to think that all they got from me was my name rank and number. I was only in there about two days and then they let me out into the camp to join up with the other prisoners who were in there.

Terence was in various PoW camps for the next four and a half years. After Dulag Luft he was moved to Oflag 9A at Spangenberg Castle in southern Germany.

This was a completely different prison camp. It was an old castle that had been a prisoner of war camp in the 1870s. It was a disagreeable sort of place. One very small courtyard with the castle surrounding it. Then there were ramparts outside above a moat which ran round it which was inhabited by three or four wild boar. It was not a pleasant place. The room in which I was put was a dormitory really where you slept and that was your only area. You could spend time in the courtyard or you could spend it in, they had a sort of library. It wasn't a library, it was more of a reading room. They called it an 'Aula'. Apart from that there were large rooms which were basically dormitories.

In 1942 Terence began his relationship with the best known of the PoW camps, Stalag Luft III.

I was in Stalag Luft III twice, 1942 for about six months and then I think 1943 till almost the end of the war.

Well, as far as the great escape is concerned it happened from Stalag Luft III but Stalag Luft III consisted of quite a number of different compounds. The Great Escape went from the North compound. On each occasion I was in the original compound which became known as the East compound and then there was the Centre compound which originally had NCOs in it but latterly had Americans in it and then there was the North compound which had RAF in it again, the South compound and another compound called Baleria for some reason which also had Americans in it.

The word went round that there had been a big escape from North compound and then of course later on some of them were brought back.

However Terence wasn't happy to sit and wait for the war to end. He took his chance on a number of occasions to try to escape.

On one escape we saw that there was a lorry parked outside the gate and the main gate was open and we thought it was an opportunity so we grabbed some hard tack rations, always a supply was kept, and got underneath this lorry. Unfortunately, he managed to get himself right out of sight but I couldn't, I couldn't get one of my legs over the rear axle and my foot was hanging down a bit. The guard looked underneath and saw it so we were caught. They came and got us and marched us round the perimeter and back into the camp. That was one. Another one was out of a tunnel which we dug from the latrines at one end of the camp which was fairly close to the barbed wire so it was obviously a good place to start digging and I was out for a couple of days and it was cold and hard and not very pleasant but at least you were free and able to do what we wanted to do. We had to keep hidden and we were given away by Hitler Youth who saw us and rushed off to tell the locals.

I was a reasonably enthusiastic joiner in escape plans. I didn't invent any of my own. I partook in tunnel digging, and all the tunnel diggers of course didn't get out. It needed too many tunnel diggers and you never had enough time to get everybody out.

Despite the escape attempts, much of the time was spent trying to alleviate boredom. He played sport, with kit being provided through Red Cross parcels. He read books, again getting reading and writing materials from the same source, and much of Terence's time was taken up reading law.

However, over the years of captivity Terence's quality of life began to suffer.

It tended to go down rather than anything. We relied enormously on Red Cross parcels and the ration was supposed to be one a week but I think only at the very end of the war were we getting anything like one a week. We were fortunate if we got one a month and didn't always get that. German rations, if they weren't so unpleasant, would be laughable. There was no, what we would call, edible meat. There was inedible meat and there were things like barley and bread but the bread was becoming more and more made with turnip flour and produced its own results.

The delivery of a parcel with a chocolate bar, or a tin of cocoa, would often be the highlight of the month.

Anything for sweetness really because that's what gave you energy, that's the thing you missed most and I found, in the hard days particularly when we were at Spangenberg, that I would mix cocoa and sugar together and make a chocolatey mix and I couldn't leave it alone. I would say I'll have a spoonful today and save the rest for tomorrow. Not on your life. I couldn't.

Somewhat surprisingly the one thing the camp was not short of was alcohol.

Oh we made our own. I don't think we used potatoes. We used raisins and we managed to get hold of yeast, and sugar and water and that was it and we made wine. We had, in one particular prison camp which was army, air force and navy, we had quite a spread of civilian experience including wine makers and distillers so we learned how to make wine. We learned how to make a still and I remember one Christmas I made myself from god knows how much of raisins and sugar, a medicine bottle that was full of alcohol, very neat alcohol, very strong proof alcohol in which I had soaked some dried apricots which gave it a flavour and a colour and it was very good. I had to dilute it with water before I could drink it. We did it on a corporate scale, we didn't do it individually.

Another surprise for Terence was when his brother, whose Whitley bomber had been shot down, arrived in the camp.

I suppose you experience loneliness but not to any marked extent. You had companionship all the time. Loneliness for your family, yes but I was fortunate, I told you that my brother joined the air force before I did, well I beat him to being a prisoner of war and he arrived a year after I did. He was a prisoner of war and we were reunited in prison camp. I couldn't believe it really. A special moment. There were few sets of brothers.

But all the way through his captivity Terence knew what was going on in the outside world.

We followed the news as best we could and there were times when it looked like it was going to be a long time and then, of course, after the invasion, we could see the beginning of the end.

The Germans made no secret of it, they published it in their newspapers, but we got English news over the radio. We had a secret radio. The Germans may have known about it but were never able to find it and we used to have news readings. Someone would take it down in shorthand, whatever the news bulletin was, and we'd have meetings round about lunchtime and somebody would read what had come over the news from the UK which was very good.

After D-Day the prisoners knew the end was near. However the prisoners now wondered what would happen to them at the hands of the Germans. In January 1945 the Russians were advancing towards Sagan, the location of Stalag Luft III, and the Germans decided to move them out.

They'd got no transport for us so we had to walk and the snow was really deep, really thick, and all we could take was what we could carry. I remember the first night. We were billeted in a church and, of course, in Nazi Germany churches had got no heating so it was a cold old building but at least there was a wall between us and the snow and the frost. Then there was quite a remarkable change. We arrived at a place called Muskau and I remember we were then billeted in a factory, they had fires on as they needed the fires for their operation. By God, it was tremendous to get in there. When we were marched out of Muskau we were walked down to Cottbus where we were put on a train.

They took us to a place called Westertimke which is half way between Bremen and Hamburg. It wasn't particularly comfortable but then none of them were. And then the British Army began advancing, or they advanced nearer to us, so they moved us again. And that was the walk we had that lasted three weeks and covered 100 km. We insisted on resting every third day so we had a certain amount of control by this time. The Germans knew it was the end and didn't want to do too much. Some of them did, some of them were perfectly happy to vent their rage on us, but on the whole they didn't.

As liberation came nearer the Germans gave many of the prisoners parole and put them onto farms which provided much more comfort. After a few days their period of captivity came to an end.

Suddenly from a copse there was the sound of firing, and we were slightly alarmed, and this was answered by gunfire from further away, and the firing from the copse stopped so we drew our own conclusions from that. Not long after that an armoured car, I suppose it was, came out from the Fife and Forfar Yeomanry of the British Army. Now we had already been out down the road to put notices up saying British Prisoners of War 500 yards ahead, rather like you see on the motorways, and of course we absolutely climbed all over this armoured car and they said it's a damn good job you left those notices back there otherwise we would have had to open fire. So that was the end of hostilities as far as we were concerned.

We were flown back and from there we were deloused and were given a cup of tea by nice ladies from the WVS. Then we went by coach up to Cosford where I spent three quarters of an hour standing under a hot shower. I hadn't had a bath since God knows when and had a sleep. Then we were given travel warrants and clothes, battledress I think and a kit bag, and used our warrant to go home.

I had no trouble readjusting to daily life but accepting life as it was. I'd had no responsibility for anything for four and a half years. I had been taken prisoner when I was exactly 20 years of age and I was now damn near 25 but I was still 20 years old because I had no experience of the world so I did have some trouble adjusting. In fact that's probably the reason I stayed in the air force. I'd been reading law in the prison camp and I had thought of taking my saved up pay and going to Oxford or some other university, preferably Oxford, to read Law but it came to making decisions and I wasn't used to making decisions. Eventually I took the easy way out and stayed in the RAF. To this day I don't know whether I did the right thing, but it doesn't matter now does it.

First of all I got a job as a staff officer at 21 Group. 21 Group was a training group, and then after I'd been there about a year I was supposed to be a pilot so I applied to go on a flying refresher course but they were loath to take me back into Fighter Command. I had so little experience as a squadron leader that they really weren't very interested in the idea. They had a command then known as Reserve Command stationed at White Waltham and I was posted there as OC of the unit, in other words the administration of the command headquarters and in command of the communications squadron. I stayed there a bit and then I went abroad, I went to Egypt.

In 1950 Terence left the RAF to join the Sultan of Oman's Armed Forces. However, four years later he rejoined the RAF, being posted to the Fighter Control Branch where he stayed until his final retirement in 1974.

Air Commodore John Ellacombe CB DFC*

28 February 1920-11 May 2014

John Ellacombe was born in Livingstone, Northern Rhodesia, and educated in Cape Town, South Africa.

When I was at school in Cape Town the brother of one of my friends was in the Royal Air Force and they were very keen to recruit people; this was in 1938. It was arranged for us to go and do some flying with a company and we flew in Tiger Moths. I got the introduction and they said why don't you come over to England and go to the Air Ministry and we'll see if we can get you into the RAF. My Dad wasn't very keen about that but we had lots of relatives who lived in England and my mother was very keen to come over so I came over with her, went to the Air Ministry and had an interview and they said yes we'd like to have you. They said, 'We'll put you down for a course,' and, as the war was about to break out, I joined a group of aircrew who were all Colonials, or Dominions, I think there were forty of us and we stayed together as a course on Tiger Moths down in the West Country.

John completed his flying training at 2FTS at Brize Norton and put as much effort into his sports as he did into his flying.

We had a very successful time there. We were the only course ever to beat the instructors. The Brize Norton Rugby instructors were the RAF champions but my lot were very good. We had two All Blacks and lots of others who were very keen rugger players.

Most of the chaps had been very keen sportsmen when they were at FTS. We had one summer there and part of the winter and we got on extremely well. In fact one of my chaps on my course was Billy Fiske who was the first American to be killed in the war. Billy was the American Cresta Run expert. He was a millionaire, a very charming bloke. He was married and his wife used to come out with us when we were going on the binge. Billy was sent down to Tangmere and he was one of the seven pilots who went straight to squadrons. Sadly his Hurricane was set on fire and he was badly burned and died.

AIR COMMODORE JOHN ELLACOMBE CB DFC*

We flew Harvards at Brize Norton. They had a front gun and we did quite a lot of air to ground firing so that gave us an impression of how to aim and all that. The Harvard was a very good trainer and we went straight from the Harvard onto Hurricanes (at the squadron) and the Hurricane was a very easy aeroplane to fly. It had wide undercarriage, ten feet, and the guns were very easily reloaded. In fact years later I got to know the designer of the Hurricane, Sydney Camm. I was then at the Central Fighter Establishment and we were flying the Hunter, checking that out. I used to go and see Sydney Camm and he was very bitter. He said the original design said you had to have an aeroplane with a ten foot wide undercarriage, over ninety gallons of fuel and the guns together so they could do a very rapid reload. You just took the cover off, put a new bunch of ammunition in and shut it up so the guns were reloaded inside two and a half minutes. He was very bitter. He used to say the Spitfire took eight minutes, had a narrower undercarriage and not enough fuel and they chose to prefer the Spitfire. He also told me the figures. If you consider the Messerschmitt 109, if that took ninety hours to build and the Hurricane took about 100. The Spitfire took 160 so in every way it was inferior but it was slightly faster however it could not out-turn the 109 which the Hurricane did. The other extremely good thing about the Hurricane was if you were shot down and were doing a forced landing you landed wheels up and the large radiator underneath took most of the bounce out of the aeroplane and you landed. You could then just climb out, hood back, knock the panel out and climb out and very little damage was done. In fact I'm told that very often they had aircraft which had force landed, a new airscrew was fitted on and various bits and you were flying again within forty-eight hours.

He was posted to 151 Squadron on 13 July 1940, three days after the start of the Battle of Britain. 151 had been at the sharp end of the battles since the French campaign in May, through Dunkirk, and was still operational. The day John and the three other pilots arrived, the squadron accounted for three Me109s destroyed. At this point John had never flown a Hurricane.

After the course the war was going and Dunkirk had happened. They posted the top seven men in the flying capabilities list direct to squadrons and four of us arrived at North Weald and were shown into Group Captain Beamish's office. He said, 'I know nothing about you but I'm delighted to see you. We can very quickly convert you onto Hurricanes and then you will be flying with me and your squadron.' So we were converted very quickly onto Hurricanes.

They were just pleased to see some new pilots and get on with it and get operational. We were taken off and instructed, put in a Hurricane and told to get on with it. They had one bloke, Barry Sutton, who was from 56 Squadron. He'd been wounded in Dunkirk so he was at the moment non-operational and he was put in charge of us. A delightful chap and no problem. And the spirit was good, I mean Victor Beamish said, 'Get training. Get on with it.'

After about two weeks I was flying and I went into combat and we attacked some bombers. It was the first time I went into action and found it very exhilarating to see all the armour and incendiaries flying around, but the squadron had had a very bad beating in Dunkirk. Teddy Donaldson (CO since Hurricanes first arrived in 1939) had been shot down and he'd decided he'd had enough. A new CO came in (Canadian John Gordon) and he was a very nice chap. On about my third or fourth sortie we were flying and they kept saying 'They are twenty miles ahead, fifteen miles ahead,' and I could see them and when we landed I said to my flight commander, John Willie Blair, 'Why did we not attack them?' He said, 'Well the CO couldn't see them. Did you see them?' and when I said yes he said, 'You have got exceptional eyesight,' and I have too, and 'You'll fly as my number two.' But the CO said 'No, you're going to fly as my number two,' and I flew as his number two on about ten sorties after that. In fact I was flying with him when he was shot down. He went down in flames and landed in a river in Essex and when he came out I thought he was taking his gloves off but what he was doing was shaking the skin off his hands.

It was known as the 'Hurricane Hand'. Most people then were used to wearing flying gauntlets which came up and zipped and in fact when I was shot down about three weeks later the only part of my hands that was burned was where the zip had pressed in.

As we flew we developed and improved what we had been told from experience. It was interesting and we found that as things went along you were doing things that you didn't want to do or hadn't done previously. But you were learning by experience and the morale was good. We knew we had to win and we were going to bloody well win and that we always had good leaders. We had exceptional leaders which made all the difference. Leadership was one of the great things that I realised later on as I grew up, that if your juniors listened to what the senior chaps were doing and respected them you would follow them regardless of what the dangers were.

151 Squadron went into lots of action. We went into many a fight with 109s. We found the Hurricane could out-turn the 109 if you saw them. It had a very good mirror above the cockpit and if you looked around and then looked in your mirror you could see 109s coming down. The technique was, as the 109s dived on you, you did an inverse turn. You put your foot across and you did a flick roll and that almost immediately meant that the Messerschmitt was then in front of you. I shot down two Messerschmitts that way. For the Heinkels, which we saw a lot of and were difficult to shoot down, we almost felt that the Hurricane did not have a heavy enough gun. The .303, we had eight .303s firing twenty rounds per second per gun, they were all armour-piercing and armour-piercing incendiary and you could see these exploding on the aircraft's wings, but a lot of the time they did not appear to be doing any damage.

It all happens very quickly. You suddenly break cloud, look around and you realise somebody's above you diving down at you so you have to break. You try and keep with your leader or your number two but it all happens very, very quickly. There's not much time to think. It's an explosive situation. When you're more in control and you're as a full squadron and you see a formation below you and you're attacking, that's much more simple and organised. I remember flying with Flight Lieutenant Smith who was the 'B' Flight commander. He had two cannons under the wing and that was the first trial they were doing for a cannon Hurricane. I was flying his number two that day and I was absolutely fascinated and I stuck with him when he attacked these bombers, these Heinkels, and blew bloody great holes in them. We were delighted to think we were at last getting a bigger gun because we realised that our .303 wasn't big enough, but when you were organised and you were attacking as a formation that was fine. The more difficult one to cope with was when you were bounced and you just broke. Sometimes you broke and you looked around and there was nobody else in sight, so the thing to do was to get back to base and rearm, refuel and be ready to rejoin your mates when they came back.

John had been with the squadron for about a month when one of the busiest days of the battle began a chain of events for him. 15 August was to be known as Adlertag, *Eagle Day, the day when the Luftwaffe used more than three quarters of its strength to attack RAF airfields. 151 had had a busy 14th so were stood down in the morning. However they were involved in fierce fighting in the afternoon and evening. Five pilots were either killed or wounded including the CO who took hits in his leg and head. John had rather a different experience.*

On that particular day we were scrambled and I was flying number two to the squadron leader. I had the oldest Hurricane in the squadron and we were told to boost which put the engine absolutely flat out. We were told there was a German force coming in and I could see them in the distance when my engine blew up so I thought that I had better force land. I could see a nice big golf course but when I got near it it had these big iron stanchions put there to stop aircraft landing and I had to force the aircraft down in a very small field. I jumped out of this Hurricane, the horn was blowing because of course the wheels were up, and as I got out a chap came out, gasping, who I realised was a brigadier. I said, 'Sir, do you have a screwdriver?' I thought we had better undo the panel and disconnect the battery which together we did. I then realised all I had to do was put the bloody throttle forward and the horn would stop blowing but I didn't want to tell the brigadier that. He had this beautiful Swiss army knife with everything on and where I had landed was an army headquarters.

They took me to this place and wined and dined me that night and they phoned North Weald but unfortunately with all the bombing that was going on the message was lost. The adjutant of 151 cabled my parents in Cape Town that I was missing. Next day they drove me to West Malling just as it was bombed and I sat in the bloody shelter not very happy. They gave me a parachute bag to put my parachute in. I was then sent by train back to North Weald. Going across London carrying my parachute bag an RAF Provost Flight Lieutenant came up and said, 'Pilot Officer, don't you know you can't take your parachute bag on leave? It's full of your clothes isn't it.' I said, 'Well open it and have a look.' Of course, when it was opened a crowd gathered round and there was this parachute. I said, 'I force landed yesterday after combat and I'm trying to get back to my fighter squadron,' and two old ladies with their walking sticks started hitting this chap on the head. The crowd was roaring at him and he disappeared. I got back to North Weald and the adjutant said, 'Oh my God. I've cabled your parents to say you're missing.' But it was an extraordinary thing, in Cape Town the chairman of my school's old boys association got the cable first in Cape Town and he rushed out to my parents' home and knocked at the door and said, 'John's alright, he's just force landed.' This was a pretty alarming episode. Now in that fight one of the pilots who was shot down was Pilot Officer Johnston who'd been flying and training with me and a very nice chap. I was told that he was going to be buried at Hawkinge so I got an aircraft, picked up one of the other blokes who had trained with us, he was at a bomber station, and we went down to Hawkinge. They had a priest there and about six airmen with rifles and they just lowered the coffin into the thing when we looked up and could see these Junkers 87s diving at us, so we screamed out 'Run!' and we jumped on top of the coffin and lay there while the place was bombed. When we jumped out again about a minute later there was no sign of the padre or the airmen, they had just disappeared. Fortunately our aircraft hadn't been damaged so we took off again, but it was a pretty alarming experience.

On 24 August John shot down a Heinkel He111 but found that North Weald had been bombed when he returned.

There was a tremendous esprit de corps there. Everybody was very keen. We had 56 Squadron and 151 and all the blokes got on very well. Of course we had the leadership of Victor Beamish and the airmen were tremendously keen and very good down at our dispersal. Sadly we were bombed because Duxford didn't turn up to cover us and in fact on that occasion the officers' mess, or part of it, was bombed and my annex that I lived in was destroyed. I landed and I didn't even have a collar. In those days you'd take your collar off and put on a silk scarf, wrap that round your neck because it was easier to turn your head when you were looking, so I had to pop into London the next day and get a new uniform, kit and all the rest of it, but it was a fine station and the spirit and the atmosphere was very good. We used to go into the Ops room quite often and you'd sit there watching all the WAAFs moving the plots around and somebody would say, 'It's coming our way. You'd better go from thirty minutes up to five minutes,' so you'd dash down to your dispersal and get in your aircraft and get scrambled.

You were very concerned for their safety. The Ops Room was finally bombed and they moved it out from North Weald to another place about six miles away. It was a very unpleasant thing when you arrived back at your base and you saw bloody great holes all over the place and sometimes ambulances and people being carried away on stretchers which was one of the things that made you much more determined to kill the bastards who were doing this to us.

We just wanted to kill the bastards. We knew if we did not win this particular battle Britain was going to be invaded. The army had very few arms left because they had all lost them in France so it was a desperate situation and we knew this was it. In fact we were down at Rochford airfield when we had just landed from one of our sorties and we had the radio turned on and that was when Winston Churchill made his speech and said 'Never in the field of human conflict' and we all looked around and said 'He means us.' We realised this was a war we had to bloody win and we hated the Germans so much we didn't need much more incentive.

151 had a lot of losses. We had six killed and eight wounded and eleven others were shot down and force landed. I was one of those. In fact I was wounded and force landed twice, so I was two of that figure.

It was the tension and the anxiety and of course your losses that were going on and then we were bombed at North Weald a second time but very little damage was done. We were all developing what we called the 'twitch' because you didn't have enough sleep and because you were so anxious your anxiety was showing. You had this bloody twitch which was not cowardice but your nerves were so shaken and you were seeing all your chums being killed. You had experienced ghastly things and very often when you landed you found there were bullet holes in your aeroplane. I know at the end of the war when I drank a pint of beer I had to pick it up with two hands. It took me about six years to lose this anxiety and all the pilots who did a lot, I mean I did three tours on operations and I didn't finish flying until September 1944 when I completed my last sortie flying Mosquitos, that one was sitting back and then you felt, well, I have survived the war and thank God for that.

I think most blokes were in the same boat, even though when you think of it some of the chaps we had in 151 had fought in France and at Dunkirk and they had been flying on operations for a long time. They had all already got DFCs or DFCs and bars, they had shot down a lot of aeroplanes and been in all sorts of things, and the one chap who saddened me in many ways was Teddy Donaldson, my first CO, because he had reached the stage where he didn't fly again in the whole war. He was so shattered and been damaged and of course he was actually shot down on one occasion and landed in the sea. He was in the water for several hours before he was picked up so there was one of the blokes, one of the outstanding pilots, who's nerve had actually gone but realised that somehow you are determined not to show fear. It was a difficult thing to describe but I suppose it's the same as facing a fast bowler with the buggers bowling ninety mph at you. You are determined, 'I'm not going to be frightened.'

John settled down into an uneasy routine which started on readiness days before dawn.

Well you were often told you were going to be up at dawn so you actually got up in the dark and you went straight down, having had a quick breakfast, to your dispersal and you sat there waiting for things to happen. Sometimes if you were told there was no activity going on we would wander up and go to the ops room and sit around looking to see what was happening or we would just stay down at dispersal and have a quick nap. There were lots of books and magazines to read and we often talked to the airmen and found out what they had been doing. A lot of very good chaps had been conscripted in and they were always very keen to talk to the pilots and we would pass the day that way. It was pretty exhausting and towards the end of the day you were absolutely shattered.

There was a certain routine when we were down at Hornchurch. If the phone would ring once, they were talking to somebody in the mess. If it rang twice, it was for you and you were going to be scrambled. If it rang three times, it was for the other squadron. So when you were sitting down and the phone suddenly rang you said 'Once...will it stop?' 'Twice...is that us?' 'Thank God it's a third time'. An extraordinary situation of tenseness. Were we going to be scrambled or weren't we? And that was the phone, but again you never knew when the phone rang what was going to happen. It was a situation where nerves began to play quite a part.

Your state of tension was such that you always found something to do and something to occupy you. You were always hearing of what had happened at the next station, so and so had been knocked down or had shot something down. Constant interest.

But humour was never too far away.

I remember one occasion we'd landed and we'd had tea and we were scrambled and I was still chewing a sandwich and I strapped in the aeroplane and I still had my mouthful and I spat and there was the poor old airman leaning over me with a face full of tomato sandwich. I got airborne and when I landed I said where's so and so, they said he's disappeared. But I apologised profusely. We had great humour with the airmen and all the others. The esprit de corps was something and I think it was the leadership integrated from the top, from Victor Beamish and the flight commanders. They were all very gallant and successful blokes and you were very willing to listen to them and follow their example.

We were all very cheerful chaps. We used to go in the bar and chat and have a drink and then when you were desperately tired you'd go to bed. What we did at North Weald, Victor Beamish made us, every third day or fourth day, you would get off the station. We used to nip down to London and go to some of the old pubs or places we had known or visit your friends or go into Ongar where we had pals and it was a very nice pub there. We'd go and have a lunch and chat to people, but Victor Beamish wanted you to get away from the thing every fourth day so that was one way we used to try and reduce the strain.

John always had a good word for the ground crew.

You mainly flew your own aeroplane. You had two different flights and if you could you stuck with your own aeroplane and you got to know the ground crew very well. You were on christian name terms with them all and they were very concerned when you landed. They said, 'Have you fired all your ammunition, Sir?' You'd say yes and they'd be very pleased and they were extremely supportive and enthusiastic and got on very well. I thought the spirit of the whole station and specially down at the squadron was superb and that's one of the things that kept you going. Had they all been morose and underconfident it would have affected your own morale but everybody was dead keen to get on with the job.

They used to put your name on your aeroplane and do various things. If you shot some aircraft down they would put the little crosses on and they were very, very supportive and very keen for you to do well.

They were tremendously quick and that comes back to what I learned years later. The design of the Hurricane, because the four guns were together, they literally took the panel off, pulled a great thing out that had the ammunition in and put a new one in and connected the guns and that literally took two minutes. There was great competitiveness for two reasons. A, we might have been scrambled again because the airfield was about to be bombed so they were jolly keen not only to do it quickly, but B to do it possibly to save their own lives.

On 30 August, 151 took part in a large number of sorties.

There was one occasion when we had broken cloud and we were bounced by 109s. Everybody broke and when I came to look around I literally couldn't see anybody. On the RT there was North Weald station: 'Bengal calling. We have a large formation heading our way,' and I looked and I saw this formation of Heinkels from a distance. They had bombed us the week before so I thought, right, this is my chance and I did a head on attack on the leader and from about 2,000 yards I just pressed the trigger and dived at the leader and as I dived underneath him all his perspex had broken away and both his engines were on fire and I thought, 'That's great!' until I realised he had put one bullet through my spinner and my engine was failing. We were told don't bale out, always land if you can, so I landed in this enormous field and jumped out of the cockpit. A bloke was rushing up at me with a pitchfork saying 'I'm going to kill you, you bloody German.' He rushed at me and was chasing me round the Hurricane when fortunately the army arrived. A sergeant said to me, 'There's your Heinkel crashing on the other side of the airfield. I'll go across and have a look.' He came back and said,

'Don't go back. They're all very badly wounded,' and in fact the pilot died very soon afterwards.

John returned to the squadron and was in action again the following day.

Towards the end we were down to six operational pilots and we were moved down to Stapleford Tawney which was only six miles south of North Weald and we were there in fact on 31 August. We were told, 'You are going to reform at Digby and then Wittering so we will try not to have any sorties,' but we were scrambled quite early on. We lost our Polish pilot, Frank Czajkowski, on the very first sortie and I think I shot down a 109. We landed and had a second sortie but that was uneventful. We were then told to pack our kit into our aircraft and take off for Digby and then they suddenly screamed out 'Scramble!' We were down to five aircraft there and we had new pilots but we didn't want to take them into action with us so the five of us went off. I attacked a German Junkers 88 but I saw his tracer bullets coming round and they hit my gravity tank which burst into flames and I was covered in burning fuel. I immediately undid everything and leaped out of the aeroplane and kept looking up to see where the German fighters were. You always looked up and I was looking up till these were tiny little aeroplanes. I suppose I dropped about 6,000 feet standing upright.

It's a very queer sensation. You just fall through the air and my face started to hurt a little bit so I took my mask off and, of course, the chamois leather on the face mask was burned. I looked down and saw I had no trousers on and my legs were partly burned so I opened my parachute and was then at about 10,000 feet.

It wasn't until I looked down and saw – and I've got a picture of my trousers. There was just the outer bit that was left. All the rest was burned. I kept those trousers and after I was married my wife said they're beginning to stink and she threw them out sadly. I've got a picture of me holding them up. It's a bit frightening to look down and realise all these blisters on your legs.

I drifted down and I landed in Essex. As I was coming down I saw a Home Guard pointing his rifle at me and he fired one shot and I was screaming 'Don't shoot, I'm British.' He fired a second one and I swear I heard a bullet pass my ear. I landed in a field and he came up. He was very apologetic and he took me to a farmhouse and the lady said 'Poor boy, your legs are burned. I'll get some vinegar.' I said, 'Just get me an old sheet please.' The farmer was very kind and they said somebody would come and pick me up, an LDV, who became the Home Guard. The door burst open and two policemen came in and one rushed up and took a swipe at me but the Home Guard hit him and stopped him and said 'He's got his RAF wings on.'

I was very thirsty and I said to the farmer 'Can I have a drink?' and he gave me a pint of water. Foolishly he put a bit of brandy in it. When I got to Southend General Hospital the consultant came out and said 'We must do something with him.' He bent down and smelt my breath and said 'You young buggers always fly pissed?' and I said 'No, I've only had a little bit of brandy in this water.' He operated on me and put me into a little side ward, and when I came to, in the other bed was Frank Czajkowski. He had a bullet in his shoulder and in his legs and he said 'Oh John, your face looks awful. They've sprayed you and you've got these awful scabs. They've taken all the mirrors out but I've got one. I'll show you what you look like,' and he came across and showed me. The doctors weren't very pleased. He used to get in a wheelchair and disappear and go round the hospital and he came back one day and he said, 'There's a ward out there and it's full of Germans and there's one in there you shot down on 24 August, one of the Heinkel bomber crew.' He said, 'They're very interesting men to talk to.' He spoke absolutely fluent German. The next day one of the young doctors came in and said, 'Ellacombe, stop that bugger going into that ward. He's telling them we're going to get them better, interrogate them and then shoot them, and they're not getting much better.' So Frank was not allowed to go back into that ward.

The Poles were very good pilots but they absolutely hated the Germans. This chap Czajkowski had fought in Poland. He'd shot down Germans there before he was shot down. He then flew with the French Air Force and managed to escape from there and come back to Britain. We had a sergeant, Sergeant Gmur, he unfortunately was killed. But we found the Poles to be very aggressive, very good pilots and in fact the Polish squadrons, 303 Squadron, were extremely good, highly efficient and had a very high rate of killing.

Throughout the conversation with John he kept returning to one subject, his station CO at North Weald, Wing Commander Victor Beamish. Unlike many others, Beamish, by this time a veteran of 36, regularly flew with the North Weald squadrons on patrol and shot down his fair share of enemy aircraft.

My view of Victor Beamish was simply astonishing. I reckoned of about five men who were great leaders in the war he was certainly the first that I met. He was an inspirational man. He sort of oozed confidence. He was always very cheerful. He used to come and have a beer in the bar and he would chat to all the chaps. We liked him because he was a leader and he used to fly and join your squadron in combat. He was always very aggressive and very keen to get on with the job.

AIR COMMODORE JOHN ELLACOMBE CB DFC*

John remembered the evening of 30 August when he returned to the squadron, now at Stapleford Tawney.

They took me back to North Weald and I went to the bar and Victor said to me, 'Good to see you John, there's another raid coming in, find a Hurricane and you'll fly as my number two,' and I said, 'Sir, when I was over on this airfield they'd just got the harvest in and they had a lot of cider and I've had three pints. I don't think I should be flying any more.' He said 'That's not very good,' and he suddenly laughed and said, 'OK we won't go and I won't go without a number two.' He was a magnificent leader and I was always sort of in tune with what he was thinking and we all admired him as a very great leader. We were terribly sad later on when we heard that he had died.

Many years later when I was at Fighter Command there was the personal staff officer to the commander in chief. (He told me) there'd been a raid up the Channel.

They were always looking to see if the *Scharnhorst* and the *Gneisenau* were coming and they used to do these Jim Crows and Victor Beamish called out one day, he broke RT silence and said, 'The *Scharnhorst* and *Gneisenau* and four escort vessels are in the Channel now.' This was reported at Fighter Command and Leigh Mallory said, 'The bloody man must be drunk. Ignore it.' So they took no notice of it and we lost about fifteen valuable minutes of this convoy coming up the Channel. Sadly he was shot down very soon after that and was killed. He was one of the greatest men and as a leader I would rate him alongside Sam Elworthy, Basil Embry and one or two others and would put them in that category of men with outstanding qualities and leadership.

That was to be the end of John's Battle of Britain. He didn't rejoin the squadron until December after his burns and injuries had healed. But that didn't stop him believing there was unfinished business.

I would very much like to have been there. By then you had several kills, you were determined to go on a bit, and we knew we were beginning to win the battle. That was the great thing. We realised that we were hitting the Germans as they were coming in and many a time before they dropped their bombs. You would see these bombs go down and you were quite determined to get on with it. In fact when I was in hospital at Southend the hospital was bombed and from there we were moved out and sent up to Bradford. We went to a very nice hospital there, Czajkowski and I, we shared this ward and there was another ward which was full of army men who had been wounded in Dunkirk and the doctors and nurses in this hospital took special care of all the military men. In fact the Bishop of Bradford came to see us one day and said, 'Oh, nice to meet you young chaps. You must come over and have tea with my daughter in my Palace,' which we did one day when we were walking. You know the whole atmosphere in this hospital with its military wing was simply superb. Fortunately mine were third degree burns but no worse. It didn't need any reconstruction at all. They just had to get better.

It was most frustrating because the chaps who had survived, Smith and one or two others who I had known very well and trained with, they were still in the squadron and the great thing when I got back to Wittering, Basil Embry was the Group Captain and he was an inspiring man. The squadron had reformed and they were good blokes. A lot of the airmen were still the same and the esprit de corps on the whole station was absolutely wonderful and it was an inspiration that started from the top. Embry was a wonderful station commander. He would go round and talk to everybody, fly with them and it was one of those things that was catching. I was at the young age that I was looking for leadership and looking for friendship and you found it.

I suppose it was the most exciting, frightening, invigorating period of my life. When you think how many blokes were shot down, I said in that three week period we had six killed, eight wounded and eleven others had baled out or force landed. When you think over that period, Frank Marlow, our intelligence officer, kept the records and showed we had destroyed thirty-five German aeroplanes in that three weeks so you take your losses and account what the Germans had and it was really quite astonishing.

John returned to the squadron in December 1940 and remained with them throughout 1941. Now based at Wittering, on the borders of Cambridgeshire and Northamptonshire, the squadron had a very different role. Still flying Hurricanes, but now with the addition of Defiants, they had slowly evolved into a night fighter squadron.

There were not many left of the original pilots. All the new boys were still there who we were converting onto operations, but the esprit de corps was still there and, of course, we still had this wonderful group captain. He was a chap with a DSO and two or three bars, which was quite outstanding. He'd been an outstanding Blenheim pilot and many years later I flew with him many a time in the transport aeroplane we had in Fighter Command. He was a great pilot and a great character but again, your spirit goes from your leaders and if you have good leaders you will follow them.

We were flying from Wittering which was sixty miles from the coast. We were doing dusk and dawn patrols over shipping and we were also doing night fighting. We had one flight with Defiants. On six occasions, during raids over Britain, I saw aircraft and I formated on them and my gunner said, 'It's no good Sir, look, it's a Wellington,' so fortunately we didn't shoot them down, but six times I intercepted these bloody aeroplanes and they were British and I never intercepted a fighter. I did when I moved up and was promoted to Flight Lieutenant. I was sent up to 253 Squadron at Hibaldstow in Lincolnshire and we used to fly sometimes alongside an aircraft, a Hudson, which had a searchlight. On one occasion the pilot said I have got my radar locked onto the thing but I said, 'Look, there's a Dornier just flown over the top of us,' and I tagged him and shot him down and he crashed into the sands just on the coast, so we never actually used this device.

Defiants were very nice to fly, a very wide undercarriage, big wing, easy to take off and land, but because of the extra weight of the gunner at the back with these four machine guns it was a lot slower than the Hurricane. My own experience was unfortunately the only four things, or six things, I ever formated on were Wellingtons, but if you found anything you could shoot them down. We did have some success with blokes finding Dorniers or other things. It was a lovely aeroplane to fly but not a good night fighter. In a way it was, but really you needed a lot more power.

The tactics were just to get underneath, let the bloke look up, and shoot into him. I mean that's really what the German night fighters were doing. They had four cannons pointing up and they would get underneath, and that's where they shot most of our poor old bombers down.

We had one astonishing bloke called Stevens and he joined the squadron at Wittering. He was an old man, he was 28 or 29, and we found out that one of his children had been killed in a bombing raid (his daughter). Steve was a professional pilot pre-war and his hatred of the Germans was such that it was unbelievable. He landed one day, he had shot down a Heinkel and the blood and guts of the night fighter was on his wing. He made the airmen leave it there. He wanted it left as a reminder of one dead bloody German. He had the most incredible eyesight and with us he shot down about sixteen aeroplanes and he was by far our most successful pilot. His hatred was just unbelievable and he finally went over to attacking German airfields and shooting them down there. But he was shot down himself and that was the end of Steve, but on one occasion he shot down a Heinkel from Wittering about twenty miles away and this aircraft was on the edge of a riverbank so he said to me to take this little transport and we will go and see. It was a standard van and we went out there and found this aeroplane. The army were guarding it and the rear gunner was in there, dead, with a machine gun through his gut, and Steve got the bloody gun and pulled it out, the smell was unbelievable, I had to go off and puke. He went out, washed the gun in the river to clean it, and said, 'We can go back now, I've got my souvenir.' But the man, his hatred and his atmosphere, his feeling was such that it was just unbelievable. He'd lost part of his family. But Steve was a very tough character. Very nice bloke, used to enjoy his beer, but when it came to killing he was the killer.

John was posted to 253 Squadron at Hibaldstow in Lincolnshire in February 1942 as a flight commander. A few weeks later he was awarded his DFC. He was yet another one of the experienced Battle of Britain pilots who believed their time was wasted flying with the Turbinlite Havoc in the experimental Havoc and Hurricane combination.

The idea used to be you would take off in your Hurricane and then this chap would take off and the back of his wing would have lights so you could see him and you would go down and formate and he would then use his big searchlight, but it was never successful.

Our morale wasn't very good because you weren't shooting things down, you weren't getting into action. It was fairly easy to fly and formate on to this aeroplane that was very steady. You flew underneath it and it had a strip of white light down the wings so you could see it very easily. There was no problem there and no problem coming back and landing separately but it was just the question that we weren't getting Germans eliminated.

There were six squadrons, there was 253 Squadron we were in and then we were sent down to Friston which was on the hill above Eastbourne.

John now undertook one of the most memorable, and most dangerous, operations of the war on 19 August 1942. The Dieppe Raid was designed to appease Stalin's demands for a second front, destroy some German coastal installations, and at the same time gain valuable information for a future major invasion of Europe.

We were told we were going into attack. The first time we went and it was cancelled. That was in early June and then when we came back we were told it was on again and that's when I went down to Tangmere from Friston, this grass airfield above Eastbourne, and we were briefed by our gallant C-in-C, Fighter Command. He said, 'We're going to attack this place, the army are going to land and I have taken the bombers out. I want my Hurricanes and Hurri-bombers to do the job,' so that was the briefing.

We flew into the Dieppe raid. On the first sortie my number two was shot down and he crashed onto the ground and burst into flames. I wrote to his mother later and said I think your son was possibly killed. In fact his

Hurricane broke up and he was thrown out and landed in a haystack and apart from severe bruising he was alright. My third sortie that day we found a battery of field guns about six miles back. As we crossed the coast we were bounced by Focke Wulf 190s and the squadron broke and I finished up with just my number two, an Australian called Dodson. I was flying a four-cannon Hurricane. He had a Hurricane IIc and as we attacked this gun battery you could see your shells exploding on the guns and on the men when I was hit by flak. My throttle was shot away and I couldn't move it. My engine was immediately pouring out glycol so I knew it would run for about thirty seconds and no more and I immediately turned out to sea. As I did that my number two was firing and he took a perfect picture of me flying through and when you think he was firing his machine guns he must have hit my aeroplane but not me.

When I was hit and damaged, I just reached the coast when the engine stopped. I managed to get up to about 600 feet, knocked everything off and baled out, and as my parachute opened I thought it was on fire because of all the tracer bullets going through. I was only about 400 yards from the shore and they were firing at me as I was swimming to Newhaven which was only sixty miles away. I was not going their way and getting shot. It was bloody frightening, and then fortunately the army sent a little assault landing craft which picked me up. They lowered the ramp and pulled me on board, and when we were turning round, Sub-Lieutenant Hall was the CO's name, I said, 'Can't we go a little faster?' and he said, 'We've only got one engine left.' We had three petty officers who were absolutely punch drunk, and as bombs dropped round us, and shells exploded, they just never turned a hair. Fortunately the main convoy sent a steam gunboat back, one of these 120-foot machines. They threw us a big rope and we set off to join the main convoy. We were bombed all the way back to Newhaven and the masses of Spitfires up top were shooting them down. When I landed at Newhaven I didn't have any boots on and an army chap said would you like a pair of army boots, I've got a lot of corpses here who died on the way home. So we went up and took a pair of boots off and I put them on and went back to Friston. Fortunately when I got there the chaps said, 'Thank God you've turned up. I'm very glad I didn't send a cable to your parents to say you were missing because I didn't bring the details down.' I said, 'Thank God you didn't as I'm sure it wouldn't have done them any good.' After that I was told to stop. My twitch was getting so bad that I was going to have a rest and do this twin-engine conversion course and then go back to Mosquitos, so that finished that tour on Hurricanes.

It was the most frightening day I have ever had. To be hit, your throttle shot away. Knowing your aircraft was riddled, flying through (our own firing), which I didn't know until the next day when they showed us the combat reports from my number two, Frank Dodson. You know, having got there, got out of the aeroplane, as the parachute opened, all the tracer bullets were flying through, and the ricochet on the water right next to me, it was the most prolonged terrifying time I ever experienced.

John now went on a rest tour until July 1943 when he rejoined 151 Squadron and converted onto the Mosquito. At that point he was posted to 487 (NZ) Squadron and was then awarded a bar to his DFC.

It was a very great moment. You were always very jealous looking around and seeing these other ace chaps with their gongs up and you were very glad when you got the bar to the thing. To my astonishment the CO of my squadron did not get a thing, he got mentioned in dispatches because he'd hit the wall at the Amiens prison and he'd led a lot of things with me there, a quite outstanding chap; but it was a thing of great pride.

You look around and you know a lot of chaps didn't get gongs because nobody put them up, but a lot of blokes who had done outstanding work, they were fellows you respected and admired.

I was in 151 Squadron and they were converted onto Mosquitos to be night fighters and we didn't mind, it was a lovely aeroplane to fly. Your navigator was sitting half back with his radar in front of him, it was a great aeroplane and very nice at night. You had excellent visibility and two engines. Then you had your four guns. The fighter bomber had four cannons and four machine guns so when you were strafing a road you really put out some firepower and that's why 151 was converted. My CO, Smith (Wing Commander Irving 'Black' Smith DFC), had finished his tour and he had gone off to 2 Group, and Embry said would he like to take over this 487 Squadron which was a bit run-down. He went there and in fact it was Smith himself who knocked down the walls of the Amiens Prison. I joined the squadron a couple of weeks later. We were down at Thorney Island and I flew my thirty-five sorties and absolutely loved it.

When you were flying in the Mosquito and you had a navigator, you were waiting for him to tell you where to go. He could pick things up at about six or eight miles and bring you right in. There's the one big joke that at Wittering was 29 Squadron, which had Beaufighters. They had a CO who was absolutely blind and his navigator would say to him, 'It's 400 yards in front of us now,' and on two occasions he had to leave his radar, come up and look over the chap's shoulder and say, 'There it is, nose up two degrees, now press the trigger,' and the aeroplane with its four cannon and six machine guns would just blast them out of the sky, but he couldn't see a bloody thing at night. He was relying entirely on his navigator. I was very lucky when I went to Charterhall in Scotland to convert onto twins, and a very nice chap, rather elderly, he was 38 and I was 22, came up to me. He had a pilot officer's badge on, he saw I had a DFC and he said, 'I'd like to be your navigator. My name is Bob Peel. I was a wing commander accountant and I had to drop all that to be aircrew,' and he flew with me on Mosquito night fighters, and then ultimately when we moved over to bombers. I joined 487 Squadron in 2 Group just after they had bombed the Amiens prison. We were up at Gravesend to begin with. We were there for the invasion of Normandy. About two days later, when the flying bombs came over, we were living in tents which was very frightening because you used to go to sleep with your helmet over your face or your armour suit, made by Wilkinson, over your body and in the morning you would find about six shrapnel holes in your tent, so when we were told we were going down to Thorney Island I've never seen the airmen pack the stuff so quickly. We flew down to Thorney Island, which was on the coast, a lovely airport, and from there we did a lot of sorties and in fact I completed my tour of thirty-five sorties in August 1944 and we had some quite outstanding attacks.

2 Group was the tactical part of Bomber Command. We had 140 Wing and another wing in Kent which again had more Mosquitos. We had three squadrons in 140 Wing. There was 21 Squadron, 487 (ourselves), and 264 who were Australians, and the Australians were very good pilots but very ill disciplined buggers. I say that unkindly; when you had a big raid going on and you were coming back and coming into land, several Australians would say, 'I've got a damaged aeroplane, I must have priority.' They didn't but they wanted to land and get into some beer. Not as well disciplined as 487 Squadron, who were wonderfully led by Bunny Smith, my great friend who I trained with all through the war, and 21 Squadron. They were very good, had a lot of extremely good pilots, some of whom were very individual and did extraordinary things. It was a great thing and I reckon that that wing did an enormous amount of damage to the Germans.

140 Wing was commanded by one of the great Mosquito leaders of the war, the then Group Captain Peter Wykeham-Barnes, later to become Air Marshal Sir Peter Wykeham KCB, DSO & bar, OBE, DFC & bar, AFC. He flew extensively in the early part of the Western Desert campaign, being awarded a DFC for leading 73 Squadron and a bar for his work in the defence of Tobruk. He received a DSO for his time during the

Italian campaign and eventually came to command 140 Wing and lead the legendary raid on the Gestapo HQ at Aarhus in Denmark for which he was awarded his second DSO.

He was a great leader, he was the CO of 140 Wing and he was a wonderful pilot. A very good leader, he led us on the raid going to the French barracks and he flew on many occasions. On two occasions I would call up and say 'I have just bombed a road here and it's burst into flames, it must be a petrol junction,' and Barnes would answer and say, 'I'm right behind you, I'm coming up to join you.' He was an inspiring leader. He already had a DSO and bar. He had been in North Africa, was a very tall good-looking man and a great inspiration and a wonderful leader. We all looked up to him.

Early on the morning of D-Day a small force of SAS was dropped well behind German lines with the purpose of disrupting travel for German reinforcements. On 10 June they reported that a train full of petrol tankers was in rail sidings at Châtellerault, north of Poitiers and almost 350km from the Normandy beaches.

One was for the SAS. The British Army had dropped their paratroopers there and they called us up one day, about four days after D-Day, and said the German tanks are running out of fuel in Normandy and there are six trains of petrol just pulled up at this junction at Châtellerault. So my CO, Smith, said, 'Let's get there first before they know we are coming,' and we flew very low and in fact the guns never even fired at us because we were flying at zero feet all the way. Three of us dropped our bombs on these trains and as we turned away we could see the huge flames bursting up. We often thought later that perhaps that helped to save D-Day as the German tanks didn't get their fuel for another three or four weeks. Another big sortie, we were told there was a big French base called Poitiers which had the barracks of the SS Division which was moving in there that evening. We got all this information from the SAS and they were due to be there at six o'clock that evening and of course we had double summertime then so just at that time, twenty-four Mosquitos arrived and bombed the bloody place and we were told later that something like 600 German soldiers were killed, so that was one of our most devastating attacks. Again we went at very low altitude and we had no anti-aircraft fire because they didn't know we were coming. In fact there was one occasion when the noise of an aircraft approaching had frightened big farm horses in a field and they ran through a fence and a piece of fencing came over my wing which, had it hit the propeller, would have brought us down, but we often got to a place, day or night, without any anti-aircraft fire because they didn't know we were coming. We were underneath the radar.

On trips we did with Mosquitos we were flying a section of three or a whole squadron, and one particular time, when we attacked the Poitiers barracks, we attacked them with twenty-four Mosquitos, so you felt you were part of a big effort. A lot of aircraft, a lot of bombs that we dropped, and we normally carried instantaneous or eleven second delay, so if you were absolutely on the ground, and you dropped your eleven second delay, you had time to pull up. You used your instantaneous when you were diving down, dropped your bombs and then heaved up. If you were sharp enough you felt the bang but it didn't do any damage to the aeroplane.

D-Day had not been a secret to John and his fellow pilots.

We knew something was coming as the south of England was absolutely packed with American soldiers wherever you went. There were great camps full of American soldiers so obviously something was going to go forward one day. The feeling was that it was just a question of building up and getting ready. We knew that one day we were going to invade. There was a great satisfaction when actually it happened because although we didn't have any real knowledge, in fact on actual D-Day itself we were told to go and patrol this part of Normandy, certain roads, and to be on the lookout for transports moving towards the coast. We were not told it was D-Day in case someone was shot down and shot his mouth off before the troops landed, but we knew obviously it was going to be.

What I saw of it was all the firing going on on the coast and a lot of explosions and a lot of searchlights. And of course we were literally ten miles inland going east to west and we realised, 'That's it! It has happened!' and it was very satisfying when you got back and landed. Of course next day the V1s came flying over us and we realised then that the Germans were getting pretty bloody desperate.

We felt we had landed and we were advancing, we were winning the war, the Germans were retreating. We had one particular thing where the Mosquitos would go over at night, it was moon period, and there was what we call the Falaise Gap. There were two roads jointly side by side and absolutely packed with Germans going. We were then carrying two bombs and two flares. You would drop your flares on one side so that the night came down and from the darkness you could attack and strafe the convoy and it was the most amazing thing to see when you went down. Your shells were exploding on vehicles and the men who got out, rather ghastly when you think of it, because a 20mm shell hitting a man in the shoulder would make a hell of a flash and I shudder to think what was left of his shoulder. There was carnage. There were cars and trucks pulled up and crashed just off the roads. You were just trying to attack the stuff that was retreating. We knew that the more we attacked them the more they would get damage. We knew then we were winning, that was the great thing, so let's blast the buggers out of the sky. We knew they were retreating.

We did this for about six days until they had retreated all the way to the river Seine and then I had just about finished my tour.

It was a great tour and I loved flying the Mosquito. We did our thirty-five sorties and the CO of flying who I knew very well and I had flown as his number two on many of them, he put me up for a bar for the DFC, which I was very pleased to receive. That was my third tour, flying in all sorts of funny places. I then went on a tour at a Mosquito OTU, Operational Training Unit, where I flew for a long time, very interesting and coaching a lot of chaps as they came through, and that was virtually the end of my war. Except I did fly Mosquitos; at the end of the war I was posted out to Aden. I found I was going to join 242 Squadron on Mosquitos. The regiment in Aden was the Patiala Lancers. They were all Sikhs. The only Englishman was Colonel Curtis, the CO, and these Sikhs were simply wonderful. They were great sportsmen, they won everything, the soccer, the cricket, athletics, tennis, and on two occasions I flew up country being top cover when they were going to destroy some forts and we would see this convoy of armoured vehicles going up and they would do their work. So my last operational sortie was in January 1945 and that completed my operational flying.

It was tremendous, tremendous, you sort of had a feeling that I might live now. It had been the height of tension going through what I had been through and all the dangerous things. You see your chums disappearing and one thing and another. People don't realise just what the tensions are. You get a fatigue, we all had the twitch because you were sleeping badly, overworked, and I say overworked but it was over-anxiety, it was an astonishing situation.

After the war John chose to stay in the RAF

A lot of people did leave, a lot of people did not get their permanent commissions. I loved the service and I was desperately keen to get a permanent commission and make a career of it from which I never looked back on.

There were two post-war events that John seemed particularly proud of. First of all he commanded No.1 Squadron flying Gloster Meteors at RAF Tangmere.

It was prestigious. I suppose having been PSO to the commander-in-chief he felt he ought to give me something decent having worked for him for eighteen months without a day off. So I went down to 1 Squadron and that was great. The reputation was very good. They had had two American COs, one was Colonel Olds, who made a big reputation for himself in Korea, and the other was a chap called Smith, not a great bloke but a pleasant enough man, so they were determined to put a Brit in there to command it for a change.

It was an astonishing feeling as the Meteor didn't have the vibration, it was a very smooth aeroplane to fly. Landing you didn't have, when you throttled back, the retraction effect of the propeller. Four guns, and when we went on our practice camps you could hit the target very easily and it was an extremely pleasant aeroplane to fly. I loved them.

I think it was pretty comparable to what the other side had. You were very confident in them. They were easy to fly, easy to formate in, good for night flying.

Secondly John was among the Battle of Britain pilots chosen as part of the guard for Sir Winston Churchill's coffin.

Winston Churchill wanted to have Battle of Britain pilots marching alongside his coffin, that was his orders, and they kept a bunch of people on their books, a list, and I was told I was on the list. In January 1965, when the dear old man died, we flew down. The funniest thing was we were going to have five days before the funeral and the warrant officer said, 'Group Captains, let's fall in and do some marching,' and we thought OMG, some of these buggers haven't been near a parade ground in years. I was still fairly fit. I'd been a station commander and had to do parades so I believe I was fairly good but it was terribly funny. The warrant officers gave us a good run down and when the funeral came we were right up in the front. We had twelve pilots, I've got a book with the inscription, led by Air Commodore Al Deere in the very front, and we marched off. It was really a very, very emotional time and I must admit I blubbed when the band started up and you had the horses going slowly in front. We started off in slow motion, then got quicker, it was a terribly emotional time. We marched all the way to Westminster Abbey and we then had a beer or two and drove back to our bases, but it was very emotional and I knew all these group captains very well and we'd always been on this list and told you were going to report and I look back with great pride as that's one of my great occasions.

John remained in the Royal Air Force until 1973. His last operational command was as Air Commander in the Gulf with his HQ at Muharraq in Bahrain. This was 1968 and British forces were withdrawing from the remains of Empire. His calmness in dealing with the withdrawal from Aden was recognised when he was made a CB.

Wing Commander Bob Foster DFC
14 May 1920-30 July 2014

Bob Foster was born in Battersea, South London and went to work for Shell BP when he left school. He joined the RAF Volunteer Reserve on 1 May 1939.

My father had been badly wounded at Ypres in 1915 as a Royal Engineer, lost a leg, amputated, and for the rest of his life he walked around on crutches. He was an old soldier and I used to meet with him and his friends and from what they told me, and because of his injuries, I had no wish to be conscripted into the army. In those days flying was a very exciting thought. I never intended to be a Biggles or anything like that but that was the sort of feeling, fighter pilot, wonderful thing. In 1938, to me and everybody else apart from Neville Chamberlain, it was fairly obvious there was going to be a war. I didn't want to be in the PBI, the poor bloody infantry, and I thought if there's going to be a war the best thing to be is a fighter pilot so I joined the RAFVR, applied to join and they accepted me and I started my flying at the beginning of 1939.

I think most young people realised it was going to happen but not many of them took the step, if you like, of volunteering rather than being conscripted later on. So I volunteered. I think I went to Hendon twice to watch the airshow in 1936 and '37, but that was my knowledge of aviation whereas other chaps knew everything about the subject. I was lucky in a way I suppose. I got away with it all.

I went up to a place called Ansty which was a civil air set up. They were training RAF pilots so most of the course was these chaps on short service commissions, but the VRs were allowed to join providing they could get time off from their employer. It was a two month course and Shellmex and BP, for whom I worked in those days, were very generous in that respect. They were very pro service so I managed to get eight weeks off, fully paid leave to do my *ab initio* flying which was very good. There were about half a dozen of us, VRs, on this course and the rest were all short service commissions.

When you joined the VR you automatically became a sergeant; you didn't have a uniform but you were called a sergeant. On my first day at Ansty we were all sitting around in the crew room all togged up in this wonderful flying clothing and a chap came in and said 'Sergeant Foster?' so I said yes and I went forward and he said, 'Oh Sergeant Foster, you must have done quite a lot of flying then?' so I said, 'I've never been in an aeroplane in my life,' and he said 'Oh Christ.' He was a man called Tribe, Pilot Officer Tribe. We didn't get off to a very good start because he said, 'Come on then, I suppose we'd better go.' We never really hit it off, just one of those things, but he got me solo after a while and after another few hours he gave me to somebody else, a chap called Smith I think. We got on famously so the flying improved from then onwards. The first flight was a little bit hairy because the instructor and myself weren't seeing eye to eye, but I enjoyed it.

I'd never been in an aeroplane in my life. It was an old Avro Tutor, or Cadet as they called them, a big open aeroplane.

3 September, the day war broke out. Yes I remember it very well because being in the VR I got my call-up papers on Friday 1 September and, because I'd trained up at Ansty outside of Coventry and the records had obviously not moved from there, I was told to report to Rugby which was the nearest VR centre, on the Saturday morning. I'd got a rail warrant, I said farewell to my parents, and got the train. They waved me goodbye to go off to war, and I got up to Rugby, went to this centre and the very harassed flying officer said, 'Who are you?' I said, 'Sergeant Foster,' and he said, 'I've never heard of you. I don't know what to do with you. Here's a rail warrant. Go home.' So on the Saturday night, it was pouring with rain, I came home on leave much to my parents' surprise and pleasure I suppose. We lived in Battersea in London in those days and so the Sunday, 3 September, I remember very well it was a beautiful day, a nice sunny day, and at eleven o'clock of course the air raid sirens went off. Everyone thought there was going to be a big bombing raid, which didn't happen as we know, but war was declared. I heard Chamberlain mentioning that we were at war with Germany, but I was home on leave then and I stayed there until November when they called me up to carry on with the flying.

Bob went to 1ITW to resume his flying, arriving at Cambridge on 10 November. After basic training he moved to 12FTS at Grantham at the end of the year.

I was still up at Grantham flying Harts and Audax and things like that when 10 May came on and the feeling was it would be like the First World

War. In another few months when we'd finished our training we'd go to France to support the army who'd be dug in in the trenches. I don't think anybody had really thought it through, including the British army commanders, that the whole thing would be over in six weeks, well that part of it anyway, and that by June the British army would be back in this country. So I was finishing my flying training when all of that happened.

We went to Kidlington for a five hour refresher course on Harvards to give us some idea about undercarriages and flaps and boost controls, which of course the Hart didn't have. So five hours on Harvards and then I was posted to Sutton Bridge on the east coast of Norfolk to a Hurricane OTU. My first flight in a Hurricane was really straightforward. My instructor was a chap called Smallwood, Flying Officer Smallwood who would later become Air Chief Marshal Sir, but then he was a flying officer who had been in France and had been brought back as an instructor. He got me in the aeroplane and leaned over the side and more or less said you push that and you pull this and off you go. I mean there were no pilots notes that I can remember, there might have been but I don't remember reading them so that was the way it was and off I went. I took off, flew around, came in and thought well this is great. Here I am, a Hurricane pilot.

Looking back on all this we were very green. As I said I joined the air force because it was the best way of fighting a war. I wasn't a terribly keen aviation enthusiast. I hadn't read a lot of books about aviation. Maybe some of my colleagues knew all about Spitfires and Hurricanes but I was a callow youth. 19 years old, and the whole thing was, not strange or exciting, I just took things as they came if that explains it. Not everybody was an aviation nut...

One particular landing stayed in Bob's mind for the rest of his life.

That was at Sutton Bridge. I'd taken off and Old Splinters was with me, we were doing formation flying and suddenly I got a glycol leak all over the windscreen. I got onto him and said, 'there's a lot of stuff all over the windscreen,' and he looked across and could see I had a glycol leak and said, 'Oh Christ, get home as quickly as possible.' We were somewhere over the Wash and I suppose I panicked a bit. Sutton Bridge was a very small airstrip and coming in I couldn't see much out of the front of the windscreen. I was coming in too fast and I landed half way down the strip, got it down but went on through the hedge and tipped up on my nose. Fortunately it didn't go over on its back because that could be serious, it could be fatal because your head stuck out the top when you rolled over in a Hurricane. It wasn't a very good show, but at least I got away with it.

WING COMMANDER BOB FOSTER DFC

After just one month at Sutton Bridge, and now commissioned as a pilot officer, Bob was posted to 605 Squadron on 8 July 1940 at Drem in Scotland.

There was one man who lived in Edinburgh on the course and I lived in London. He was posted to Kenley and I was posted to Drem just outside Edinburgh and we thought this was quite ridiculous. It would be nice if we were near our homes, we thought. So we went to see the CO and said can we swap the postings? And he said, 'No, they've got to stand.' So this chap went down to Kenley, this was in July 1940 right at the beginning of the battle, very inexperienced only having about thirty hours on Hurricanes. I don't say it would have happened to me but he only lasted a few days. He got clobbered. I went up to Drem to join 605 and we were up there until September so I had five weeks of flying Hurricanes, beginning to know the aeroplane, and by the time we were sent south I had about eighty hours on Hurricanes which was a lot for those days. I hadn't fired a shot in anger but at least I knew more about the aeroplane and what it could do so in that respect it was a good posting.

While he was at Drem Bob was initiated into the ways a squadron flew rather than just an individual.

605 was rather prosaic in their flying. We kept to this vic formation which we'd been trained to do anyway, tight formation flying and scrambling in that way. The training I got went on through the squadron so we were very good at formation flying but not very good at seeing the enemy. This rigid formation meant that only one chap, the squadron commander, was looking around the sky. The rest of us were intent on formating with your section leader and so on. With hindsight it wasn't a very good thing. We had a couple of weavers at the back of the squadron. They were the eyes of the squadron but even they couldn't or didn't necessarily see anything. It did mean on odd occasions you were jumped by 109s without knowing anything about it and I think a lot of chaps were shot down in that respect.

There was no discussion about it, not in those days, not that I remember. Actually we weren't bounced very often, I mean I was only bounced once. Providing you had time as you went into attack your bombers, you had what was called the attack formation, in other words the vic would become starboard or port echelon and then we'd peel off to go into the bombers. If you had time for that it worked very well whereas with the finger four you couldn't do that so I think as a defensive thing it wasn't good but offensively it was fine. And of course you could get airborne quickly. At Croydon we'd take off as a squadron because it was a grass airfield and you could get all twelve aeroplanes lined up right across the airfield, a wonderful sight.

All twelve Hurricanes would get airborne at the same time and then form up into four vics and climb together. It was quite efficient in that respect, but not as good if there were 109s about.

But however much training Bob had, he knew it would not prepare him for actual combat.

You can do your dummy runs and so on but you don't know what's going to happen. You use your own... not common sense, you don't know what's going to happen, you can't train for it.

It was basically this Sailor Malan sort of thing. Height is essential, don't hang around in the sky congratulating yourself, never fly straight and level in the combat area, get in, hit the bombers hard and get out again, and keep your eyes open all the time. That's about the basics of the thing and if you did that you stood a better chance of getting away with it. I think a lot of chaps, having attacked, thought well that's it, let's go home, and they didn't make it.

Bob well-remembered a number of the characters at 605 Squadron.

The CO, of course, was Squadron Leader (Walter) Churchill, ex-605, an older man, in his 30s I should think. He had been an auxiliary with 605 and at the outbreak of war he'd gone to France, I can't remember the squadron, but he joined a squadron in France and had a distinguished few weeks after the Phoney War, got a DSO and DFC by the time he came back to join, rejoin, 605 as the CO. He was an ace, if you like, the first time we had met anybody like him. He and I never really hit it off, I don't know why, some sort of lack of empathy. There was nothing bad about it, there was just a lack of feeling between the two of us, but he was a great man.

Then the two flight commanders, Gerry Edge, another auxiliary who'd done very well over Dunkirk so he had quite a lot of experience, quiet man, gentleman, very nice indeed. The other flight commander was a chap called Archie McKellar who was about 5ft 2in tall, Scotsman, a Glaswegian who had been with 602 Squadron flying Spitfires and had transferred to us. He was a livewire and a brilliant pilot and had a very distinguished career later on in the battle. Then the other two chaps I remember were Bunny Currant and Jock Muirhead, both of whom had been Halton Brats who had come up as apprentices, regulars, and both had had experience over France. They were the people we looked up to, us rookies. Nice men, wonderful chaps and very helpful with advice. And the rest of us were pretty new and they were our guide, comforter and friend if you like. I remember them very particularly.

Archie McKellar claims an interesting place in the annals of air fighting, having claimed twenty-one enemy aircraft by 1 November including four on one day and five on another.

Yes there were five. I don't know which day it was but if I looked in my logbook I could probably find out. I wasn't flying with him on any of these occasions but he came back and claimed them. The other one of course, which we do know about, was when he got three Heinkels in one go when the squadron, accidentally or deliberately, did a head-on attack and Archie opened fire on the front one which bounced off onto the second and the third and all three came down so that was three in one go. So at least that helped his score. He was a very forceful little man, very forceful, so it could well be that he got all these. He certainly got one at night, which was unusual.

We were wondering when we were going to go south. After all we were there as fighter pilots. All the action was going on down south and there were we stuck up at Drem, having a good time but the whole idea was let's get into the action.

On 15 August 605 were called into action when an enemy bomber force from Norway and Denmark tried to attack northern cities.

Well this was a bit of a letdown. 15th August? That was a bit of a cock-up. They sent this lot over from Norway to attack Newcastle, Sunderland, and so on and the whole squadron was scrambled, A flight and B flight. Archie McKellar was leading one flight and a chap called Scott was leading the other flight and I was with Scott. He was another auxiliary and the two flights went off separately and we'd lost the other flight. We could hear all the instructions on the radio and we were in our usual six formation as a flight with Douglas Scott leading us and for some reason he either didn't get the messages or he didn't vector the way he was told and we never saw a damn thing. We were out over the North Sea and our flight never got involved which was very annoying because the others got into it and had a great time but I never knew how or why Douglas missed it.

The other flight did pretty well. Archie got a couple, but for some of them it was the first time they'd been in action anyway and it was quite a good blooding, although one did get shot down, forced landing on the beach and got away with it, Ken Law, but it was a nice easy way in I suppose, for the ones that did get into the action.

Finally 605 Squadron returned to the fray in the south with a posting to Croydon, the airfield that had been London's main airport throughout the pre-war years.

Croydon, well we first saw Croydon on the night of 7 September. We flew down from Drem to Abingdon, refuelled and then flew in towards Croydon from that direction. It was about six at night, and it was the day of course when the Germans got through and bombed the docks, so from miles away before we got to Croydon we could see the flames and the smoke as the whole of London seemed to be on fire. A huge volume of smoke, black smoke, and planes and so on, and when we landed at Croydon just about as it was getting dusk, that's what we could see. So that was our introduction to what it was going to be like. Bunny Currant said, 'We're in for trouble now,' and there we were; but that's what we wanted, what we had come down for.

I had all these worries as my parents lived in Battersea, about a mile from Clapham Junction, and there was always a feeling that they were in more danger than I was, in some respects, but I don't think it affected my flying. It was always at the back of your mind because they had the bombing all round there. At Croydon, apart from the daytime raids, we weren't there then as they were in August, we really weren't affected at all. The odd bomb would drop around the place but it didn't affect our sleep or anything like that, not mine anyway.

Normally one would be sitting around on the grass because we'd be at readiness. You'd read a book or sit around talking or walk around. We had a radio, but chaps more or less sat around, read and talked or wrote letters maybe. To have a scramble, you could be on fifteen or thirty minutes readiness and then you'd be called in but if you were on instant readiness the bell would ring, you'd run to your aeroplane, get in, strap in and so on. Sometimes it would be a flight or section take-off or even a squadron take-off and you were concentrating on getting out onto the airfield, getting into formation, taking off, settling down and formating on your section or flight commander, wondering what the hell was going to happen. You didn't know. Every time you were scrambled you didn't know whether you were going to be involved in action or not. Quite often you didn't but the feeling was always there that life was going to get a bit dicey.

You knew roughly the night before what was going to happen and if you were on readiness you'd get up, wash, dress, have breakfast and go down to dispersal, look at your aeroplane and make sure everything was right and then sit down and wait. Sometimes you could sit there all day long, sometimes you'd sit there for half an hour. The tension did build up at times when you were just sitting around with nothing much to do, and in fact it was released when the bell went.

Bob had a slightly different relationship with the ground crew than many other pilots.

It's so long ago I can't recall their names, but they were always there. Your aeroplane was there. It had been run up. Everything had been checked and, to the best of my knowledge, everything always worked. The oxygen was always filled up. Of course I didn't have a particular aeroplane. OK Archie McKellar had UP-A all the time and the same crew, but I seemed to be a bit of a dogsbody. Until the morning I didn't know which aeroplane I was going to fly, so therefore you didn't have that bonding with your fitter and your rigger or your armourer because it could change day after day, but whoever it was they were all auxiliaries, it was an auxiliary squadron and they were all regular auxiliaries. A good bunch and no complaints whatsoever. As far as I was concerned everything went well.

Well you're all doing the same sort of job, aren't you. The object is the same, and I've said this many a time that throughout my RAF career anyway I never came across, well maybe later, but in 605 a bad apple for want of a better word, and looking back on it, and I've said this before too, I never really got intimate with any of these chaps. You know people have often said was it dreadful when you lost one of your friends, and I would say well of course it was but they were only friends for a few weeks. I'd never met anyone in 605 until I went there in July and by September we'd lost some of them but we were really people passing in the night, if you like. It wasn't like old friendships where you'd known each other for years and years. Maybe I wasn't an inquisitive sort of person but I couldn't tell you whether they were married or whether they had brothers and sisters. We were eighteen chaps together and even nationality didn't come into it. The Poles and the Czechs who came later on just fitted into the squadron. I found that all through my RAF career that there's that bond of friendship, we were all doing the same job and we bonded together to do that.

The day later, regarded as Battle of Britain Day, 15 September, had no special memories for Bob.

I remember it because I was on leave. We didn't fly every day. 605 was lucky that we always had a full complement of pilots, in other words eighteen or so with twelve aeroplanes. There were always four or five chaps who weren't flying and so you would have a day off and Sunday the 15th was just another Sunday and the CO said you're not on today. Have the day off. Saturday night and tomorrow you're not on. Most unusually for a Battle of Britain pilot I was at home. I went back to see my parents and when I came back to the squadron in the afternoon, of course, they'd been in action twice already; so that's my memory of the 15th, which is not a very noble one. Just the luck of the draw.

However, 27 September was a much more notable day.

That was the only time I really got clobbered; well I thought I'd got clobbered anyway. We were scrambled to intercept some aircraft over Sussex and got up to about 20,000ft and there was a bunch of 110s. Obviously they'd either lost their escort or the escort had missed them, one or the other. Anyway they were in this defensive circle and we went, one defending the other one in this circle, and we went in to attack them. Just as I opened fire the whole of my engine blew up on me and I thought I had been shot down, but subsequently it was just the engine had blown up. It was still just the same, plenty of glycol, oil and stuff all over the place so I thought about baling out and then decided no because I wasn't burning and I saw a big field below me and thought well that's the thing to do. I still had controls and things so I glided down, landed in this big field and much to my surprise an airman came up to me and I said, 'Where am I?' and he said, 'You're at Gatwick, Sir,' which was a big airfield, it wasn't the same as it is now. Anyway, I got away with it and in the end it was just that something had happened to the engine, but it was still a bit scary. Of course we did pretty well that day. The Germans lost some fifty-seven aircraft I think, and to me that weekend was the turning point of the battle. The 15th is always reckoned to be. But that was the last time, that weekend, they sent over loads of bombers. I think we shot down 104 confirmed on those three days and I think that really broke the back of their intentions.

September was a vital month for Bob, but it took a while for the impact to sink in.

At the time it didn't make any difference whether it was July, August, September or October. In fact we had just as much action, different sort of action, in October as we did in September, except the bombers stopped coming. We had a lot of 109s coming over all the time so we were just as active in October, but I suppose it didn't enter our minds that we had won a battle because the battle went on and the war went on. It's only with hindsight, and in the last few years, that people have started to say this was the definitive battle of the war, the first one. If it hadn't been for that the war wouldn't have gone on, but that wasn't obvious, not at that time.

In fact Bob destroyed or damaged four 109s during October. The first of these was on the 7th.

Oh yes, of course I remember it. We were jumped by some 109s out of the sun. The first we knew about it was a frantic shout, 'break, break, break!' which meant you didn't sit around arguing, you just broke. I broke down and the 109s came down on us, shot down a chap called Charles English and damaged somebody else. I went down and pulled out of the dive, looked around, and ahead of me was a 109, flying straight and level, heading south and going home. Whether he saw me I don't know but I got straight behind him and shot him down. He could have been one of the ones that attacked us and thought it was all over and done with and was going home. As I said, it didn't matter which side you were on, you couldn't afford to relax. So that was that occasion, I remember quite well.

This combat was much like many of the others Bob became involved in.

It doesn't last very long generally speaking. To start with it's chaotic. I'm talking personally, I've never confessed to being an ace pilot, one of these chaps who just pointed, fired a short burst, saw one go down, turned round, fired at another, it didn't happen to me. A dogfight only lasted a couple of minutes at the most and it's all energy at the time. You try to shoot down something ahead of you and at the same time you're conscious of what might be going on behind you. It's difficult to describe but my fighting prowess probably wasn't as good as some of the others, not in results anyway, but I did my best.

For a few seconds you're focusing on the aircraft in front of you but not for much longer than that. After all, whatever you do it's not quite like the First World War where you were dicing around, looping the loop and all this sort of thing. The whole thing is over and done with in seconds. You go in, you attack, you either hit or you don't, and you break away. And then you're conscious that someone may be after you. It's difficult to describe. The adrenalin's flowing and you're trying to do two things at once. You're trying to shoot down something else but on the other hand you're conscious that someone else may be after you. And I think obviously with a lot of chaps who were shot down the second thing happened. You forgot about the chap behind you.

Touch wood it never happened to me. Obviously if you're hit, you're in flames, you're burning, you don't even think about it, but I think the other reaction is if everything seems to be working alright the last thing in the world you want to do is bale out. And I think, with Jock Muirhead who was one of our chaps who was shot down and killed in October, I think his situation from what I hear was a bit similar to mine. An eyewitness saw this Hurricane coming down, obviously attempting to land somewhere, well it seemed like it, but at about 1,500ft it suddenly burst into flames and the pilot got out but he got out too late, his chute didn't open and he was killed. That was Jock Muirhead, and the situation was exactly similar to mine. Nothing was wrong and, rather than bale out, he was trying to force land, but unfortunately he caught on fire and it was too late to bale out. And he was a chap who had baled out over France anyway so he knew the situation. He'd done it before but this time the instinct was to sit there where you're reasonably comfortable and force land the thing.

EMPTY SKY

Every pilot had a different reaction to danger.

Everything (scared me) I suppose. No, there was apprehension. I mean every time you took off you didn't know whether you were going to come back again or not but I never got to feeling scared as such. Apprehensive, frightened maybe because until you get into action you don't know what's going to happen, but everything is so unlike, what shall I say, unlike Bomber Command who sat there for hour after hour not knowing what's going to happen, a different thing altogether. With fighter pilots the thing is over and done with in a few seconds, in a few minutes, and the worry is when you take off not knowing what you're up against when you get up there and possibly relief when nothing happens or when it's all over.

Yes, I got stressed but not to the extent of losing any sleep for instance. I don't know whether some chaps couldn't sleep but I, it's difficult to say this, maybe I wasn't as sensitive as some other people. I mean we all react differently to situations and I don't personally remember ever getting stressed, or argumentative, or awkward, or worried in particular. I always slept well, so I coped fairly well with it.

We'd have a few beers in the evening. Our local was The Greyhound in Croydon and most evenings, when we'd finished. that was the thing to do, go out to the pub and have something to eat and drink and come back and go to sleep or stay in the mess. Croydon was a funny situation because we were in houses on the other side of the airfield. We didn't have a proper mess so one house turned into a mess. We had plenty of beer. In those days it was fairly straightforward, you drank pints of beer. Well I suppose fighter pilots do the same now, not much different really.

Croydon was different to most RAF stations, having been an international airport before the war.

There wasn't anything luxurious but it was different in that firstly we were there on our own, just one squadron, and because it was a satellite of Kenley, we were literally on our own. There wasn't a station commander. There wasn't any admin or anything at all. We were just there. It was rather pleasant. We didn't have any things that other RAF stations had so in that respect it was very pleasant. A nice large airfield and you did your own thing so it was different to an RAF station and very relaxing too.

By the end of October Bob had been in the front line for almost two months, but even though the Battle of Britain was virtually over, nothing really changed.

The war just went on. I don't think we realised in those days that we had been engaged in this definitive battle. It was a job to do and we felt we had done pretty well because they stopped coming over, in daylight anyway, so I suppose we had that satisfaction, but on the other hand we were still on readiness wherever we were. Of course the RAF then went on to the offensive in 1941 so for a fighter pilot there was no beginning and end of this thing. You just went on and on until you were posted away.

I think we did pretty well, I can't tell you about comparisons. I mean some squadrons were in the thick of the action a lot longer. As a squadron I think we acquitted ourselves pretty well with what went on but I honestly can't compare it to the others. It depends a lot on the claims from a certain squadron. We had McKellar who claimed a lot, but other people didn't. Other squadrons had their Tucks and Laceys, so on the scoreline, if you like, some appeared to be more successful than others. Others you don't hear about but I think 605 had as good a reputation as anyone else that I know of.

Bob was flying in Archie McKellar's flight on 1 November when McKellar was shot down and killed. He had already been awarded two DFCs and was now awarded a posthumous DSO.

In February 1941 605 Squadron was moved to Martlesham Heath, Suffolk. In March Bob attacked a Heinkel He111 and although badly damaged the bomber escaped into cloud.

I wasn't involved much by then. For this particular one, in February 1941, we went up to Martlesham Heath and we were not involved in any of these sweeps over France at all but we were looking after convoys going up the east coast.

It was very quiet, very pleasant, really very relaxing. Difficult to explain. You didn't live for the day but you didn't look forward much either. You took life as it came and being posted to Martlesham was on the edge but the Germans had finished coming over, except once when they bombed Martlesham, and then 605 went north to reform again and I left them and went to an OTU so I wasn't involved in the war much afterwards, the luck of the draw again.

Bob was posted to 55 OTU, a Hurricane unit, at Usworth in Durham.

I quite enjoyed it up to a point but it wasn't a rest tour. There was no danger but it was jolly hard work being an instructor because we had all these chaps coming in all the time, mostly from Canada, on the Empire Air Training Scheme, a lot of Canadians who were great chaps, but it was hard work. I did more flying as an instructor on the OTU than we did on the squadron. On the squadron some days you didn't fly at all, some days you'd be on readiness, but instructing is day after day while the weather was good. It was jolly hard work being an instructor.

Bob was now able to compare his own training with the instruction he provided after the Battle of Britain.

At Sutton Bridge it was the luck of the draw. Some chaps went south after about thirty hours on Hurricanes, and people have written how they only had seven hours on a Spitfire before they went into action. In 1940 the emphasis was to get people into action as quickly as possible but I don't think it affected the standards of training. I think this seven hour thing was unusual. Most people, at least out of Sutton Bridge, had thirty to forty hours on a Hurricane. I think the air force was very sensible in that they didn't feed you like lambs to the slaughter. They did what they could to make sure you had enough flying training before you went into action, such as 605. They were sent north after Dunkirk and were up there for five months reforming and training before being sent south again, so if things had been really grim, or worse, then they would have obviously been sent down earlier. However, the chaps in 11 Group were. I think August was the real peak period of time when they really had it hard. By the time we got down there, although the action was still there, the airfields weren't being bombed. When I was instructing at the end of '41, '42, there was no great urgency at all. The chaps came in and had their two months training and then they went off to squadrons. There was no great 'Get these chaps through!' We flew as much as we could, weather permitting, and when they'd done their fifty or sixty hours they went off to their squadrons. It was just like a sausage machine in a way.

In March 1942 Bob was posted again, this time to 54 Squadron as a flight commander. The squadron had a fearsome reputation for being in the heat of battle. Their baptism of fire had been over Dunkirk and through the first half of the battle. Withdrawn to the north to recover they were sent south again in early 1941 and took part in many of the sweeps across France.

I went to 54 Squadron flying Spitfires at Castletown in the north of Scotland. My luck again! But that was a good posting actually. Castletown was a pleasant airfield and 54 is a well known squadron, had a brilliant history during the battle, had been withdrawn, and back again to Hornchurch and then they were back in Scotland reforming. I was sent up from a Hurricane OTU to join a Spitfire squadron which was fine. There was no problem there. Converting from a Hurricane to a Spitfire was a non-event really. We had two or three months up there, very pleasant, looking after the Navy going in and out of Scapa Flow. We didn't have any action as such but that was why we were there, waiting to be sent south, that was the thought on everybody's mind, eventually we would finish up in the south of England somewhere.

But 54 Squadron was not sent to the south again. This time it would be a much longer journey and the second phase of Bob's wartime career.

By February 1942 the Japanese were in Papua New Guinea and Timor and everywhere else and the Australians were panicking a bit, quite rightly so. The Americans were not there in great force and the Australians sent a chap called Dr. Evatt, who was the Minister for Foreign Affairs, to Washington to start with and then to London for help. They wanted us to send a division of troops to Australia to help defend it. It happened to be the beginning of 1942 when the 8th Army was running backwards as fast as they could towards Alexandria, so there weren't any troops. Then they wanted some ships. We didn't have much of a navy in those days. To cut a long story short Churchill said to Dr. Evatt that we couldn't help them much but what we would do is send a wing of Spitfires to defend Australia and he had to be content with that. Churchill said there were two RAAF squadrons in England, 452 and 457, and also, he said, we will send you a very famous, well known RAF squadron to make up the wing, a political gesture obviously, and just by the luck of the draw it happened to be 54 Squadron. We set sail from Liverpool in the middle of June on board a troopship, with our Spitfires on another ship, and got as far as Freetown.

There had been a big argument with Churchill and Portal who was the Chief of the Air Staff. Portal didn't want to send any Spitfires to Australia. He said he hadn't got enough to spare, but Churchill had promised them and said he couldn't let them down, they had to go. Portal lost the argument so we set sail on the Stirling Castle. We got as far as Freetown at the time when the 8th Army was retreating and being pursued by Rommel right back almost to Alexandria and Cairo and things were really serious in the Middle East. Portal apparently went back to Churchill and said, 'I must have these Spitfires,' so reluctantly the ship with all our Spitfires was diverted to Takoradi and they were flown across to the Middle East. We sailed gaily on in our convoy to Durban and on to Australia, three squadrons of men and no Spitfires. We landed in Australia in August or September 1942 without any aeroplanes and it took another three months for new aircraft to dribble in from the UK. They didn't come on one ship, they came on various ships and it wasn't until January 1943 that we were fully equipped and we flew up to Darwin. By that time the war had turned. Midway had happened and the Japanese were on retreat. By the time we got to Darwin the need for it was really over. There wasn't any threat to start with but it was certainly over by the time we got there.

Darwin was empty. 19th of February when they bombed Darwin, they used the same four carriers they used to bomb Pearl Harbor, the same aircraft and the same leader, Fuchida. Yes they really plastered Darwin, which was just a little town at the top end of Australia with a port with a few ships in it. The Australians evacuated Darwin completely of all civilians and turned it into a military camp and the harbour was hardly used at all so there was no real reason to defend Darwin, there wasn't much to defend. That was what we were sent for.

We flew up in January 1943 in the middle of the wet season which is not very pleasant. We were based at the RAAF airfield in Darwin which was a good strip but we were stuck out in the bush about five miles away, hacked out of the bush, in tents, all a new experience to us but we settled in quite well. In fact Darwin was not a bad posting in that respect. OK it wasn't very pleasant but there were no diseases or anything, no malaria, nothing that the people in India and Burma had or even the Middle East a bit. As soon as the weather cleared in the dry season, as they called it in April, it became a pleasant but rather boring posting. We settled in alright but again we were a squadron on our own. The Australian command was fifty miles down the road and we did our own thing in our own time but people got fed up in the end because there was literally nothing to do. OK we were able to fly. Extraordinarily enough we were never really stood down even though the chances of them coming over were nil. For days on end, weeks on end, we were always on some sort of readiness just in case, but at least by about three o'clock in the afternoon you knew the Japanese weren't going to come if they were ever going to come at all so you were stood down and you could do some flying then. At least the pilots had the opportunity to fly around and have a good time, but for the ground crew there was just nothing to do, week after week.

I was lucky, going ahead, that I finished my tour out there at the end of 1943 and came home, but the squadron and the pilots were there to the end of the war, 1945, and they were completely demoralised. There they were, Spitfire pilots, highly trained, sitting around on their backsides with literally nothing to do and no chance of anything ever happening. By 1945 the Japanese were back in Tokyo, almost so, I think the last raid was July 1943 on Darwin and they never came over after that. For two years the squadron sat there with nothing to do. It was very bad and I'm glad I didn't stay out there. They changed the pilots certainly but a lot of the ground crew were up there all that time.

Despite his lack of regard for the posting, he found the Australians reacted very well to them.

They were very good. The wing arrived in Australia in September 1942 in Melbourne and the two Australian squadrons were sent home. Fair enough they went on leave. We were sent to a place called Richmond about twenty to thirty miles outside Sydney, an RAAF base. We were then sent on leave and we went by train into Sydney. The news had got round that we were coming and, although I didn't get involved in this, there were Australians there waiting on the station to take people home. Anybody who wanted a home for the fortnight's leave, they found it. The Australians couldn't have done more for us.

The three-squadron wing was commanded by Clive 'Killer' Caldwell, a man who arrived in Australia having gained a fine reputation in the Western Desert.

Clive was fine. He wasn't known over here but he was a Middle East man. He was an Australian who had had a good career in the Middle East. We didn't know anything about him, not when we arrived in Australia. He was sent back from the Middle East to run the wing and I got on very well with him. He had a distinguished record, he was a good leader, a good chap. He was a bit 'bolshie' as far as higher echelons were concerned and he had a very sticky relationship with the VIPs of the Australian air force, they didn't get on at all. That was not our problem, but he upset a lot of people, but as a pilot and a leader he was a good man.

Despite his modesty about his time in Darwin, Bob shot down the squadron's first aircraft in Australia. He then went on to attack a further eight Japanese aircraft, shooting down four of them.

It wasn't anything very brave. Two of us were scrambled over Darwin in February 1943 and the Japanese were sending over these high level fast reconnaissance aircraft called 'Dinahs'. They were faster than anything the Americans had, faster than the Kittyhawks, a bit like a Mosquito, a high-flying fast aircraft. They came over photographing. We were scrambled that day and we were vectored onto them just north of Darwin. We saw this thing and it turned to get away but, with the Spit at full boost, we were as fast as it was, so I shot it down. So it wasn't anything very brave, it just happened and it made the headlines that a Spitfire had shot down a Japanese aircraft. A lot of fuss made, I think, over very little, but it just happened to be myself who shot it down.

The squadron was flying the Spitfire Vc, the first time Bob had operated an aircraft armed with cannon.

You could fire any amount of 303s into a bomber and unless you hit something vital it would keep on flying. If you hit it with cannon then it normally went down. If we'd had cannon in the Battle of Britain it would have made a lot of difference. The Germans had cannon. So when it worked the cannon was very effective, it really hit an aeroplane. Of course the Japanese were easier because they had no self-sealing tanks, no armour plating, nothing at all, so if you hit a Japanese bomber the chances were that it would go down, whereas the Germans, you could put hundreds of rounds in, as was proved, and providing you didn't hit something vital they could get it home, so the cannon was a great advantage

What helped more than anything was the early warning system which picked up the enemy aircraft out to sea.

It was pretty good for those days. We didn't know it at the time but they were intercepting a lot of Japanese traffic. The Japanese would move their bombers down from Singapore, or somewhere like that, towards Timor, and sometimes we would intercept that twenty 'Bettys' were being based somewhere on Timor which usually meant they were going to attack Darwin. We normally got advice the night before to be on standby the next day as something might happen. It didn't always happen but normally they had advance warning of it. They would pick them up sixty or seventy miles out so most of the occasions they came over we were at height to intercept; not every time, but usually we did.

They didn't come very often. They still had a feeling that Darwin as a port would be used as a launching pad possibly and there was always shipping in the harbour so a couple of times they attacked Darwin, the oil tanks and so on. On other occasions they came over to attack the American air bases that were up there. There was a place called Fenton and so on. It was retaliation because by then the Americans were using those bases to attack so the Japanese came over three or four times, that's all, to attack these bases. I don't know why they did it because it made no difference to the war at all. They weren't doing anything to draw forces away from anywhere else. The Americans weren't interested.

They'd send over twenty-seven bombers as a rule, three lots of nine with their fighter cover 5 or 6,000 feet above and normally, even though it only happened three or four times, the Zeros would stay up above until you started to attack the bombers. They wouldn't come down onto you before you started to go into the bombers, but our tactics were to have one or maybe two squadrons attack the bombers with one squadron to go into the Zeros which worked reasonably well but it happened so rarely that it was like a one-off job. If it happened all the time you could get used to the attack but you'd have this one raid and then sit down on your backside for four weeks with nothing to do and then you'd get another raid. Somehow you never really got into it.

Myself and Robin Norwood were the only people who had fired a shot in action when we went out there. Although 54 was a famous squadron by name, all the famous pilots had gone so these chaps went into action for the first time without any background whatsoever. We did reasonably well for what it was worth but the whole exercise was, I shouldn't say a complete waste of time, it was a good exercise, but it rebounded on us too as the Americans were fighting all through Guadalcanal with God knows what losses, but as soon as we went into action it hit the headlines in Australia. 'Australian Spitfires down Japanese' and so on. The poor bloody Americans in the jungle didn't get a mention so there was no love lost between the Americans and us unfortunately.

We achieved the object, we achieved the moral boost that Churchill wanted. We did shoot down a few Japanese aircraft. What we achieved is probably negligible in terms of the total war but in terms of an exercise it was worthwhile and it was appreciated by the Australians. We made a lot of friends, I did anyway. Looking back on it it was an unnecessary exercise but having taken part in it I wouldn't have missed it. I liked Australia, I didn't like Darwin very much but I liked Australia and the Australians. So from a personal point of view it was a good posting.

Bob was awarded the DFC in August 1943 and finally left the squadron, and Australia, in early 1944.

I came back the other way courtesy of His Majesty. I'd finished a tour out there and I wasn't very interested in staying in Australia as an instructor or anything like that so they sent me home. I came home via the States on a US ship from Brisbane to San Francisco. We had a week or so leave in San Francisco then we caught the train across the Rockies. Four days on the train to New York where we again stayed for a couple of weeks and then we caught the *Queen Mary* home so it was an interesting journey and I got back in the UK in March 1944 with no job.

The *Queen Mary* was used as a trooper. They would do the Atlantic crossing on their own. They didn't go in convoy, it was much too slow for that. So she would leave New York, or Greenock, and just head out into the Atlantic without any escort, or without any seen escort anyway, and just head straight across as fast as she could. We were lucky enough to be there when she was returning to Scotland so we joined the *Queen Mary* in New York and sailed for four and a half days at full speed across the Atlantic with, I think, about eight to ten thousand US troops on board. Obviously she had been stripped down to nothing and they were sleeping in the corridors. You had two meals a day, breakfast at about ten o'clock and a meal in the evening at about six, it wasn't bad. We had a good cabin, the cabin Churchill had used when he went across for one of the meetings. It was a big cabin and Churchill had it on his own but we had, I think, ten or twelve people in it on bunks so it was slightly busy but it was more comfortable than lying in the corridor.

The country had changed in the two years since Bob had left for Australia.

When I left in '42 the war was pretty grim and nothing was going right. Singapore had fallen. The Middle East was dicey. The Germans were just about still attacking in Russia and everything was on a knife edge. Things were really grim. By the time we got back in '44 the war had changed completely. The Russians were half way back towards Berlin. The Middle East had been cleared and we were in Italy and the war was going to be over soon. D-Day was coming sometime, nobody knew but the whole country was full of Americans. Unfortunately my father had died while I was away in Australia so I wasn't able to meet him again, but my mother was around. I suppose the general feeling in the country when I got back was certainly more optimistic than when I went. The end was coming, we didn't know how long it would take and of course we knew nothing about V1s and V2s in those days which was a good thing, so it was a very optimistic country when I came back.

Bob went on leave and then contemplated his next job. So began the third phase of his war.

Well I wasn't interested at all in flying. I wasn't offered a flying job and I didn't bother about it. So I went on the usual leave and then went back up to the Air Ministry to find a job and a chap said, 'well, no flying so I don't know what to do.' And then he said that there was an interesting thing coming and he went on to explain that because of the coming invasion of Europe the air force, or at least Tedder who was deputy C-in-C under Eisenhower, wanted more coverage for the RAF who he thought in the Middle East never got any coverage because all war correspondents were attached to the army. He wanted to set up his own what was called Air Information Unit whenever the invasion took place to cover stories about the air force, to make sure the air force got their share of the news. He was setting up this little unit of war correspondents from the national papers, BBC and so on, and they wanted a few RAF officers to escort them around, look after them and point them in the right direction.

Was I interested? So I thought, 'sounds good to me,' and I said yes. We had Dimbleby with us, the old father Dimbleby, and one or two other people, so we formed this unit and waited for the invasion. We didn't know when it was going to be or where but in the end it did happen, Normandy. We packed our bags and eventually got across as a unit to cover the RAF who were then arriving on the airstrips. The first one didn't land until about D+10 or something like that and we were there to cover the actions of the Spitfires, Typhoons and whatever went on in the RAF.

Naturally we would get foreknowledge of what was going on and we were based at a little village called Creully which is some fifteen miles from Caen towards Bayeux. We were told on the night before that Montgomery was stuck outside Caen, the Germans were defending it strongly so the idea was to bomb their way in. At the beginning of July we were told that evening the RAF would come over and bomb the western side of Caen and then the army would advance and take the town so we sat about half a mile behind the bomb line and the bombers came over and plastered the outskirts of Caen which was a frightening sight in a way. But they made such a good job of it of course that with the bombs and the craters and so on the army couldn't move through it at all and it was the next day before they started to advance and by then the Germans were back. Eventually they did get through but it wasn't a classical piece of tactical bombing. It didn't achieve the object; it killed a lot of Frenchmen and it killed a lot of Germans and eventually the army did get through but it was a hard slog because of the cratering of all the roads and everything else.

Even the fact that many hundreds of French were killed, there was no reaction to that, not at the time. Now of course everybody says the same thing, but funnily enough I don't remember much reaction from the French either. There were no demonstrations outside Caen, no Frenchmen saying 'Look how many you've killed!'

The city of Caen is surrounded by high ground, it's quite an amphitheatre, and Bob and his journalists had a grandstand view of the attack.

The noise was tremendous to start with. The bombing was half a mile away and they didn't bomb short. It wasn't horrible at the time, it's horrible thinking about it now. I don't say we cheered, of course we didn't. The feeling was, and we didn't know it was going to be chaos at the end anyway, that the RAF had come over, they had bombed where they had been told to bomb, and everyone thought what a jolly good job. And of course it sounds a bit cynical but when it was all over we went back to dinner. We didn't stay around to see the army go in. Of course their thoughts were completely different.

Next was the offensive at Falaise.

Again the army was stuck and the Germans were dug in and this was another big bombing raid. We were told about that at dawn. The Caen one was in the evening and the Germans had all night to recover. This time it would begin at dawn and Bomber Command would bomb. Instead of bombing solidly they would bomb a line on the right hand side, for want of a better description, near a factory called Colombelles, which is on the outskirts of Caen. They would drop their bombs there in a line and about a mile away, to the left if you like; the American 8th Air Force would come in and bomb a similar line down there. I remember sitting on the grass in a big field with Montgomery, with his little stick and a map, saying 'the RAF will come in and then the Americans will come in and then the army will move in, the tanks are all ready, we will drive through and we will be in Falaise in forty-eight hours,' or words to that effect. We all went away and at dawn we found ourselves on a hill just behind the bomb line and at dawn the Lancs came in and they bombed a perfect line down.

The Americans followed about an hour or so later and we were then about four or five miles away from the action. It wasn't like Caen. We were further away but we could see everything. Well, the long story is that the army moved in with their tanks but things didn't go as well as they planned. Everything went well for the first five miles. Then they got bogged down again, the whole thing petered out after forty-eight hours and it was another three weeks before they actually got to Falaise. They brought the Poles in, and the Canadians, and our last experience of bombing was a week or two later, just before the Falaise Gap battle, when the Polish Armoured Div was going into action, and we were told that Bomber Command would come over in daylight and bomb ahead of the Poles who would then sweep in.

It was a sunny day, a lovely sunny day but a bit hazy, and unfortunately, the only time we experienced it, Bomber Command missed it a bit and they bombed short. They bombed right in the middle of the Polish Armoured Division. They hit the Poles, but they still went through and hit their objective. But it wasn't a very good start.

Of course it was great access for the press, but the main reason for that was to have good coverage of the RAF and their actions.

Well, they did it to the best of their ability, which sounds a bit unkind. My friend Tompkins, who I seemed to get attached to, was a *Sunday Dispatch* airman who'd flown an aeroplane and had a private pilot's licence. These other chaps had been brought in by their papers – you haven't got anything to do so why don't you become part of this – and they didn't really know much about what they were doing. They did their best. They wrote good stories but they were mainly human interest stories and things like that. With hindsight I don't think they really achieved the object that Tedder wanted. It was all favourable to the RAF and they got coverage but when all these reports were coming back to the editor or whoever it may be, he sorted out the headlines and there were a lot bigger ones, the row between Montgomery and Eisenhower say, or the big advance the Americans were making. The job the RAF was doing was a bit down the line. So they did what they could, it achieved the object but not as strongly as Tedder hoped. In fact I think he lost interest after a while.

There were five of us looking after these chaps. I had my Tompkins and a chap called Scott and we seemed to be up in the action a bit more than some of the others. We were given a free rein really, what do you want to do? and I don't say that all of the units went up to watch the bombing, some would say they weren't very interested.

After Falaise the air war in Normandy was obviously coming to an end and the next step was to sweep up towards Brussels I suppose. After Falaise news came round that the people in Paris had risen. This was on the Tuesday or Wednesday of that week, and Paris was about to fall. Tompkins said, 'There's not much happening round here now because the Germans are retreating all over the place and the big story is going to be Paris. Can we go there?' We had this old Humber staff car so I said, 'I don't know why not,' so we had this CO, a chap called Squadron Leader Bell, who didn't know much about what was going on either. We said, 'Do you mind if we push off for a day or so?' and he said, 'No, go on.' On the morning of the Friday we said let's head towards Paris from Caen so we set off at the crack of dawn and we drove up through Falaise which had then been cleared and on to the next town called Argentan where we stopped for breakfast and met up with a lot of Americans who had just advanced up through the area. We then decided to head off towards Paris and we only had an aviation map but we asked one of the Americans, Military Police, what was going on ahead and he didn't know but we thought, 'Off we go.'

To this day I still don't know how we navigated but we headed in the right direction and went on for hours and hours, through various towns, saw women with shaven heads, the usual thing that was going on. Of course with the Germans having retreated people were taking their revenge, rightly or wrongly. In the middle of the afternoon we came to a village called Rambouillet and as we drove into it we saw a lot of tanks ahead. We were stopped by a chap in American uniform who asked us in fluent French what we were doing there and where were we going. Well the reaction was why was this American talking to us in French with us in RAF uniform. We later found out he was speaking fluent French because he wasn't American, he was part of General LeClerc's 2nd Armoured Division which was a French division with American tanks. They were waiting to go into Paris. The advance elements were ahead and when he said where were we going we said we were hoping to go to Paris. Well he said 'You can't go now because it's too dangerous so wait around here.'

He was a very polite young man. He said, 'If you hang around here when we get the order we shall be advancing into Paris and if you like you can come with us. 'It was a lovely afternoon, very hot, so we sat around and waited and in the middle of the afternoon he came up and asked if we had room in our car for some other people. We said yes and he said, 'We have two young French ladies here, attached to the French forces who would like a lift. Do you mind?' So we said if they were young French ladies we wouldn't mind. Anyway he said, 'When we get ready to move I'll introduce you to them.' At about six or seven o'clock at night or maybe a bit later things started rolling and this chap came over and said they were ready to move and introduced us to the mademoiselles, two lovely young French girls, who came and joined us. We put them in the back of the car and they waved us on. We had one tank ahead and we had another tank behind us and we headed towards Paris with the 2nd Armoured Division spearheading the advance and it was an interesting run in. For the first few miles nothing much happened but when we got nearer to the suburbs the whole of Paris came out to welcome us because the Tricolor was flying all over the place and we were in this convoy.

I've never known and never will see again the reaction of a crowd of people who had been relieved. It was really quite extraordinary. I've never drunk more champagne and been kissed by more pretty girls. It was really quite an experience, it really was. Eventually we arrived in the centre of Paris, the Place de la Concord, at about nine o'clock at night and we found ourselves in a hotel called the Grand, just near the Opera, for the night, bedded down there and that was the start of a weekend. It was really a tremendous ride in.

The shooting was still going on. Coming along the Left Bank there were signs of a lot of damage. There were still some fires burning, and in fact along by the Louvre there was still a bit of action, but it had more or less quietened down, that was on the Friday. But Saturday we had an interesting day. Tompkins suggested it. He said, 'Let's go and see the tomb of Napoleon,' and I'd never been to Paris in my life so we went to Les Invalides and so on and the man in charge let us in in the end. We stood there and looked down at this tomb and it was quite moving really. It was just the two of us, we were the only people in there, and then we went up to Sacre Coeur at the top of the hill, again for something to do.

When we came out we were met by a young Frenchman who said 'RAF?' because we were in RAF uniform, Tompkins and I. We said yes and – he obviously spoke very good English – and he said what were we doing and we explained. He said would we be interested in seeing the headquarters of the French resistance, and so we said 'Yes.' By the Sacre Coeur there's a big waterworks and apparently in the cellars underneath the waterworks they'd set up the Montmartre resistance headquarters. We went down a lot of steps and almost underneath Sacre Coeur was this Ops room all set up just like you'd see in the films with radio. They had a logbook that I signed and then we came up and he said it was time for a drink so they all piled into this car of ours and we drove down the hill to a café which had obviously been a letter drop or something I suppose because the resistance people knew the owner and we started drinking. The news got round that we were there and we started off with half a dozen people in this bar and after about a quarter of an hour you couldn't move in there. The owner must have got carried away because he started giving drinks away. You could have anything you wanted and I said to somebody 'There's a lot of people in here, where do they all come from?'

He said that news had got round that the owner was giving away drinks and he'd never been known to do that for the last twenty years, so the poor man, we drunk him dry, quite literally, us and about another forty or fifty Frenchmen. Then they started singing *The Marseillaise* and we sang *God Save the King*. It was really quite an experience. Then at lunchtime Tompkins decided he ought to do some work. They'd set up a news office in the Hotel Scribe and I took the staff car up to the Champs Élysées to watch De Gaulle's parade. I was sitting in this car on my own and someone said in front of a lot of people, 'Do you mind if we get in the car?' 'Yes if you want to,' and then they joined me and then De Gaulle came past with his entourage walking down to the Place de La Concord and one of the Frenchmen said 'Go on, go and join in,' so I thought nothing lost so I started the car and nobody bothered us at all. About twenty metres or so behind De Gaulle there were a lot of people and we just joined in the procession and drove down the Champs Élysées. By then people were packed in the car, there must have been about twenty Frenchmen boys and girls in the car and we drove all the way down in the procession taking all the plaudits and so on.

It was a wonderful day and then of course firing broke out when he was nearly down the bottom so everybody panicked and everybody got down inside the car. I was behind the wheel and I couldn't move at all so I just sat there and it was afterwards, when the shooting was all over, one chap said, 'You're very brave sitting like that,' and I thought, 'Well I'm not brave. I couldn't bloody well move!' Eventually they all got out and said thank you very much and that was the end of a good day. I was very privileged in a way. Probably the only person there.

We stayed there for two or three days enjoying ourselves and then we got a very irate message from Caen saying 'What are you doing up there? You're supposed to be covering the Air Force.' So we came home and that was the end of any excitement really. We followed the air force as far up as Brussels and stayed there for a while on the periphery of Arnhem.

Bob remained with the unit until early October 1944 when he was posted to HQ Fighter Command where he stayed for the rest of the war. He finally left the service in 1947 and rejoined both Shell BP and the Royal Auxiliary Air Force.

After the war I was a VR, I was never a regular officer and never wanted to be particularly, so at the end of the war I came out. I was literally a wartime airman and came out in 1947 like many others. I went back into the Auxiliary Air Force as I had an interest in it, but a lot of chaps just wanted to forget all about it. I think that went on for twenty or thirty years after the war and then suddenly the public interest came into it and people started writing books, controversial books, did we win or did we lose, and it was only then and with all the books to start with and then with documentaries the interest is growing and growing. I think history has now said it was an important battle whereas in the '50s and '60s it was just something that happened over the south of England. That's what's happened because of all the publicity and the historians.

On his retirement he took an ever-increasing role in the Battle of Britain Fighter Association. He became its chairman in 2009 where he remained until his death in 2014.

There was one further link with the past for Bob. In 1996 renowned pilot and aircraft restorer Peter Vacher found and eventually returned to England a Hurricane which had lain unwanted near Bombay since the war. This turned out to be R4118, a Hurricane I which Bob had flown with 605 Squadron during the Battle of Britain. Perhaps Britain's most historic and original 1940 airworthy aircraft, Bob was reunited with it in 2004. He sat in the cockpit for the first time since 2 October 1940.

I sat in the thing when it was first launched in Cambridge. Oh yes, it did bring it back. I was amazed how old and small it was. I mean the cockpit, I could hardly get into it. They were small you know. I suppose there weren't many fat fighter pilots. There were some tall ones and I don't know how they got into them, there wasn't a lot of headroom.

It was exactly the same. It's extraordinary isn't it? A sort of oily smell. It is there. It's not castor oil but it is an oily smell. And the instrument panel is original. Someone said I could fly it and I said no way. But it's a great thing, after all these years.

This reunion also made Bob consider his opinions on the Battle of Britain.

I think the main thing, if you live in the UK, it's the only thing that happened over England so therefore it's very personal to people here. What happened in Malta and the Middle East is something a long way away and so if you're having an air show at Biggin Hill you obviously concentrate on the Battle of Britain and the two aeroplanes in the battle were the Hurricane and the Spitfire. You don't see poor old Defiants there. You don't see any Blenheims there which did part of this, and it's also been built up over the years, in the last twenty years I would say. We had our association, and there was always Battle of Britain Day on 15 September, but there wasn't all this emphasis that there has been over the last twenty or thirty years when people started writing books about it and then they made a film about it, *Battle of Britain*, in 1969, and now it's become, not a myth, but it's been brought forward as the definitive battle, which it probably was. I think that's another thing, to us the battle went on, but it did have an effect on the rest of the war. Had we lost, had the Germans either invaded or bombed us to oblivion we wouldn't be here now. I think that is generally accepted as a possibility and to people living in this area of England it is the Trafalgar or the Armada, it's one of these great things of British history.

Squadron Leader Geoffrey Wellum DFC
4 August 1921-18 July 2018

Well I always wanted to fly since I was a small boy and joining the air force was the cheapest way of learning to fly that I knew. It didn't cost me anything and in fact they started to pay me. I always wanted to fly and the cheapest way of doing that was in the air force.

Geoffrey Wellum was born in Walthamstow, on the border between East London and Essex. He was educated at Forest School in Snaresbrook and was still in the sixth form when he applied to join the Royal Air Force.

As a young kid I used to go to North Weald aerodrome, as it was called, and see all the Siskins and Bulldogs in the 1920s and '30s, all painted in their squadron colours, gaily painted, and their pilots in their white overalls and they were my heroes. I just thought I'm going to try to do that if they'll have me and that's as it started and as it continued, and I applied for a short service commission in 1938. I was underage but they said they would accept me. 'Could I go back to school for another term?' and I said yes, because I wanted to be captain of cricket. They said, 'Oh we don't want to interfere with the cricket, old boy, but when you're not playing cricket will you brush up on your maths a little bit.' And so that was what happened.

I did a term at school, I captained the cricket eleven, I did absolutely nothing at all in the way of work and I went up to Desford in Leicestershire in July of 1939 and in fact war was declared half way through our *ab initio* training. Yes, I always wanted to fly since I saw those gaily painted little aircraft tumbling around in the sky in the 1920s and '30s. Simple as that.

The day war broke out stuck in Geoffrey's mind for the rest of his life but not, perhaps, for the usual reasons.

We were sitting in the anteroom, Reid and Sigrist ran the flying school. In those days, diverting a little bit, when they taught you to fly you weren't in the Royal Air Force, you were a civilian pupil pilot and you had to do fifty hours *ab initio* training and pass that course before they would accept you, and in fact a good third fell by the wayside, probably a little bit more. We were sitting in the anteroom and we heard this plaintive voice. I was rather amazed: was this really the Prime Minister of this great country saying that war was declared? And it didn't register, not really, you know, nothing changed.

The countryside was still the same and then some chap came in who was the director of the flying school. He was rather pompous (and talked) about attacking the Hun and then some said well look obviously we, on our little grass airfield in the middle of Leicestershire, our little Tiger Moths, twenty chaps learning to fly, are high on the list of priority targets for the Luftwaffe and so obviously we must be a great worry to them so we are going to be attacked. They made us taxi all the Tiger Moths and park them round the edge of the airfield, and this you've got to believe, we were issued with pickaxe handles to defend those aeroplanes to the last man.

Of course, eventually, after two or three days, that was day and night, and when the Luftwaffe didn't turn up and the German paratroopers didn't turn up, we started flying again. It was all a bit, that's my reaction, I thought it was silly. As for the war, and that very few of us, if any, would get through it, never occurred to me. No, it didn't really come into the equation. I was far too busy being happy. I was learning to fly. I'd had a lovely last term at school and, no, it just did not register. Not until, in fact, I got to Biggin Hill and that was early September '40 and then I thought this looks a bit dangerous.

Geoffrey completed his training and was posted to his first front-line unit, 92 Squadron at Northolt, although during the Dunkirk operations the squadron operated from Duxford in Cambridgeshire.

I got an above average assessment and I found myself in a Spitfire squadron within ten and a half months of leaving the cloistered existence of school. The training in those days was as it was in peacetime. You learned to fight your aeroplane, whatever it was, fighter or bomber, on the squadron, and when I first went to a fighter squadron, I had never fired my guns. I was never told how to use the reflector gunsight and I didn't know the first thing about it. The first time I fired my guns in anger was at 150+ Heinkels over Maidstone and that was the first time that I started to know what it was all about. But no, our training did not prepare us to operate a fighter aircraft in a fighter squadron. Fly? Yes, they taught us to fly very well, but it ended there.

They never told me about deflection (shooting). It became obvious but they never told me how to use our reflector gunsight. I knew afterwards and I thought if they'd only taught me this in training, I would have done a far better job than I did. We were never taught how to fight our aeroplanes. Using it as a fighter, as a gun platform, is a very different thing from doing a perfect slow roll and the examiner saying that's very good, old boy, you didn't lose any height. That's got nothing to do with it. It's a different world. Forget all the training. Forget all that instruction. Just get in the aeroplane and fly it to its limits.

When I first went to a squadron it was just before Dunkirk and I'd never even seen a Spitfire, let alone flown it, so I couldn't be of much use to them. Well it was all a bit daunting. I joined at Northolt the night before they went off to Dunkirk and I realised that I had achieved an ambition to be in a fighter squadron. There I was in the anteroom and they were all accomplished Spitfire pilots and I wasn't but the same steward that brought them their drinks brought me my drinks. I was a member of a fighter squadron which was what I had endeavoured to be since I was a small boy and I had finally got there. So that took up all my thinking rather than being daunted by the prospect of having to get into a single seater fighter for the first time and hurl it into the sky. It was a feeling of thankfulness really that I had finally got there and here I was in a fighter mess with a fighter squadron.

At this point Geoffrey was introduced to one of the most famous RAF pilots of the war. Roger Bushell had been CO of 92 Squadron for more than six months and would make his name not as a successful fighter pilot but as a persistent escaper from German PoW camps and for his subsequent leadership of the organising team for the 'Great Escape' from Stalag Luft III in March 1944. Bushell was one of the first out of the tunnel but was recaptured within days and murdered by the Gestapo along with forty-nine other escapers.

I only met him for one interview where he put the fear of God in me quite frankly, but he was a tremendous character, very forceful. A barrister, and I thought well if ever I end up in a court of law, he can take me to the cleaners any time. He looked at me and said, 'I can't be bothered with you. We're just about to be made operational and you haven't done this, you haven't flown that and look at your logbook, it isn't very bright, is it?' I thought I'm about average, what do you want? But in the end I had a little, not a go at him exactly but I said, 'Well look, if you send me away to fly a Spitfire for the first time somewhere else I would ask to come back to 92 Squadron.'

'Why?' I said, 'Because the Air Ministry have said so, I've been posted to it, you've got my posting notice on your desk.' 'You cocky little so-and-so,' he said, not to me but to the adjutant, a chap called Burgoyne who was

First World War, a dear old chap he really was. I was dismissed and I went and sat down and Mac was called in and he came back grinning all over his face. He said, 'I gather you told the big white chief that 92 was your squadron as much as his?' I said, 'Well not quite like that but something like that.' And he said, 'I don't think you'll be going anywhere. I think he likes the cut of your gib.'

After Dunkirk the squadron was moved from Duxford, first to Hornchurch, then back to Northolt, until finally they arrived at Pembrey in South Wales where they stayed until early September 1940.

They were cock-a-hoop as they'd shot down quite a few but I think they'd probably learned that some of their number weren't coming back, they weren't going to see them again, and I was watching them and they were transformed really from being 'hey nonny no' to fighting a war in a Spitfire. It became a reality as opposed to 'Let's get at 'em!' It was a serious business and it showed on their faces.

The first day I think they were over Dunkirk three times and we lost four including the CO who was Roger Bushell, who was shot down and taken prisoner, Paddy Green who was my first flight commander for a day, who was wounded and managed to get back into Lympne, Pat Learmont, who was shot down in flames, and he was the chap who looked after me on my first night with the squadron and I felt that quite a bit because one minute he was there and next he wasn't. And the other chap who was made a prisoner was a fellow called John Gillies who was the son of a plastic surgeon who helped Macindoe.

At Duxford Geoffrey had begun to learn the ways of the Spitfire. He flew his first solo there and the memory of that day never left him.

The thing flew me to start with. Oh yes, these things stand out vividly in your mind. Diverting just a little bit – a bloke asked me a short time ago and he said he couldn't understand how I could remember such detail, and I said well I don't understand why you can't understand that if you get an 18½ -year-old lad and say there's a Spitfire, go and fly it and if you break it there'll be bloody hell to pay, are you trying to tell me that you can't understand that I can remember everything? I can see it. I can remember walking out to it and looking at it and there was this lithe single-seater, almost delicate in appearance, no instructor in the back of that thing.

You had to get in and fly it all with a maximum of 140 hours flying and I can remember my oxygen mask as I walked banging, I can feel it banging across my face and the two-ground crew looking at me as if to say 'Oh God, another sprog.' I can also remember, almost with resignation, taxying out down wind and turning into wind and thinking, 'well there's no excuse now. I might as well get going,' and I opened the throttle and the acceleration was something I'd never experienced.

The next thing I knew the thing had leaped into the air with me hanging onto it. In those days you had to change your hands on the stick to pump up the undercarriage. I took my hand off the throttle and I hadn't tightened the throttle friction nut enough and as I took my hand off the throttle it came back and I lost power so there were hands and things all over the place. But once I got it into the air, and the aircraft cleaned up, I got it up to about 10,000, it was a lovely day with lots of fluffy white clouds around, and I remember floating round the sky in this wonderful aeroplane and the thought came into your brain that you wanted to do something and somehow the thought transmitted itself to the aeroplane and it did it. Then of course there was the question of getting over the euphoria and getting it back on the ground.

It was the most important part of the sortie and I undershot a bit, because in Harvards where I was trained you came in with a lot of motor but if you did that in a Spitfire, with wheels and flaps down, it assumed a tail-down attitude, quite stable, didn't drop a wing on you or anything like that, and that meant ten feet of nose came up and you couldn't see ahead and that was off-putting. I remember seeing, I can see it now, the hedge going by underneath, 'I hope that's the airfield,' and there was the grass coming up quickly and I can remember pulling the stick back and she went straight on the ground. Not a bump anywhere, stable, a lovely, lovely pilot's aeroplane. I suddenly got into dispersal and had a little think about it all, and in the end I got to know a Spitfire beautifully doing almost glide approaches and landings and in the end I could almost three point it on a three-penny bit. The aeroplane flew me on take-off and landing but I had quite a lot of fun with it when I was in the air so, yes, it's very, very vivid. I know I've gone on a bit about this but, you know, it is very vivid.

I think I knew my way around in a Spitfire after I'd been on the squadron about a month. It took a little bit of time but I was always slow on the uptake, as it were, and towards the end I seemed to accelerate and by the time I'd been at Biggin for a fortnight I think I knew my way around in a Spit because if I could see my antagonist I always thought, in a Spitfire, half of it was done, I always thought I could outfly him. It was the chap you did not see who got you. And therefore, with my tiny little mind, I suddenly thought well the answer is, even if you never see an enemy, never stay still – chuck it around, never stay still – twenty seconds, thirty seconds – if you did, nine times out of ten you were killed because you did not see the chap who hit you.

I was shot up very badly once, it really was quite off-putting because I did not see the chap. I was flying home at the end of a day, 'Thank goodness that's over', and there was the most almighty bang. Luckily I got back to Biggin with it. It's the chap you don't see who gets you every time, so never stay still and chuck the thing around. Forget the flying rule book, slow rolls, keep the needles in the middle, hands and feet you know, be brutal with the thing and then you stood a chance.

When Geoffrey forgot his own rules, he became a hard taskmaster on himself.

At least I realised I was doing something wrong. You know if you want to exist mate, if you want to survive in this bloody lot, don't do that again. You're jolly lucky to get away with it. Oh yes, I think you've got to be self-critical. That's why you mustn't really, if you think you can fly the thing, you mustn't take it for granted, that there's not somebody else in a black crossed aeroplane who's just as good as you are. And you've got to be aware that things can go haywire, particularly if you're in the middle of a gaggle of aeroplanes all shooting at each other. It was just like a load of gnats on a summer evening, you're getting mixed up all over, tracers, it's mad, war, it really was.

You mustn't be too reckless. By all means go for him but don't get carried away. If you think you've got him but you're not quite certain, I'll take another burst, that sort of thing, don't necessarily do that because there again you're back to the old adage, if you fly straight or in a steady old turn you'd be shot down because the Germans had been trained in combat flying. They'd experienced combat flying, evaluated their aeroplanes and their tactics in the Spanish Civil War. They had fine-tuned things in the Polish campaign so really they had a head start when our chaps went over to France in their nice Hendon display-type formations, where you should have had a finger four formation where everybody covers everybody else, but when you're in tight formation you're concentrating on the leader so if the leader doesn't see something... we lost so many top quality fighter pilots through that basic error.

On 8 September the squadron made its big move from South Wales to Biggin Hill on the border between London and Kent, right in the path of oncoming formations of German aircraft. From there Geoffrey made his first ever sortie against enemy aircraft.

During this time 92 Squadron had three further commanding officers, Philip Sanders DFC, Robert Lister and Alan MacLachlan. However, the heart of the squadron for many was Brian Kingcome, Geoffrey's flight commander.

We got off from Biggin. I can tell you the date, it was September 11, and somehow the squadron had to get airborne very quickly. We went up through a little bit of cloud and we got separated. I was number two to Brian and I was hanging onto him and the two of us were going up there climbing like bats out of hell because we never really had enough time to get up to them.

We weren't scrambled early enough, and I can remember seeing Brian up there and he looked at me and the controller came on, and I can hear him now, Bill Igo his name was, Brian was leading, he said, 'Gannic leader, 150 plus, Dungeness, Vector so-and-so, Buster.' I looked ahead and there was this mass of aircraft, again like gnats on a summer evening, with 109s above and I'd never seen so many of them. Brian and I were underneath, climbing up for a head-on attack and I sat there and thought, 'Well, what the hell do I do now? Where do you start on this lot? Well the first thing, Geoff, is to turn your gun button to fire because if you don't it won't go bang.'

Well I did that and I tightened my straps, I can feel it, got down behind the armour-plated glass and we went straight into them. I was in Spitfire 1 QJ-K for King serial number K9998. And that was the first time I went into action, it's as clear as I can see you. You never forget it. You never get over it. It stays in your mind for the whole of your life but it's when you're doing things like this, interviews or you write a book, it all comes back.

Before the book was successful, I put it in the back of my mind but when things started to happen the dreams came back. It's something that stays in your mind forever. Those early days in September 1940, those early days of the war when life was very, very crucial. There was a national crisis and one was very aware that if we lost that battle there was nothing that could stop those dreadful people coming over. They would have had air superiority.

People say the navy would have saved us but they wouldn't, they wouldn't, not without air cover and the Germans would have knocked hell out of them. Look what happened earlier in the war. Look what happened coming back from Norway. *Glorious* was sunk, all by air attack. Look what happened to *Repulse* and *Prince of Wales* in the Far East – air attack. Unless we've got air cover, our ships were sitting ducks, particularly in a place like the English Channel, and that's where the problem was.

So, people say we didn't win the Battle of Britain, the Germans lost it rather than we won it, and that Hitler didn't intend to invade anyway. They weren't even alive these people so what the hell do they know about it, but the constant bombing, mortal combat and the threat of invasion in September 1940, those things were very real indeed, believe me. Perhaps we didn't realise quite the importance of it but when one had time to think about it, which you didn't then, you had other things to think about, self-preservation, but when you had time to think about it you realised that the chips were well and truly down. No quarter asked or given against an utterly ruthless and evil regime, and they had to be stopped.

And that is one of the reasons why pilots such as Geoffrey Wellum went up to meet the enemy day after day.

Like an automaton. In the end you didn't think about it. You were tired. I can always see dawn readiness. I can see Spitfires standing in the gloom at dispersal. I can hear the airmen and the clank of petrol bowsers and I can remember sort of looking up at the sky and thinking, 'Oh, it's going to be a lovely day again, oh God, another dawn.' Said a little prayer, 'it's going to be another busy day. If I forget you don't forget me. Just give me this day, please just give me this day.'

My view of the enemy? My view was what the earth are you doing over here? Why are you stirring all this up? What do you want? You've got most of Europe. I don't understand. If I can prevent you, I'm bloody well going to. I can't understand why any race of people should upset the peace of the world, which it did, one stupid little corporal madman with a small moustache who for some reason had the whole country of Germany at his fingertips. They were indoctrinated, they were so for the Fatherland and die for the Führer, we don't understand that sort of thing and I thought why does a seemingly intelligent people, why do they do this? What is it? Why do they put on a uniform and strut about the place in their jackboots? I don't understand. But the thought of these people doing the goosestep up the Mall to Buckingham Palace to install Goering, who I think was earmarked, it appalled me. Why? I didn't understand it and therefore I didn't go much on the enemy.

I've met one or two German fighter pilots recently, in the last three or four years. Some of them are nice blokes but some of them are arrogant sods. They go around with their Knight's Cross round their neck. They go around with their wings on, and one chap, somebody told him that the bus was leaving at nine and it left at quarter to nine and he came down at twenty to nine and said you told me quarter to nine, went to the restaurant and ordered an English breakfast keeping the rest of us waiting. That is what I detest about the Germans. But again some of their fighter pilots, Gunther Rall, I met him at Aces High, a nice chap. He could be mistaken for an English fighter pilot.

No. 92 Squadron became the highest scoring fighter squadron in the Royal Air Force during the war, but at the beginning of the Battle of Britain its reputation as a successful squadron was still to be created. However, create it they did, the fighter pilots, the ground crews, the antics they got up to and the battles they fought.

No. 92 had only just been re-formed. It was a squadron in the First World War, a Canadian squadron with SE5s on the Western Front, and after the war, like everything else, it was disbanded and it had only been re-formed for a few months when I joined it. They weren't operational, and in fact they were made operational on the night I joined them because they were told to go on dawn readiness the next morning to go to Dunkirk.

I felt part of 92 Fighter Squadron Royal Air Force. 92 Squadron was a law unto itself and, although I say it myself, it was a fighter squadron of the very highest quality. We were in the forefront, in the front line at Biggin Hill. I can't remember the exact date, but it was very early in September, the 5th or 6th or something like that, and we stayed in the front line longer than any other squadron has ever stayed at any time, and when I left the squadron in 1941, August, September, something like that, they were still there then. Shortly after, they went out to the Middle East, but we stayed on the front line longer than any other squadron. We took casualties but we also did quite a bit of damage to our antagonists.

Comradeship. Love of one's fellow man. We lived hard, we played hard. It was just a question of not letting the bastards grind you down basically. It was great, you can't define it. Brian Kingcome in his book gets as close to it as anyone can. It was an unforgettable collection of people, and somehow they had an atmosphere about them.

Many was the time I've gone straight to dispersal having been chucked out of the White Hart at Brasted or even gone up to a night club and gone straight to dispersal at three in the morning because we were on dawn readiness, and one did that, parties most nights, pretty ladies around. We went to Manston after the battle, and that was like a haven although Manston was as near to the French occupied territory as it was possible to get. The weather clamped while we were there and we used to go to a pub called the Fleur de Lis in Canterbury and I can see it now, the chaps in this very old thirteenth century pub, best brews, cigarette smoke rising to the ceiling, tinkling jewelry, comradeship, buying each other drinks and being together. Didn't want to go with anybody else, forget them, no other squadron except 92. Together we lived and fought and played very hard.

It was full of characters. Bob Holland who was a pianist. He could play anything from Beethoven to Boogie Woogie and many's the time, at dances and things with a few bevies inside you, we used to take over the orchestra and Bob would play the piano and the perspiration would pour off him. So, there was Bob Holland, Tony Bartley, who was ridiculously good looking and a right playboy, but an exceptional pilot.

Then there was Brian, steady and always there. Brian basically lead 92 throughout the Battle of Britain. Johnny Kent then came towards the end and tried to instill a bit of discipline. He says he did in his book, but I think what happened was we didn't succumb to him, he succumbed to 92. And then, of course, we had Jamie Rankin. But although I've been going on, you can't put your finger on it. It was a comradeship and a love of fellow man. We loved each other, don't take that word wrong, we loved each other's company, we would do anything for each other, and we lived and played hard together, and indeed, without being too dramatic, we fought hard too.

Johnny Kent had made his reputation as a fearless pilot and outstanding leader at 303 Squadron. It was a squadron full of Polish pilots, but from its formation on 2 August 1940 Kent created a highly successful and well-disciplined group of fliers in just a few weeks. On 26 October he was posted as the new CO at No. 92 Squadron.

Oh yes it had a reputation. In fact, I think we were known throughout Fighter Command as a load of playboys. Ill disciplined, red linings to our tunics and that sort of thing. Yes we had a bit of a reputation for being a bloody-minded lot. Well you see, in a way, it's understandable. We'd lost four COs who'd spent a couple of days in the chair, been shot down and then pushed off. And Brian did all the fighting and leading until about October, I think it was, when Johnny Kent came.

Now our attitude was here's a new chap, Johnny Kent, is he going to occupy the seat for three or four days and then push off somewhere? Or get killed? Or shot down? You know, let him adapt to us, which was probably the wrong attitude but that's what it was and you can understand it. We'd been leaderless, by which I mean a squadron without a leader, CO, since Dunkirk and Brian Kingcome was 92 Squadron and we'd follow him anywhere, and then Johnny Kent came along and tried to read the riot act which caused quite a lot of unhappiness. But in the end we got used to each other and he became one of the boys and took us through the initial fighter sweeps of 1940, '41.

Early on at 92 Geoffrey got himself a nickname.

Boy – yes. Well there's a bit of a story about that. Firstly, when I joined the squadron, I was under the age of 19 and secondly, although we'd learned how to drink at flying training school you couldn't keep up with 92 Squadron. I had three or four pints one night, and I suppose got a bit ridiculous, and Brian Kingcome said, 'We're going out again tonight boy, now no more than three pints because if you don't we'll have to call you the boy drunkard.' So I said, 'Thank you very much indeed, I shall have more than three pints if I want to.' He said, 'Alright boy but just remember what I said.' And thereafter everybody called me 'Boy', as simple as that, but I'd like to think largely because of age.

High up on Geoffrey's list of memories was the day he first shot down an enemy aircraft.

11.00 hours on 11 September 1940. Brian and I going into 150 plus. That sums up the Battle of Britain for me. My mind, I can see it as clear as I'm seeing you, that about sums it up.

Heinkel 111, Dungeness. It was the first time I was in action. I followed Brian into this mass and it broke away and I was a little bit 'What's going on?' and then below I saw a Heinkel that had obviously left its formation going full bore back towards Dungeness and so I had a go at him and was fortunate enough to get a confirmation. It crashed on Dungeness and that was when I got shot up in 'K' because I was so keen on 'Aren't you a clever boy!' But there was this enormous bang and there was a 109 sitting behind me, very very close indeed. I could see the paint peeling off the leading edge. He must have been no more than, it's terribly easy to exaggerate, but I reckon thirty yards, and I remember automatically thumping the Spitfire into the most brutal turn and thinking I'm going to be killed, so what, make it clean if you can, and then I thought, well sod it because I can out-turn him.

I knew he was on the limit and all the time I kept the Spit on the limit and you knew it was on the limit because, dear aeroplane that it was, before it stalled, in a high speed stall, it would judder, the Spit would judder. Now if you were good you could hold it on that judder, lots of power, stick right back, hard over, and the 109 couldn't stay with you. I remember seeing, I'm pretty certain that I didn't imagine it, but they had slats all the way along the leading edge to ease off. They had quite a vicious stall, and they used to come out and I thought, 'You're on the limit mate,' and if I keep going like this I'm going to be a very difficult target. And eventually that's what I did and I got back, in K, that aeroplane.

In fact, I think I might have had two that day because I shot at a Dornier, a jolly good burst it was too, and when I got back on the ground I didn't remember a thing. I remembered the Heinkel and then the intelligence officer said to me, 'Didn't you mention something about a Dornier?' I said, 'Oh yes, didn't I put that down?' So he said put it on the list and I said, 'No I can't be bothered.'

Air Commodore Peter
Brothers CBE DSO DFC.

Group Captain Billy
Drake DSO DFC*
DFC (USA).

Above: Wing Commander Peter Ayerst DFC.

Below: Wing Commander John Freeborn DFC*.

Above: Group Captain Allan Wright DFC* AFC.

Below: Flight Lieutenant Terry Clark DFM AE.

Above: Wing Commander Terence Kane.

Below: Air Commodore John Ellacombe CB DFC*.

Above: Wing Commander Bob Foster DFC.

Below: Squadron Leader Geoffrey Wellum DFC.

Left: Squadron Leader John Gard'ner.

Below: Flight Lieutenant Hazel Gregory.

Squadron Leader
Tony Pickering.

Warrant Officer David Denchfield.

Above: Squadron Leader Keith Lawrence DFC.

Below: Flight Lieutenant William Walker AE.

It never worried me, what did it matter. If Bill got eight, Jim got two and Geoff Wellum got one, what mattered is we stopped them. That's the big thing, not individual victories. I couldn't be bothered with it.

It's almost impossible to describe [a dogfight]. It's just a mass of aeroplanes coming and going in all directions, very close to you, you can hear their engines and then you try and chase somebody. The thrill of having a good burst at him and knowing you've hit him. You haven't got time to claim him because you break away because there's somebody about to have a go at you. And this is coming back to what I said at the beginning. Never stay still for more than twenty seconds. Don't get carried away if you think you've got somebody. If you tickle him up a bit at least you've put him off, but if you follow him down, nine times out of ten he would have a number two and they'd have a go at you. So it was just total confusion.

Warm work. I remember thinking clearly one day what am I doing in this lot? This is bloody dangerous. But you react differently in every combat really. If it's a general mix-up you were far too busy shooting and avoiding being shot at.

In a mass like that you get split up so leadership doesn't really come into it. Leadership takes you into the battle but once you're there and you get split up it's a free-for-all and sometimes you think Good God what's going on, is this twentieth century civilisation? You see aircraft on fire, aircraft breaking up, people baling out, sometimes maybe half a dozen at a time, people baling out and their parachutes don't open. They stream with the shroud lines twisted and therefore they roman candle straight down and the ground's 20,000 feet, you're thinking poor chap. What's all this about?

I remember, and this is another thing, I can see him now, a German aircrew man had baled out of his Heinkel 111 too early. It was going down and his parachute got caught up round the tailplane and he went plummeting down streaming out the back like a rag doll, you know, alive, waiting until the ground got in the way. And I remember quite clearly thinking, Great God, what are you doing allowing this to go on, this is crazy, and then there would be a bit of tracer over your head so you stopped doing that and hammered around to try to see who was shooting at you. Once you got in there you were on your own.

Geoffrey's memory of a 'typical' day during the battle has many similarities to other. pilots.

Normally you were up at dawn, you were at readiness. You were scrambled to go into quite a large number of enemy aircraft. You were fighting in the skies over Kent and Sussex. You probably didn't have time for breakfast. Sometimes it was brought round to dispersal, other times, after say a trip, you'd be put to fifteen minutes available and you could get in a transport and go off to the mess and get yourself lunch and then back and I think probably... people say five or six times a day, well I don't know about that; I think a more realistic number is three. I mean by the time you'd got airborne that was five or six hours in the air, pretty hectic combat, by the time the aeroplane had got back on the ground, been rearmed, refuelled, checked over, this five or six business I think is a lot of media hype on that. I have done four but I think three trips is probably more accurate, and two of the big combats, one in the morning and one in the afternoon because the Germans had to refuel, rearm, in between that you'd probably do a convoy escort if there was one going up the east coast or something like that, but that was a more normal day I think, but certainly you were down at dispersal from early dawn until dusk.

Luckily, if things had quietened down ops used to send us back to thirty minutes which meant we could go back to the mess, have a cup of tea or something and a sit down in comfort, but that happened day after day after day.

It was total resignation. Let's go. In fact, the first thing to do when you got to dispersal was to get in the cockpit and take a whiff of oxygen which helped tremendously. It had to be done, it became a routine, it had to be done. You didn't know if you were going to come back or not so you just accepted it. Total resignation. If you've got to go, you've got to go. We had armchairs and chairs that collapsed into beds and the scene at readiness was everybody was reclining on them, some smoking, some reading, some fidgeting, and the odd chap would get up, walk to the door, look up at the sky and there was this feeling 'Come on, let's get on with it', but generally speaking it was one of just sitting and waiting. Not a great deal of conversation, a little bit here and there but all your mates round you, all in the same boat, all paddling the same canoe, all waiting to be hurled off into the great blue yonder, and there it was. The telephone orderly sitting at his table with the phone that went straight to the ops room and it would ring and if it wasn't a scramble it was that the NAAFI van's going to be late because it's got a flat battery, 'Oh sod them!' But there it was, it wasn't an awful lot, it was just an atmosphere of waiting and a little bit of let's get on with it. If we've got to go then let's go.

Everybody would look round at the telephone orderly and if it wasn't a scramble then there would be a collective sigh, that sort of thing but if it was a scramble then all he did was 'Scramble Base 12' and we were out of that door, 'Out of the way...quickly!' and outside you'd hear the flight sergeant,

'Start up! Start up!' and all the way down the track airscrews would turn, and by the time you got to your Spitfire the engine was running, the fitter was looking at you from the cockpit. You had your parachute hanging on the wing so as soon as you'd got it on and were walking round the trailing edge of the wing towards the cockpit he'd get out of the cockpit quickly, lift you onto the wing, almost put you in the damn cockpit, and standing already on the other side was your rigger and he would help put on your straps.

Once the engine had started the rigger unplugged the starter battery and then he would come straight round and stand on the other side to help you put your straps on and quite often they'd pat you on the head and it would be chocks away and they'd stand at the wingtip with expectations on their faces. It was a drill. We had it absolutely weighed off. Certainly my crew and I did. They knew exactly where to put my parachute, exactly what I would do, how long it would take me to hobble round with my parachute on, up onto the wing and he would just be getting out of the cockpit to help me in, straps on, door shut.

The ground crew were part of the squadron. You were their pilot. You had a rapport with them. You gave them a bottle of whisky if you could get it as a Christmas present. You'd have a chat with them about their problems, but they were always there and you'd see them, if they were waiting for someone to come back and they didn't turn up, you could see them looking out to the south, south-east, and then when he didn't turn up they'd go and give a hand somewhere else, all the time aware. Mine, they were always waiting for me.

The moment the aircraft stopped in dispersal they'd jump up on the wings, undo my straps, undo the door for me, help me out, all that sort of thing. You were their pilot and I can see them now, bless their hearts, taxying out standing on your wingtips, helping you round, coming out to meet you as you taxied in. 'Get anything today Sir?' 'No, I sprayed bullets all over Kent.' 'What, again?'

This is a great thing about a fighter squadron in war. It's a very tight community from the ground crew who look after you, a fitter, a rigger, each aeroplane had its own, it was their aeroplane and you were permitted to fly it. You always tried to fly the same aeroplane if you could and after I got 'K' shot up, K9998, I was given 'G' and they took over 'G' from 'K' as 'K' had to go away to be repaired as it had one or two holes in it.

A major aspect of 92 Squadron's day to day routine was the airfield itself. Biggin Hill had been an RAF airfield since the First World War days when air defence squadrons countered the threat from Zeppelins and Gotha bombers. The interwar years saw fighter squadrons in residence, equipped with the classic biplanes of the day, Sopwith Snipe, Gloster Gauntlet, Bristol Bulldog, Armstrong Whitworth Siskin and Hawker Demon, in fact the aircraft that had so captivated Geoffrey Wellum.

[I remember] with great affection. Biggin Hill was in the forefront of the battle. Biggin Hill was a station that was thoroughly devoted to its squadrons, to its ops room, everybody knew everybody else and Biggin had the most wonderful atmosphere of comradeship at the height of the battle and, as I say, we were at the forefront. Biggin was scrambled first.

We had forward landing grounds of course, West Malling, Detling and Manston if we were really pushed, but of course Manston was under constant attack. People have no idea. If you got up and flew, say, towards the south coast it was a bloody silly thing to do. They were all over the place, these black crossed so-and-sos. But Biggin with great affection. It was a fighter station for its fighter squadrons and a community. It had its own ops room of course and they used to be there so you knew your controllers, they knew you individually. I called up for a homing one night. I'd had a bit of a rough time and 'Nice to hear you Geoffrey, come on Geoff, in you come,' and I saw them and I said, 'Coming in to land now', 'Come on in old boy', you know, that sort of thing. Because it was getting dusk and we'd been out late and the wing had been split up and the controller was a bit worried and it was dear old Bill, 'Come right on in Geoff.'

Key to that good relationship with the squadron pilots was Wing Commander Richard 'Dickie' Grice who had won a DFC in the First World War and had witnessed the shooting down of Manfred von Richthofen. His interwar period was dominated by service in the Middle East flying Bristol Fighters and Armstrong Whitworth Atlases. He was promoted to Wing Commander in November 1938, the month he took over command of Biggin Hill, a vital station in Britain's air defence.

It was often Grice's calm voice on the station tannoy or a friendly arm round a shoulder that helped the hundreds of RAF crew and WAAFs maintain their sanity in a sometimes desperate situation.

He came up to me one night when I'd been on the squadron a bit and I hadn't had any leave and we were having a few jugs in the mess because we had a bit of a dance going on and about 10 o'clock one night he came up to me. He was a tall chap and always had a pipe, tapped me on the shoulder and said, 'Geoffrey, how about a week's leave?' 'Oh, thank God for that.'

The adjutant came up and said there's your warrant. He said, 'Get off the station first thing in the morning, have a lovely seven days and then come back to us,' and he did that to one or two people who had, I think they call it combat fatigue now but in those days we called it just getting a bit twitchy, and it did the job. I came back ready to go down to Manston where we went for the winter and starting the sweeps.

We did the first fighter sweep ever from Manston. The Biggin Hill wing leading as always. That was Boulogne. I remember the usual thing. You had a chap up there: 'Well chaps, this is the day we've all been waiting for.' Christ you'd think we were going to bloody Berchtesgaden rather than Boulogne. Its only across there, you can see it.

Dickie Grice had rather a strange end to his time at Biggin. There had been a devastating series of attacks on Biggin Hill at the end of August and into the first week of September. By 4 September these major bombing raids on the airfield had resulted in extensive damage to almost all the airfield buildings. Grice believed that the sole remaining section of one hangar still standing would be too tempting a target for future raids so ordered that the remains should be destroyed. Grice was censured at a court of enquiry for what the Air Ministry believed was an unorthodox decision but then exonerated. By this time he was a Group Captain and after the war was made CO of Manston and subsequently Tengah in Singapore.

Geoffrey almost seemed to live a charmed life during the Battle of Britain, but he knew many pilots who weren't so lucky. They would arrive full of enthusiasm but become another statistic on the losses list.

You have no option. By the time we'd got to Manston we'd got through quite a lot of people. It seemed to ease off a bit towards the beginning of October November. Most of the big fights, big combats, had gone. They'd stopped their bomber offensive. They used to send their 109s over. Chaps were still getting picked off because 109s used to come over very high, drop a bomb any old where and then do a sweep round while you were climbing up to them, so they had a height advantage. But you had no option. You put it behind you, and you didn't think about it. You know you might in a more sombre moment be in the pub having a pint and say 'Cheers mate'. You missed absent friends but you accepted it. You had no option. It would drive you nuts if you did. It was stiff upper lip stuff.

It had to be total acceptance, there's nothing you can do about it so go out in the evenings after we were released and have a few beers in the pub with locals, darts, you got to know them in the end and they knew you and you were their heroes in fact and you got to know them and it took your mind away from an RAF station, from the dispersal point, from Spitfires. OK you were in uniform, but you were in a civilian local pub. We used to go out to all sorts of places when there were one or two ladies around. A place called Hilden Manor I think, but we just used to get off the station basically.

But did Geoffrey ever think that the battle, and perhaps the war, might be lost?

No. Well you never thought for a moment you would lose it. You became aware that you were denying them their aim. I always had great satisfaction if I saw a formation of Dorniers, I remember one evening, jettisoning their bombs. You'd stopped them getting to London or wherever it was they were going, jettisoning their bombs over open countryside.

They weren't particular, these chaps, if they saw a little village and they were getting hammered they would jettison over it, it wouldn't matter; but that I found very satisfactory, that you denied them their aim for the first time. They had not achieved what they set out to do. In fact, in spite of the self-styled intellectuals and visionaries of today, we defeated them, we beat them, and we stopped them doing what they wanted to do.

But that is not what gave Geoffrey most joy during the battle.

Being a member of 92 Fighter Squadron, that's the simple answer to that. A very great privilege to be in the best squadron in Fighter Command, which it was, and a fully qualified combat-ready Spitfire fighter pilot. That was my aim in life. The only snag was that I was at my peak and I'd achieved my aim, and I was a pretty good fighter pilot, although I say it myself, before I had reached the age of 20. After that the graph goes downwards.

Nothing can come up against being a member of 92 Squadron at Biggin Hill during those days of 1940 and 1941, nothing. Nothing will ever replace it, nothing can ever replace it, and you never ever forget or get over it. You never get over it. You ask me these questions and I'm giving you answers but I'm seeing those answers. I'm seeing the aircraft. I'm seeing the blokes. I'm seeing the pub. I'm seeing the sky at dawn. I remember my reactions, 'Oh God here we go again', but nothing will ever replace those days at Biggin Hill in 92 Squadron at the height of the Battle of Britain, in the dark days of the war, nothing will ever replace that in my life. I'm over the top.

Of course, it wasn't just the Spitfire squadrons that helped to win the Battle of Britain. There was also the more numerous Hawker Hurricane.

Well they complemented each other. A Spitfire had a better performance and it was the most delightful aeroplane to fly. It was a pilot's aeroplane. The Spitfire was a thoroughbred, the Hurricane was a thorough jolly good workhorse. It was a better gun platform because it had its guns close together. I got to like the Hurricane. I never flew it operationally but I tested it for Hawker's and I went to an OTU after I'd been taken off ops, that was a

Hurricane OTU in the beginning which converted to Spitfires but if you're asking me which of the two I would prefer to go to war in it was the Spitfire because it was the most delightful aeroplane to fly.

You didn't get in it, you strapped it on, and it was a friendly aeroplane, it wouldn't let you down. It had no nasty habits whatsoever. It didn't drop a wing. I got into a spin in cloud one day trying to be clever and I came out and there was the earth, I thought it shouldn't be there, straight down, and I took corrective action, and a single seater fighter, high powered, it just came out like that, just like that. And I did a lot of stupid things in a Spitfire because I was stupid, precocious I suppose, and it got me out every time, totally stable, beautiful, beautiful aeroplane. My first and only love really.

The Spitfire meant a tremendous amount. The Spitfire was a wonderful aeroplane that took you into battle and, God willing, it brought you back again so it meant something very close to you. You didn't like to fly anybody else's Spitfire. You wanted to fly yours and the ground crews didn't like another pilot flying their aeroplane so that's what it meant to me. It was all part of the team. It was part of the team, the fitter, the rigger, you and the aeroplane. I used to talk to it. When I was in combat, for some reason, I used to shout, yell, all sorts of obscenities, God knows what it did. Black crosses? What are you doing over here? I used to yell at the top of my voice, normally when I was frightened, which was continually.

The smell of the oil and the 100 octane. Each aeroplane had its own smell. A Spitfire smelt different from a Hurricane which smelt different from a Harvard. It had its own smell. It was all part of it. Of course, you didn't realise and you got used to it but yes, it had its own smell, its own character. Each had its own idiosyncrasies, but you got to know it and had it trimmed as you wanted it. You knew how to get the best out of the engine, which never faltered. Thank God for Rolls-Royce.

The Hurricane did not have our performance, but it was ideal for anti-bomber. We had to take on the 109s. Mind you, if we got a bomber, obviously we had a go but generally speaking we tried to keep the 109s away. Whether we really succeeded I don't know because it became just a general mix-up. Sometimes, if we were lucky, the 109s had to go back to base because they were out of fuel.

I remember one evening we caught a squadron of Junkers 88s and I think there were about three RAF squadrons having a go at these 88s and the last I saw of that lot, out of a whole formation, was just three 88s going back over Dungeness towards France, and that was one evening and I think we must have shot down eight or nine, not 92 but they were breaking up all over the place. It was great to watch.

During the winter of 1940, 92 Squadron's task changed. The Luftwaffe was coming over at night, and Spitfires were not great night fighters, so Fighter Command went on the offensive. The plan was to wrestle air superiority from the Luftwaffe, engage the enemy, entice them up to fight, and prevent squadrons from being withdrawn to reinforce German forces building up ready for an attack on Russia.

Initially the RAF tried sending pairs of fighters at low-level to shoot up any target of opportunity on the ground. These were called 'Rhubarbs'. When this had little effect, they tried larger sweeps, called 'Rodeos', involving more aircraft but at high level. But these had no real effect either. German fighters just ignored them. So something else was needed and the answer seemed to be the 'Circus', a large number of fighters escorting a small bomber force. The bombers were the bait and the fighters waited to pounce.

Well we should have learned, but Goering told the Germans to keep close into the bombers. I think that was wrong. The fighters should be free to roam and shoot down whatever got in the way. Not be confined to a bomber where you could be easy pickings. We didn't learn from that. We had a close escort that did not leave the bombers.

The Biggin Wing was often doing that because we were bloody good at it, but we lost a lot of blokes. You had an escort cover just above us and then a top cover. We had about three wings of Spitfires to escort twelve bombers and sometimes only eight and that's an awful lot of effort, so presumably we felt we were taking the war to them but that's probably the only benefit there was.

By this time, 92 Squadron had become part of what was called the Biggin Hill Wing. Up to six Spitfire squadrons operating from Biggin or its satellite airfields could be deployed on sweeps across the channel. But this change in tactics seemingly had very little effect on 92 Squadron.

We kept very much to ourselves and other squadrons were rotated but we stuck it so we rather felt one above them and Biggin belonged to us. It's jolly kind of us to allow you to come and use the other dispersal. We must have been an arrogant lot of chaps but that's the way it was.

The Wing also received a new Wing Leader in the form of Adolph 'Sailor' Malan, the older, highly-successful South African CO of 74 Squadron during the Battle of Britain. He was a strict disciplinarian.

Dour South African. A very good leader, solid as an oak. Lacking in a sense of humour but nevertheless he knew his way around and he led the

Biggin Wing very well. He'd get us into the right position if ever we came up. 'They're 109s, lads, not Hurricanes, they're 109s. Stay with me, I'll tell you when to break. Go in, a quick, quick burst and then away.'

The war took it out of him, there's no doubt about that. In fact I think the war, those days of the war, I'm talking now of '40 to '42, particularly the Battle of Britain in 1940, took far more out of us than anyone ever realised. Sailor went back to South Africa and died very shortly after.

Two of my COs became alcoholics. I don't know. With me it's something, I can't ever forget the detail. Sometimes it depresses me a bit, but I don't know really. Everybody's different, but I know, in spite of what the people who came out of the caves in the Welsh hills having done nothing in the war, after the war I know that those first years in a fighter squadron in those days took far more out of me than I ever thought. I reached my peak before I was 20 and thereafter whether I was ever the same quality of fighter pilot on my second tour as I was with my tour with 92 I've got a certain number of doubts.

Geoffrey saw nothing memorable in his first 'Circus'.

We were at Manston. We were briefed as if we were going to Berchtesgaden but in fact all we were doing was escorting six Blenheims to Boulogne, to the docks. I think we were escort cover, we may have been close escort, I can't remember, and the Blenheims went in, they went in at 8,000 feet. We stuck with them. They bombed, a bit of flak, we turned round, and came out again. I think it only took about an hour. We rendezvoused over North Foreland, picked up the Blenheims, stayed with them and that was it. Didn't see a German fighter anywhere near us.

With 92 I must have done about seventy or eighty and then I did a lot more when I went to 65 Squadron but probably in the end about 100, something just over.

We got a bit wiser by the time we were doing sweeps. We were tied to the bombers. You had a close escort, an escort cover and a top cover. Now the close escort were tied to the bombers and if a 109 got through, well we lost a lot of bloody good blokes there. Whether it was worth it or not I don't know. I suppose it must have been because at least we were taking the war over to the Germans and eventually they shifted a lot of their fighter squadrons over to the eastern front ready for the Russian campaign. I can remember, I can't remember who it was, but the day that they invaded Russia it was a briefing or something and I think the station commander came in and it was Russia had been invaded and he said, 'Gentlemen, we have won the war.'

In February 1942 Geoffrey's long period at 92 Squadron came to an end.

I'd been operational since June – about sixteen months. I felt very upset, I got very emotional at leaving the squadron. During my short time on the earth at that time I'd always had an awareness of the passing of time. When I left home to go to boarding school I realised that infant days were behind me. I had reached a milestone and I was going away to boarding school.

Similarly, when I left school to join the Air Force I realised it was another big milestone in my life, and when I left 92 Squadron I was physically sick. I was acutely aware that a very important era in my life had come to an end. I'd survived, God knows why, I had survived and nothing could ever be the same again, and I realised that I had reached a peak in my life at the age of just twenty – twenty years and one month – and I thought this is a silly time to reach a peak in my life because the graph, the curve in the graph, is going to go down from here on, and it did.

I was promoted and got a flight in 65 Squadron, with Tony Bartley an old friend of mine, and again we were a bloody good squadron but whether I was ever the quality of fighter pilot (I don't know). I talked to Tony about this and he didn't think he was either. We were doing sweeps two or three times a day, getting knocked hell out of by the 190s but we were doing quite long penetrations, very short of fuel and it was taken for granted that we had to land forward and one of them was across the North Sea to Flushing. Now, there was no land and you only wanted a bit of flak to hit the wrong bit and half way back home everything went off the clock and temperatures and the pressures and there was the sea and it's a cruel place the sea. It's such a cruel place to endure days in, be it in a dinghy or strapped in the cockpit of a Spitfire that wouldn't ditch anyway. You had to bale out if you were capable of it.

In April 1942, while flying as a flight commander with 65 Squadron, Geoffrey flew on what would be one of his hardest days of combat so far.

Ah yes, we were escorting Bostons. I think I remember we were escorting Bostons to Lille which is a long way and we were close escort and the Bostons were bombing from a relatively low height. After bombing they were turning left which meant that my squadron out of the wing that was giving the close escort was on the outside of the turn. I didn't like it one little bit and it so happened that a squadron of 190s did just what I thought they would do and they cut us off. I could see now the rest of the circus turning for home, and there were we turning the other way into the attacking 190s.

I blame myself because two of my section got shot down just like that. If I'd have seen those 190s ten seconds earlier I could have probably done something about it but my number two was out of position. He was a lovely bloke and I yelled to him on the RT. I can't remember whether I pressed the transmit button, and there was this 190 shooting hell out of him and I looked behind and there was one doing it to me and the next thing I knew I was fighting this chap behind me. Dear old Freddie blew up.

It has haunted me to this day. If I'd done my real job as a leader, I would have seen those 190s just a few seconds earlier. It's all very well now keeping position and all the rest of it, but I still blame myself to a large degree because that was a pretty bad bit of leadership I reckon. I should have seen them earlier but there we are, that's another thing that's very much in my mind. Two other blokes collided, two Rhodesians we had with us, because all hell was let loose.

Spits were breaking into them and breaking out and we lost four out of the squadron that day. I had this 190 that was onto me, shot me up well and truly, and I can remember, how I got there I don't know, literally without overdramatising it too much we had to fight our way out, and eventually I did a roll off the top because that would point me back in the way I going towards the French coast which I could see and in the distance were the white cliffs. I can remember thinking that's my home and I left the throttle right up to the gate, plus 18, dropped the nose and I went like the clappers.

The next thing I really knew was that I was over England. Don't ask me how I got there, it's a blank, a total blank, because I was pouring with perspiration, I was very frightened, I thought I was going to be bumped off and I thought of girlfriends, Mum and Dad, and I found myself over Hawkinge and I thought I know I've been shot up, I'm going in there and I went in there, taxied up to where I thought I ought to, got out and rested on the grass, I don't know for how long.

Then I heard a voice say 'You alright?' and it was an airman so I said 'Yeah, a bit tired, but get me some fuel and is there an engineering officer about?' and he said, 'Well I think you should have a look at this, Sir,' and I said, 'No, I don't want to look.' The 190 had hit me in the tailplane and I suppose there was a 20mm cannon hole there, I don't know, not exaggerating, nine inches across. I just wanted to check that I had full control as I wasn't going to push it further and eventually an engineering chap came along and he said, 'Yes, it's alright but don't over-stress it,' and I took it back to our base at a place called Great Sandford which was a satellite of Debden.

Our squadron was at the satellite and there were two other squadrons at Debden. I went back there and that was it. They gave me a new aeroplane and that afternoon we went out again which I didn't like. That shook me more than I think it would have done in my early days in 92.

These cross-channel sweeps were a completely different way of waging war as far as Geoffrey was concerned.

We didn't know what to think. The great thing in our mind was at least we were flying over there as opposed to them flying over here. In other words, we shoved them back across the channel. That was how I felt. Whether that was a sensible thing I don't know. Basically, that was how I felt. Mind you there were times when our penetrations were a bit deeper, Lille, Lens, Bethune, we thought Christ it's a long way from home. If you get shot down there, you haven't got a hope. You're a prisoner at best.

[I remember] turning around from Lens where we saw a Stirling shot down; we took Stirlings on raids after the Blenheims and it was a long drawn out thing. He got hit in the port outer and it caught fire and it was horrible, but I remember turning around and covering him and you couldn't see the cliffs. You could just make out the French coast and you thought, God, it's a long way back.

Many was the time I've landed, we used to call it landing forward, to either Lympne, Hawkinge or Manston. Many's the time I've lobbed in there with five gallons and that's stretching it and I'm sure we lost one or two in the channel running out of fuel. You couldn't ditch a Spitfire. It would go under like a torpedo. It was nose heavy. It wouldn't ditch. But many's the time I've landed there with five gallons.

The distance was a danger particularly if you got involved with some 109s over Lille or somewhere. Lille's a bloody long way and if you got involved with them there using boost override plus twelve or sixteen pounds of boost, full throttle, fine pitch, chucking it around and end up facing the wrong way it's not very nice because you've got to come back. In 1942, with 65 Squadron, we had Spitfire Vbs, and good as it was it was outflown by the 190 and they were coming into service and the 190 was a very, very good and tough antagonist. Had terrific roll rate and a good performance.

In July 1942 Geoffrey was tasked with leading a flight of eight Spitfires off the aircraft carrier HMS Furious *to reinforce the air contingent on the beleaguered island of Malta in the Mediterranean. The seemingly daunting task of taking off his Spitfire from a carrier deck held no fears.*

I had no trouble whatsoever. You had to pay attention. You didn't want to get a swing on or anything like that but generally speaking you revved up on the brakes to as much throttle as possible and the moment she started to edge forward, overriding the brakes with the stick back in your tummy to keep the tail on the ground.

The moment she did that you bashed it through the gate and the ship was steaming at 32 knots so basically with what little wind there was, which was about 10 to 15 knots, you had 45 knots over the deck and the moment you let the brakes off you had feel and I thought this was a piece of cake. All you had to do was keep it straight, hope the fan in front keeps turning round because if it doesn't you're going to splash over the end and that was fine. No great problems taking off from a carrier, at least I didn't find it.

But the task of preparing the aircraft for the flight was something completely different.

Malta was a hot spot, we knew we were going there, and we were confined to the ship for about a week because they had to get special airscrews for us. We didn't have enough revs to get off the deck with the airscrews they'd fitted to the Spits they had waiting for us, they were tropical. Added to that we had to take off with ninety-gallon overload tanks to get us to Malta and we had to wait for hydromatic airscrews to come because we had not been able to get them. Hydromatic airscrews came with 3,000 revs on take-off, the ordinary de Havilland airscrew that we had on the Spitfire had 2,650 maximum. It wasn't power you wanted it was revs, so they gave us these hydromatic airscrews, untried, but that was fine.

It was a typical British botch-up really. One sort of know-all said, 'So why don't you put down twenty-five degrees of flap to get you off the deck, and somebody said, 'Excuse me Sir but in a Spitfire the flaps are either fully down or fully up so you can't get twenty-five degrees,' so some other bright spark said, 'Why don't we get a chippie to make a little wedge of wood at twenty-five degrees?' Right so then what do you do? 'Well you let your flaps fall down and then you get the junior rating on the ship who doesn't mind losing his fingers to hold these wedges and then let the flaps up and they won't come fully up, just 25 degrees,' and that's what we did. It was typical, only the British could have done this sort of thing, so when you got airborne you had to let the flaps down so that your wedges of wood dropped into the sea and then let the flaps up again.

I went down the day before take-off to look at my Spitfire which I had been allocated, 465 it was, and there was a little airman taking all the ammunition out and I said, 'Corporal, what's going on here?' 'Well Sir,' he said, 'It's a question of weight. We've got to reduce the weight to get you off the deck.' Fair enough, I could accept that, and then another one came up with packets of cigarettes. All our ammunition trays were full of cigarettes, short of cigarettes they were in Malta.

We flew all the way through the Mediterranean, past Pantelleria, where they had 109s, and we didn't have a bullet between us, not one. If we had been attacked from Sicily or somewhere like that there was nothing we could have done about it and that's how we got my squadron of Spitfires to Malta, not a bullet between us and with our little wedges of wood. It's unbelievable. Can you imagine that happening today with all this computer business and goodness knows what? But, nevertheless, we did it.

Geoffrey had very vivid memories of the convoy in which HMS Furious *was a major part.*

Very moving. The first attack on the convoy happened just after we left but there were five carriers there, which was all the Navy had, thirty-two destroyers was it and some cruisers, and I must say that the Navy were most professional. I found it very moving.

It impresses me, the sea and the colours. Our personal escort was the cruiser *Manchester* which was later sunk. She was sunk off the Sicilian narrows, but she was a beautiful Town-class cruiser, raked funnels; looked absolutely beautiful. We were coming across Biscay and dear old *Furious* was steady as a rock, but *Manchester* was sticking her nose into the sea, throwing the spray right back to her B turret. It was a wonderful, wonderful sight. There were these graceful ships and alongside us was the tanker *Ohio* of fame, that had the fuel on, and the *Melbourne Star* which finally got through to Malta. Only four of them did and the fifth was the *Ohio* to which a couple of destroyers lashed themselves either side and motored her at two knots for the last few miles and got her into Grand Harbour with her cargo intact and that saved us.

I got to Malta and a chap said, 'Sorry about this chaps.' We'd done this long trip at first light, all down here, and four o'clock in the morning (we had to) take off to bring the convoy through the Sicilian narrows and at six o'clock the next morning I was right over the Sicilian narrows with my overload tanks on, and with bullets this time, escorting the convoy which was being bombed hell out of. I think it was 87s had a go at it and E-boats and things like that. There wasn't an awful lot we could do.

We stopped the high-level stuff getting them but I didn't see a Junkers 87 at all. But there were these wonderful ships of the navy, thirty knots plus, very, very moving, and after about two and a half hours I was pouring with perspiration. I'd lost my number two, where he'd gone, I don't know, and I found myself stooging around the unknown over the Sicilian narrows and I thought, 'This is bloody silly,' and so I headed off back to Malta. I saw a cruiser below, she was zigzagging, and one or two merchant ships, and

I went back to Malta to find the rest of the boys there. Whether we achieved anything I don't know. We might have prevented people from getting there, but at least we did what we were asked to do. The next morning the ships came in, *Melbourne Star*, *Brisbane Star*, *Port Chalmers*, *Rochester Castle*, and then the next day *Ohio* got in.

[We were] cheering and waving things and all the rest of it, and in fact we had some Beaufighters on Malta that did a standing patrol throughout the night over the Grand Harbour because they wanted to unload the ships as quickly as possible to save them from being bombed and all the cargos lost, so the whole of Grand Harbour was floodlit and they unloaded these ships.

After the convoy got in there was a lull in Luftwaffe operations and we used to be at readiness most of the day. We didn't do many standing patrols because of the petrol side of it but each ship had petrol on it, but the tanker *Ohio* was full of it, aviation fuel. I was doing one or two sweeps over Sicily and I got this sort of tremendous pain over my eyes that I'd been having for some time and it was this sinusitis business and they took me into hospital and stuck needles all over me. I was told that I was finished. In a way I was pleased because nothing had ever come up to 92 Squadron but at the same time, I was just 21. I thought, 'Finished, over the hill.'

So the doc told me. He said I wanted a prolonged rest from operational flying. I'd been going, except for a short break, since I joined 92 Squadron, June, July 1940, so it was quite a time putting your neck out really.

I got home and it was all unreal. They looked at me in hospital and sent me home on a month's leave. I got home and there again was my room all waiting for me and something snapped inside. Yeah, and I broke down I suppose, and then the next phase was I thought this was bloody silly behaviour. Mother was there, obviously upset I suppose, but no, it had knocked, those three years had knocked hell out of me and, well it would do anybody. You recover from these things, but I can never ever forget those three years. It's vivid, I can feel it, I can remember it and I can see it, I can see it.

After his recovery from sinusitis and complete exhaustion Geoffrey found a new opening for his flying ability.

I was seconded to Gloster Aircraft Company as a test pilot. I knew my way around in fighters by that time. I could contribute something, and they were civilians of course, but the early Typhoons had a lot of trouble. It used to get elevator flutter because, I am told by the boffins, it was trouble with the internal mass balance. I didn't quite understand what that meant.

As far as I was concerned you used to get elevator flutter and tails used to come off. On a Typhoon the tail unit was bolted onto the back of the monocoque, the fuselage, with a lot of bolts round a big flange, and it used to break there, and if you go to the Typhoon in Hendon and look round that fixture, round that joint, you will see little plates all the way round. Whether that did any good I don't know but I put a Typhoon off test one day and a week later she was on ops from Manston.

The chap came back, he had his wheels and flaps down on the final approach and his tail came off just like that, and I had to be a witness, now why? It must have been the conditions of the flight. Whether he'd been hit I don't know, but tails used to come off and engines weren't terribly reliable. They had a life of sixty hours because they were sleeve valve Sabres. The aeroplane went pretty fast considering it was built like a brick, but it had its problems. In the end, of course, it turned out to be a first-class ground attack aeroplane developed by Roly Beamont.

Geoffrey remained in the Royal Air Force after the war until his retirement in 1960 when he took over the family business. Twenty-five years later, now divorced from his wartime sweetheart Grace and with the business failing, he retired to Cornwall and 'got it out of his system' by writing his memoirs. He put the completed manuscript in a drawer and got on with his life quietly. It was many years later that author James Holland went to talk with Geoffrey about the Battle of Britain. Geoffrey lent him the manuscript, and a short time later, while enjoying a pint in his local, Penguin Books rang and offered him a contract to publish his book. And, as they say, the rest is history. First Light *became a huge bestseller, as befitted perhaps the most honest and hard-hitting memoir of the battle ever written.*

My days revolved around dawns and pre-dawns, first light, going around to dispersal in the pre-dawn in the transport, getting out and seeing just a faint glow of first light and thinking, 'God, another day.'

It seemed an obvious name. It's very clear in my mind. The ghostly images of the Spits at dispersal, the clank of spanners. 'Lofty, got any anti-freeze?' you know, that sort of thing. 'Chiefy?', 'Yes boy', 'We're pissing glycol out of this seam here, look,' and so on.

I can hear it. I can see it. I can feel it. And I can feel that total resignation. Nothing more to be done about it. Here we are, 'If we're gonna go, let's go.'

Squadron Leader John Gard'ner
14 June 1918-6 May 2011

John Gard'ner was born in Dunedin, New Zealand, and had his first experience of flying when aircraft landed near his house.

I think it would have started when I was about 10 or 11 years old and we lived in Dunedin. One day three aeroplanes flew over and they looked exciting so they landed on the mudflats at the end of the road where we lived, the mudflats at Anderson's Bay, I think it might have been, and so my friend and I leapt on our bicycles and charged off down there to see what appeared to be great big aeroplanes. They were like Bristol Fighters and out of these aeroplanes came chaps that looked like gods dressed in white overalls and I thought, 'God, look at these fellows here.' That was it and I thought about those aeroplanes for a long time.

Well shortly after that my mother remarried and we moved from Dunedin up to Nelson and about a year or two later, the time when (Charles) Ulm, Kingsford-Smith and Ulm, were flying round New Zealand in their Fokker three engined job and they came and landed at Nelson. I was one of the first to get out there, and got myself ten shillings, and we went for a ride in this thing around the Nelson area and I thought, 'This is marvellous.'

In about 1937 they started the Civil Reserve of Pilots and I thought this was a good chance to learn to fly so I applied and to my delight I was accepted. I was the first boy in Nelson to be accepted in the Civil Reserve of Pilots and I started towards the end of 1937 in a Gypsy Moth out of the so-called Nelson airfield which actually was a long strip of paddock. I suppose I got maybe two hours, maybe three flights. At that time I was working in the New Zealand Public Works Department, I had left school and then along came advertising for short service commissions in the Royal Air Force. I thought, 'Well this is it. I'm going to have a go at that.' So I applied for the short service commission, and from Nelson I had to fly over to Wellington to be interviewed. I do remember a man, a Squadron Leader Cochran interviewed me, I've always remembered his name. By the time I got over there I was feeling very ill and they told me I had the flu and then said, 'Terribly sorry old boy. Come back when you're better again,' so disappointedly I went back to Nelson.

I think it was six months later I went back again, but that had put me back a bit. Then I passed and over the course of time I was accepted and so right at the end of 1938, twenty I was, we were gathered together in Auckland. Actually I did my first train ride ever from Wellington up to Auckland, never been on the rail like that before, and I must have met up with all the other seventeen when we went on board the ship. I don't remember any of the details about how we got together except we were on that ship, the good ship *Rangitata*. I do know that included amongst us was Colin Gray who became a top ace. I got to Britain and we went to Hatfield.

John went to Number 1 Elementary and Reserve Training School on 23 January 1939.

My first impression of England. I didn't see much of it. In my memory we went straight to Hatfield which was the Elementary Flying Training School and I can't recall much about it but I do remember being in London, somewhere around Piccadilly Circus, and I think I was pretty impressed with Piccadilly Circus. We were staying at Dolphin Square and there were about three of us put up there. Well to me that was a completely new sort of surroundings because I was a bit of a country boy. We lived out in the country and to be in a city surrounded by buildings, I mean to go to a place like Wellington from where I lived in Nelson, meant going to the big time, so you can just picture what it was. It was huge and it was most unusual for me.

I remember this. The war broke out as far as I was concerned, I recall being called into the officers' mess by our instructor, his name was 'Flossie' Farmer, he was a flight lieutenant. He'd obviously seen some action because he had a DFC so he was very impressive. He was sitting on the edge of the billiard table and swinging his legs and we sort of, acting pilot officers on probation, were asked to gather round him and he was sitting there swinging his legs backwards and forwards and then he said solemnly, 'Gentlemen, we are at war,' and I don't know what the reaction was, I don't know whether we jumped up and down with excitement or what.

I joined up to fly to see the world. I had no idea there was going to be a war. I suppose I pleaded ignorance about it but I recall, prior to working for the government, I had another friend and we had a boat on the Nelson harbour. There were rusting ships in the harbour and I recall us seriously discussing the fact that the rusting ship over there, the Japanese are going to be buying it and they are going to turn it into guns and one day that stuff is going to be shot back at us. I suppose I was a raw youth of 15 or 16 years old.

When war actually came I had no feelings of fear or anything like that. It was just something there was. I'd been trained to fly. I was doing what I wanted to do. My only thoughts were that I was being trained on Airspeed Oxfords and chaps like Colin Gray were on single-engined Harts and Hinds so we were a little bit envious. I was very envious of him because it indicated to me that I was going to go to a twin engined aircraft, a bigger aircraft, in other words a bomber, whereas Colin was going into the fighter world. It didn't upset me but I just felt a little disappointed.

141 Squadron had been originally formed on 1 January 1918 but had been disbanded within two years. It was reformed on 4 October 1939, nineteen days before John was posted to the squadron at Grangemouth in Stirlingshire, Scotland.

I was posted to 141 when it had no aircraft whatsoever. We arrived up there and there was just a gathering of the ground crews and the new fresh young pilots. It was at a little grass strip called Grangemouth which belonged to Scottish Airways and somehow or other the air force commandeered some Anson aircraft and we continued flying, keeping our flying training going on twin engines. Gradually the Ansons were used then to fly south. Once the more experienced pilots came along we started to be flown south to pick up aircraft, and the first ones we picked up were Blenheims, as far as I was concerned, fighter Blenheims. The other people got Gladiators. Again we were envious, but I got the Blenheims and we started our training. We were given an instructor, an experienced officer who got into the left-hand side of the cockpit. We new people got in and we went through all the knobs and tits and explained what it was all about, then we took off. He showed us round, how to get your undercart up and that sort of stuff, and the usual stuff on how to land the thing. You got back down on to the ground after a bit of a demonstration of what the Blenheim would do. Then he said 'Move over,' and so he got out of the aeroplane, we moved over and we took off. That was my conversion onto a Blenheim fighter.

My first flight by myself was rather terrifying in the sense that we started night flying almost immediately and there you flew by yourself, you didn't take your navigator with you. You simply experienced the idea of taking off into what I say was Stygian blackness. I recall vividly the first time I took off I had my eyes glued onto the artificial horizon to make sure I stayed going up and put full power until I thought I was well clear of the ground and began to throttle back and put the wheels up. After that it was alright but it was the first moment which was so terrifying in the dark. From then on we did patrols. We patrolled the Firth of Forth and I recall not seeing anything. We never had anything to go and chase but we were up there on patrols. That didn't last very long because the powers that be decided that the squadron should convert to the Boulton Paul Defiant.

I don't really remember giving it a thought that I would be going to fight the war in the Blenheim. It was biggest aeroplane I'd flown. There was a lot of power in it. I think I felt confident about the aeroplane. I found it easy to take off and land and manoeuvre it around and fly on one engine, but thinking I would actually go into war with it and be shot at, or try to shoot someone with it, it didn't seem to enter my head.

During the winter of 1939-40 John settled into the daily squadron routine. He also found a social life he wasn't expecting.

The winter of 1940 we were stationed at Grangemouth. We were fogged in day after day and I learned to ice skate. We had a number of Canadian officers in the squadron and they took us all out to the Falkirk ice rink and I learned to ice skate there; I learned to dance there as well. We learned to play ice hockey, and we would go along there, play darts and meet the local girls on the ice rink.

I didn't go to the pubs. I was never a pub bloke, but I used to enjoy going down to the ice rink there and just skating. They were still playing ice hockey tournaments, mainly Canadians, so we saw some good matches going on there and I was able to get a seat in the director's box simply because I was friendly with the director's daughter. When we went and did the ice skating we'd go as a group but then when I became friendly with this young lady and I was able to go to the ice rink and sit in the director's box and watch the ice hockey, I was the only one that did that. Actually I got into a fight with her boyfriend. I can remember a fist coming towards me and I couldn't ride it off and he broke a tooth. He was a bit drunk and he apologised for striking me but after all I was escorting his girlfriend, at the ice rink, and he thought I was after taking her affectations away from him. But I thought it was jolly good, I had the opportunity of getting the best seat, watching all these matches and being up there in the director's box.

My recollection is that there was a lot of fog there. When it came to the actual flying there were no aids for flying at all in the bad weather so we just didn't fly. The airfield layout for night flying was a row of paraffin flares along the runway with a big one at the end. I think it was at the landing end, the big one, and the duty officer's duties were to go out there with a flat truck with these flares on it, go out onto this big grass paddock which is what the airfield was, put a finger in the air and go around to feel which way the wind was blowing. He would start walking out, pacing out so far and dropping a flare and that was what we did our night flying with at Grangemouth. It was very primitive.

When we were flying the Blenheims round the Firth of Forth, we were up on patrol. They had decided we were operational. My recollection is there always seemed to be moonlight. You could see the Firth of Forth and the bridge quite clearly so it seemed to me if the Germans were coming over they could see their targets just as well as we could. During my time there I don't recall anybody in the squadron being told to be vectored, you just went up and you were literally looking. There was no ground control other than when you took off you reported you were airborne and you went onto a frequency that told you where you were going to patrol and that was that.

I did have a bit of a problem with a Blenheim. I can't recall exactly why I did it but I do remember the very low cloud and whether I got into a panic situation or decided I was clever enough – I decided I would land it in a big field. I landed safely enough but the field wasn't quite long enough and I went through a few trees and I think the aircraft was rather bent at the end of it. The wheels weren't up or anything but it was slightly bent and my radio operator seemed to be stuck in there so I thought if this thing catches fire he's going to be in difficulty. I rushed back to him and helped him get out of the aeroplane and we ran away from it. It might have been more damaged than I thought and it was, I suppose, a blot in my copybook. Rather than fly back through the cloud I think I must have elected to land the thing so I could see the ground. An experience.

I do recall when we converted to the Defiants being up there at night and flying around and being caught in the searchlights. I'm aware that at one time I got into crossed searchlights, and you very quickly lose your sense of attitude trying to avoid them. I was told that one time they saw a Defiant come roaring down the searchlight and they thought he was going to go into the ground. I apparently got into a searchlight and, trying to avoid it, without realising it, found I was going down it, but I was lucky enough to realise that I was doing that and pulled out of it. The duty officer at the time was, I remember his name, Ian MacDougall, and he went on to be an air commodore, but he was the duty officer and he saw all this.

141 Squadron became the second squadron to receive Defiants after 264 which brought the aircraft into service at Martlesham Heath.

We were told, after we'd been made operational on the Blenheims, we were going to get the Defiant. It was a single engined aeroplane. It was a brand new aircraft for us and we just thought that this was marvellous, a step forward. It was all beautiful, shiny, new and with a huge gun turret with those massive-looking guns sticking out. When they first started arriving we had to be converted from the twin engined, which I'd always been trained on, to the single engined aircraft. To do that we had a couple of Harvards, so we flew the Harvard to get back to single engines and then an old Fairey Battle came along and with that we did circuits and bumps. My recollection is that you took the thing off, you were told not to bother to bring your wheels up, as you had to wind them up as I recall in the early ones, just to fly around and land it; in other words, to make sure you could take a single engined aeroplane off, make a circuit and come in and land. After that we got straight into the Defiants and there you were, a pilot in a brand new aeroplane, and my thoughts were, this is magnificent, but giving no real thought to the fact that we didn't have guns to fire forward and that we had the chap in the back in the turret.

I had flown nothing else until much later on when I got the opportunity of cadging a ride in a Spitfire. I've flown the Spitfire a couple of times and I've flown the Hurricane a few times too but these were all in the quiet periods so I had nothing to compare it with. To me it seemed to have lots of power, but when you hear the aces, Colin Gray when he wrote his book, he had no thought at all about the Defiant except that it was a useless aeroplane, under-powered and all this sort of stuff compared to him flying around in his Hurricane I suppose. I can't say that I had any impressions, as I had nothing to compare it with.

Unlike the other two frontline fighters, the Defiant was not cramped in the slightest for the pilot, but for the gunner it was a different story.

The gunner came in to the aeroplane quite a different way, through the side of the aeroplane beside of where the gun was, so once you were in the aeroplane there was no physical connection at all. He was a long way behind you. But the complications – I didn't realise until fairly recently how complicated it was for that air gunner to get into his turret and do all the things he had to do to finally get his guns loaded. The switches and things, each gun had its own box of shells and each one was individually put in, and finally with the right taps and switches he was able to make the gun live. All the time we were getting in and all we had to do was get strapped in. That was all done at a leisurely pace because there was no scrambling, so you got in, you got into the parachute, then you put on your other stuff, and then you leisurely did your check and you're ready to go. The chap in the back is going through all the stuff there. He was very cramped and he had this sort of, he looked a bit like a beetle, with his parachute and stuff all strapped onto him.

The communication was different. Sometimes you had a very good communication, all by wire from front to back. It was in the early days, it seems, that in the actual battle, the time that we were caught out was when the communication was virtually nil. Each lot of equipment got superseded by something else so it got better and better and when we were over Glasgow chasing that Junkers we were talking quite happily to each other.

At night the pilots had their planned mode of attack.

If you were lucky enough you came in from the rear and underneath and you hoped that the rear gunner didn't spot you.

But during daylight there was a strange plan to attack from alongside the intended target.

The initial idea was that you would fly alongside and you'd actually have several aeroplanes there. You'd have two or three of them all in different positions all being able to attack from the side. That would have been the ideal situation and if your target was not able to fire back at you, or you could knock out their gun turrets immediately, it would create the perfect target. I'm not sure how 264 Squadron actually made their attacks. We were never told, I was never told, how to go about attacking anything that we saw. We weren't in action long enough to have done anything in the way we might have been told how to do it.

In early July 141 Squadron was sent down south in a rush.

We were going on to a brand new aeroplane, but we had no idea. We knew there was another squadron down in the south. We had no idea how that squadron was getting on and I think on the day we were told we were operational and were going south to replace the other squadron I don't recall being told or warned that we were going to be replacing a squadron that had been battered about. We just took off and I know now that there is a history of the move of 141 Squadron from Ayr down to this little airstrip at West Malling, a satellite piece of ground near Biggin Hill, just with one squadron on it. It was just a grass field, and at one end of the field, in my memory, there was a white building which became our squadron headquarters. When we got down there we finally got told we were operational and we'd fly the aeroplanes out. They'd go down to Hawkinge or Manston and in the evening they'd be flown back again if you hadn't been lost.

The other squadron, our sister squadron, 264, did extraordinarily well. I learned that later of course. The first week to ten days they had great success because the enemy thought they looked like Hurricanes and were making their usual sort of attack on a Hurricane. They soon realised that this was a different thing and they got to work on 264 and as a result of 264 being so battered we came down to replace them. There was some sort of debate at high level as to whether 141 should be put into the line or not. In the end, whoever made the decision won out. I don't know whether it was a decision made as high as Churchill and old Stuffy Dowding, but what we heard was that it was put into the line with some reluctance at some high level.

As a young pilot officer I don't recall that we were going 'gosh, when we get down there we're going to relish it and have success.' In the event we know what happened. I think I was on my third patrol. Previous patrols the squadron went on were quite ineffective, nothing happened.

During their short time with the Defiants the squadron had managed to develop a form of rudimentary defensive tactics.

If we were going to be attacked we were to go into a circle, and I recall that, when going back to our training in Scotland, it was the only tactics we were asked to do. If you were going out on patrol you'd fly in these vic formations of three, your leader would tell you to go into line astern and from line astern he would go off, depending on what he wanted to do, and go into a circle. I remember being tail Charlie, and in any of our training there the greatest difficulty was to keep into the circle as you were pulling harder and harder G to maintain it. To be quite frank about the whole thing I don't recall ever going anywhere, and having the air gunner fire the guns, so when it came to the actual battle which I was involved in, when I realised I was being hit, I described it as a thumping noise on the aircraft, but thinking back it could well have been the air gunner firing off a burst before he was obviously hit.

John's third patrol was in response to reported enemy activity near a Channel convoy. It was a bright clear afternoon as the Defiant formation crossed the Kent coast. John was flying Defiant L7016. His gunner was Dudley Slatter, a newly-commissioned pilot officer who had been in the RAF since 1935.

On 19 July we were ordered on patrol, there were twelve aircraft. In the event three of them, in the run ups, found there was something wrong with the engines and the answer was that only nine got airborne. Somehow we were organised into the vics of three. I do know that the intercom was poor between the pilot and the air gunner and as far as hearing anything being ordered by your squadron leader everything was done, more or less, by hand signals. The radio communication was almost non-existent. It was a simple patrol in the area where the convoys were coming through. We were in the middle of the shortest part of the crossing, the straits of Dover, where the convoys had to gather together and that's where the Germans attacked.

Literally we were going happily along and suddenly thump, thump thump and I saw tracers coming through. I have recollection of tracers coming under my armpits and going out through the front of the aircraft. That was what I thought I heard at the time, this thumping noise, then suddenly there was the smell of oil and cordite, this is why I think the gunner got a burst off, and that was it. Suddenly my engine just stopped, nothing there, and the other thing I felt was 'God, I'm being hit.' I turned over quickly and the rudder bar felt floppy at my feet and I thought, 'Haven't got any rudder here', the engine is dying away and what can I do except go down, so I turned over and went down as steep as I could go. I said, 'How do you feel?' to the back, no response, so down I went and it just seemed to me there I was, suddenly nothing to be seen anywhere. We weren't very high, 8,000 to 10,000 feet if that, and I'd made that in one big swoop. I saw a naval vessel and I thought I'm obviously going to land here so I thought I'll try and land beside this naval vessel. I went by it at quite a speed, I overshot it, and I thought I'll try going round again. It's a miracle to me, I don't know how I kept the aeroplane level because I could still feel I wasn't getting anything out of the rudder. I know from the pictures that I came around in a descending swoop, streaming black smoke out of the back, and that was how it was pictured, and as I got close to the water I thought, 'I'm going into the water and I've got to get out of here quickly.' For some stupid reason I undid my straps thinking I'd got to get out quickly. Well obviously I hit the water and the next thing I knew was I was in black water. I'd obviously been knocked out and the aeroplane had sunk and I was well down in the water but I was able to get myself out of the cockpit. I could see light above and I managed to get myself to the top and then I saw blood all round the place and I realised my face was hanging down and then I blacked out again. Apparently I was picked up by a motor torpedo boat and again I remember coming to and saying to the chaps for some reason or other my flying boots had come off and whether it was my imagination or whether they were actually there I can picture my two flying boots side by side in the water. In those day we wore those beautiful shiny black ones which were changed later on and I said, 'Will you please get my flying boots out?' and nobody took any notice of that so I faded out. I came to next time and I was lying in hospital in Dover. I was told it was Dover hospital and I was swathed in bandages, feeling very sorry for myself. I was there for ten days before they finally discharged me and I was sent off on sick leave where I met up with my friend and we spent the next two months recuperating together.

During our battle I didn't see a thing. I had no idea who hit us. I saw no other aeroplanes. The sky was empty as far as I was concerned. I do remember lying in the hospital, I had a bed right beside the window, and I was able to move over and look up and I saw lots of vapour trails and I said, 'That's where the battle is and here am I here.' I felt a bit unhappy about that but I didn't feel depressed. I can't recall feeling afraid at any time. It must have been excitement and running on adrenalin.

This single engagement effectively ended 141 Squadron's Battle of Britain in less than a week. They had been pounced on by Me109s from III/ JG51. Seven of the Defiants were lost. Just two made it back to base. It also marked the end of the Defiant, the RAF's most recent arrival, as a frontline fighter. The type had been operational for just two months.

I wondered what had happened to the rest of the chaps because I had no idea really that people had been shot down in flames. I know I heard reported that there were flamers going down all around me and that's been taken up as if I'd seen them but in fact I never saw a thing. The sky was empty except for me trying to save myself and my gunner. That's how it was.

I can only think, as he fired off his burst, it may have been done in the actual moment of being hit – a squeeze of the trigger, as it was a thumping noise with a very short-lived thumping. All I can think of was, those were what appeared to be tracers going through out in front and, as I say, some of them appeared to be coming under my armpits, that's my recollection of it. I've always thought he was probably hit in the very first attack as the others were, the flamers were. I was lucky that I wasn't a flamer, but the other three, remember there were four aircraft at the back, tail-end charlies you might say. I can't remember where I was in those four, but three of the back four went down in flames, so I heard, and I didn't.

Dudley Slatter, John's gunner, was lost in the crash. John spent the next three months convalescing in a succession of grand stately homes across the country.

I was pleased to get back. Really I'd had two months with my friend Terry Orchard and we'd stayed in stately homes in Scotland, in west England, northern and southern Ireland, and every time I reported back to wherever it was in London they'd say not wanted, not required as yet, so we'd go down to the Lady Frances Ryder organisation. She and the Miss MacDonald of the Isles, their war effort was to entertain the colonials and we were colonials so we'd go in there and she'd say, or Miss MacDonald would say, 'Where would you like to go this time?' and we would say, 'Well we haven't been down to the west country yet so we'd like to go there.' They would dish out third class rail tickets and off we'd go. Each time we went away they'd say report back in so many weeks, a month or whatever it was, which we duly did, both myself and Terry Orchard. I had no idea when he finally got back to flying but he was still with me when I had to say goodbye to him and I went back and reported up in Scotland.

I often wondered why it took so long for me to get back to flying, and I could only assume I was supposed to have been more concussed or something. It's only as I got older all the scars have disappeared. I nearly lost my eye but there's only a faint thing now. My face was all bashed in and down the back of my head was battered so I can only assume they must have thought I was still unfit, or didn't have the right mentality or something, but when I was finally posted back, I wouldn't say it was with relief, but I was glad to go back and when I did get back I discovered they were still on Defiants. They were back at Ayr and they were doing night fighter duties so I was able to get back and do the odd patrol over Glasgow and that area before we started to re-equip with the Beaufighter.

My air gunner became a chap called Freddie Lammer who was a German who had been recruited into the air force prior to the war; he was a bit older than I was. Freddie became a very well known photographer when he finally retired. He was my best man when I got married.

Alfred Ritter von Lammer was a fascinating man. Born in Austria in 1909 he had grown up with wealthy parents. His father was high up in Austrian railways and his mother, thirty years younger than his father, ran a travel company and a bank. Both were shattered by Hitler's impositions of tax in 1935 and when Austria was annexed in 1938 Freddie decided to stay in London. He dropped the 'Ritter' and the 'von' from his name and became plain Freddie Lammer.

Freddie Lammer came from a well-to-do German aristocracy family. He moved in the same circles as the Von Trapps. He moved in that sort of circle. In fact Freddie Lammer learned to drive a car on Von Trapp's Mercedes Benz. Now I understand his whole family were eradicated and he escaped to Britain. He was a very well educated man and he made application to fight against, as he called it, the Nazi tyranny, and somehow he got through and got a commission in the Royal Air Force. I think he was a flight lieutenant when I joined up with him and I was a flying officer. He went on and after he left me he went on out as a gunner with other squadrons, did quite well, DFC and bar.

We were on patrols and again nobody ever shot anything down in the short period I was back there. I did have a slight engagement with a Junkers 88 but I could not make the aeroplane, this is what did annoy me, I could not make the aeroplane go fast enough to creep up underneath it so that my gunner, Freddie Lammer, could get a shot at this thing. The Junkers, obviously, hadn't seen us and I thought this was going to be it, however suddenly a whacking great big balloon appeared in front of me and I thought I was going to go into that. He must have been flying along the top of the balloons and I had to pull away and of course I lost sight of it. That was my one and only viewing of a Junkers 88 up until that point in my life which was a very disappointing thing. It did infuriate me that the aeroplane would not go fast enough. I had to dive it down, pull it up and, of course, I couldn't get close enough for him to swing the guns around. It may have been my fault as the pilot not being able to get the best out of the aeroplane, I don't know, but that was a big disappointment.

Being a night fighter pilot afforded John the ability to see what was going on from the air night after night.

When I was flying over Glasgow, and various other places I've been flying at night time, there were lots of fires going on, fires everywhere. Over Britain, at night time, particularly in the moonlight, you can see the ground easily. You can see the railway tracks, you can see all this sort of thing. It depends how high you go but in the early days we didn't fly very high, certainly under 20,000 feet, so it was easy to see the ground and any little lakes and things all showed up. You would see over the countryside these beacons, they were coded beacons and they changed the codes regularly, but when we took off at night time, as part of your briefing you took your piece of rice paper with the codes on and they were an identification if you were up at night and you wanted to get back to your base. You looked around and you saw the beacon that had the code you were after and you knew you flew on a certain vector from that beacon towards where your base was. You couldn't see your bases. On a bright night you could see it was an airfield, you can't disguise it, but in the dark you couldn't see anything at all.

By September, 141 Squadron would send detachments down south, to Gatwick, to help out with night fighter duties as the Luftwaffe struck more and more at night. However in November the squadron was finally posted to their new permanent base at Gravesend.

When we were stationed at Gravesend with 141 Squadron we were flying over London. At this stage we were under ground control so we were sent off over London, and the night London got her first big blitz I was airborne over there. I never saw any enemy aircraft but it would have been so easy to have seen them because certainly if you were above, or anywhere really, the whole sky was lit up. I do recall the frustration in the ground controller's voice when he was telling you 'We've got a target for you, he's straight ahead of you, you must be able to see him,' but of course they had no idea how high up or down it was and I personally never saw a thing. A chap like 'Cats Eyes' Cunningham gets up there and every time he's airborne he sees something, but I didn't. Over London that was a fantastic sight and a couple of days later I had leave and another chap and I went up to London. We went and looked in the area round St Paul's Cathedral to see the damage that was done there and it was interesting to see that apparently St Paul's Cathedral was unmarked. We know it was a bit but it survived that terrific blitz. It may have been the big night or several big nights, but as far as I was concerned it was a big night, and we went up two days later and were able to get up into that area and just see for ourselves the damage that had been done.

I think you know when you see the damage that is done like that you feel a bitter sort of hatred for the people that were doing it, but you know throughout the war I never had that feeling that I was fighting for my country. I suppose it might have been the fact that you might even have considered yourself being a sort of mercenary, but I never had that feeling that a lot of people who have written about it have expressed that they wanted to kill the people who were doing it. You talk to the bomber boys and they had no compunction if you were an Englishman of going out and dropping stuff on German cities. But I can't recall ever having that sort of antagonism.

I had hardly got back to the squadron and was doing our patrols over Glasgow when we started re-equipping with the Beaufighters. People like myself (who had trained on twins) had no trouble at all. We went on to the Beaufighters, and that, to us, was a big powerful aeroplane. Huge engines with a lot of oomph, and it started off with primitive radar. Admittedly it was just fore and aft and not much up and down but I had only just got going when I got posted away to a Canadian squadron, 409, where I became a flight commander.

409 Squadron was stationed at Coleby Grange in Lincolnshire and was equipped, at that time, with Beaufighter Mk.IIIs.

I was posted to a Canadian squadron simply because they needed an experienced, or inexperienced in my case, new deputy flight commander, and I was simply uplifted from 141. I went off down there and I don't know how long I was there but I was with that squadron and did quite a lot of patrols as a deputy flight commander.

This was November 1941, more than a year after the Battle of Britain, but the night war routine had remained very similar all the way through despite the arrival of new aircraft.

Flying at night time was a completely different war really. We never had scrambling. I never scrambled during the war at all. It was always going off on a patrol. You were allocated the time to go and that was it. When I got to the point of being a flight commander and getting the people to go off on patrol there was a certain degree of jealousy as to what patrol you got because you went off, say, in the early evening or at dawn, those were the most likely times you would get a contact, and so to keep the peace, I never personally said I'm going to have him, or him, going every time. I spread my patrols when I was organising them so everybody got their chance because, in a way, you might look upon it as sort of a game. We had fun. I must admit we had fun in the war. We also had excitement, and I liked to be fair about distributing the possibilities of some chap getting his first contact or making his first kill. I didn't have that (type of) mind that I'd got to put the ace on to be sure he's going to kill what he was after.

But it didn't seem to matter which aircraft John flew, he never seemed to find the enemy or shoot anything down.

I never got anywhere. When I got back to Ayr for the patrolling over Glasgow, my life in the squadron was simply easy patrolling, no scrambling, nothing like that at all. It got a bit hairy. We did fly in some pretty bad weather and at the Canadian squadron we were about ten miles from a big bomber squadron in Lincolnshire, and many a time when you took off we couldn't get back there because I didn't have much in the way of blind landing facilities and we'd land back at this big bomber field. So we'd go in there and that was it. You'd fly in the following morning if the fog had lifted, you'd fly it back to our base.

John stayed with 409 until Summer 1942 when he was promoted to acting squadron leader and posted to 488 (NZ) Squadron, still flying Beaufighters.

I went from the Canadian squadron and at some stage 488 (NZ) Squadron was being re-formed and I went back to Ayr as a flight commander in 488. I was selected for that of course because I was a New Zealander and the ground crew were mainly New Zealanders, but we had a lot of other nationalities. We had Canadians, I think we had an Australian, we had some British crews there, so I went to 488. Now at some stage there I must have finished my tour and I was sent to 13 Group headquarters at Newcastle upon Tyne as a squadron leader ops and my immediate boss was Al Deere. He was a wing commander at that point and it was while we were there that the air officer, AOA, the Air Officer Admin, said, 'I'm going to send you to staff college.' I said, 'I don't want to go to staff college, I want to get back to my squadron.' He said, 'No Gard'ner, you're for staff college,' so to staff college I went.

I was probably the most junior officer there. They were all wing commanders and above and I was a lowly squadron leader at this point. Anyway I went to staff college which was an interesting one as it was the period when Mountbatten, Montgomery and Trenchard, they all came to the staff college and gave us talks about what had been going on over in Africa and the Far East. One of my fellow students was a chap called Whittle, so as far as I was concerned one of the most interesting lectures was when he gave a talk about how the jet engine developed and how he was pre-war as a pilot officer and had this great idea and was at Cranwell or somewhere and they set him aside to carry on with his development. It was when we were there that a WAAF officer, Intelligence, at the Air Ministry realised from photographs that the Germans were already flying jet aircraft way back in East Germany whereas Frank Whittle's jet had flown for the first time around Farnborough. The Germans were way ahead on that and that came to light in that period when I was at staff college and it created quite a stir as you can imagine.

I went back to 13 Group headquarters which had moved from Newcastle upon Tyne to Inverness and I went back there as Squadron Leader Ops. I stayed up there for nearly a year during which time we had mainly Polish squadrons under our control. We got ticked off by the Air Ministry because we were sending the Poles out and they were shooting down the Germans who were sending up their long range aircraft reporting back the weather. Apparently their weather reports were being picked up by our side and we were told, in the end, to stop going out and shooting them down, which was a bit ironical. My job there was, I flew around the various bases as the ops staff, flew up and down to try and see the Loch Ness monster, and up into the Orkneys and Shetlands. They were all out stations, radar and reporting stations, they were all part of the job I was involved in. It was during that period when my wife presented me, down in Edinburgh, with a brand new daughter. I was able to fly down to see my daughter and back up there and then for the rest of the war I hardly saw her again.

I did some refresher flying after that tour with headquarters. I went to Bedford for refresher flying on Beaufighters and then I came down to 488 Squadron again but via 219 Squadron. While I was on 219 Squadron I had been converted on to Mosquitos and was initially flying over the Normandy beachhead. From there I was posted back to 488 Squadron which had moved down with Mosquitos. I was a flight commander in 488 and went across three weeks after the D-Day landings to Amiens. We couldn't go earlier than that because the runways were in bad shape and you couldn't fly the Mosquitos unless the runways were in reasonably good condition.

So we went down to Amiens and as the ground forces moved we finally moved up into Gilze-Rijen and operated from there.

All my flying was always in the straight night fighter world. I never fired anything into the ground. At the time I got into them we were sent over as pure night fighters and that's how I personally operated. I never had any of that business of firing my guns or shooting up trains or doing anything like that at all. When I first joined 488 again they were in southern England and they were doing rhubarbs and things like that but I never got involved in that at all.

Now that was the frightening time of my flying. We seemed to be ordered off on patrol in bad weather and all you could see was lightning and flashing around you and my memory of it is I always got a bad weather patrol. During that time I never had a contact. When we finally got posted from 219 to 488 and moved across to France I never got a contact anywhere during that time.

Finally I did get a contact on a 190 one night and that, as far as I was concerned, was plain murder. They counted and I had fired ten shells that all went off in one short burst and away he went and that was my kill, a 190.

When I did it that particular time it was a target. You gave no thought to the man in it, it was just this was your target and this is what you wanted to hit and that's what I thought about it. As he went over and down I thought, 'That's good. I've got him.' I didn't see him hit the ground or anything but they reported the next day that this thing hit the ground and the pilot was in it when they found him. Right where I said, there was no question of it really. Ten shells, one short burst and that was it.

John flew with a number of different navigators during his time on Beaufighters and Mosquitos.

There were so many different blokes. During the period you are together you just were Tom and Bill, you were a pair and you did everything together. Once the war had started you never really went off duty. Once you went over the other side there were no pubs you went to. You weren't chums, as it were, you were a professional pair. I recall the last man I had was called Perfect, Dickie Perfect, and he had been with some other squadron before, so with the addition of the 190 I was able to get him up to the score where he could be put up for a DFC.

I enjoyed flying the Mosquito. It was a bit ungainly on the ground. For taking off and landing you had to use a certain degree of brakes and throttle control to keep it straight because those big engines, you got great torque from them, and if you're taking off, particularly with a bit of a side wind, it became a bit difficult to take it off and keep it going straight until you'd got your tail up. Once your tail was up you got some air through the tail and you got control. I personally never had any problems with it. Some chaps sort of spun off you might say but I never did and landing was the same way. Once you'd landed it was alright but once your tail dropped down you still had to manoeuvre your brakes and engine power. Once you're in the air my recollection of it was that it was lovely to fly but you have to remember I had the night fighter version with a huge great radar dish on the front of the fuselage so we were less manoeuvrable than the Mosquitos that were just plain without that great big cumbersome radar thing. I suppose that all gave it extra weight, but I went through various marks of Mosquito, and as I recall the last Mosquito I flew was the Mk.38 version.

Prior to that was the Beaufighter and the Beaufighter in my days flying them still had rather primitive radar. As soon as you pointed it down, any picture you had was lost in the returns from the ground. Now the Mosquito had gone much much further than that and had the dish, but the old Beaufighter just had things in the wings. I seem to remember a pole sticking up the top and one coming down underneath it and that was how your radar operated, where the beams went out and came back.

When I was flying a Mosquito, for some reason I always felt sort of safe, and yet you're surrounded by a lot of wood. I did have one incident when we were flying out of Amiens. We actually had a target and we were drawing up slowly on this target when suddenly I was surrounded by heavy ack-ack. One went off more or less under the nose of the aeroplane and I recall the next minute being upside down and trying to get the aeroplane back on an even keel. I got it back and then my navigator said to me, 'I've got something here,' and he reached down and he had a piece of shrapnel which he'd got out, it hadn't gone into him but it had gone beside him and then I realised the starboard engine was overheating and so I said to him, 'I think we're in trouble. I'm going to close the engine down,' so I closed it down and I was heading back.

We had taken off in fog, we were the only aeroplane that had taken off in fog from Amiens with the idea that in an emergency we might be able to get back into Brussels-Melsbroek. So we took off in fog but up above was a beautiful clear sky, one of those nights that was as clear as anything while down below it was thick fog. They gave me a vector and I was heading back on one engine to Brussels. Of course we still had plenty of fuel, and there seemed to be nothing else wrong other than the engine had been hit and bits of shrapnel had come into the aeroplane. But luckily neither of us had been hit. We got back towards the airfield and said, 'We've got to land,' and they said the visibility was 100 metres or less but we'll turn the lights on. So at 500 feet we came around and I still couldn't see things. Of course on the Mosquito, once you've got your wheels down and your flaps down, you're committed. There was no way you could go round again, so we came around on a heading. They told me what the runway was and you could faintly see some lights so we had a rough idea where we were going and I was descending. As we came closer we got down to about 300 feet and it started to black out and I thought, 'God, here it is, we're committed now. I can't go round again. We're committed to land.' I kept going on the dead setting on the gyroscope and finally as we came down low, and we were getting lower and lower, just at the right moment I was lucky, I'd hit straight onto the end of the runway. With a huge sigh of relief I pulled back the throttles and we landed. But we were some distance up the runway and I realised then that once you were on the ground, and you could see a few lights again, I got towards the end of the runway, and I knew I wasn't going to stop in time so I went to put the brakes on and swung. Luckily it didn't pull the undercarriage off. We stopped and turned along a sort of taxi way. I stopped there and switched off the engine and that was it.

After a while we thought we would get out of the aeroplane and some jeep came along and picked us up. I was wearing a shirt and a pair of trousers, nothing else. I do recall that I had my binoculars in the back and I had my field cap and I left them in the aeroplane. I think we must have been shaken up because they carted us away and it was on New Year's Eve of 1944 and there was a party going on in the mess. Of course the station was virtually closed. Nobody was doing anything. No flying was going on. On New Year's Day we were put up in the hotel and the Germans sent in a last desperate attack on Brussels Melsbroek and my aeroplane was shot up. When we eventually went back to see it there were just a couple of engines lying on the ground because it had just burned up. They came over and on that attack they destroyed a helluva lot of aircraft on the airfield. It was one of their last desperate attacks at that time of the war. My aeroplane was completely beaten up. I lost my binoculars and my field cap.

John was still with 488 Squadron when they were disbanded at Gilze-Rijen in April 1945. During 1944, while at 488 he had rejoined the RNZAF so returned to New Zealand in 1947. However, just a few months later he was offered a permanent commission in the RAF and returned to England. He remained in the RAF until his retirement as a Group Captain in 1965. In 1950 he was seconded to the US Marine Corps where he trained Meteor pilots and flew Skyknight fighters in action in Korea.

Flight Lieutenant Hazel Gregory
1922-16 August 2012

I was living in France just before the war, my father had had a job in Paris from which he retired in 1938 and I stayed on as I'd been offered a place at the Sorbonne; I was studying modern languages and I was there when war broke out. In April 1940 I had a cable from him to say that my mother was very ill so I had to get permission from the embassy to travel. I came back to England and she did recover, in fact she lived until 1979, but by the time she was well enough for me to leave again France had fallen so I joined the WAAF.

Everybody was very very depressed in Paris. There was a strong feeling that they couldn't go through it all again because they had suffered very badly in the First World War. The pessimism was absolutely noticeable. It was so different in England. Everybody was firmly convinced that we were going to win come what may and nobody was pessimistic at all.

Hazel Gregory (née Fuller) was born in Clapham in south London and was 18 years old in 1940. She had no specific idea of what job she wanted to do when she joined the RAF.

I liked the look of the uniform so in May 1940 I joined the WAAF. I was quite willing to do anything that came along but we weren't given a choice of what we were going to do. They allocated us and if you had a reasonable education you became something called a Clerk, Special Duties which turned out to be a plotter in the operations room.

We were interviewed and everyone had a fairly good education. I suppose they thought we needed to understand how things were done. Then we were interviewed by a psychologist and then we had a manual dexterity test. It was like a Fisher-Price game now. You had coloured blocks which you had to put quickly into various shapes and then they said, oh yes, you'll be a clerk, special duties.

We went to Leighton Buzzard for a fortnight's training where they taught us to read maps and interpret the map co-ordinates. That was about all and you just practised plotting, you had to be very fast and very accurate, it was no good putting one on that was in the wrong place. It didn't teach us much, you learned by doing it. Then I was posted to Uxbridge, 11 Group.

It was a very large camp and the operations staff didn't mix much with the other people. We had our own quarters which were small wooden bungalows which had been officers' married quarters before and we had our own mess and the food was very good but then if you're cooking for ten people you can cook good food whereas down in the main halls where they were cooking for 500 it was a different story.

This was pre-Battle of Britain, just about the same time as Dunkirk. We were all expecting trouble to come and everyone was determined that we were going to get through it. Nobody for a moment felt that we wouldn't. It was just unquestionable.

It was very quiet in the operations room. We had very little work but it was like a big board game. The only thing we were doing really at that time was providing air cover for shipping in the channel and using little wooden ships that we pushed along to represent the convoys. Then after that the attacks on the airfields started and we became very busy. But for the first few weeks I was there we used to have an exercise once every shift to keep our hand in.

We knew about radar – it was called RDF in those days – Radio Direction Finding – and we were told we must never discuss it outside of the Ops Room. There were four or five plotters who were dealing with the reports that came in from the radar stations. Radar only worked as far as the coast. The plots came through on tape on the teleprinter and you could have a headset if you were busy and hadn't got time, very heavy, uncomfortable ones.

The first thing that came through was a raid number. The information came from Stanmore from the Filter Room and they sent us through the details of where the aircraft were, the map coordinates, the direction and the height and immediately you transferred it onto the table. The number of aircraft was on little wooden blocks with plastic numbers and you had to keep it pretty tidy. You had a box full of them and orderlies came round to keep your supplies up. The plots were plastic arrows in three colours and the clock changed every five minutes. You took off the oldest colouring and started on a new one – red, yellow and blue. Later they had magnetic blocks and magnetic metal plots with sticks that came on and off but in those days we just had wooden ones and plastic plots.

The controllers would then direct the aircraft from the various sectors to combat it and that was the end and it came off the table, off for five minutes, every plot came off because it's no good if it's not up to date.

There were about ten of us. We worked shift patterns which was very difficult. We worked one day from eight in the morning until four in the afternoon and came back that night at midnight till eight the next morning and then you had a complete day off until four o'clock the following day and you were on from four till eight that day. This was very tiring, you never ate or slept at the same time in any given day and so your body clock never got used to it. However, most people found it very easy to deal with, unlike some of the people later with the Y service which was a very stressful, difficult job. There were a lot of mental breakdowns among the people who worked in it, but it wasn't so in Fighter Ops.

The plotting table showed the whole of south-east England and 10 Group, which was Devon and Somerset, and 12 Group which was based in Nottingham. It was a big map. You sat down when there was nothing happening and we were allowed to read books and write letters and do our knitting. Everybody was making really fancy underwear as you could buy silk and satin then, it was the in thing, we were all making this underwear which greatly interested all the men. But as soon as anything came up you threw it under the table and got it out of the way.

We could hear the controllers talking and you had to keep a close eye on the table all the time even if you were doing other things. You had to watch what was happening and as soon as anything came through on the teleprinter or the headset everybody immediately put down what they were doing and got to their feet ready to work.

You were allocated an area. I was at the top of the table working so all the stuff was backwards working away from me. You had the place that was usually your station but you had to be a bit flexible about that because if anyone was off sick the NCOs would have to rearrange where people were detailed to.

You would see a raid build up over the Channel but later, when the battle actually started, you were too busy looking after your own sector, you didn't have time to look at anybody else. You would take the raid over from the next plotter. As soon as the number of the raid came up that you were to deal with then you would take it over. You would take off the box for the raids that had disappeared for whatever reason, they'd either lost them or they'd shot them down or whatever. You just plotted your geographical sector. Mine was based at Watford and I plotted everything from the river northwards in that sector.

The raids were frequent and they were attacking the fighter airfields, all the sectors, and most of them were very badly damaged but everybody pulled together and got them going again straight away.

Hazel found she had a particular interest in the fate of one specific airfield.

I felt that about Biggin Hill as I'd been there for a short time on attachment when someone had been killed and they sent two or three experienced plotters down and so I felt Biggin was special. It was much smaller. Sector ops rooms were mainly above ground in little huts and things and were much smaller than Uxbridge. Otherwise the job was the same.

As was to be expected, Hazel's busiest day was 15 September.

The mass attack on London, we didn't know the dates at the time because we never saw a newspaper, but it was just procedure and we got on with what we were doing. I think it was 15 September and we went off duty at four. Mr Churchill spoke to us and he said, 'Well done young ladies. This has been a momentous day and one in years to come you'll tell your grandchildren about.' And he was right. I was 18 years old and you don't think about having grandchildren at that age do you? But all the girls were young and all the plotters were girls. Some of the orderlies who used to bring us supplies and keep us going with everything, some of those were men, but all the plotters were girls. Our youngest member was 15. She'd lied about her age and sent her elder sister's birth certificate which taught me that a document may be genuine but you've no proof it belongs to the person who's showing it to you. They never found out. When you joined up they looked at your birth certificate but you could easily be showing them the wrong one. The eldest girl on the watch was 26 and we all thought she was a bit over the hill as we were all late teens or early twenties.

It was a bigger operation than we'd ever dealt with before. Mr Churchill was there all day and it was very exciting but it was business as usual. The whole table was covered with raids. It wasn't just that one, they were everywhere, coming in from everywhere, and at one point in the afternoon all the lights at the back of the ops room which showed the state of the squadrons, every single one showed airborne. Mr Churchill turned to Sir Keith and said, 'What reserves do you have, Air Vice-Marshal?' and he replied, 'None Sir.' It was that close.

Hazel received her own nickname from Winston Churchill. Due to her auburn hair he called her 'copper knob'.

Mr Churchill was there with a lady that we subsequently discovered was his wife but we didn't know that at the time. General Ismay was with him too and they were obviously fascinated. They were there all day. But he was a very friendly and very nice man. Obviously liked the girls quite well though he was a devoted family man.

FLIGHT LIEUTENANT HAZEL GREGORY

We were so busy we didn't really have time to think about it, we just did the best that we could, everybody was working flat out. We didn't even have time for a lunch break that day, we were there from eight to four. If you wanted to go to the toilet you had to get one of the NCOs to come and take your place over and you ran there and ran back. I've never forgotten it. We were busy for two or three months all during that period but that was the busiest. It was bombers with fighter cover and they were coming in from the east, from Holland. Of course the radar was a great boon to us because fighter aircraft, specially in those days, could only stay up for a short period of time and this meant we could plot them from when they started out so that the aircraft didn't have to hang around in the air waiting to see what happened. We were able to scramble and direct them as needed and that made all the difference.

The man in charge was Air Vice Marshal Keith Park, CO of 11 Group and directly responsible for the air defence of London and the south-east.

Sir Keith was a man in whom we all had great confidence. He was a great leader and very informal and very pleasant but very determined that things were going to be done properly and done in the way he approved of. He was a very pleasant man to work for. We all thought a great deal of him. He would be sitting up on the dais and controlling the squadrons. We could hear him talking. He was very concerned that day. He went off duty after we did, we didn't know how long he was there as we went off at four o'clock.

Hazel went off duty at four and had her eight hours break before coming back to the plotting table at midnight.

And then we went back on duty and there was nothing, nothing at all. The table was completely bare and it was a great anti-climax. But when they came down on that night at about three o'clock in the morning of 16 September and put up the numbers of aircraft, enemy and RAF, the RAF had lost 27 planes with 13 pilots killed and we were told I think it was 185 German planes had been destroyed. Although that figure was disputed later we realised this was really important and there was never another mass raid on London in the daytime. They switched to night bombing after that and the plans for the invasion were abandoned. I don't know how but we did know that. I can't remember how we learned it but we did, we knew that. We were aware of all the German barges in the Channel ports ready to come over and they were all disbanded, they were all stood down.

From that point on, Hazel's days got progressively quieter.

This was such a change from the day raids. Of course you were on 24/7 and that's when the Germans turned their attention to bombing London at night.

There were big fire raids to start with and though we plotted all these aircraft coming in we had very little night fighting defence. I think there were about two Beaufighters or something like that. We did develop it later, but at that point there was very little the air force could do. The anti-aircraft guns and the balloon barrage were the only defences. We came up for a break, we used to come up as they had a small canteen at the top of the stairs, and we came up for a break in the middle of that night and we looked towards London and the whole sky was on fire and we were in tears. Most of us had friends and family in London and there was absolutely nothing the air force could do, nothing at all.

We seemed to have a lot of information but not so much as during the daytime. For instance the numbers of aircraft in a raid. I seem to remember having the height of a raid on the daytime ones but we didn't have that information at night. But not having the night fighter defences meant they didn't need the information so much.

It got a bit boring. We found that, having had all the excitement, war was like that. You had periods of utter excitement followed by long periods of complete boredom.

However Hazel's periods of boredom were easily dealt with by her sparkling social life.

We had a great social life because we had the break in our duties from eight o'clock one morning to four o'clock the following day. We were supposed to sleep but we didn't do always and, of course, we were on the tube line to London. We used to meet friends and go to London most evenings when we weren't on duty. We used to go to local pubs. We went to the one at Northolt with all the Canadians, one of my friends married one of them. It was a very exciting life.

We went up to London a lot because of the underground line to Uxbridge and in fact it was sheer fortune that we weren't in that big raid on the Café de Paris when that was bombed. We used to go there a lot and we used to go to the Savoy and the Dorchester and the Mayfair hotel. We had a really good time and nobody took much notice of the raids even when they were on. They were more of a nuisance than anything. We used to meet pilots as we used to make dates over the phone with them and then you'd meet somebody and the next time they wouldn't turn up. Their friend would say oh so-and-so's bought it; that was just the way it went at the time.

We would go up on the underground which took nearly an hour because it's right at the end of the underground, the Piccadilly line, and then we would go into various hotels and nightclubs which were much smaller.

They were little places then. We would dance, there were dance bands, and if there was a raid it was a nuisance because it made it difficult to get about. The underground didn't stop but most of the buses stopped running. Whenever we were off duty we used to go up town or to somewhere local.

There was a strange spirit about. People accepted the fact that it was dangerous and you thought nothing of it.

Only once did Hazel feel in danger while working at Uxbridge.

The only time I did we were coming back, my friend and I had been down to the shops in Uxbridge and we were coming back when a German machine gunned us from the air. We dived into one of the blocks and found a bunch of WAAFs sitting at the end of a billiard table. 'Come and join us,' and they asked what do you do and we said, 'We are plotters,' and they said, 'Oh, not those stuck-up tarts,' because we were treated rather specially. We didn't have any other duties and we had our own mess and our own quarters and I think it was Sir Keith who said the people who worked in ops should be treated specially and we were but it didn't make us popular with the other people on the camp.

We had very few raids on Uxbridge but they had developed a special land mine which came down by parachute and it was eight foot long and I think it was aimed at shutting off the entrance and exit from the Ops Room. If they couldn't get in or out it would be inoperable. It fell in the WAAF quarters and hung on a tree and eventually they realised that our watch was unaccounted for and two intrepid ladies, an officer and sergeant, came down and found us all asleep in bed and the lights had gone. When this land mine fell it had brought down the overhead lighting circuits and the blackout was up which were wooden shutters in each window. They came in and said, 'Everybody out in two minutes.'

Fortunately it was quite a warm night and we congregated by the gate. They rounded everybody up and one of the girls had what was very unfashionable which was a very large bosom and she was struggling underneath her clothes to get her bra on. She managed to do it and told her friend who said, 'Not to worry girls, the balloon barrage is definitely up.'

We went to Hillingdon Hospital and spent the night on the floor in an empty room and then we couldn't get back to our quarters because the bomb was still there. It was three days before a naval contingent came and took it away to Hackney Marshes and exploded it, and so we all went on duty in what we were wearing which in my case was pale green satin pyjamas. None of us had got anything, we hadn't got our special passes but they let us into the Ops Room because they knew us. Nobody had got any money or anything at all sensible but we'd all got our make-up! When anybody said what would you take if there was a fire in those days: that was the answer, our make-up.

When we went off duty at four they took us up to stores and issued us with new shoes, new hat and everything including all that awful underwear.

In 1941 Hazel was given a commission due to her ability with languages. She had a special feeling about the importance of the period and the vital roles they had undertaken.

That's what we felt like, yes, I must say. Probably erroneously but that's how we felt. We did feel that we were doing something special and that it was important for the country, that it made a difference. It was a nice thing to feel.

At that point they hadn't had any women officers in the control room so I became an intelligence officer and was posted to Bletchley Park.

I knew nothing. In fact I wasn't officially posted there. I was officially posted to RAF Cheadle which is an outstation of Bletchley and I was in the Y service. It was in a big mansion and I went there two or three times but I wasn't actually on the official books, I was RAF Cheadle. I went there and they said you're not working here you're working somewhere else but we'll give you transport, which they did. It was the rations van and when I got there they were much more pleased to see the bacon than they were to see me.

There was no training for it. There was a training school but they didn't do much and you did it by a system known in the trades unions as 'sitting by Nellie' (picking up the job by sitting with an experienced member of staff).

You were quite at liberty to do whatever you thought would work, and if it didn't, well too bad, but if it did everybody was pleased, whether you could get some results by getting plain language out of the code. The cribs worked for me. I liked that system and then they built the computer Colossus and brought in 100 Wrens to work it because it worked on very old fashioned valves, radio valves. They were always breaking down and they had to be taken out and replaced. The Wrens were billeted in Woburn Abbey.

I worked in Hut 6 decoding the Luftwaffe messages. Hut 8 did the German naval work and we did the Luftwaffe. We would get these great sheafs of figures through and we would have to try and turn them into plain language. We had something we called a crib which was like a big sheet of paper with holes in it and you moved it about. (These messages gave us) location of squadrons, where they were going to, where they were coming from, what their task would be, so that you could build up a picture of what the Luftwaffe was doing.

FLIGHT LIEUTENANT HAZEL GREGORY

Of course, key to this decoding was the capture of the German Enigma machine and the breaking of the German codes. Enigma was a system of rotors and a plugboard in a typewriter-style machine that had been adopted by the German military from the mid-twenties. An Enigma Research Section was formed headed by First World War codebreaker Dilly Knox, together with Alan Turing, Tony Kendrick, Peter Twinn and Hazel's immediate boss, Gordon Welchman. The first code was broken early in 1940 and messages were deciphered from then until the end of the war.

We had six Enigma machines in Hut 6. When we saw this American film about obtaining a machine, that was nonsense. We had one, the Poles gave us one in August 1939, Dilly Knox, who was our boss, went over to Poland and the Poles were very co-operative and very helpful. They had done a lot of mathematical work on the Enigma and they gave him a complete machine which he brought back via Victoria Station in a suitcase; it was like an old film. We had that, and various technical wizards built copies of it and also we'd captured several so we had plenty of machines. What we needed was the codebooks for the settings, so every day at midnight the code changed and you took a pencil and pulled it round, it had cogs on it and you pulled it round with a pencil and set it to the new setting for the day. Once you'd got those you could decode the stuff and that was what they captured that was so valuable, the settings books. The Germans had got them for several years in one book and that was what our people captured. The people who had to work it, they were firmly convinced it was unbreakable, which it wasn't because we did it. But the permutations were enormous, several million because there were twenty-six letters and the permutations work out at a huge figure. Once you'd got the settings you could decode. They came out in groups of five letters and you could decode those once you knew the settings of the machine. You had what we called the insets which we put in every day and we had a machine of our own called Type X that had five drums on it. The German one had four. This was our own encoding device and we used it for everything.

The Enigma machine never ever produced one letter as itself. So it was never reproduced. But most of the German mentality was very disciplined. Everything would be in the same format so you could quite often get into the message by decoding the first bits. They were always in the same format.

Nobody in Hut 6 spoke very good German. Most of us knew a little but not a lot, but we could recognise it and so it went through to Hut 3 to be interpreted and evaluated. They had a little wooden tunnel between the two and you put all your stuff in a wicker basket and pushed it through with a broom handle. It was very hi-tech in those days. From then on they would decide where the work would go to, either to the Cabinet Office if it was really vital, or just to the relative Ministry, and anything really urgent was sent by dispatch rider or special armoured car. The rest went by teleprinter which is very secure because it's a landline. It's not radio.

Security was fantastic. We were told that never ever were we to discuss it in any way, not for the rest of our lives. Literally you did your own job and you never asked anyone else what they did, you never discussed it, and everybody lived out because there were no quarters but even local landladies didn't know what we were doing. Everybody was so security minded that we never ever mentioned anything about our work.

The biggest surprise I ever had was when it all came out about twenty years ago now I suppose because we were told never ever must we discuss it. We weren't allowed to tell anyone where we were or what we were doing. My parents never knew that I had been doing that work. I was very sorry about that. I would like them to have known. My husband knew because I met him at Bletchley. He was an engineer and part of the Long Range Desert Group and they were establishing Y service to go along with Montgomery and because he was an Arabic interpreter they were given empty vans, I think by the Americans, and he equipped them. He got it done in the civilian workshops in Cairo because he was able to tell them what he wanted because of his Arabic. So he came over to find out what exactly they wanted to have put into these vans and that was when I met him.

Many of Hazel's intercepts were to do with the war in North Africa.

That was the big thing happening at that time and then Alamein came along. My husband was there. When he left Bletchley he went back by convoy and went right round the Cape. It took them weeks, and he arrived at Alamein the day before the battle started. He always said they were waiting for him.

Bletchley Park itself was a late nineteenth century mansion purchased in 1938 by Admiral Sir Hugh Sinclair, head of MI6, to be used by British Intelligence in the event of war.

Its situation was perfect due to its seclusion but with excellent rail communications to Oxford and Cambridge, the source of many of the wartime codebreakers.

It was a very attractive site. There was a lake and a lot of ground. We were in wooden huts and they are still there but they are falling down. Then they built new concrete buildings we moved into and there was the mansion which was a big Victorian building and is still there and they are doing it up now. It was a very attractive place and very safe. We were only ever bombed once, a dispatch rider was killed by the main gate, but that was the only time. I think it was a stray bomb that somebody dumped on their way home but otherwise I think the Germans couldn't have known a lot about it or otherwise they would have bombed it. It was very safe, a very attractive site and there was a tremendous lot of people. More than 1,200 people by the end of the war. Everybody lived out, anywhere within the neighbourhood, and we all came in by train or by lorry or bus. There was a lot of traffic coming and going and we worked the same shifts. It was common this shift system and very uncomfortable to work. You never ever ate or slept at the same time on any successive day so you never had time to get used to anything.

There were all ranks, depending on what your job was, men and women. Whereas in Fighter Command, when I was first commissioned there were no women officers in the control room. They went there later as many of my friends were working in Fighter Command. But Bletchley was a strange place and it illustrated to me very much that it never works well to have a lot of people working under different conditions. They had different hours, different pay, different holiday entitlement and everyone always thought everyone else was getting away with murder. We had watches at Bletchley because we worked round the clock on these shift hours so you were always on with your own watch.

Throughout her time at Bletchley Park Hazel was given no information about the impact of her work.

Nobody ever said that it was valuable then. It was later they said this had been successful. We knew a lot of the people, particularly at the War Ministry, didn't feel that the money being spent on what we were doing was worth it, but we had one person who always thought it was well worth it and that was Winston Churchill, he was a great supporter. He didn't ever come up to Bletchley, not to my knowledge, I never saw him there.

Bletchley Park was too secret. Nobody was allowed to come really. The King and Queen came to Uxbridge while I was there. You did feel cut off really from the main war effort. At Fighter Command you didn't, you felt you were right in the centre of things but at Bletchley we felt somehow cut off.

We knew and said nothing about it and it was only under the thirty year rule when they brought things out and started publicising it that the full picture dawned on us. It was the biggest surprise I ever had when they announced this because they had told us never, for the rest of our lives, ever mention what we were doing. All the equipment and everything was dismantled.

Sometimes something would come up on the news later and you would think, 'Oh, I know all about that.' Malta was a big preoccupation at the time because when they started they only had three aircraft to defend them. I was doing a lot of the early message work for Malta, the movements of Italian naval ships mainly.

It made the penny drop. We didn't realise at the time the significance of what we were doing and nobody ever said to us we were doing anything valuable, we were just slogging away on what was really fairly mechanical.

It was strange. I missed the air force, because it wasn't an air force establishment and I was sorry I couldn't get back to Fighter Command which I really liked. I was pleased to leave. I didn't like it there very much. I was posted there so you just went where you were sent. It was a lot of hard work and we didn't get much feedback from it and there wasn't the same atmosphere there as there had been in the air force itself. When I was posted to the Air Ministry I was glad to go really and for the following year I was in London, in the Air Ministry in King Charles Street which is parallel with Downing Street. There was a tremendous labyrinth of underground passages between the two which we were always told were bomb-proof, but just recently they have said that they weren't so we were living in a fool's paradise.

I was on the staff of the Chief of the Air Staff, Sir Charles Portal, dogsbodying really. I was working for the Director of Intelligence, Sir Frank Ingalls. We were supplying information through to the cabinet office and I was what the Americans call a dogcatcher, which means if the great man wants a dog you go out and catch one, you just do whatever you need to do. I was a dogsbody.

In fact, far from the modest description of her work, Hazel's job was personal assistant to the Director. During her time at the Air Ministry, they were planning, and then executing, the Normandy landings, D-Day.

We weren't allowed to leave the building. Nobody who knew the date was going to be was allowed to leave the country or was allowed to get anywhere where the Germans might catch you. For several days over the period, D-Day had to be postponed for twenty-four hours because the weather was so bad and you weren't allowed to leave the building. You were told to bring in a suitcase with sufficient stuff for a few nights and there were restrooms down in the underground tunnels with bunk beds. You slept there and there was a shower room and a washroom. When some men came in to build a new wall map they weren't allowed to leave, they were told they'd got to stay; it was because the map in the war cabinet office was of the actual landings and because they had seen this and knew what the actual place was. There was a big security scam going on to make the Germans believe we were going to land in the Calais area which we weren't and it was very successful.

One of the reasons Hazel had been chosen was her experience of the secrecy at Bletchley Park. Subsequently she never divulged much of what she heard and saw during those D-Day planning meetings.

It was the work I was doing. I often used to take the minutes of the Joint Intelligence Committee and this was what they decided. The actual date itself was fairly flexible for quite a long time. We were working towards early June, but the actual date wasn't decided completely immediately. In the end it was going to be the previous day, but it had to be postponed.

I then went to Cairo. I was in the intelligence office in headquarters Middle East Command in Cairo, but we hadn't got a lot to do at the time. Things were more or less over by then and we hadn't got a tremendous lot of work. We spent most of our time censoring the troops' mail, which is a deadly dull job. I asked for it and Sir Charles always said I could when things had settled and D-Day was over. I was there at that time, and when it was all finished and everything was going well, and obviously the war was coming to its end, then he arranged a posting for me to Cairo. When I said thank you to him and said goodbye he said, 'You've earned it.'

Against her expectations when she joined up Hazel had spent time doing vital work in three of the most important places and periods of time during the war.

Squadron Leader Tony Pickering
25 August 1920-24 March 2016

I joined the Royal Air Force before the war, the Royal Air Force Volunteer Reserve, and to be quite honest, before the war they brought in conscription which meant that you were conscripted into the army when you were 18 years of age. I was at that age and I decided, along with one or two other of my colleagues who were working as engineering apprentices with the old BTH company, the forerunner of the General Electric Company GEC, and we decided as apprentices that we didn't want to go into the army and be conscripted so we decided to join the Royal Air Force Volunteer Reserve. We were, of course, interested in aircraft. All the youngsters of those days were really interested in aircraft and I joined the RAFVR. That is why I joined. I wanted to get into something because we knew there was a war coming on, everybody knew that. Churchill warned us of it of course, and I wanted to get into somewhere I knew I could enjoy myself flying.

Tony Pickering was born in Foxton in Leicestershire and educated at Market Harborough Grammar School. He became an apprentice at British Thomson-Houston, a heavy industrial company based in Rugby that built engines for ocean liners, steam turbines and generators. Hence Tony moved to live in Rugby.

I wanted to become a fighter pilot and my height was just about right. I decided that I would go to Ansty aerodrome, which is only five or six miles from Rugby, and fly at weekends. I flew on a Saturday from Coventry, Ansty aerodrome Coventry, and the chief instructor took me up, flew me around, showed me the countryside and I was really keen to get into the aircraft and fly it myself. Of course we had to have dual instruction for about thirteen hours. If you weren't capable of going solo after about fifteen hours you were tested, and either you survived for a few more hours or you were out. I went solo after thirteen hours.

We flew on Saturday afternoons in actual fact, as we worked Saturday mornings. In those days it was a five and a half day week and as an apprentice

I had to really get down to work. I had to study at night school three nights a week to get my engineering qualifications.

Like so many others, Tony remembered the day war was declared.

I remember very well because on the Friday night, previous to the Sunday when war broke out, they called us all up. We were told by the BBC, that was in those days on the radio. We were told to report to our centres and my centre was at Coventry and I reported to Coventry on the Friday evening. Then they said OK, sign here and go back, and on the Sunday we were actually at war, but again I sat on my bottom for two weeks before they decided what they were going to do with us. It was something like 20,000 people in the RAFVR, a lot of people and a lot of young men. They couldn't cope with them all at first.

The day war was declared I was ringing the bells on Sunday morning as usual, being a campanologist, and remember walking from Rugby town centre to where my digs were. My father supplied me with digs in Rugby as I lived in Leicestershire at the time and to enable me to work and study in Rugby I had to live in Rugby. I was walking back to my digs and someone said to me Neville Chamberlain is going to talk to us at midday so of course we all went to the radio and listened to Neville Chamberlain who told us we were at war.

It was more of an excitement knowing we were going to be involved in a war. We wanted to get moving, to get started. It was frustrating for quite a few weeks because of course they didn't know what to do with us, there were so many of us in the RAFVR it took time for us to get moving.

I think most of us were sensible enough to realise that we'd got to be taught to fly and we realised also that the Royal Air Force itself could not accommodate us all immediately. Quite a few people waited until about Christmas before they moved on to fly but nevertheless we realised, again, that this was coming and we'd just got to be patient.

With about 1,000 others I was sent to Hastings where we marched up and down the promenade for a few weeks as they didn't know what to do with us, but eventually I arrived at Redhill in Surrey to fly the Miles Magister.

After more than two months 'square-bashing' at 3 ITW in Hastings, Tony was posted to 15 Elementary Flying Training School at Redhill in Surrey.

When I first started at Ansty near Coventry I was flying in the Tiger Moth and then, when the war started, and after moving from Hastings to Redhill, I went onto the low wing monoplane which was a Miles Magister, a nice little aircraft. We were down at Redhill from about October to April before we moved on to a flying training school at Sealand near Chester.

Well of course the war started in France, somewhere about May. At that time I was at Sealand learning to fly the Miles Master which was the trainer before the Hurricane or the Spitfire. I finished there in July, round about 20 July, 1940. The war of course was then going on and it was rather hectic at that time. I moved from Sealand to Biggin Hill to fly the Hurricane.

In 1940 very few trainees were given the chance to fly their front-line fighter before they reached their squadron. However, many went to resting and refitting squadrons for a slightly more gentle introduction to the art of being a fighter pilot. In Tony's case he went straight from Sealand to Biggin Hill to join 32 Squadron, commanded by John Worrall, and in the thick of the action. Tony arrived with two other new sergeant pilots from Sealand: Ray Gent and Tony Whitehouse.

My first experience of the Hurricane was when I arrived at Biggin Hill in July 1940, on a Friday morning, and I could see the Hurricane sitting on the ground. The squadron itself was down at Hawkinge, the forward base, but there was one Hurricane there on the aerodrome at Biggin and we reported to the squadron commander, who wasn't actually with the squadron at Hawkinge, he was at Biggin Hill on that day. Three of us walked into the squadron commander's office and he said to me, 'How many hours have you done on Hurricanes, Pickering?' I said, 'I've never even seen one until today, Sir.' He said, 'Well this afternoon you will fly that aircraft, do three circuits and bumps at Biggin Hill and tomorrow morning at four o'clock you will be awoken and you will fly with us down to Hawkinge forward base and you will fly number two to Hector Proctor, the flight commander, and he will direct you as to what to do.'

We took off on the next morning, the Saturday morning, and went down to Hawkinge. I flew number two to Hector Proctor, the flight commander, who a fortnight before had been a sergeant pilot with 501 Squadron. An ex-Halton boy, a flight lieutenant by that time, he'd gone up from sergeant pilot to acting flight lieutenant and he said to me, 'Don't put your gun button on fire, sit behind me and watch what I do, but you're not to use your gun button. I don't want to be shot out of the sky.' I think he thought I'd sit behind him and get too excited and press the button.

Tony formed an early opinion about the Hurricane.

A good stable aircraft. An easier aircraft to fly than the Spitfire, which I flew later, because you had a better view forward. Sitting in the Hurricane you were higher up and you got a good view forward for taking off or landing. It could take a lot of punishment and take a lot of machine gun bullets through the fuselage and the wings and still fly. A good stable aircraft.

We knew we were in the front line, there was no doubt about that, at Hawkinge. We would land there, they'd refuel the aircraft for us to make sure we were fully topped up with fuel and we'd sit there by our aircraft, sometimes in small groups, sometimes individually by your aircraft, because we only got a few seconds warning and you were in the aircraft and taking off. Quite often we were not on the ground an awful lot because we were immediately sent off. There was I sitting behind my friend Hector Proctor. I can remember it quite easily. I can remember Hector firing his guns and there was I still sitting behind him.

32 Squadron had already created a reputation in the early weeks of the air war. Throughout the Battle of France they had stayed in England but had flown daily out to France and operated from various airfields. They had suffered losses and many of the pilots were tired.

Actually it was daunting because they were a well known front line Royal Air Force squadron with some excellent pilots and I was very humble as I realised I was only a number really; just making a team up. More like in cricket you have a long stop who stands behind the wicket keeper, that was my sort of job, just making the numbers up, because quite frankly I had not a clue, let's be honest about it, coming straight from the training school to that. The squadron commander realised that because I think I only did about three trips with 32 and he said, to the three of us, 'You three sergeant pilots are useless. I can't have you here,' and he sent us to Sutton Bridge to continue our training where we flew our Hurricanes in training.

Some people might consider that we might have been depressed but I think the three of us were sensible enough to realise that we weren't going to last if we were carrying on in the front line at that time. We'd never fired a gun in our lives. We'd got no idea what to do really. Never been taught how to use your gunsights or anything like that and to be put into the front line, as the squadron commander realised, was ridiculous. We should never have been sent there. Very few of the Royal Air Force Volunteer pilots, such as myself and the other two, were sent immediately to a front line squadron. We were usually sent to squadrons that were just outside the front line and had the opportunity to do some training. But there was no opportunity; he couldn't give us any training at all, the squadron commander.

Pete Brothers was a friend of mine for some years. He was one of the fellows we looked up to and my leader, Hector Proctor. He'd flown through France so he knew all about how a Hurricane operated on the front line so I would have learned a lot from him. But they couldn't afford someone like myself sitting behind them. We were more of a nuisance.

At Sutton Bridge Tony and his two friends were given the training they should have had earlier.

When we eventually went on to a Hurricane operational training unit at Sutton Bridge then we did receive first class instruction because the instructors there were all ex-France; they'd been in France when the war first started, all the instructors.

They taught us air firing, we didn't have any bombing or anything like that, it was purely air firing and we were shown how to fly in formation. We were shown the tactics of attacking bombers, things like that, but generally we were taught how to use the Hurricane as a fighting machine because we'd never been taught that before. You'd got everything you needed, fully armed.

After his time at Sutton Bridge Tony returned to 32 Squadron, now commanded by Squadron Leader Mike Crossley, an experienced pilot who had won the DFC after the Battle of France.

By the time I got there we were defending our own country, defending Dover and the south coast. I don't think I flew over the sea, not at that time. They'd already been pushed back by the time I arrived, but later of course, after I'd done about twenty days at Sutton Bridge and moved back to 32, the same day that I moved back, the squadron moved to Acklington in the north. The squadron commander said, 'You three, you've been trained now, we're not taking you to Acklington. You're going over to 501 Squadron at Gravesend.' So we moved back in the morning and in the afternoon we were on the way to Gravesend because the squadron, that very day, moved up to Acklington.

501 Squadron was another veteran of the French campaign and another Hurricane squadron.

When I went to 501 with the other two gentlemen, Tony Whitehouse and Ray Gent – Tony is still around and Ray unfortunately was killed – nevertheless we, the three of us, I'm certain, felt completely confident to be used as fighter pilots. There was no question of taking off and not having your gun button on fire. Our tactics were to attack the bombers. The Hurricanes were there to attack the bombers and that was our job and that is what we did.

We were sensible enough to realise that we'd got a lot to learn even then and you felt confident but nevertheless you were only a number at first. There were some excellent pilots there, Ginger Lacey, for instance, Hogan, Holden, Morfill, Paul Farnes, names I could mention who'd knocked a few down. We'd realised we were not in the same category as them and we'd got to learn. I think most of us realised we weren't in their position and we were flying number two or number three to these experienced pilots. They were the first ones to press the button when you went in. You followed them in when we were attacking bombers at that time, in and out quickly.

501 was well led by Squadron Leader Hogan, our CO, a very experienced pilot and aggressive man, aggressive pilot, which is what you wanted. He looked after us, we young 19 or 20-year-old boys, he was a few years older than us and he actually looked after us, the social side as well, he made sure we were well fed and looked after which was a good thing.

One of the hoary old subjects that raises its head at this early stage of the war is the difference in treatment between the NCO pilots, such as Tony, and the officers.

When we were in the air we were well looked after. You were a pilot and you were treated the same as an officer completely. On the ground, unfortunately, at Gravesend, with all due respect to the British Army, the army fed the sergeant pilots, the officers were in the clubhouse and were fed by service men, RAF cooks and people like that. But we were fed by the army and quite frankly the food we were given, if I'd given it to pigs or sheep I'd have been in trouble because it was terrible. I'd never had food like it in my life. But Squadron Leader Hogan realised what was going on and then every evening after we'd done our flying, because now we were going into September and October 1940, Squadron Leader Hogan realised we were not getting correct food and we had dinner every night in the officers' mess. All the sergeant pilots were told to go to the officers' mess and have dinner with the officers, which actually gave us a good meal every day.

I had a lot of respect for the young pilots who had come through the Royal Air Force college at Halton and, of course, they were more experienced, they were better disciplined than we were. We were civilians really who were coming into the Royal Air Force. We hadn't received the basic training, and in particular a man called Percy Morfill, who I remember very well indeed, he was the senior sergeant pilot and we had to do as we were told, no doubt about it. He was the same rank as ourselves but we had to do as we were told.

The day started very early for the fighter pilots during the summer of 1940.

First of all we were woken up in bed by a beautiful WAAF girl with a cup of tea. Never forgotten that. And you were a bit fed up having to get up early. If you'd been a bit older you'd have been grumpy I suppose. Nevertheless we knew we'd got a job to do. It was drilled into us. We were disciplined to know we'd got a job to do and we were young enough to be able to take it without falling out with everybody.

The only impression I can remember was it was so early in the morning to be up. I had never been used to being up at that time in the morning. There was so little activity going on anywhere, even at that time. Remember we were going to dispersal at five o'clock in the morning. It was still dark when you got there and then gradually it would get light. You had to be there with all your kit on and ready before it got light.

Now I tell you what, you did feel good if the CO said to you, 'I want this aircraft testing. I won't put you with the squadron. We've got that spare aircraft. You're not flying with the squadron this morning. You're the reserve. Take that aircraft and give it a test, put it through its paces.' And you went up early in the morning just as it was getting light all by yourself and you felt as if you ruled the world. You were there up in space all by yourself. It's a wonderful feeling that, when you're up there by yourself in the sky without a soul about. You can't see anybody, no other aircraft or anything and you're going up high, because you could go up to 30,000 feet if you're doing a test, and you felt on top of the world. You felt like you were looking into space.

But these were some of the hardest days and Tony's sole focus was the air battle against the enemy.

I scrambled from Hawkinge earlier on but then from Gravesend with 501, difficult to remember the first time, but I do remember it was a grass airfield. As long as you were more or less into the wind it didn't really matter, but we didn't take off strictly speaking in formation. If we took off as a squadron, then you did take off in formation, three of you together. Each squadron was split into four threes and you joined up in the air, but occasionally, if you were scrambled, you just went off, turned the aircraft into wind and went off and we formed up in the air.

Well we'd got to get into the air. We knew that the Hun was very close to us as we were being scrambled. It was only getting into the air as quickly as possible and forming up as a squadron. It wasn't really a tactic. We knew what to do. We were well trained by that time.

We were usually in the dispersal hut, sitting in chairs comfortably, playing cards or something like that, suddenly get the scramble, the alarm would go. Your parachute would be in the aircraft, your fitters would be standing by the aircraft because they didn't go and sit in the hut as well. They stood by the aircraft at all times when you were on duty. A fitter and a rigger were there and with the starter battery alongside plugged in your aircraft and immediately you got the scramble you just probably ran about thirty or forty yards, jumped into the aircraft, pulled your parachute on, and within possibly two minutes you were taking off, probably less than two minutes in lots of cases.

You just got to your aircraft as quickly as possible. You would have your backside kicked, there's no doubt about that. You had to run. On occasions we did sit in the aircraft. We were brought to readiness sitting in our aircraft. We were sitting there with our parachutes on, helmets on, and then you'd get the signal to scramble and suddenly a Verey pistol would fire a signal, a light would go up, and you'd go off.

Hogan used to bring the squadron up to head-on attacks. It was always going in from the front and in the distance you'd see a big black cloud, looked like a thunderstorm, but it actually was a formation of probably 200 German bombers coming in. Above them you could see the 109s as they were turning and twisting above the bombers to protect them, and he would take us in on these head-on attacks when we hoped we could get there before the 109s could come down onto us to protect their bombers. You'd go straight through the bombers. You'd fire your guns. If there was any knocked down, of course the senior blokes would claim them and down you'd go and that was it. You'd then be attacked by these 109s and it was a matter of looking after yourself then. It was every man for himself then, and eventually, after a few minutes, Hogan would call up and say 'Re-form', using coded words of course, re-form over Ashford or somewhere, but using code all the time and telling us to re-form at a certain height and we'd go back as a squadron again. Then he'd call us together and we'd go in for another attack, that's what used to happen.

Those tactics were adopted certainly by the younger members of the squadron who would then go in, fire their guns, and then go straight through because we knew the 109s would be sitting up there waiting to come onto us, but you'd have to watch your step for the next two or three minutes and make sure a 109 didn't get behind you. You had to climb up and do a quick turn or something. The sky's very large, very large, because you'd see these things going on one minute, and twenty seconds later you wouldn't see an aircraft for some reason, only the big black cloud of the bombers, you'd see them going, but the sky would empty very quickly. That was the difference between the First and Second World Wars. We were firing our guns and flying at a higher speed, considerably higher speed, than they did in the First World War. When you see films of the First World War they were fighting around each other and waving their guns at each other and things like that; but of course ours was so quick, everything moved so quick.

I think we were sensible enough to realise that probably we missed them anyway, but I suppose we must have hit some of them. The senior blokes were better pilots, there's no doubt about it. They were entitled to them. If plenty of heat went down we felt the more senior pilots were entitled to them.

I think we felt more experienced, but even at that time, right through the Battle of Britain until I left the squadron at Christmas, I always felt a junior man. Whether it was because some of the senior men were a little bit more aggressive than I was and they sort of looked down on us as young people, they probably thought we hadn't got a clue and to a certain extent they were right. At least we could fly the aircraft and we could press the button but probably we hadn't got that aggressive spirit one or two of them had, I'll be honest about that. We'd got a job to do but some people took it very very seriously indeed.

Lacey was the type of fighter pilot, I think, who studied people who had been fighter pilots in the First World War. He was determined he was going to make a name for himself and he went into it very seriously. I could just imagine him lying in bed in the evenings and going through dogfights and realising he'd done something and he'd say to himself, no, I shouldn't have done that, I made that mistake, I won't make it again, things like that. He studied, he went into the tactics more than we did. Although Ginger was only a few years older than me he was a man and I was a boy, that's the difference.

On 1 September Tony was in action over Caterham in Surrey when he was shot down by a German bomber gunner.

I've seen in a book somewhere that I was shot down by 109s, but I was not. I was shot down by bombers. We were going in on a head-on attack and the front gunners on this aircraft shot my sump away, the Hurricane's sump. I lost all my oil and there was smoke. I had to go vertically down, more or less, until I could straighten out and keep the smoke away from me. There was mostly smoke to start with, complete black smoke was filling the cockpit and I had to sort of sideslip a bit to send the smoke away and then I got down to about 3,000 feet and flames appeared and as soon as I saw flames I was over the side, I didn't wait.

The canopy was already open. All I did was pull the clip, lift myself up, and out I came like a cork out of a bottle. I didn't have to climb out, you didn't climb out of Hurricanes or Spitfires, fighter aircraft, you just eased yourself out of the seat and the slipstream of the aircraft would pull you straight out.

I landed in the Guards depot at Caterham. That was quite a story really because I had no badges of rank, I'd just got a shirt, I hadn't even got a tie,

I'd got a silk scarf round my neck just to keep my neck clean and a shirt and a pair of slacks and I was picked up by Irish Guardsmen. They'd got their guns and pointed them at me as they didn't know whether I was British or a hun, because they were falling out of the sky, the huns were, in fairly large numbers in those days. I identified myself and they said right we'll take you to our commanding officer and they took me to an Irish Colonel. He gave me a drink. He said, 'Would you like a whiskey?' and he gave me a whiskey. 'You can have my car to take you back to Kenley' – the aerodrome at Kenley where I was based then. I had that and then two years later when I was a flight lieutenant I was sitting in a train from Euston to Rugby and two gentlemen sat opposite me in civilian clothes, military men obviously. One of them suddenly said to me, 'Excuse me, Sir, did you get shot down over the Guards depot at Caterham?' I said, 'Yes, I did, as a matter of fact, two years ago.' They said, 'We are the two guardsmen who picked you up that day. We are two Irish guardsmen. We are going to Ireland on leave and we recognised you.' I always remember that.

On 29 October Tony managed to get his own back when he shot down a 109.

Well the strange thing was we'd been attacking Ju88s, bombers, and I got myself nicely positioned behind this Ju88 and he suddenly saw me. I was in a Hurricane, he suddenly saw me and he knew I was behind him. I don't know whether I gave him a quick burst and he just opened his taps, I'd got my throttle fully open and he went faster than me by at least 50mph. Absolutely amazed me, that did. What type of Ju88 it was I don't know but he just opened his throttles completely and before I could do anything more about it he shot away from me. I bent my throttle lever over as far as I could get – it was metal and you could push it and get a bit more – but I couldn't get near him. Then I saw this 109 coming and I got behind him and shot him down. I don't think he was trying to attack me, I think he'd been attacked. I think somebody had had a go at this 109, but there was no-one else in the sky because again the sky suddenly became empty except I saw this 109 coming. So I thought, 'Right, just the job,' and I got behind him and I got to shoot him down. He was a darn sight slower than the Ju88. He couldn't get away from me. I was able to hold my speed such as I stayed behind him but I couldn't with the Ju88. I've never forgotten that. It's a bit strange.

That was a fairly simple case, I must be honest. I think he'd been knocked about by some Spitfires or Hurricanes. Someone had had a go at him but he'd got away and there wasn't another aircraft in sight. No-one was behind him, nobody was near him, he was all by himself and I got behind him and knocked him down.

Sometimes even the youngsters needed an occasional day off.

I do remember that we were working hard, really working hard. We knew what we'd got to do. We did get a day off occasionally. About every eight or nine days the CO would say 'You can have a day off, 24 hours off.' Even at that hectic time we were given 24 hours off and you would probably go and visit some friends, but get off the station, that was the main thing. Most important, get off the station for 24 hours. You couldn't sit on your bottom and stay on the station. It was most important you got away.

At about six or seven o'clock in the evening you got off which meant travelling through London and I've never forgotten going on the underground and seeing these hundreds of people lying on the platform sleeping. A lot of them were elderly ladies with children. I can remember more than once when these elderly ladies would see my RAF uniform with my wings and they'd get up and put their arms round me and say to me: 'You boys carry on, you boys carry on. We rely so much on you.' I've never forgotten that and then getting to Euston station where I would get a train to Rugby for a few hours, going to Euston station, bombs would be falling around and these elderly ladies again would be serving us cups of tea in the canteen, inviting us in to have a cup of tea. They were all elderly people. I've never forgotten these elderly ladies. It was wonderful. It was humbling. And I remember getting taxis through London where they were dodging the bombs in the road – terrible.

When I was going, usually by taxi, through London to get from one station to another, you'd see fire engines all over the road, you'd hear bombs going off, you'd see buildings collapsed into the road and the taxi driver would try and get round these buildings. It was pretty hectic, but being very young it seems strange, I mean today I'd be very worried about it but I wasn't worried at all.

At other times, specially as it neared Autumn, they just needed an evening off.

We used to go down to the local pub because by that time the evenings were coming in. We were a day fighter squadron, we were not equipped to fly as night fighters. Some of the more senior pilots did try and do this but it was never successful. One or two of the very senior pilots would be sent off at night time in Hurricanes to try and attack the bombers, but it was done rarely because they were just not equipped. They had no radar or anything like that. They just had to look out of a Hurricane and try and find the bombers. It just didn't work. It was not successful.

So we invariably would go out as small groups of sergeants together and the officers together but the sergeants had the advantage over the officers. I've always mentioned this before to people. We as sergeants were allowed to mix with the WAAF girls, these young girls of 18 and 19 years of age. The officers were not allowed to do it. They were very strict. Officers were not allowed to mix with the WAAFs. We were, so the few sergeant pilots in the squadron had the pick of the girls on the station. They were lovely girls and I've always admired those girls because they were well brought up, well educated, and quite frankly they behaved themselves, and we, to a large extent, behaved ourselves. Quite frankly the evenings we spent with them were really enjoyable and I've never forgotten them. They were the ones who got bombed. We didn't. We took off, but these young girls were on the aerodrome. Later on we moved to Kenley and they got bombed. There weren't any bombs dropped at Gravesend but when we moved at the beginning of September to Kenley, the Royal Air Force permanent station, the WAAFs there looked after us and they looked after us very well.

I think that we, as young men, respected these girls. We'd been taught by our parents to respect girls and we were young lads and I think there's always a black sheep in a family, we knew that, but generally, to a very large extent, we respected the girls and they respected us. We had some lovely times together, walking back from the pub at about 10.30 at night back to the aerodrome, a mile, OK we used to stop and have a cuddle or something like that, but nevertheless they were nice girls. But they were the ones who suffered, we didn't, and those girls stuck it out. There were a lot killed at Biggin, lot of WAAFs killed at Biggin. I don't know whether any were killed at Kenley, but certainly these girls were very brave. Always admired them.

They were plotters. And some of them worked on aircraft. They did a lot of clerical work and when we were at Kenley we had dances about three days a week in the sergeants' mess and these girls used to come in and we'd be dancing away. There was always some bright individual who could play the piano or play an instrument. But these girls were strictly controlled by the WAAF officers. I'll give the WAAF officers' credit. They were elderly ladies, as far as I was concerned, they were probably only in their late twenties but they were elderly as far as I was concerned. They looked after these girls and they were disciplined, they had to be in their billets at a certain time and they weren't allowed to take any of us to their billets or anything like that.

After a few weeks on the squadron the constant intensity started to take its toll.

We were certainly very overworked, there was no doubt about that. We had lost quite a few people; 501 lost a lot of pilots but nevertheless morale never went so low that we ever thought we would lose this battle. It never entered our heads. You felt tired, and you were. We were physically tired because you were getting up early in the morning, you weren't getting any rest until early in the evening, but of course, thank goodness, we appreciated the dark nights coming in. It meant that instead of being on duty for about fifteen hours or something like that the times were getting shorter, certainly daylight was getting shorter and shorter, and I think we did appreciate the fact that that improved our morale. Morale was improved because we were receiving a hammering, we must be honest about it.

I've never forgotten one Saturday evening round about the end of September, I suppose, when Dowding put up about twelve squadrons on the Saturday evening. There wasn't a hun in sight. I don't think the hun had left their aerodromes in France. It was later in the year and about an hour before dusk. We flew up and down, these squadrons, on the railway line between Ashford in Kent and up towards Croydon; there's a stretch of straight railway line. We would patrol that line quite often and he put these squadrons up on either side of this line and everywhere you went you could see a squadron of Hurricanes, a squadron of Spitfires... just on that, the one occasion. I felt the morale of the squadron was getting a bit low; we'd taken punishment and morale leapt up immediately when you could see nothing but your own fighters all over, squadron there, squadron here, and I've never forgotten it. I don't know the date of it but I know it was a Saturday and I've never seen that written in a book anywhere. No-one's ever mentioned it to me but I do remember it vividly. Certainly my morale had gone down and I felt that it had for a lot of us. On that Saturday night, in my opinion, that's when Dowding really showed himself. He put us up and we could see nothing; we had about three quarters of an hour of flying, and there was nothing but Spitfires and Hurricanes to be seen all in beautiful squadron form, all tightly together, and then we landed and I don't think the hun crossed the coast. That was a magnificent move on the part of Dowding.

As well as his personal milestones, some other events also stuck in Tony's mind.

The big bombing of the docks of London when we were at Gravesend, that must have been the very early part of September. I've never forgotten that because it was terrible. There was smoke and flames coming up all over the place. I don't know why we'd missed them. I have a feeling we were late taking off for some reason, not only us but the other squadrons as well, and they got right through to the docks and they played havoc. I remember that one in particular. We couldn't stop them that day.

The success with 501 Squadron was to stop the bombers getting to London, making them drop their bombs into the Thames or into the fields. That was where you had success. I don't say on every occasion because there were so many of them, but we did turn them and that was our job, to turn them. On lots of occasions they did drop their bombs at random into the fields and on the Thames, but of course I'm not denying the fact that they heavily bombed London.

Another event that stayed with him for the rest of his life involved another 501 pilot of a similar age to Tony. His name was Eddie Egan. Eddie was posted from 615 Squadron to 501 on 3 September 1940. On the 15th he shot down a 109. Just two days later he was out on patrol with Tony.

Eddie and I were young fellows of a similar nature, similar education in the squadron, two young sergeant pilots who used to read books, play music, go and have a half pint, no heavy drinking, just a small drink, and mix with the girls, but we lived a similar sort of life. We were probably two lads who'd lived a sheltered life, ex-grammar school boys, not used to the rough and tumble of civilian life, and we got on well together. Of course he was shot down flying alongside me. We were flying together and what I thought were Spitfires came down and picked him off, but they weren't, they were 109s and it was too late. I thought there were three Spitfires above us but they were 109s.

Yes it did upset me because I never knew why they picked him and not me. Because they could have got me the same way. We'd been talking to each other. We'd been split up from the squadron, told what to do to get back into the squadron again, fly to a certain position at a certain height. We were both endeavouring to do that but these 109s picked him off.

Later on the Battle of Britain was given what sometimes seem to be arbitrary start and end dates, but at the time there was no end as far as the pilots were concerned.

It was no different as far as I was concerned. We were still flying in November and right up until Christmas. Probably not quite so hectic, but November was quite busy as far as I remember. I wouldn't have cut it off at the end of October. I would have said November, but certainly by Christmas time it had got quieter. It was Christmas, the 29th I think. It was the end of December when I was at Northolt with 601 Squadron and they bombed the city of London that night, they set fire to London. You could read a newspaper at midnight as the flames were such. London was absolutely ablaze on that night.

On 20 December Tony was posted to 601 Squadron. But less than two months later, now tour expired, he went to 57 OTU at Hawarden near Chester to instruct and test aircraft from the maintenance unit there. It was also Tony's first chance to fly a Spitfire and compare it with his experience on Hurricanes.

Well I enjoyed it from the experience that I survived obviously, but secondly I felt a lot older, a lot more competent, after going through the Battle of Britain. When I was asked to become a test pilot at a maintenance unit to fly Spitfires, the first time I flew Spitfires, I felt confident I could do the job, and being basically a very young and inexperienced engineer I was a success as a test pilot. I was interested in the aircraft, I was interested in the engine. I was interested in who made this part, who made that part. There were very few, apart from the ex-Halton boys, that had got an engineering background. They'd taught them engineering, but generally most of the pilots didn't know one end of a hammer from the other end or a spanner.

When I took this test pilot's job I realised it was Spitfires and I said, 'Good gracious, I've never flown one of them but I've seen them, I know a bit about them.' I was fully conversant with the Hurricanes and I knew I'd only got to get in and just look at the taps. I didn't need anybody to show me anything. I think I'd probably sat in a Spitfire before but I'd never flown one. So I flew it and I was really impressed with it.

I think it was a better fighter aircraft than the Hurricane. The Hurricane was a good stable aircraft, could take a lot of punishment. It was like comparing a racehorse with a farm horse. The farm horse could pull a lot of loads, do all its work on the farm, the racehorse would do the racing. It was about 50 mph faster, you see, than the Hurricane. I bet they tell you in the books it was only about ten or fifteen, but in actual fact it was about 50 mph faster.

Tony spent two years at Hawarden, but finally it was time for him to go back on operations.

The Wing Commander said to me, 'We want a flight lieutenant in 131 Squadron' – by that time I was a flight lieutenant – he said, 'Would you like the flight commander's job?' and I said yes, and I went with Sampson.

Ralph 'Sammy' Sampson had been in the army until 1940 but transferred to the RAF and finished his training in March 1942. He joined 602 Squadron, taking part in the Dieppe operations in August the same year. At the end of 1942 he became a flight commander with 131 Squadron based at Castletown in northern Scotland.

It wasn't so hectic, of course, not to start with. We started doing sweeps and we sometimes did two sweeps a day over France later on but when

I first joined them they were up at Castletown in Scotland and it was a nice little job flying these Spitfires round and looking after Scapa Flow, that was our job to look after Scapa Flow. I enjoyed it there and even went off and did a bit of deck landing on an aircraft carrier. That's quite a story too because I was a junior flight commander, Sampson was a senior flight commander, Squadron Leader Jimmy O'Meara was the CO, and a message came in from Fighter Command. They wanted one officer and six other pilots trained to fly off aircraft carriers just before the invasion of Sicily as a reserve which they could transfer to the navy straight away. So in the mess one night this message came in. The adjutant showed it to Jimmy O'Meara, the CO. They wanted the squadron leader I think and he said, 'I'm not bloody well going,' and Sampson says, 'I'm not bloody well going,' and they both pointed to me and said, 'You're going,' and I had to go and take these boys flying Seafires, and that's the story of how I came to fly Seafires on aircraft carriers. But they didn't need us because they landed in Sicily and they didn't get the casualties they expected so they didn't need us and after about six months they said we were no longer held as reserves for the navy. We were held as reserves but they did offer us commissions, they said we could go into the navy with the same rank and the same seniority.

No, I didn't want to go on bloody carriers. We broke a few aircraft training, I can tell you. I don't think I did. I didn't because I had a year testing Spitfires and a year as an instructor so I was very experienced as regards Spitfires and Seafires. I didn't break one but some of them did because you were only allowed to come in at a certain speed, you see. And some of the chaps got the speed a bit low and they dropped it from about twenty feet, and on the Spitfire, if you dropped it from twenty feet, the undercarriage came up straight through your wings. That was the difference between that and a Hurricane. The Hurricane would bounce, if you dropped it from twenty feet it would bounce, but the Spitfire, the ruddy undercarriage went ping! straight through the wing.

We re-formed, got new pilots, not completely but probably four or five new pilots, and the CO, Squadron Leader Jimmy O'Meara, an Irishman, brought us down. We came down to Exeter and by that time we were joining in sweeps going over Brest and the western side of France. It was fairly quiet because the hun was not interested in knocking Spitfires down at that time. Most of his squadrons had gone to Russia and they didn't want to waste any of their 190s or 109s by mixing it with Spitfires. They were there to stop the bombers and the Americans were bombing that part of France, Brest and La Pallice a bit further down, various ports on the Biscay coast.

The Americans were going in and bombing them and our job was to escort the Americans. Invariably we couldn't escort them all the way because it was a long way. We had only got two hours. We had long range tanks which gave us about two and a half hours and we dropped the tanks when we got over to France. You had them under the fuselage and you pulled a lever and they dropped. When you emptied it, you emptied that first, and then went onto your main tanks. We used to do these trips over there but we weren't interfered with by the huns, not as a rule. I did fire my guns over Brest once and then a bloody stupid Spitfire got in front of me and I put about twenty or thirty holes in him and we had to stop and the hun got away because he interfered with me. I remember that. It's one trip I do remember.

Rodeo was usually a fighter do where we escorted. They were bombing what they called Noball targets, which were those flying bomb targets in France. We moved up from Exeter to various stations like Redhill or Kenley, as a forward base, or Hawkinge or Manston. We got take-off early in the morning and move up. Sometimes we would go overnight, come to a forward base overnight. There would be a wing of us, two squadrons, 131 and the one Ken Wilkinson was in, 253.

It was like a busman's holiday, I suppose you'd say. Providing the Merlin engine ran, there wasn't any fear of not coming back because we weren't attacking, at that time, we were not attacking anti-aircraft posts. Now the old hun was bloody good with anti-aircraft. You never mixed it with their anti-aircraft people. If you went into an aerodrome to machine gun it, if you found anything on the ground to machine gun, you never went back a second time, you only went in once. That's why poor old Ken MacKenzie became a prisoner of war. He was attacking an aerodrome in Brest, went in, machine gunned it and they fired back at him. Being an Irishman Ken thought, 'Right, I'm going back and having a go at them,' and they shot him down. I always pull his leg about that.

Jimmy O'Meara had been all through the Battle of Britain and was a good pilot. An excellent pilot, a good leader, he flew us as a squadron through some very bad weather coming back from trips over France getting back to England, and you know what England's like, mist and fog coming down. He'd bring us back to the aerodrome, he was very good. You couldn't see your hand in front of you but he'd bring us all in very tight together and he'd take us straight to the aerodrome. He hadn't got radar in those days. He was given a course to fly but no guarantee you were going to be within five miles of your aerodrome, but Jimmy used to come straight over the middle, he was good.

These fighter operations over occupied Europe were flown almost daily from the spring of 1941 until the early part of 1944 but they were treated as a 'battle' and were never well documented after the war.

Well it was successful from a fighter pilot's point of view in so much as we got control over Europe. We could fly around Europe as long as you were in large numbers, and we were in large numbers. We were flying Spitfire Vs for quite a bit of the time, we did have IXs later on but we had Vs to start with, and Johnnie Johnson, with his IXs from Kenley, he had three Canadian squadrons at Kenley, Johnson was flying above us and looking after us. We were supposed to be escorting the bombers but Johnson and his boys from Kenley were looking after us. If any huns appeared he'd drive them off before they came near us.

Perhaps the biggest danger was from itchy-fingered American gunners.

Well, it was a bit of a bind. The trouble was you were told not to get within a mile of the Americans because they were a bit trigger-happy. OK I can understand it because if there weren't any British aircraft around, or American fighters around for that matter, they were attacked pretty heavily. They had a rough time, the Americans did, so you can understand them being a bit trigger-happy – so we didn't go within a mile of them.

(We also went on) Rhubarbs, which was just flying around in twos and threes. You'd say to some young pilots coming into the squadron, 'We've got some rhubarbs tomorrow. You'll go with Bill, the two of you. Take off, go in at deck level all the way, attack cars, buses, anything you see over there, lorries or anything like that. Attack aerodromes, get back quickly, don't stay about. Attack trains, transport and things like that.' We didn't do many of them but we did a few.

They were more exciting. Flying as an escort to a bomber was just a day job to do, but going in you'd got to be a bit brighter when you were attacking things on the ground because you knew very well if you made a mistake you could get shot down, but you very rarely got shot down when you were escorting bombers. Even the anti-aircraft fire was directed at the bombers, not us. The hun knew the bombers would do the damage and we wouldn't. We couldn't do any damage up there.

With your cannons and machine guns you would go in sweeping over the fields and the forests and trees and looking out for something going along a road, a big lorry or a train. You put your nose down, press the button, give it a two second burst, that was about all, and away you'd come and go and look for something else. Just two of you.

Initially we flew Spitfire Mk.Vs but they were underpowered. Nice aircraft, but bear in mind it was underpowered. At that time the hun with the late 109s and the 190s were superior to us. Thank goodness we weren't doing a very exciting job and we weren't interfered with escorting these bombers, but when we got the IXs, that was a different story. We'd got it on the hun then once we got the IXs, especially the IXBs. The IXA was good but that was for high flying, but the IXB, Johnnie Johnson had the IXBs at Kenley and you could hear him. We'd be on the same wavelength as we were escorting the bombers and he was higher up. You could hear Johnson giving his instructions to his Canadians. They were having a wonderful time. They were good.

By the beginning of 1944 Tony was getting tired, having flown continuously either testing, instructing or on his two tours of operations for three and a half years.

At the end of the second tour I'd had enough. I felt a bit weary. I'd got the responsibility of being a flight commander. Occasionally when the CO was away and Sammy Sampson would say to me 'It's your turn to lead the squadron today,' and I'd lead. You'd got more responsibility and I think you felt that responsibility. You were pretty young, still only 24 years of age. It was a big responsibility looking after the chaps and occasionally you lost a man. Invariably it was probably an accident. I remember one fellow in particular being killed down at Culmhead. A young pilot came and landed behind a Spitfire and the propeller hit the fellow in the cockpit, tore him to pieces. He landed too close behind the other one and went straight into the back. That sort of thing wasn't very pleasant. You didn't mind a fellow landing without his undercarriage or getting a cut on his face, or even breaking an arm or something, but you didn't like the idea of someone being churned up by a propeller. It wasn't very nice.

For most of 1944 Tony stayed in the south-west taking on a variety of roles from controller to gunnery officer. However, there was a possibility that he could get back into the action. 616 Squadron was re-forming and testing their new Gloster Meteor jets at Culmhead in Somerset.

It was a rest period at the end of my second tour and I met this man, Squadron Leader Watts, a very nice gentleman. I had met him before as a fighter pilot when he was a flight lieutenant and I was a sergeant pilot and we got on well. Together with one or two of his other pilots we would sit and have drinks together in the mess at Colerne. I was at headquarters of 10 Group at Rudloe Manor and we used to meet in the mess. They'd got these Meteors, the first squadron to get them, and they were starting to get operational and he said, 'We could just do with you in our squadron, Pick.' I said, 'Well I can't make any effort at that because if I'm found out

I'm going to be in trouble because they've told us disciplinary action will be taken against anyone who makes any effort to use influence.' But anyhow he thought he could get me in. He said, 'Pick, don't worry, you're in,' and forty-eight hours later, more or less, I was on the way to Egypt.

I never saw him again, Squadron Leader Watts. A good guy but he was outdone by the people in Fighter Command. 'Oh he wants that fellow Pickering does he? What's Pickering been doing?' and somebody would say, 'He's that fellow at 10 Group. He's trying to get in through the back door. We'll send him out to Egypt.' I have a feeling I knew the fellow who did it too. He'd been out in Egypt and had a rough time. I met him earlier before all this happened and he said, 'Haven't you been overseas yet?' I said, 'No, I've been spending my time in the UK. I've been doing sweeps and things like that.' He said, 'You chaps, sitting here and enjoying life. You should go out into the desert and do a bit of real flying.' He was a bit aggressive to me. He was at headquarters Fighter Command and I thought afterwards that somebody had mentioned my name to him and he's getting his own back. Anyway I didn't mind. I appreciated it afterwards. I really enjoyed it out there.

After going through headquarters Middle East at Cairo and then at Alexandria I went out for a few days to El Ballah to the Gunnery school there. I did a gunnery course because when I was an instructor I'd been sent on a gunnery course to Sutton Bridge. I'd been flying and I got a good assessment as a gunnery instructor. My logbook would tell you I got one of my best assessments there and I must have been alright as a gunnery instructor because then they moved me back to 131 Squadron, to a fighter squadron, and that must have been on my records.

I met Hector Proctor out there but he didn't know what my records were. They didn't even know I was going out there, but he said, 'What have you done?' and I told him what I'd done after leaving him as a sergeant pilot years before, told him what I'd been through and he said, 'Right, we've got a post at the gunnery school that would just suit you,' as I must have told him I had done the gunnery course and been a gunnery instructor flying Spitfires. Dropping bombs as well, firing rockets and things like that. He said, 'You're just the man I want. There's a squadron leader's post up there. You can have that.'

Tony finished his war in Egypt. He returned to the UK in December 1945 and was demobbed the same month. He rejoined his former company, now GEC, and worked for them all over the world. Tony was convinced that the RAF and his wartime experiences made a huge difference to his post-war life.

I was only a sergeant pilot during the Battle of Britain and therefore I didn't progress very far generally in life but once I got my commission and I ended up out in Egypt and various places I met people who were better educated than I was and more experienced than me. I felt that, when I came back after the war and went into engineering, I didn't intentionally try to stand out among people. I think I've always realised in life that lots of people know more about engineering and know more about life than I do and I've always respected that. I did find, however, that people were pulling me out to do things.

It's very funny, I'd go to a massive power station in Hong Kong to discuss the operation of the turbines and I'd get on well with the senior men there. For some reason I got on well. I remember once in Hong Kong I went out there and they were in trouble on this turbine and it was making a lot of vibration. They wanted to know what the trouble was. They were only generating about half the power and they asked me and I diagnosed what was wrong and told them how they could put it right and how we could do this and how we could do that. In the evening the chief engineer said to me, 'It's all settled now, Tony, we're quite happy. We'll go and have a drink,' and we went to a place called the Harvest Moon, a lowdown place in Hong Kong, to meet the other engineers, a lot of the young engineers who hadn't got their wives out there with them, and we had a couple of drinks. Then he put his hand on my shoulder and said, 'Tony, this is not the place for you and I. We'll go to the Hyatt Hotel or somewhere like that,' and we went out of this lowdown dirty place and I thought, well, why did he say that to me. I'm sure he could see in me that I had experienced life and I think that's what I can thank the air force for. He picked me out and it happened all over the world; I went all over the world with GEC, any country you like. The only country I haven't been to is South America, I've been everywhere else, and I feel that people who I've met, people in senior positions, have gone out of their way to make themselves known to me and discuss with me and I think they could see something I'd got which the ordinary man in the street hadn't got. I'm trying to be modest anyway. I don't want to make out I was anyone special, but it was that there was something the air force had built into me. Only six and a half years but they had done something.

It means to me that I was somehow chosen in life to take part in something which did affect the welfare of this country and the survival of this country and why I was picked out to do that I don't know. I think our destiny is decided by someone greater than us, you know. I'm a church man obviously and I think our destiny is all laid out for us. I've had a wonderful life, how much more I've got I don't know, maybe a lot maybe a little, but I do feel that I've enjoyed every minute and I've no regrets whatsoever in this life. As I told you I never fall out with anybody. You can't do it, we don't live long enough for that.

He was also in no doubt about the importance of the Battle of Britain and the British forces in the war.

I think that it's good that the youngsters of today do appreciate that we went through a very serious period. The British people went through a very serious period during 1939 to 1945 and without Winston Churchill leading us I don't think we would have succeeded, no doubt about that, in my opinion. It's not just the Battle of Britain, there was El Alamein as well. They have got to know what happened, thousands of men sacrificed their lives at Alamein. The navy, in their episodes, the people who were destroyed by U-boats and things like that, the people of the navy who were killed in battle. And of course the air force did their bit as well, but I think the youngsters of today ought to know, schools ought to teach them more. It was a critical period. We came very, very close to disappearing off the face of this earth as a nation.

Warrant Officer David Denchfield
2 November 1919-5 December 2012

David Denchfield was born in Eckington near Staveley in Derbyshire and later completed his education at Hemel Hempstead in Hertfordshire.

I was mad on aircraft. There wasn't the same amount of material that was available then as there is now but there were certain books in which the various aces, Mannock, McCudden, Ball, were written about and it fascinated me that somebody could fly up into the sky and do this so I thought right that's going to be for me.

I had tried to get my father to sign the necessary documents allowing me to go into the RAF itself when I became, I think, 17, but remembrances of the First World War were very strong particularly for those that fought on the Western Front and there was a great spirit of 'We won't get caught in this again' among them, certainly not if it meant going overseas. I was unlucky in getting my father to sign the necessary form but luckily the RAF had just recently instigated a system of building up a reserve of trained, well partially trained anyway, pilots, air gunners, air observers plus various ground crews in a scheme which was based around certain large towns and cities and drew their input from around that area.

They had scheduled apparently to have about fifty-three of these working but I think at the time the Second World War started there were thirty-six in operation. My father signed quite happily after the Munich Crisis so I sent away the forms thinking I was going to get to a centre at Hatfield which was quite near my home in Hemel, but, to my surprise, and I suppose some pleasure, I was answered by the town centre at Luton which I didn't know was in existence.

They had only just opened up and they used to fly from the nearby Luton Airport which was almost a private airfield. It had that look about it but they'd certainly got people that used to operate aircraft from there. They'd got the Percival Aircraft company on one side of the entrance road and the Napier Engine Company had formed a flight centre on the other side of the road so I joined that.

18 May 1939 it was. We went for our medical checks etc. I think it was an old hat factory place and I know the girls were getting a great deal of enjoyment from staring from their windows into ours where blokes were walking exposing their backsides etc.

There were an awful lot of disappointed people there. 'I've been mixing bloody paint at so and so's for donkey's years now they tell me I'm colour blind.' At the end of the day I think that there'd been about seven of us signed up for it and we were due to be taken up for a ride, but the last two, this bloke called Brown was so late that they said 'oh no we can't do it today but you have to turn up at Luton Airport,' which we did, and we flew in a Magister made of matchsticks and plywood all glued together. Tremendously strong. I remember it had like an ordinary bolt to operate the flaps. You hoiked it along to put the flaps down and clicked it back down and if it didn't click back down properly it used to work up and you'd suddenly find yourself on the approach and think what the bloody hell's happening here; but it was a nice aircraft really. Spun like nobody's business. Didn't let you do more than three turns.

This was Spring/Summer of 1939 and David was flying at weekends at 29 E&RFTS. He went solo in July 1939 but as his flying progressed, and the news got worse, there was little thought of any forthcoming conflict.

The fact that I joined the VR, it didn't really worry me. I'd done what I wanted to do and I was all prepared whatever happened to do what the circumstances decided. If we stopped to think seriously about it I suppose a certain apprehension came in, bound to with anybody whatever job they're doing. But no, I wasn't unduly worried.

David continued with his day-to-day work until the day war broke out.

I was down at Dickinsons, envelope manufacturing etc, down in Apsley in Hemel. I was working with a girl called 'Ditches', her real name was Miss Hedges. She was about two years older than I was and I was 18 at the time. We worked on the section print from stock which meant we arranged for printing of whatever people wanted. I was only there for three years.

On that particular day, which I think was 1 September, when Hitler marched into Poland, it was an odd day really. Everybody got cracking with their work but from about midday onwards it got distracted quite a bit because the Territorial Army and other reserves were calling for their people. The radio was full of messages through various people to get up and go and I seemed to be the only one not getting any sort of message at all. My friends in the Territorial Army had long since gone, some perhaps home, and of course the Special Reserves that were built in with the Army Service, which did come under the Territorial Army, they'd automatically gone. I remember 'Ditch' Hedges coming to me early afternoon and she looked awful, she was drawn, she'd got mascara stains running down from her eyes where she'd been crying. She said, 'I can't bear it. The people we're seeing go, haven't you got anything yet?' I said, 'No, don't worry Ditches they'll come sooner or later.' And really it wasn't a very normal day. It started off being normal but there was something subnormal about it in the end.

I was packing up to go home and my boss said, 'Where are you going, Dave?' I said, 'I'm going home, Mr So and So.' 'Well,' he said, 'Clear your desk first.' I said, 'If you want my bloody desk cleared, you can come across and clear the bugger yourself because I won't and I won't be here on Monday so you can do what the hell you like with it. Cheerio,' and with that I pissed off.

I was at church that Sunday morning and I was in the choir at St Mary's Parish church. My kid brother was also in it. I was at one end of the pew and he was at the far end. And we'd only been going for about five or six minutes when the parson announced that they'd just heard that there'd been no reply or acceptance of the ultimatum given to Germany and so we were now at war with them and we'll just say a prayer and then he advised us to go home. There'd be an evensong that night. And so we went home. But halfway down the hill from the church the sirens went so Tony started to run. I said, 'What are you running for?' He said, 'Well we were always taught to run and get to the nearest shelter.' I said, 'Oh stuff that. I'm not bloody running, probably a false alarm anyway.' We walked down and, just before we got to the junction, right in the middle of this bloody road were some Territorial Army blokes and a local unit. I said, 'What are you doing?' He said, 'We're on anti-aircraft duty, we're putting a machine gun up.' I said, 'What the bloody hell do you expect to hit from here? The first you'll see of them is when they suddenly go past and they're gone. Why don't you get up on top of the hill somewhere?' 'Oh no, that's not what we've been taught.' Well I said, 'You've been bloody taught wrong then.' And then wandered off up the hill.

I then met the girl who would be my first girlfriend, Peggy. I went to see a friend off as he was going to join the Territorial Army at Watford. I think it was an anti-aircraft group, and I saw him off and I became aware there were two girls standing in the doorway so I wandered across to enquire whether the complimentary remarks they had been making had anything to do with me and that's how I met my first girlfriend.

WARRANT OFFICER DAVID DENCHFIELD

In November 1939 David, having finally had the call-up, was posted to 4ITW at Bexhill on the south coast. He was a sergeant and he remembered the way he was treated compared to officers.

On a fighter squadron the blokes that had to tie together in the air to work were either sergeants or officers. Some of the more lowly officers used to borrow money from the sergeants to keep them going because although we both paid mess fees those poor buggers paid a bloody lot. So there was quite a feeling of acceptance between the various ranks in a fighter squadron anyway.

I didn't fare too badly at that time because my instructor was a Sergeant Pilot, and they only had, I think, two pupils each, but we still lost about seven or eight people thrown off the course, one because he queried the conclusion that one of the ground instructors had come to and the next thing he was off.

At the end of April 1940 David went to 15EFTS at Redhill before moving to 15FTS at Brize Norton six weeks later.

When we arrived at Brize Norton to join 15FTS we were told we were on Oxfords. 'I don't want to be on a bloody Oxford. I've sat in one and it's bloody huge. Everything's around you in open space, I like a tight cockpit.' 'Sorry mate but that's what you're doing.' 'What are we going to be flying afterwards?' 'Well you can take a choice on that.' So we all made a choice and like an idiot I put down Blenheims. Thank God I didn't arrive there cause they went down in droves over France. Droves.

Shortly after we started flying Oxfords, I think we'd been flying them about a week, I got to dispersal and said to one of the ground crew, 'Where the bloody hell are all the Oxfords?' 'They've all gone,' he said, 'Yes, they've been flown over to South Cerney or somewhere to join a flying school there. We're going to get Harvards. We're an all Harvards school now.'

My flying instructor started with four pupils. At the end of the first day they got rid of two of them and he was just left with Jack Tibbles and myself. One flew in the morning and the other in the afternoon. It remained that way for two months until the night we did night flying.

That evening, 26 July, David and Jack were flying their Harvards from RAF Windrush, a diversionary airfield in Gloucestershire,.

He took off with Jack Tibbles and was with him an hour and then he said, apparently, 'Well that's it, Jack. I'll get out now and I'll take Denchfield up and you go away and do an hour's circuits and landings. Remember all I've taught you.' Well we were flying not from Brize Norton then but from a grass airfield up north of Brize Norton, and they'd put landing lamps down, they'd got various lighting arrangements there, and I had to walk back to get my chute from the bus that brought us as soon as I saw they were taxiing back. By the time I'd got it, and walked up to the airstrip with it, Jack Tibbles was just about to take off on his first solo. We saw him take off – I can see it now – straight down, straight up, and he started to bank. I thought, 'What the bloody hell's he doing?' We could see a red light gradually making a circle on the tail light on his rudder and at the same time it was going downwards and this continued until suddenly the whole bloody lot went and hit the deck.

They found out later that the reason for that was that we'd been told on take-off to sit there, let the magnetic compass settle down then set the setting on the automatic gyro compass and unplug it. Just check that things are running alright and then you take off down the runway, heading zero according to what you've set on it and that enables you then to turn onto 270 on the first leg, 180, 090 and back on zero to land.

We were told to take off watching that like a hawk but nobody thought to ask what happens if things aren't quite right, and that's what happened to Jack Tibbles. He was so intent on watching this bloody silly gauge that was reading zero zero zero he must have thought 'I'm keeping this bloody straight.' Of course he was because it wasn't unplugged so it was drifting away, and at the same time, as he started to drift away, because he wasn't making a proper turn, it started to lift, and as it started to lift so that encouraged it to get even bigger until eventually it was too late. He couldn't have done anything about it, he was too low to do anything about it. So that wasn't a very pleasant night. We spent a long time looking for him and I'm glad we didn't find him.

About four days after that I was sent off on the first solo. Landed it back and he said 'What was it like?' 'Lovely, it really was.'

That afternoon I was told you're seeing Flight Lieutenant So and So. He's the one that did all the checks if someone said I think we should check that man as to whether he was going to be a decent pilot or not. He was the one who said, no he won't, get rid of him. I was told get an aircraft, take it and wait outside the building. I strapped up. He said, 'Right Denchfield, just taxi off and take off,' so I did the usual taxiing very carefully so I could see what was coming. He said, 'Okay, take off, turn left, turn right, steep turn to the right. Okay take me back.' He got out. Didn't even say a word. They said, 'Did he say you hadn't passed?' and I said, 'No, he didn't. He didn't say much at all.' My instructor comes in all smiles. 'Ah, Denchfield,' he says, 'You've got your wings. You've passed your wings flying test.'

What we needed next was specific training on the type of job we had to do and that I'm afraid we didn't quite get. The training on Spitfires, that was quite a lot different to what we expected. We went up to No 7 OTU at Chester airfield and when we got there we were told we had to fly a Master for an hour.

I duly took off my first trip in a Master. It was quite good really. It's a wooden matchsticks aircraft with, I think, a Rolls Royce Kestrel engine, which was a V-shaped water-cooled engine and roomy cockpit and, best of all, if you're acting safety pilot at the back, they had this wonderful device where you turn a little knob in the cockpit canopy and push it up and then you could pull the lever and you went up in your seat until you actually had your head outside the cockpit canopy area. You sat there behind this windscreen and, cor, what a lovely view I got.

I was acting safety pilot one day. We went soaring up in the air (and I thought) oh that's trouble, and just then a voice said, 'Dave have you noticed anything?' I said, 'You mean like the temperature gauge of the engine going up?' He said, 'Yes, better get back then.' And straight away we went back and the engine was making all sorts of noises as we came in to land. The factory at Chester had a roof that was made like a saw, one vertical side and then a slanting side along for about ten rows I suppose, and I swear blind that as we came in to land my eyes were level with the tops of these slopes on this roof. Later on the Chief Engineer at Chester, because I used to go up there regularly with De Havillands, used to boast that he'd built the factory. I said to him, 'Now you may have built this but I was one of the three that nearly knocked the whole bloody lot down again.'

Anyway, after the trip on the Master we were then sent to the other hangar where they had a Spitfire on trestles with power laid on in the form of hydraulics and you could sit in the cockpit and operate things. They worked – all bar one thing. The engine starter wasn't connected to anything, so you pressed the button and lights and nothing happened.

A marvellous sergeant went through everything with us and I don't think there was much on the list he left off. I was there about an hour and at the end he said, 'Well do you reckon you've got it, Sarge?' and I said, 'Yes, just about.' So I got out and walked back to our dispersal. 'Well Sir. He says you can trust me with it.' 'Right, take that one out there and don't bloody bend it.'

I was then delayed for about ten minutes. My friend Ollie Cooper had done a similar check on another Spit and we used to have a bet every flying school we were at who would get first solo. He got it usually and this time I saw him walking out with a chute and I thought, 'Sod it, I'll have to pay the bugger half a crown again.' Anyway, I was delayed for about five or ten minutes, I got in this aircraft and taxied out and of course with the Spit you had limited time in which to taxi, you couldn't bugger about because the radiators were underneath the wing so they were completely blocked off from the airflows. Hurricanes are different, radiators in full view of the propeller draft. I taxied up past a Spitfire up on its nose and took off. Bloody marvellous, you felt you'd been flying it all your life, so training must have been some good. Came back in, floated in past this bloody aircraft, switched off the engine with about 100 yards to go and shut the fuel off and then she ran on the fuel that was in the carburettor and if you didn't do that you could be sitting at dispersal with the temperature going up and up and up and you couldn't do anything about it, even turning the fuel off it had to get rid of that fuel in the carburettor. And I walked in, saw Ollie there, 'How'd it go Ollie?' 'Well it may have gone alright with you but it didn't go alright for me.' I said, 'Sorry to hear that. What's happened?' Then I said, 'Don't tell me that aircraft on its nose was anything to do with you!' 'Well yes it was,' he said. He said, 'The biggest trouble was getting out the bloody thing.'

David remembered everything about that time in detail, and in particular his feelings about the Spitfire.

The feel of sheer joy that here was an aircraft which did everything you wanted. If you wanted to get up there fast you went up there fast. She was so precise, so precise and lovely.

At no point did David ever feel his training was being rushed so he could get through the system and into a squadron.

Look at it this way: we had three eight-week sessions, one on Magisters, two on Harvards, and then the final one on Spitfires. Those twenty-four weeks they had cut to twenty-one, and for the final time on Spits we had three weeks I think. That had originally been eight so they chopped our training quite a bit but we still did the same number of hours and were forever spending hours each night doing bloody homework because for those three lots of eight weeks we also did ground training as well, things like navigation and air worthiness and god knows what else. We had to pass exams before we got the wings so I think we got the training as regards general airmanship and flying itself. What we did not get was specialist training in the formations we used, and how they could be bettered to enable us to do more to finding out where enemy aircraft were than worrying about what else we were supposed to be doing. We'd got the ability to do that on top of flying the aircraft, we just hadn't got the know-how.

Towards the end of his training David was given an opportunity to become an instructor.

We were asked before we left the last stage of our Harvard flying whether we'd like to go in for instructing as they had a great need for instructors and I was asked and I said 'No. The one thing I joined the RAF for was to fly fighter aircraft,' and particularly after Hitler went into Poland my object in life was to shoot down as many of the buggers as possible. I think we were all of that mentality.

Following his conversion onto Spitfires at Hawarden David was posted to 610 Squadron which had been taken out of the front line at Biggin Hill and sent to rest at Acklington in Northumberland.

There were six of us being sent up to Acklington. We turned up and had breakfast then waited for our transport that would take us to a railway station in Oxford. While we were waiting a Spitfire came into land. He started holding off at about twenty feet up and the aircraft stalled as it was meant to do. He came down with a hell of a thud, shit and crap flew up and out of the mist a solitary wheel went rolling across until it hit the De Havilland factory in the far distance. The aircraft just schussed along the ground, a tangled mass of rubble, and somebody said, 'He's lost them. He's lost them.' And we all burst into maniacal laughter because the pilots' room was plastered with official posters which said 'Lose your so and so and lose your wings', 'Do this and lose your wings.' That was how we left and it was followed later on by the best friend I could ever have, Ollie Cooper. We dated back to VR and we were two of the six. We got on this train and of course it was a no-corridor train, once you were in that compartment that's where you stopped. We'd had a bit of a do the night before and Ollie was a bit of a beer specialist in that he used to pee like mad the next day. He suddenly gets up and starts wandering the aisle in between the two seats. So I said, 'For God's sake Ollie sit down. What's wrong?' And he's like, 'I think I want to pee.' And I say, 'It's easy, drop the window in the door and just stand there and pee out into the open.' 'Can't do that,' he says, 'it's not right.' So this carried on until the train began to slow and we suddenly shot into a tunnel. About a hundred yards or so we stopped so I said, 'Come on Ollie. Can you manage to do it without peeing yourself?' Somebody opened the window so he started, a great gush and the train went chuff chuff chuff, went forward about fifteen or twenty yards and he was piddling into a crowd of people that were absolutely crowded on this platform and the look of horror on their faces. All these people getting out of the way! Phil Goddard, in his usual calm way, said, 'Well they hardly thought it was a welcome from the fire services' Thames barge did they?' And so that put us in a good mood the whole way and, in fact, when we went into a hotel in Newcastle for a meal at midday they had a sort of head waiter wandering around. He didn't do any waiting, just swanned around, and he said, 'Calling Mr Thomas, Calling Mr Thomas,' and someone said, 'Calling John, Calling John Thomas,' so that put us in a good mood again.

David and his five friends settled in at Acklington to learn about squadron life.

I think everybody wanted to be there, they wanted to get to know the way the squadron worked because obviously they didn't want to get turned out by doing something bloody silly. As regards flying ability, well, you've either got it or you haven't and the powers that be reckoned we had. I think that our group enjoyed it immensely, they settled in with it, it was a bit difficult at times because people came people went. You could see what they were trying to do, trying to hold on to whichever people they thought might benefit the squadron and other people they got rid of fairly quickly.

We had one pilot I remember. I flew with Joe Pegge, Flight Lieutenant, and this other pilot was supposed to be flying tight formation which meant flying with wing tips not touching and not overlapping at all but very, very tight. This bloke sat about thirty yards out and Joe kept saying, 'Come on number two, come on, come in close, tight.' He didn't budge. If anything he went further away. So Joe gave up talking to him. They got rid of him because they said he wants further training.

We still did the orderly watch duties where we'd have people sitting, waiting to take off if we got a call, and we did get quite a number. Looking back I think a lot of those were probably training exercises and nothing to do with enemy aircraft at all because we seemed to get a lot of calls, so we'd take off and fly over, fly up and down looking, and then eventually they'd say, 'No, forget it, it's all finished.'

The previously mentioned Joe Pegge was the pilot who David remembered most from those days. His full name was Constantine Oliver Joseph Pegge and he gained something of a legendary status at 610, flying through the hardest days of the battle. He was awarded a DFC for destroying seven enemy aircraft and even survived an attack from an Me109 and then running into a bomb crater as he landed at Biggin Hill.

Joe Pegge was one of the original members who had flown with 610 down at Biggin Hill and elsewhere and he was a bloody superb pilot. He was like (Ronnie) Hamlyn the sergeant pilot, senior sergeant, who had flown the same number of operations and they both belonged to the old school.

They seldom used their RT, did hand movements for everything, which was great, particularly if your RT at the moment was turned onto the IFF mode so you could neither hear or receive messages for fifteen seconds. We were flying one day in tight formation up the sea coast, Northumberland coast, at virtually twenty-five feet hopping over groynes and things like that, and Joe was saying, 'Lift up a little bit number three, I'm trying to miss the obstructions. I hope you'll miss too. If you get down there I can't be sure.' It takes a lot of concentration to fly tides at low level and he said, 'I don't want to distract you at all, don't move your eyes from where you're looking.' He said, 'I'm going to read you an excerpt from a little book I've got.' And I had a quick look and I could see him with this bloody book held in his left hand and he was flying with his right hand. It was an extract from the *Kama Sutra*. He said, 'Are you enjoying this? I'll read some more,' and he carried on and he was reading at the same time he was watching, pulling up and across, and eventually he said, 'Well I think we're a little too near the station now for me to read anymore particularly as I want to go up a bit, so that's all.' We'd had about twenty minutes of this. Bloody marvellous, he really was.

On 15 August the Luftwaffe had launched an attack against northern cities from their bases in Scandinavia. Arriving without proper fighter escort, they had received a bloody nose and it proved to be the last attack of its kind. That meant that, for squadrons based in the north later in the battle, there was little enemy activity.

Our predecessors had virtually cut the involvement we had up there to a minimum when they carried out that tremendous fight on that big formation they sent across. They didn't have 109s, just 110s, but they lost a fair number that day and those were only the ones we know about because they came down on British soil. Some additionally must have come down during the long trip back to Norway so we didn't have quite as much involvement, but we were on standby most of the time. Some of us were training and the others were on standby and so on. I think we had people on standby duty almost every day.

Our usual readiness was thirty minutes and this meant that people had got their parachutes already on the aircraft; if it was mine it would be hanging off the port wing. I used to keep it on the port tailplane until they put our bloody silly IFF on and I couldn't dangle it over the IFF aerial so it used to go on the port wing which was just as well as you walk up and under it, grab the two straps, pull away, it fell on your back, came round, click click, bent down, strap between your legs, click click and you're finished.

Ten seconds and you're on your way to get in. Most people, like myself, used to go out if we knew we were going to be on readiness from seven till twelve, something like that, put the chute in place, climb up on the wing – when it got icy it got a bit troublesome. I tried once four times to get up on the wing and slid off every time but eventually you managed to get your hand over the canopy and press the little button down which meant you could slide the hood back; you were away then. So you climbed on board, people adopted various habits after that. Most people did as I did, get their feet inside and sit comfortably on the empty seat, and I mean empty because there was no cushion on it, we relied on the parachute for that. Our helmet was hung, against all regulations, over the mirror sight, the RT lead was plugged into the connection on the front of the seat and the oxygen tube was hung on a loop into the little connector on the side of the cockpit just behind the right-hand side of the dashboard. I stuffed my gloves back behind the gunsight and just dragged them out when we got on board. We then sat and prepared the aircraft, made sure the brakes were on and operated them and read the readings on the dial to make sure they were operating correctly and were hard on. We checked the throttle, that it was not locked hard, and set it to where we wanted it to be, about half an inch open, and then locked it. The propeller, we made sure that was in the starting position, and there were various other bits and pieces to make sure the aircraft was ready for immediate take-off, and then we got out, shut the hood again and went over to the hut.

There was a lot of talking going on. Of course we had Joe Pegge's bloody gramophone. *She had to go and lose it at the Astor*, that was Joe Pegge's favourite. It was on the go incessantly. It was a wind-up type, used to play about two records before it needed winding again. They'd got a bulletin board. We used to get a day off a week when we used to disappear into Newcastle for a day and get back early morning the next day and we used to bring back any magazine or picture we could which would go on this board and had some of the most atrocious photographs you'd ever seen. In fact, if we got visitors, say from army cadets or RAF cadets, whose officers had brought their wives up, Joe Pegge used to make an immediate dash for the wife and say, 'Come and see our bulletin board.' What they thought of these pictures I don't know. There was an awful lot of talking going on. Some people read but I couldn't be bothered to read as there was so much going on besides. You could wander outside and watch what's going on. There were things of interest all the time because we had about thirty odd accidents up there, stupid accidents. I think I had two, or maybe three.

There were also interesting people who used to come in other aircraft. There was the day a Beaufighter landed and Joe Pegge walked across to ask the pilot for his opinion on the weather, as it had been pretty bloody awful, we had a heavy sea fog roll in. He was quite pleased he had done when she took her helmet off, it was a woman pilot, and of course she didn't have radio on board.

One particular day the North Sea delivered a heavy sea mist that would cause problems over the airfield at Acklington.

It started off quite well and I'd taken off round about ten o'clock and gone up to do what was laughably called a reconnaissance, so I was doing my usual thing. I'd gone up north of Newcastle to the next largest town up there. I used to choose that because it had a lovely straight rail track that I used to line up with to do aerobatics. I got up to about 12,000 feet, lined up on this and did about two loops and thought that was enough. I used to do two or three more things like spins, steep turns and then just have a general look round, but I suddenly got a radio call: 'All elfin aircraft return to base immediately.' I thought we must have something coming over so I went belting down and thought, 'What's this bloody cloud. It's sea mist, you can't see through it.' We had a big waste heap from the nearby pits which stuck up nearly 800 feet near us at Acklington but I couldn't see it. The next thing I remember seeing was the balloon barrage and thought 'no, I'd better turn back.' I started to pick up whatever pinpoints I could and I managed to find the railway line that split from the mainline and went round the airfield so that was my great saviour then. By this time I was down at about 400 feet, just above the stuff, and I remember seeing a hangar and thinking it was bloody close. Anyway I did a couple of dummy runs to try and see whether I had a clear run or not and I settled on landing east to west and some silly sod thought it would be a good idea to cause confusion by saying, 'No more landing east west, land north to south,' so I went round and I heard another call: 'This is elfin, can you get a starter ack to me, my engine's stopped.' If you were lucky it would start off the batteries, and that was Joe Doley, so I had to do another dummy run. I did two more and thought if I hang onto that one I should be clear. There's no-one else on the airfield, no-one else landing, Joe won't be moving, so round I went, picked up the pinpoints I'd got and came into land, a beautiful landing. Landing uphill too. And so I gently trundled up the slope and down the other side and I stopped rather violently. Luckily I was only doing five or ten mph. I saw the back end of an aircraft with my wing stuffed into it. I got out, walked round, kicked my aircraft, the tyres, walked across to the other aircraft, kicked it and swore at it and thought it was a good job the pilot wasn't in it because the prop had come in across the back of the seat and was embedded in the instrument panel. It was Joe Doley and so we had a few words. Mine was alright apart from a busted prop and by this time we had a crowd of people round us.

David spent the rest of the time during the battle making regular patrols and waiting for something to happen. Autumn turned to Winter, and finally in December 1940 the squadron returned south and took up residence at Westhampnett, part of the Goodwood estate in Sussex.

Well I only did one would-be interception while I was up north. I was in the Battle of Britain from early October 1940 to the end of October. I did loads of take-offs which I thought at the time were genuine but I now think were training exercises and it didn't get much better when we got down south. I remember being half way across the bloody Channel with a formation of twelve with the CO getting hot under the collar, talking to the control area saying 'Where the hell's this bloody formation?' 'You're over the top of them' he said. 'Well if I am they must be invisible because I can't see them.' It turned out the lot we were looking for were twenty miles further along the coast. So that sort of thing happened only too often. But things were changing. They weren't operating in the same massive formations they had done because Hitler was getting himself ready for the attack on Russia and he was moving heavy bomber units so the whole picture was changing really and it was changing even further the fact that we, having seen the mess he made trying to get to this country, we were going to do the same bloody thing with our pilots by moving them to France.

If anything life was easier because we'd lost all these bloody exercises. The only exercises we did were done as solo exercises after we'd finished another flight and we were more of a cohesive unit than we had been. We no longer had people coming in, stop three days and disappear. We were a collection of pilots and we each knew the others and, oddly enough, we stopped having these bloody foolish accidents. They stopped overnight the minute we set foot in Westhampnett.

And with the reduced pressure the daily routine seemed a bit more relaxed too.

Well it varied of course, depending on what the other people were involved in. If they were involved with you at the same time you used to get up round about seven o'clock. We had two LACs quartered with us who used to do the housework for us and they were very good. Looked after us, brought cups of tea in the morning before we got up, and we'd get up, walk across to the farmhouse to have breakfast, which was nothing to write home about, cornflakes and stuff, toast, sometimes bacon or sausage, egg occasionally, tea or coffee, and wander from there into dispersal. There were two such places. B Flight had a dispersal up at the north end of the airfield while A Flight was in among the general air force buildings along the west side. Take our chutes out, walk across to the aircraft, set the aircraft up, wander back, say hello to anyone we hadn't seen there before and sit down listening to the bloke answering the telephone. The officers used to appear and we used to revert to the usual while we were on readiness.

It was now 1941 and time for the RAF to go on the offensive.

We didn't really get to know anything until a short time into January. We had a sector meeting at Tangmere where there were all sorts of top brass telling us what they had in mind for us as the year went on. We were going to start an array of entries into Europe. The first ones were going to be individual aircraft that were going to dash in, shoot something up and dash out. There were then the sweeps which would entail a load of bomber aircraft, perhaps twelve, being escorted on a bombing raid by about twelve squadrons, the idea being to get German fighters up where they could be dealt with. The trouble is it didn't quite work that way. The other item we were told about was the arrangements for night fighting. As of now, they said, Spitfires, although they had been kept off night fighting, would be doing it. We're arranging for a number of fighter units, Spitfires and Hurricanes, all to be on the same night, every night, to operate a night fighting force which would entail taking say three squadrons, with a range of height bands from zero to nine, and one aircraft from each squadron would go in each height band. Then on the night when it happens the controller would arrange a datum height at which all the aircraft would band, the lowest at the datum height and then at 1,000-foot intervals. You'd have, at any one time, nine aircraft from each squadron operating, and that should bear results. Trouble is you've got to see the bastards first and yes, I know we did have results but they would have done better to keep the ack ack.

I remember Hamlyn saying, 'What happens if one of the aircraft that comes into our orbit on night fighting is a British bomber, apart from the fact they've got gun turrets at the back.' And he said, 'You just shoot it down as it's not supposed to be there, 'That's a bit harsh. What if it's bombers coming back from a trip and it's not quite sure where it is?' 'That's his lark.'

The bomber escort operations were called Circuses and David took his place on Circus 3 on 5 February 1941. 610 Squadron was joined by the Polish 302 Squadron, also from Westhampnett, and 65 Squadron from

Tangmere, among others, to escort twelve Blenheims which would bomb the airfield at St Omer in northern France.

Oh dear, it all started very well really. It started about ten o'clock when the CO comes in and says 'All here? All happy? I've got something to cheer you up a bit. You will all be released from one o'clock today until 0800 tomorrow morning.' Big cheer. 'Only one snag, twelve of you will be going on a trip to France today.' And while he's saying this someone at the back was copying from a sheet onto a blackboard the list of names that were going. He said, 'It's quite straightforward really. We'll take off about twelve o'clock to an assembly place about twenty miles further east and we shall wait there and join various other squadrons and eventually we will have three squadrons of Hurricanes and nine squadrons of Spits. We will be joined at twelve thirty by twelve Blenheims from Norfolk and we'll then go across when the Blenheims will bomb St Omer and we'll all come home. Any questions?' And that was it. We all went out and when I saw the list I thought, 'Oh Christ.'

We all wandered out and got in the aircraft, emptying our pockets first, and we set off. What a mess it turned out to be. We were off the coast dead on time at twelve thirty and we circled, we circled and we circled, and I heard the CO call and say, 'Ground control, where are these bloody Blenheims? Are we at the right place?' 'Yes you are. they'll be with you.' Well they finally turned up at a quarter to one so we quickly fell into shape and we started off over the channel. Our Hurricane friends had gone to join the close support with the Blenheims and we and our other people from Westhampnett, another Spitfire Squadron, they were up above us, we were under them. I can't remember seeing any of them at all. It's not surprising because only four got up through the cloud. We had snow all over the countryside and thick cloud above us and we climbed up through it. From my position as number three on the formation I could see the number two of the squadron commander's section, so the visibility wasn't all that bad, but we broke cloud at about 12,000 feet I suppose and got just above the clouds. Only four of them got above us, the other eight decided they couldn't get through the cloud and did a mid-channel up and down survey. What they thought that would do I don't know. We had two other squadrons that failed to break through the cloud so we set off as a depleted support group to Blenheims that turned up late. We'd given everybody on the other side of the channel the chance to see that something was coming that day. We had two formations here. In fact the reserve group was over Hastings way, that was supposed to take off fifteen minutes after us but in fact they took off a minute before us, they'd already gone. We crossed the channel alright and I was getting a bit uncertain as I kept falling behind. I realise now I was adopting the wrong policy and should have done it differently. I tried to catch up. I suppose we must have been about twenty-five miles south of St Omer when I dropped behind for the next time, partly cause and effect from the last sweep I did to the north, and caught sight of a flash so when I turned back the next time I held onto the curve a bit and that put me behind. I thought they were about 400 yards in front of me so I would catch them up. I did a quick check both ways, opened throttles and went steaming up to get in my place when suddenly I heard a bang, bang, bang...'where did that come from?' ...and tracer going past. I put the stick hard over and put lots of rudder on so I was turning and going down at the same time. There was a loud bang as I did that but nobody followed me. I straightened up eventually, about 8,000 feet I suppose, and I found these things out at different times. I'd obviously got some trouble up front because I was losing revs. I hadn't got the power I should have had. The fuel seemed to have disappeared from the top tank and I'd got no rudder control at all, it was just pushing at empty pedals and the elevator control, I sensed it wasn't half as sensitive as it used to be. Then I also found I had wet legs and that was because I had the contents of the fuel tank, or what was left of it, in the cockpit with me. I caught sight of it as I was checking round the cockpit. It was round my feet sloshing backwards and forwards and it was at that point I said, 'Whatever happens I will not, under any circumstances, make a forced landing. It's bale out or nothing.' So off came the safety harness, I tucked the safety straps away so I'd got no obstructions to getting out, made sure my parachute was hard in, and that was about it. I sat watching all around me eagerly because I was on my own. I then saw the Blenheims just above me going hell for leather. They had made two dummy runs and they were on their last attempt when they would drop their bombs. They caught me up and left me standing so I thought this was a good place to be. I dropped down a bit and maybe the rear gunners would take care of anything coming up behind but I'd only just started when there was a series of queer banging noises from up front and a bloody great flash and I was gone. I couldn't wait any longer. Just as well I did. If I'd left it to get my straps undone it would have been too late. So that was it.

I landed, got rid of my harness and parachute, pushing it under the snow. Took my helmet and discarded the RT stuff. I left the rubber tubing on, I put that on my foot and wound the rubber tube round. And as I was having a pee I saw a bloke in a green uniform coming up the hill because I was in open countryside. There were some houses a short distance away but nothing else. This bloke comes up with a gun in his hand and says, 'For you the war is over.' I thought I remembered reading that phrase, and they took me through, I met a young French boy who told me how old he was and I stopped and thought, 'How long was I doing French at school? Five years?' So they took me up to St Omer airfield.

After that it was a bit of a...I don't say nightmare...more like a comedy act I suppose. I was taken to the airfield at St Omer where we stopped in between two buildings, one of which looked like a haystack but was a camouflaged building, and then suddenly from the building to my right a crowd of German pilots appeared and they all came to a stop and saluted and walked away. I kept saluting until the last one came and thought I couldn't be bothered anymore but the last one turned out to be the commanding officer. Anyway I was given an officer to accompany me while I was there and he took me for a trip round to get a replacement boot and then he realised there was a war on so didn't give me the pair, just the missing boot. So I walked round Germany for the rest of the time in odd boots and I came back with them. He took me for a tour after that, took great delight in showing me the meat store and then took me back into their little mess where we had a cup of tea. They switched onto an English programme on the wireless that I had mentioned and listened to that for about ten minutes and the pilots started to appear and the air was full of words like 'I'm claiming one...he's claiming two,' and I thought they've shot down the bloody lot if it's true. And then I got a companion called Hill, Pilot Officer Hill. He'd been one of the four from 65 who had made it through the cloud above us and he said, 'You know the buggers came straight through us as though we weren't there.' I think he was the first one to be hit and he had the advantage of being able to speak German which did help. We came to the conclusion in the end that they were claiming something like twenty odd shot down, so we didn't believe that and in fact I think it was about five in total. I had the unearthly feeling when we sat in the mess listening to the chatter going on, if I close my eyes and forget about the language I could very well be back at home. The atmosphere was the same, you could tell. Forget the arrogance of the sods, the atmosphere here was the same.

From then I was just trying to control myself so I didn't make any glitches, say anything I ought not to say, get rid of these bloody letters I had in my pocket because I had read them in the toilet there. One was from Ollie Cooper who was with a squadron of Spits that had just moved south and the other one was from a friend of mine who was turfed off flying, waited for about six months and still hadn't been given an air gunner's post so he asked if he could go back to flying and they said yes, sure thing, why didn't you ask? They sent him back to the same flying school that had turned him out, not the same instructor, and this time he went through without trouble. I did manage to get rid of them. I tore them up into little bits and dropped a few bits here and a few bits there.

David was taken to Dulag Luft near Frankfurt. It was to be his first of seven camps over the next four years.

It's just like an army camp really. Much the same as it would be over here except that they had rules and regulations and you have to obey them before you can get the gates opened. But once you're in there you can virtually do what you like. There were some things you had to be careful about... but unless they've got the means of finding out, and with all their prowess at it they weren't so good as they reckoned they were.

They kept us moving from camp to camp to stop us getting stabilised in a particular area because it wasn't long before certain people with the ability could get organised on things like tools or bits of material and so on so they used to keep us moving and stop that happening.

I was lucky. When I arrived at Dulag Luft I teamed up with another pilot, a Hurricane pilot, Flip Jones, Kenneth Jones actually, but when we got to our first proper camp one of the RAF blokes said, 'What's wrong with your voice? You sound just like Flip the Frog.' And from then on he was called Flip. He had had an operation on his larynx. He had been a Hurricane pilot and was on an experimental mission and he ended up above cloud, out of radio touch, and he had to land somewhere and he went down on what seemed to be an airfield, and it wasn't until he was rolling across the grass that he realised that the aircraft had funny markings on them. But we teamed up as a pair and we stuck it like that all the way through.

I tried to escape once but it didn't work so Flip and myself said this war can't last forever. Let's just sit it out. We'd been there about a year and we were on a train. We decided we would get in a carriage with big windows and one bloke said, 'These windows are held down by catches and if we lift the catches we can lift the window and jump out so long as the train's going slow enough.' There were about three guards. The train began to slow down so we lifted the catches to go but as soon as we lifted the window the noise of the wind was terrific and there were a few words from the corridor and a guard ran in with his rifle. And we all said, 'Good evening, officer, how are you? Can you tell me who opened this bloody window?' But that was it.

Like so many other prisoners, David looked out for the delivery of Red Cross parcels.

Well the big thing about the food, the thing that made it edible and made it suitable for us to eat, was the Red Cross food parcels. If we'd had to rely on the German food we'd have starved to death because we went that way in the early days of the war before they got things running properly and then for the last year of the war it was bloody awful, it really was. And when we were out on the march, the last couple of months, we got food which was mainly obtained from the farms where we stopped. Rough and ready food like potatoes and things like that. When I was weighed after I came home I was six stone two pounds and I had been ten stone ten pounds. It's amazing we had any strength at all.

Through occasional news items David and the other prisoners learned that the war was beginning to go the way of the Allies.

I think it was when the news came through about Stalingrad, after that the Germans didn't seem half as confident as they had been before. After Stalingrad one felt if our people do it right they've got this done and dusted. If they make a cock-up of it then they should take the bloody lot out and shoot them. That's the way we felt.

David continued his existence in the various camps until the late winter of 1945 when, fearing capture by the Russians, the German guards started marching the prisoners westwards.

On the last day I spent in captivity we were sleeping on the top floor of a hayloft, three floors of it. When you went to bed, or woke up, you saw little red lights glowing throughout the place (of the guards smoking) and it was hay. (The hayloft) was made from scaffold poles and ladders tied together and that was it so any chance of a mass exodus, you could forget it. So we went to get into our bed space at about nine o'clock at night and we were sitting there smoking when someone came through and said 'Right, get down, we're on the march again.' He was one of those English-speaking ones and he said, 'Our feldwebel has spent the last week trying to get in touch with those in Berlin from whom we get orders. That place is now no longer available.' So he had been left on his own and he had decided he was going to march all of us west to a spot where we can be picked up by our own troops. 'Well I suppose we'd better come then,' and we marched back during the night for about three or four hours until eventually we turned up a longish lane and at the top was a farm and they moved us into this and said 'You spend the night in this.' Flip, myself and Tex – we'd formed a triumvirate – said, 'We're not going in there, not with diseased sheep.' So Flip said, 'Can we not sleep on this heap of straw in the courtyard?' He said, 'Yes, if you like.' So we spread two blankets across it and slept,

Tex in the middle because he was only about five foot four, and us on the outside. We spread our greatcoats across the top, took our boots off and went to sleep and I had the best night's sleep I'd had for years, I really did, and I woke up feeling warm – we used to wake up feeling bloody cold normally – and relaxed. And I'd got something on my face – it was bloody snow and we were covered in it. Added to that we then made the alarming discovery that what we were sleeping on was not a hay mound, it was the farm pile of manure, and it says a lot for our sense of smell that we couldn't discern it, but during that day the British Army came past so our thanks go mostly to the feldwebel in charge who took the decision, both for his own sake and ours, to move back west and I'd shake his hand if I met him.

We'd been taken back by lorries which were on the supply train going back for more and we eventually turned up in a little town which had been bombed to glory and while we were there the American and British troops had come through so we were told to get our own transport to get back to another town. This we did and while we were there the war had been finished about a day. We went into the nearby little town where they had set up a hostel caring for troops on the move and this was great. We were able to listen to British radio, British news, have cups of coffee and generally relax in decent armchairs and I remember I'd got a book, one of these pictorial magazines that had a mass of pictorial information in it, and I remember Flip saying, 'Dave, it's time to go,' and I said, 'OK I'll be with you in a minute,' and I couldn't leave this magazine and the next thing I knew someone said, 'Excuse me Sarge but we've got to turn you out, we're shutting.' 'OK, which way do I go?' I was standing on the steps of this bloody hall and it was pitch black, absolutely pitch black. Wait a minute, we came up that road down there so I'll go there and see what happens. By this time I had acquired a gun, and a knife which Flip Jones had ground on both edges, so I set off down the road with this pistol in my hand. I had it still until about three years ago when I realised I couldn't maintain it any longer so I buried the ammunition in the back garden and took the pistol down to the police station and said 'I want to hand this in please.'

I was walking very steadily down the middle of the road, as quietly as I could, keeping periodic glances behind and to my right and left thinking if there was any problem I would open fire first and ask questions second. And as I walked down this road I came to a school where we had been before and there was a guard on the gate there: 'Hello sarge, you're late.' I said, 'I know, I was too busy reading about the war,' and walked in, got into bed and went to sleep. We'd been classified by that time, Flip and myself had been classified, as most suitable to be taken home or something – that meant that due to the time we had been in, about four and a quarter years. We turned up at an airfield and we were put into flight number so-and-so and were told to go and get some food. Anyway we were both standing there, we had got the plates, had a wash and suddenly the tannoy went 'flight number so-and-so, come now,' and we were gone. On the way we hardly broke step as we picked up a parachute from a pile and we were the last two on board the Lancaster. That was a 22,000-pounder bomb carrier, Grand Slam Lancaster from 617 Squadron. Anyway we tumbled on, we were sitting on a single riveted circular panel under which was the H2S, or had been, we took off, they told us not to interfere with things, not to pull that rod, not to do this, not to do the other. Rear gunner was quite reasonable really. He stood outside his turret and when we approached the English coast he said, 'Anyone want to get in the turret, two at a time?' I didn't bother, nor did Flip, and we had a lot of engine noise changes and then I said to Flip, 'What's he doing now?' as by the attitude and the quietness he was about to put his flaps down, and sure enough we heard the whirr of the machinery as the flaps came down and I just said, 'If he doesn't put it down pretty quick he's going to run out of room,' when the rear door was opened and two voices said, 'Welcome to the airfield near Reading. You're back home.' So we seized our gear and got out.

I should have said that at different stages in our transfer we had had TCP sprayed into us to kill lice. The RAF did it differently. They had an automatic powered spray which they stuck up our trouser legs and into the armpits and three hours later I was gasping for breath as a cloud shot up. They took us into the big hangar and it was actually VE night. We sat at a table with about eight other people and they put all this mass of tables laid out down this hangar-like building and each one had about ten people plus one of the various women's voluntary services that were on duty including WAAFs from the station. Now this is the worst thing I experienced I think, when you want to say fuck off the difficulty of stopping yourself swearing. It had become second nature to garnish your ordinary language with swear words, to add a bit of substance to it. That is something to worry about, but I managed to do it and so did Flip and so did all the other people on the table except one bloke. He said, 'Pass the fucking mustard down mate will you?' and then he went all red. We all burst out laughing, including the girl. Then they called us up, and we went out in dribs and drabs, and from there we went in a bus to the station and from there we travelled around London and up and into the Birmingham district area. We stopped at one station and there was an elderly porter, and I mean elderly, on the other platform and a voice from the carriage said, 'Eh Mate, can you do anything to get this train to go a bit bloody faster?' 'If you want to go faster get out and bloody walk.' 'Oh no,' he said, 'I don't want to get there that quick.' And I thought, thank God we were back in the England of proper humour, and we ended up at the station at Cosford near Birmingham.

We arrived in there about six o'clock in the morning and they said, 'Bath and bed. And you don't go anywhere until you've had both.' I said, 'Alright.' So I had a bath, then they had breakfast for us and then we went to bed about eight o'clock in the morning. I woke up about twelve o'clock and had another bath, something else to eat, and then they took us on a tour of investigations, table by table. Then we got to the awkward bit: 'Were you wearing a flying suit?' 'Well, what was I doing?' 'Ah yes, you were wearing a flying suit. And so that presumably is in Germany now?' which was a bloody lie as I had taken it back home and left it there. After that they gave us money, I think about four or five hundred quid, which wasn't the sole amount, it was just from it, and various forms and paperwork that we had to get down to. We got new uniforms so we spent the night sewing on our emblems because I had gone from being a sergeant pilot to a warrant officer pilot so for the first time went to a mess for warrant officers. We went to bed, got up, had breakfast, got dressed and by nine o'clock we were back at the station. Flip was waiting for a train to go even further into the west country because he lived in Gloucester and I was waiting for one to take me back to London. So we said cheerio, I got on the train which went to Euston, picked up the next train, a local bus and a train through to Hemel Hempstead, stopped outside the Co-op, climbed the stairs to Dad's office, the door was open so I looked in and said, 'Ah, you've got a decent secretary for a change, a nice new one,' and he said, 'When did you come in?' As I went out to go to Dad's car I looked across and there was a Mr Collier there. He was the father of my wife's boyfriend, well he was engaged to be married to her but was killed in '43, so I went across to him and said, 'Sorry Jack can't be coming home as well. I'll look after the wife he would have had anyway if I get half a chance,' as I hadn't met up with Babs then and came home. Dad's secretary had phoned my mother so she was outside on the pavement and my kid brother turned up later on. Bloody annoying as he was now two inches taller than I was. And that was it.

David settled back into peacetime life, joined AV Roe as a draughtsman, and eventually rejoined the RAFVR. He finally left the RAF in 1953 but continued his involvement with aviation, working at De Havilland (later British Aerospace) Hatfield until his retirement in 1984. A talented painter and model-maker David lived in Cambridgeshire until he passed away in 2012.

Squadron Leader Keith Lawrence DFC

25 November 1919-2 June 2016

Keith Lawrence was born in Waitara on New Zealand's north island but went to school, and subsequently worked, at Invercargill, the southernmost city in the country.

It was just the fascination of flying which in those days was in its very early years. That would be in the 1920s and '30s. I suppose it was my interest in flying and what every young person at that age, the late teens and early twenties, all they wanted to do was to learn to fly. Just at that time I was stuck in a very boring job working as a bank clerk and along came the man from the air ministry who was a recruiting officer on a Commonwealth recruiting drive, Australia, New Zealand, Canada, Rhodesia, South Africa, and looking for young chaps who could be trained as aircrew for what was known to be then an inevitable war. Providing you were fit and passed a medical, had passed what was called in those days a School Certificate, had the aptitude and ability to enable you to go solo within a very short time, they were signing up these young chaps to take short service commissions in the RAF. The inducement was to take a commission for four years and then two years on the reserve of air force officers and either to be given the option of doing a certain amount of training with the New Zealand Air Force or going direct to England to complete the training with the RAF. Being of a certain temperament I thought this is what I've been waiting for so I signed up in 1938 and at the beginning of 1939 I set off, set sail.

Keith took very little time to decide which was the best option for him.

The New Zealand Air Force was equipped with the most ancient of old biplanes discarded by the RAF. Wapitis and Vildebeests and such aircraft as that didn't appeal to me as aircraft on which to train so I took the option of electing to train in England and set sail with about thirty others in this old steam ship, forty-two days at sea before we reached Southampton. This was via Panama of course

I had travelled to the north. I lived in the south and travelled to the north but I hadn't travelled outside New Zealand so life wandering off to Panama and to Kingston through Panama of course was an eye-opener where we were allowed off and were guests of the Army Air Force which had a base at Panama and were able to see all these modern, wonderful aircraft that we'd only seen in pictures in magazines.

A few days later we sailed on to the West Indies where we stopped at Kingston, Jamaica, to take on a fresh load of coal to get us across the Atlantic and of course the port life of Kingston Jamaica was a real eye-opener.

Some of the young fellows were introduced to the facts of life, which hadn't been properly explained to them, and what they lost there they gained in other ways only to lose that when they went to the medical quarters in England.

Arriving on the RMS Tainui, Keith was posted to 10 E&RFTS at Yatesbury not far from the site of RAF Lyneham in Wiltshire.

When we arrived in Southampton we were immediately taken off to where we were to do our initial training. I'd never given a thought to what sort of aircraft we would train on except that it would be on a Moth aircraft of some kind. I was so familiar with the local aero-club which I'd frequented as a curious teenager at the flying club and knew the trainers that would be used and in fact they were Tiger Moths.

Our very first stop was the Elementary & Reserve Flying Training School. There were Elementary & Reserves and there were Flying Training schools. The Elementary & Reserves were for training *ab initio*s and the reserve parts were for training volunteer reserve pilots who went for so many months training every year at these particular airfields. The Elementary & Reserves were all run by private companies, one by De Havilland and another by the Bristol Aeroplane Company, and I went to the one run by Bristol which was at Yatesbury in Wiltshire. Although I'd flown only once, as a passenger in a Fox Moth with the local flying club in New Zealand, they had a fleet of Tiger Moths and Ansons for the VRs and the Tiger Moths were a familiar sight. We set about our training almost immediately we got to Yatesbury as civilians because if we weren't found to have the aptitude for pilots as required by the Air Ministry, or the air force, you could be told politely we'll offer you a job as a fitter or an aircraftsman or you can return to civilian life as you please. If you could solo within eight hours you were able to complete the course of fifty hours.

Our instructors at the Elementary and Reserve FTS were in fact ex-RAF officers who were all pilots who had been trained as instructors and were able to give us some idea of what service life would be like and what service training on service aircraft would be when we were given our next posting to a flying training school, an RAF flying training school run by RAF personnel in uniform on a working RAF station.

It was every bit as exciting as what we hoped it would be, the experience of learning to fly in a Tiger Moth. The training was, of course, first of all just take-offs and landings, as simple as that. It sounds a simple thing to a civilian but there's a lot of skill required and quite a few hours before you complete this to the instructor's satisfaction. The very first essential was once you get airborne to keep the aircraft in the air and to know what to do if you lose flying speed and stall it so we learned stalling and recovery from stalls and then spinning because you could accidentally, or inadvertently, get into a spin and if you didn't know the correct drill and the use of controls for coming out of a spin you finished up in the ground as many a First World War pilot did. Then there was aerobatics and finishing up with map reading and aerial navigation.

I passed the CFI's test, the chief instructor's test, and when you completed your course you were assessed as exceptional, above average, average, or the one below that, below average of course. I passed out as average which I thought I was OK. I was competent to do everything I was asked to do and had a great deal of pleasure in doing it. Flying is a very pleasurable accomplishment.

So we could be treated as service personnel when we were posted to our next flying training school, we first of all had to be inducted into the air force and we were posted to the No.1 RAF Depot at Uxbridge to undergo the training that would turn us into servicemen who could drill on the parade ground, take parades and the other duties of air force officers as were needed. Also to have uniforms made, so when we finished our induction and were given our commissions before we left Uxbridge after two weeks we could join the RAF at our flying training school in uniform and be ready to train.

All the uniforms had to be made to a high quality that would satisfy the CO of the depot or his adjutant and for this purpose London military tailors were invited down to take the measurements and make the uniforms of those who were on the course. This required several fittings but eventually they passed the satisfaction of the adjutant and then we were thought to be fit to face service life on an RAF station and were given our commissions.

We knew we were on the bottom rung of the ladder because we were commissioned as acting pilot officers and it would mean a certain amount of probation, six months, before we were granted our full status of pilot officers. At that stage, of course, we had no flying brevet. The wings were still to be earned at the flying training school we went to where wings weren't awarded after fifty hours of solo flying or fifty hours on Tiger Moths, it had to be something more exacting.

Keith knew he would receive a commission as part of the agreement when he joined up in New Zealand, but it was still a special, and formal, occasion.

It was special in a way that we knew that other aircrew joining the RAF came in by means of the Volunteer Reserve. They were always non-commissioned as were many of the Halton-trained tradesmen who were remustering to flying duties.

Officers and other ranks lived very differently. The officers' mess, the sergeants' mess and the way the other ranks lived were very different and we only were aware at that time of life as officers and the way life was lived in the officers' mess.

On 28 May 1939 Keith went on to No.40 Course at 5FTS Sealand in north Wales.

At No.5 Flying Training School Sealand we found ourselves on a course of about fifty trainees. We were split two thirds onto one type of aircraft and one third onto the other. The two thirds were to be trained on Airspeed Oxfords, the twin engined aircraft, and the other third would be trained on Hawker Harts, Audaxes and Hawker Furies and that one third of the course were expected to become fighter pilots in the RAF. I was selected to be trained on twins so I was trained on Airspeed Oxfords and did day and night training, dual and solo, for the next six months which included a lot of classroom training.

I had no ambition to be a fighter pilot although the high speed aircraft and the glamour aircraft of those days were the Hawker Hurricane and the early days of the Spitfire whereas the bombers were lumbering old things like Whitleys, Heyfords and such like, which, in the back of one's mind, you hoped not to be posted to or to be trained for. However, one was selected for one or the other and I was selected for twins, so apart from a lot of time spent in the classroom studying things like meteorology, gunnery, navigation and lots of other associated subjects, all a bit boring but all very necessary, we worked up to the granting of the wings at the end of the course which consisted of a final flying test with the chief flying instructor; first of all one's flight commander then with the chief flying instructor.

It was a very proud moment. We had been in training for all the weeks at EFTS and the flying training school and we'd completed our six months plus, so it was a very proud moment to be able to pin wings on your uniform and be part of the flying fraternity in the RAF.

I think my training on twins led to a certain number of us who were on that course being posted to twin engined Blenheim fighter squadrons, Blenheim F.1s, fighters which could be day or night fighters, and in fact that turned out to be the case. At the end of the course, when I had been awarded my wings, I was posted to No. 234 Squadron which was to be equipped with twin-engined Blenheim fighters. But when we got to Leconfield in South Yorkshire near Beverley we found that in the hangar, allocated to our squadron, were a few old Avro Tutor trainers that had been trainers for the RAF in the early thirties, Magisters which were single engined monoplane trainers, the equivalent of Tiger Moths, and a few Fairey Battles, the old light bomber, very much under-powered even with its Merlin engine. So until our Blenheims arrived, our flying skills were kept in hand by lots of flying on the Magisters and the Avro Tutors; a beautiful aircraft it was to fly too, one of the most pleasurable I have ever flown. Before we received our Blenheims we started training in, for what reason I don't know, service aircraft which were in service. We were given instruction in flying the Fairey Battle which, at the end of the canopy at the top, had an air gunner's equipment. This was stripped out and dual controls for an instructor were put in and we were given dual instruction by our flight commander to the extent that after two or three landings we could make a reasonable landing and we were sent solo in the Fairey Battle. So it continued for less than a month, this nondescript training, before our first Blenheims arrived. Before that we were introduced to formation flying in the Fairey Battles, and with the flight commander instructors in the back each pilot was given the instruction he needed for flying formations at a reasonable distance, flying in proximity to another aircraft and then in very close formation. But at this stage our Blenheims were delivered.

The Blenheim had already been flown by the flight commander. He'd flown a couple of take-offs, and in fact I soloed on a Blenheim after three periods of instruction with my flight commander. After that it was flying with a co-pilot who was a squadron pilot or flying with the flight commander on all sorts of exercises which might bring us up to operational standard on Blenheims.

This was the winter leading into spring 1940 and the Blenheim bombers had already gained a dubious reputation. However Keith rejoiced in this new aircraft.

Because we were fighters I suppose we had an impression that the Blenheim would behave more or less like a fighter. The Blenheim as a bomber we were very well aware of, but it was a delight for any pilot to fly. I think anything after a lumbering old Fairey Battle or Airspeed Oxford, seeing 180 or 200 on the clock made you feel it was really a service aircraft, but we did things, at least I did, which fighter pilots were not supposed to be able to do with their aircraft. When I'd been at FTS I'd looped an Airspeed Oxford, which wasn't part of the training but which a couple of other chaps and I did. When I was first pilot I said 'What about it?' and he said 'Yes, we'll do it,' so I looped the Oxford, and similarly when we got our Blenheims I was talking to a chap in the mess over a few beers one night and I said, 'Do you know what I did with an Oxford when I was at FTS?' and he said, 'We should be able to do it in a Blenheim as well.' So next day I found myself with this very chap, a New Zealander called Pat Horton, and we were doing an exercise and he said, 'Are you telling me you can loop one of these things? Let's see you try.' So we did; we looped the Blenheim which I don't suppose many other chaps in the squadron did. This was part of Blenheim flying when it was equipping a fighter squadron and not a bomber squadron. We did hear about the vulnerability of the Blenheim as a bomber and that it was hardly an aircraft to go to war in matched up against German fighters like Me109s and Me110s. At this stage after just one month on Blenheims it was a time when Spitfires were rolling off the production lines of the factories. They found that they needed the aircrew to fly the Spitfires that were then in production in such numbers that they must be given priority over such things as fighter Blenheims. So one morning the ATA arrived to fly our Blenheims away. They arrived flying in Spitfires and we were given the order to learn to fly these. So the Fairey Battle, having been a good conversion aircraft, we were all ready to get into our Spitfires the very next day. We were told to go and draw our pilot's notes – every aircraft has its pilot's notes which tell you every last thing you can and cannot do with the aircraft you are told to fly – swot up, and when we were done to report back to the flight commander down at dispersal. You would be taken by him, take a seat in a Spitfire, get strapped in, have your parachute and your Sutton harness strapped on, you'd be given a tour of the cockpit, told what to expect and what not to expect on your first solo and how the undercarriage had to be pumped up and down and the fact that you were going to swing on take-off in a certain way and if you didn't correct the swing you'd finish up in the hedge. Anyway, having taken all this on board, and being pilots with, I suppose, 160 hours experience behind us, we found going solo no trouble at all. It was just a thrill, that everybody who's ever flown a Spitfire expected it to be. After flying Blenheims you'd find speeds like 300 on the clock and this sort of thing; here was an aircraft that at the slightest touch would do what you asked it to do.

We liked flying our Blenheims, but then to be given the opportunity of flying Spitfires it was something else entirely, something beyond what we could have hoped for.

When we received our Spitfires they still weren't in dispersals round the airfield, they were lined up in nice straight lines in front of the hangar so when we were on our first solo we had no taxying to do. All we had to do was just open up the throttle, go off to the take-off point on the grass field and take off. It was only later we found that taxying the Spitfire, or even getting it back onto the flight line, was no easy job because of this huge expanse of the engine. The nose of the aircraft obscured at least forty-five degrees of your forward vision, so you had to be fishtailing backwards and forwards to judge your position from other aircraft and from the perimeters of the taxiways.

In May 1940 Keith was sent on a short air navigation course as a precursor to him becoming the squadron's navigation officer. While he was away the squadron moved from Leconfield to Church Fenton in North Yorkshire and then down to the recently opened RAF St Eval on the north Cornwall coast.

The squadron life at Leconfield, which was far removed from the war, was lived as a peacetime squadron. After about six hours of training on Spitfires at Leconfield our squadron was posted to St Eval in Cornwall, which was very much an operational station at which we found ourselves doing convoy patrols, escorting convoys up the Channel on their way to Southampton or the Port of London. These convoys were so often attacked by German raiders that we found ourselves introduced to engaging enemy aircraft, and on the ground being introduced to being bombed by German bombers, which we did suffer at St Eval. After, I would say, another four weeks on patrols when raids were reported approaching Plymouth, we were scrambled for those sort of engagements, there was no real action against the Luftwaffe in force until we were posted at the beginning of August to Middle Wallop in Hampshire as part of 10 Group. We were one of three squadrons which were defending the ports of Southampton and the airfields which the Luftwaffe could reach along the south coast. There was Tangmere and the Coastal Command airfields all taking considerable raids from the Luftwaffe during that August.

Perhaps the few weeks spent at St Eval were more of a gentle introduction to the coming combats in the south-east.

Was it a gentle approach? Yes, an introduction, not first of all being asked to meet the German raids in great numbers and all we were doing was engaging the lone raider off convoys, but it was nonetheless an introduction to being fired at by defending gunners from bombers. We knew what we were going to face, of course we didn't know at that time that we were going to be posted into the thick of it.

Keith's first shared success came against a German Ju88 attacking a convoy on 8 July 1940. This was the squadron's first victory.

My first sight of an enemy aircraft was a Ju88 with black crosses on it. In so far as I concerned it was just something that was attempting to bomb the ships in the convoy and we were going to shoot it down. And that's what we got on with doing.

There were three of us on patrol when the squadron got its first 88, and I was in on it when that first enemy aircraft was destroyed. I got the first shot at it. I didn't bring it down but my number two had his go and then in came the flight commander who had been furthest from it at the time we were manoeuvring onto it. Then we saw its propellers stop and it landed in the sea several thousand feet below.

It was all over in the course of about... I suppose from the first shot to the last was probably no more than two minutes long, and a very satisfying sight it was to see this enemy aircraft ditch in the sea, it being the first aircraft 234 had engaged.

The Battle of Britain began on 7 July but at St Eval we had already done several engagements against the Germans prior to 7 July and after that it was classed as the Battle of Britain at St Eval until we were posted to Middle Wallop when more squadrons were needed.

In these few weeks at St Eval Keith and the rest of the squadron were able to learn a lot about their aircraft and the best way to take on an enemy.

At this stage we were still teaching ourselves how to shoot and how to use our machine guns and the temptation was to open fire much sooner than one needed to. The temptation was to open fire at 400 yards, or even 500 yards, at which range the spread of fire from the machine guns was virtually ineffective. To make any great impression on the aircraft one needed to close right in to the closest, densest fire, which was set at 250 yards, and it was only then, with machine guns of only .303 calibre, that you were able to do a lot of damage to an enemy aircraft. This was all part of the learning process and I think in that first engagement it became obvious, very obvious to the flight commander first of all, and to the other two pilots, that this was what was needed. We did bring it down but I wouldn't say we were at the ideal range for making a great success of shooting down an enemy bomber.

The Spitfire was a wonderful aeroplane to fly, and to think that you had eight machine guns, but then when you found that you weren't at the right range your eight machine guns would put bullet holes in your enemy target rather than disable it or destroy it and bring it down. Although you might see pieces coming off it it needed a very high concentration of fire of .303 bullets to bring it down, whereas the Germans, the 109 pilots, had cannon which were much higher calibre than the .303s and they had machine guns also so they were much more heavily armed than a Spitfire, or the Hurricane. I think that's where they got a lot of their success with the Spitfires and Hurricanes which they brought down, their firepower being so good.

We did have tracer, but it also taught us – which we hadn't been given a great amount of practice at, or hadn't had any practice at – about deflection shooting. You didn't shoot at the aircraft, you shot at where the aircraft was going to be in two or three seconds. With the aircraft flying at 300mph this could be many yards in front of the aircraft, and this is where you had to fire so your enemy aircraft ran into your hail of fire, your cone of fire after you had pressed the firing button, but to many this had not been taught as a skill. I hadn't fired at an enemy aircraft. The only time I had fired my guns in the Spitfire was once at a ground target to give me experience of what the guns felt like as they fired, and the next time I fired the guns was at this particular enemy aircraft. I think there must have been many other pilots in Fighter Command who's first live firing of their machine guns were at enemy aircraft. In those early days there was no such thing as flying at drones for practice, this came later, but for those chaps who were the hunting, shooting, fishing types, who had been used to shooting grouse, duck or whatever, this became second nature to them and they were the chaps who did not need to teach themselves deflection shooting as did a lot of us just by force of having to learn the hard way.

The recoil of eight .303 Browning guns is very slight. There is a slight reduction in speed I suppose, but perhaps no more than one or two mph, but one feels that one is retarded by the recoil of the guns being shot. The aircraft reacts to this and then you regain your acceleration straight away.

The Spitfire Vs came in after the battle, they came in 1941, and the recoil from the two 20mm cannons and four machine guns was quite considerable. It was very noticeable that your guns were firing and you could realise what force there was when your ammunition left the aircraft.

Once you picked out your target you separated, your sections would separate from each other, and then the aircraft within your section separated and picked out their target. If you had been vectored onto the bombers particularly you'd go in and shoot until you have to pull away because you overtake, you've got overtaking speed. You get in as much firing at the target as you can and after that you pull up hoping to find some of your fellow squadron pilots, but as like as not you will be left alone with the sight of a few enemy aircraft and it's then that you've got to start to weave, not to fly straight and level but to be on the alert and take a complete lookout, looking for any remaining targets there might be and fighters that might still be hunting for whatever Hurricanes and Spitfires they could find. This is where we learned very fast how one needed to fly to disengage and return to base from an empty sky. As often as not you'd return by yourself as did all the others in ones or in pairs as we'd been split up by either dogfights or having gone through the bombers. We'd been broken up by individual engagements and then had to find our own way home. The squadron would take perhaps twenty minutes to arrive back and after twenty minutes those of us that were gathered together in the dispersal hut began to wonder why so and so wasn't back, or so and so still hasn't phoned. As often as not he'd baled out or had been shot down and force landed somewhere. The odd time he'd bought it but that's the way it was. The squadron would be gathered together, the spare aircraft would be put into the line, and we'd go back on readiness ready for the next scramble, the aircraft having been rearmed and refuelled.

It was a very slow learning process in that with each scramble and each engagement, and they were all different, you were becoming more accustomed and more experienced to what could happen, what you could do, what you must do and the fact that you had to be alert beyond the normal sense of being alert with all that was going on around you from every dimension.

One did have to be very much aware of this. Heightened awareness dispelled all other feelings of the danger there might be, although admittedly it does become a part of you which I suppose you develop, and have to develop, to escape the attentions of being bounced or being engaged by something you hadn't seen or had missed during a dogfight.

Yes there was a good deal of discussion after every scramble about what each pilot had managed to do, what he'd managed to shoot at, and I suppose we learned from talking with other pilots about the best ways of doing things, what were the ranges, the angles etc.

By this time most were able to throw the aircraft around and do what you needed to do with it. It was knowing your aircraft and what it was capable of that was one of the primary requirements of a good fighter pilot, knowing what the aeroplane would do and wouldn't do and when it was close to the stall and if you were doing high speed turns you could get into a high speed stall and learning to gauge just how much G-force you could put on in a tight turn. We could out-turn the Me109s and easily out-turn the Me110s but you needed to be able to do this to eventually either with a couple of turns get round and get him in your sights or if he tried to outclimb you or if you had to escape his guns. You had to be able to out-turn at the maximum tightness of turn, which was absolutely essential but it was very quickly learned. When you greyed out you learned you had to ease off on the stick a bit and for most pilots a rate of turn was easily able to turn inside the radius of a 109.

Once pilots had learned their business of manoeuvring their aircraft, it was then a partnership between squadron and ground control as to how an attack might be made.

It was really up to your controller, your ground controller, who was watching your squadron and where it was in relation to the raid he was vectoring you on to. First of all, if it's possible he gave you enough height to be above the German fighters or the bombers so he could vector you down onto them and put you up-sun first of all, but it depended on the fighter controller, and they varied greatly in skills, to manoeuvre their squadrons into the right positions. It was hardly ever for a head-on attack because the closing speeds of the two aircraft would be something like 700mph I suppose and the length of burst a fighter could get in at a closing speed of 700mph was pretty well ineffectual unless he happened to hit the pilot head-on. So the normal was for the fighter controller to bring the squadron abeam of the formation. He was bringing you in abeam of the formation he was going to attack so that you could quarter onto the enemy targets and gradually coming round onto the line astern position but with the possibility of being able to lay off deflection shooting and get a shot in before they reached that line astern position.

To help make an attack a successful one, the Air Ministry had developed a reflector gun sight before the war. Almost unbelievably, with British optical factories at full capacity in 1938, an order was placed with Austrian factory CP Goerz and drawings were sent to Vienna. Despite many sceptical critics, the complete order was delivered and there was no evidence that the Austrians passed information to the Luftwaffe.

The reflector gunsight was a great improvement on the old iron ring and bead sight of the old days which partially obscured the forward view of the pilot. In this case the gunsight was an electric or electronic one which was mounted below the cowling of the cockpit and projected a light onto the windscreen of the Hurricane or Spitfire which showed up as a red, or pink, ring and bead which acted exactly the same as the old fashioned ring and bead sight of the old days but in addition to that it was marked off so that the radius of the cross bars could be varied and, if you had them set at a certain distance, you knew that you were within 250 yards of the tail of an Me109 and that's of course the range you always hoped to be. If the target was far from filling that gap you were too far away and you shouldn't be firing, shouldn't be wasting your ammunition.

There were also upgrades for the old De Havilland two-pitch propellers.

Modifications were going onto the Spitfire during the course of the battle. The first Spitfires just had the coarse and fine pitch, coarse pitch for cruising and fine pitch for take-off and landing in case you had to go round again, but otherwise it was coarse with no variation and the only variation in power would be through the throttle lever. In August 1940, when we were at Middle Wallop, we got the very first modification which made so much difference to us. The big difference from the coarse pitch only to a variable pitch was that the Merlin immediately turned all of the power into an acceleration or climb that you needed and then all you had to do was set your revs at fighting revs and the propeller would change its pitch as was needed and there was no thought necessary from the pilot to gain absolutely maximum effect from all the power that was obtainable in your engine.

With variable pitch one could vary the pitch to whatever was needed. In the case of a close engagement with the enemy where you needed maximum response from the engine you set your revs at 2700. Cruising revs were something like 2000 by comparison and for climbing in formation you were perhaps at 2200 or 2300 which was a choice up to the pilot, but always once you were into action you went up to 2700 revs which gave you the optimum power from the engine. By another comparison the take-off revs were something like 3000, but for ideal fighting conditions it was 2700.

Between 24 June and 20 July 1940 all Spitfire squadrons were upgraded, a fantastic achievement by De Havilland's engineers. But there was more to come later in the war.

The later modification to that one of course, was the hydromatic airscrew which was the complete automation of throttle and optimum pitch so that if you were at a certain power, a certain number of pounds of boost, or inches of mercury, pounds of boost in our case, the engine would set itself at the best pitch to make the most of whatever boost you were putting into the engine, whatever power you were putting in through the throttle. This didn't come in until 1941 but I flew my first Spitfire with the hydromatic airscrew in Malta. Spitfires which relieved the Hurricanes were fitted with hydromatics and they were very superior to the performance we had got out of our Merlins when we were flying variable or even the old two-pitch.

On 13 August the squadron was sent from the Cornish coast to the sleepy Hampshire station at Middle Wallop. However, this put the squadron right in the heat of the battle.

At Middle Wallop, the very day we landed there, we were scrambled against a raid of probably forty or fifty plus with Me109 and Me110 escort. We flew what was in those days the accepted formation for flying into action, that was flying four vics of three in very close formation with no other lookout than the squadron leader who, when he sighted the aircraft, got us into position for attack, gave us the tallyho when we spread out, and it was each man find his own target and that turned out to be the way we flew during the battle which was, as it turned out to be, a very extravagant way (of flying into action).

Each morning the squadron was in the line. Readiness started at daybreak or at dawn. The first raids were never known to be that early so one flight would be detailed to go on readiness at dawn and they'd be at readiness with parachutes, to scramble within five minutes or whatever, and the rest of the squadron would then come down after taking an ordinary breakfast in the mess and join the flight that was already there which would then be relieved for their break and a new set of pilots would be written up on the readiness board. The CO would leave it to the flight commanders to choose those pilots he put down in each flight, six from each flight, A flight and B flight, and those would be the chaps who knew if there was a scramble they would be the next off. They'd have their parachutes all ready. In the case of Spitfires, they'd have their parachutes all ready in the cockpit so that when you scrambled you jumped into the cockpit, your rigger was there to hand you the straps and buckle you in and then likewise the straps of your Sutton harness and then each pilot put his own oxygen and RT chords into the sockets and, with the hood still open, signal to his fitter who was using the trolley ack – that was the 24-volt accumulator which started the engine of most Spitfires. When you gave him the thumbs up you started the engine, the engine fired up, and the trolley ack was disconnected.

Getting out of bed at that time and knowing there was always the possibility of having to get up and get stuck in within the hour was not the sort of thing you wanted to contend with at that early hour of the morning, but you very quickly got used to it and it was just part of life. You were there to do what you were asked to do and told to do, ordered to do. I don't know, with me, it just washed over me, I did what I had to get on with and what I was expected to do.

We were always met with squadron transport. We went round the billets of those chaps, we usually were with a WAAF driver in a pickup truck or, I won't call it a people carrier, a personnel carrier shall we call it, which would pick up the chaps from the flights that had been detailed to go on earlier and take them directly to the dispersal area which would be maybe one third round the aerodrome or two-thirds of the way round depending on where the squadron was sited. We had three squadrons to share our airfield, always three squadrons. We would find, in those days, the aircraft weren't dispersed in pens but were just lined up ready for action facing the way we would taxi off to the take-off point and the ground crew had already run the engines up. They were warm and they were rewarmed up every so often so that there was no coughing and spluttering from the engines when we were asked to scramble. Life was already very much a going thing. And then the NAAFI came round soon after that with cups of tea for those chaps who'd had to get up early and weren't perhaps in the best frame of mind at that early hour and usually were inside the dispersal hut at that time. It was only on the summer days when it got hotter that we spent our waiting time out of the flight hut. It was a matter of just settling down to wait either for a telephone call or the scramble instruction or just to whittle away the hours with games of cards, reading or dozing or whatever.

I liked getting up early in the morning at that age but some liked to lie in and were a bit loath to get out of bed. I wasn't that sort of chap and in any case I was a New Zealander, I was an outdoors chap if you like, and they didn't bother me. The dawn readiness lot, when it got towards nine o'clock were always on the lookout for the relief so they could get a decent breakfast.

We lived together, that first squadron, for nine-odd months. We knew each other's characteristics and we knew who we liked and who we didn't like and so on, and the chaps that we liked to have flying with us, next to us, or the chaps that were going to do better than others and the ones that would really get stuck in, and it became like a rugger team in a way. You knew all the individual strengths and weaknesses of all the chaps around you.

As squadron pilots we were immersed purely in the business of our own squadron or the squadrons who we saw being scrambled who were also on the same airfield with us. As to what was happening in the other parts of the group or the adjacent group was not passed on to us as pilots. Our sole concern was with what we had to do in our own squadron. Very rarely were we ever scrambled with other squadrons on the field. We found ourselves with another squadron perhaps when we reached the place where we were being asked to patrol. In the case of Middle Wallop nearly two-thirds of our flying was done in support of 11 Group. Our AOC was very supportive of the AOC of 11 Group, Sir Keith Park, and when he asked for squadrons he got them. When we got airborne the CO would call up, 'Crecy squadron airborne,' and we would get 'Crecy squadron, patrol Brooklands, angels 20' or 'Patrol Guildford, angels 20' or Tangmere or Kenley, and as soon as we got to angels 20 we would be vectored off by our own controller. This controller who was in 10 Group, his ops room was the same as the one in Bentley Priory that Dowding was looking at or the AOC of 11 Group was looking at and he took charge of the squadron from down near Bath somewhere although he was talking to us. We might have been over Surrey or Kent or anywhere and, because they were all ex-pilots, they already had some fighter squadron experience and they were pretty good most of them, but some of them were better than others, at putting you in the right position at the right height to escape the attentions of their 109s first of all and then to engage the bombers. Inevitably, being in Spitfires, if they could get the height, they had to take on the 109s. I am sure they all had in view first of all, whether Spitfires or Hurricanes, to get at the bombers.

Keith's view on leadership within a squadron varied depending on the quality of the individual commander.

We had one outstanding chap in 234 Squadron, but we had a non-flying CO to begin with. He just brought the squadron together, got it going as a flying unit, but he had seen service out in the Middle East and he was rather older than the rest of us and when we went into action he was unable to fly due to invalidity or whatever it was. We were left without a CO and we were left with two flight commanders. Pat Hughes was a flight lieutenant in the Australian Air Force who had been seconded to the RAF and was a flight commander, first at 64 Squadron and then in 234. He was a man who was outstanding in every way in his flying ability. He was a rugger player who'd played not only for Fighter Command but for the air force against other service teams and he was a chap that everybody looked up to. The A flight commander was an equally good chap but being my flight commander, and all of us being of the age of about twenty, we relied on the leadership of our flight commanders to begin with before we learned the ropes ourselves and so in that way it was very important. Pat Hughes was a very successful fighter pilot who in the course of the six weeks we were up at Middle Wallop had fifteen destroyed to his credit, and there were one or two others who were hotshots who had successes. Half way through Middle Wallop we had a squadron commander, O'Brien, who was posted to us from another squadron and who inevitably had seen quite a lot of action. Squadron Leader O'Brien then led the squadron. He had already been awarded the DFC, so there was a leader along with our own Pat Hughes who we were only too happy to fly into action with. At the end of the first week in September we were on a scramble over Kent when I was flying number two to my flight commander and we had gone into the back of a lot of DO17s. He was already firing, he'd picked out his target and I'd seen bits flying off the aircraft he was attacking. In that sort of close formation it's each man to his own target, so I'd picked out my target, and then after that had finished we were all spread out, split up all over the place, spread to the four winds, and we all made our way back eventually from this engagement to Middle Wallop and the two that didn't return...

Keith was a very emotional man and this emotion came out when he was talking about the loss of both O'Brien and Hughes. Keith had shared that first squadron success with Pat Hughes on 8 July. In just twenty-four days of intense combat Hughes' tally had reached fifteen. In the first week of September Hughes had flown twelve sorties, but the afternoon of 7 September saw the largest Luftwaffe raid yet. A force of some 900 enemy aircraft approached Britain and every RAF fighter was needed. Pat Hughes led his flight into a force of Dornier 17s. Various explanations have been used but it is not known exactly what happened. Keith saw him attack and bits fly off Hughes' target. Hughes may have collided, or been hit by debris. What is known is that his Spitfire crashed into a field west of Sevenoaks in Kent. He baled out but his parachute failed to open and he fell into a back garden. Joe O'Brien was also lost that day, shot down in combat with an Me109 over St Mary Cray a few miles north of Sevenoaks.

Keith was hard hit by the loss of these two close colleagues but he was given no time to think about it. Two days later the squadron was withdrawn to St Eval to rest after such a tough period but Keith was sent straight back to the front line.

Four of us didn't go back to Middle Wallop to re-form and retrain the new pilots. Four of us were posted on to operational squadrons. Two remained at Middle Wallop, one went to 609 and one to 238 on Hurricanes. Myself and Bill Bailey, a sergeant pilot, went to Hornchurch to join 603. We went straight into the thick of it there. I saw as much action, or even more action, in the three or four weeks I was with 603 Squadron as I saw at 234 in Middle Wallop. But what we found out later was that four pilots from each retiring squadron, each squadron being rested, were posted on, always as a part of a policy devised by Air Chief Marshall Dowding and Sir Keith Park so that the squadrons in the line were always topped up with experienced pilots and I just happened to be one of the four. I think the other chap who went to 609 was one of our Poles, Zurakowski, who later became a very famous test pilot. He had had a good deal of success at Middle Wallop, he was certainly very experienced, and so it was. We just fitted straight into 603. They were all a bunch of strangers to us but we soon got to know them, living in the mess with them cheek by jowl for those weeks, but it was not so far to have to fly before we were already where we needed to be. Hornchurch was right on the edge of London, right in the midst of 11 Group you might say.

We were doing exactly the same as when we were in support of 11 Group from Middle Wallop. It was a smaller airfield, it seemed more hemmed in. I was there when 54 Squadron got bombed on a scramble and Wing Commander Al Deere did a few cartwheels before he reached the far hedge but was picked out alive and was able to carry on. It was very much the same except there were quite a number of New Zealanders at the mess from those three squadrons and we began to feel a little bit more 'at home' as a group. We had a great CO there called George Denholm. He was a bit older than the rest of us, a bit like a father figure, but goodness he could fly and he could lead and he was held in the greatest regard by his pilots. We also had Peter Pease, James 'Black' Morton and George 'Sheep' Gilroy. I was only there for four weeks and was getting to know the characters as opposed to going into a complete new set of fifty-odd pilots living in the mess. It was a pretty crowded place.

Hornchurch was very close to London and it gave Keith the opportunity to get into the West End.

On off-duty time we were able to get into the West End being a half-hour tube ride from Hornchurch. During those nights we did go into London we were at the receiving end of the bombing, we could hear that going on, the anti-aircraft going, and in the mornings when we came home or even when we got into London after stand-down it was those people who were taking refuge in the tube stations. They were all there with their bedding and places lined up ready to spend a night in the underground shelters of the tube stations. It was the same in the morning going back to go on duty. You could see the terrible life that a lot of the civilians had to cope with. If they'd been either chosen to go into the shelters or forced into the shelters by lack of housing of their own or their own houses having been damaged, we were very close to what civilians were having to put up with. Everywhere of course there were fire wardens about and ARP personnel going about their jobs and duties.

On 8 October, one month after moving to 603 Squadron, Keith was posted again. This time he went to the newly formed 421 Flight, initially based at Gravesend.

It was for a different purpose entirely. It was said at the time, or shortly afterwards, that it was instigated by Dowding and Churchill as a blind for the fact that we had cracked the Enigma code and at the late stage in the Battle of Britain we were privy to the orders that were going out to the Luftwaffe overnight for the next day's raids. If we'd made absolutely full use of that they couldn't give the game away, so what they did was this 'Jim Crow' flight, as it was called. We were equipped with Hurricane IIs, the first aircraft to get high-speed blowers, and these were meant to be better than any Spitfire there had been so far. We were given these aircraft down at Gravesend and we very soon found that the job was to fly out over the enemy coast and to give a running commentary, a dicey business, on the raids that were coming in without being shot down yourself. It was a crazy business. We were all pilots who had been several months in the Battle of Britain squadrons and we were giving this running commentary. We knew that the Germans were monitoring all of our RT transmissions as we monitored theirs so they would think this was how the information was getting back or reinforcing the radar and the other intelligence they might have with the reports from the Jim Crow squadron. We found that the Hurricanes were no good after a while. Paddy Green, who was our CO, he was flight commander. He was a skier of great repute who was a pre-war pilot and I think from a University Air Squadron. He marched up to the Air Ministry as he knew a few people up there, thumped the desk and said these Hurricanes are no good, we want Spitfires back. We were allotted half the Spitfires that belonged to 66 Squadron which was at Gravesend and we used the same squadron letters, LZ, as 66 Squadron and that's where we got to know 66 Squadron and their various characters. But then we went a bit closer to the coast. We went down to West Malling; that got waterlogged so we went to Biggin Hill; and finally Hawkinge was reopened after having been closed due to enemy action. We operated from Hawkinge on what was called this Jim Crow. It was really a reconnaissance, looking for pilots that had been brought down in the water in the straits of Dover, or the North Sea, off the coast of Belgium and so on. We were doing weather flights and that sort of thing when the weather wasn't good enough for the Germans to mount raids. By that time, this was October and November, the weather was getting so autumn-like that the Germans, although the raids went on and on they got less and less and fewer and fewer because of the deteriorating weather, the autumnal weather arrived and they couldn't mount the assaults.

Keith felt, as did a number of the pilots, that they were almost sacrificial lambs.

Well we were in a way. Ask Billy Drake. He got shot down. Billy Drake, as you know, he got shot down over there but he had enough height to get himself back without an engine to Hawkinge in one piece in a Spitfire that had no engine. That was a case in point of course, but that side of 421's duties were a bit hair-raising, but 421 remained in being. I was shot down at the end of November in 421 but I rejoined them when they had become 91 Squadron one year later and they were still doing the same duties except that they were doing lots of one-man or two-man rhubarbs and that sort of thing over France. They were going in pairs, not working as a wing or anything, but absolutely as an individual squadron doing reconnaissance over the airfields of France where they were sending up the sweeps, the 109s which were engaged in the sweeps at that time.

Keith had led a charmed life during the Battle of Britain but even he could not avoid enemy guns forever. On 23 November he attacked and damaged an Me110. Three days later he went off on a weather reconnaissance on his own.

One chap was detailed on the flight every day to get airborne between first light and sunrise, which was recognised as being before the sun got over the horizon, get airborne before that, before sunrise, and report on the weather between North Foreland and Dungeness, that's where most of the raids came in, and to report back to the Met office after you were down to tell them what the cloud conditions were. On this particular morning I got off pretty well on time.

Ten or fifteen minutes into the flight I'd reached North Foreland and by that time reached 8,000 feet on a pretty cloudy day – the cloud was in broken layers – and turned south-west to go down to Dungeness. I'd just reached Deal and there had been no warning in the headphones of any enemy activity. Nothing from the controller that there was anything amiss, and I saw, very suddenly as I was keeping a reasonable lookout, I saw down on my ten o'clock side three aircraft, three that were obviously 109s, pass underneath me and were heading out towards the channel, towards the straits of Dover. This was just about off Deal, and having height on them, and realising what they were, all I had to do was stuff the nose down and get after them, not remembering, or knowing, these chaps always operated in fours. That was the unit: two pairs but used as a four. They must have seen when I was stooging down back towards the south-west and I think one of them must have said to his mates, 'Leave this chap to me,' and he must have slid out from the formation, come in behind me, they went under and he came in behind me, and the next thing I knew was that I had lost a wing. There I was one minute shooting, I had the button pressed for a nice good long burst about three or four seconds, and the next thing there I was in mid-air and all I could see of the aircraft was a wing fluttering down as if it was a leaf. I was in stockinged feet, having been in flying boots, falling through the air, wings off, and obviously the first thing you think of is, 'Well crikey, if I'm falling to the ground I'd better get my parachute open.' So off I start with the procedure of opening the parachute and I go to pull it with my right hand. The D ring was always on the left and one always used the right hand to pull it, it's easy to grab and easy to find. The right hand and arm was useless, wouldn't work. Lifted it up and it still didn't work, so I had to scrabble around with my left hand, got it open, and by that time I was down to, I suppose, 4,000 feet and just about over the coast. I'd seen them when they were perhaps a mile or two inland, perhaps less than that, and as I went down I could see the coast drifting further and further away. I finished up, as I landed in the sea, about a mile offshore and then the problems began. I had to get rid of the parachute, shrouds seemed to be everywhere, but I finally got rid of them. Wind got into the parachute and carried it away and then I had to blow up the Mae West to keep myself above water, no CO_2 bottles in those days or compressed air bottles. I was blowing and blowing but nothing was happening and realised the bladder of the Mae West was split. What buoyancy I did get came from kapok pads inside, built into the Mae West, and there was I with one hand trying to keep myself above water, I didn't know it at that time but my right leg was broken in pieces, the calf of the left leg was hanging off and all I had was the one good hand that had opened the parachute, and there was me taking on water.

Suddenly a big hulk appears next to me and then over the side comes a hand which I gripped and I'm lifted on deck to what I thought was a trawler but it was a lifeboat which had happened to be out there on a patrol before dawn. This was just as the sun was rising, this happened at eight thirty in the morning which at that time of year was sunrise, and got lifted on by this brawny sailor who was an RNR man. Lifeboats were then manned by the Royal Naval Reserve, and they were all servicemen. They got me on board and plied me with a drink, but they could see I was in such a state with the two legs and only one arm I couldn't do much for myself, so they set sail for Ramsgate and unloaded me into an ambulance. I was taken to

Ramsgate hospital in a pretty sorry state, mostly getting over the effects of being nearly drowned and with the injuries I had just staying alive.

There again another coincidence. On that particular morning I hadn't allowed myself quite enough time to get airborne as I should have done at first light. I was in a bit of a panic, I suppose, to get airborne, grabbed the first Mae West I could see and put it on. It so happened that at this time our Mae Wests were being modified, having fluorescein dye bags sewn into them so if a pilot landed in the sea he could be found from the fluorescing sea patch. It so happened I picked up a Mae West with the dye in it and after I'd landed in the sea, and before I was picked up by the crew of the lifeboat, they saw the parachute of course, went to the parachute and no bod, and then they spotted the fluorescein dye patch fifty yards away, came straight to me and picked me out. So it was I escaped that day, goodness knows how. To be ejected from an aircraft when you're strapped in with Sutton harness, radio communication chord, oxygen tube, hood closed, canopy closed. Somebody's got to be with you to allow you to survive that. And then the coincidence was that I had the fluorescein dye and the fact that I landed at that hour of the morning next to a boat on a search.

One fact at a time, Keith later managed to piece together what had happened to him.

Well, afterwards, miles after the event of course, I wanted to find out about where my crashing aircraft landed and whether it did any damage to other property, or more seriously to people on the ground, and so I started delving into it. I found that the aviation archaeologists had discovered where my plane landed and that was in boggy ground of a farmyard in a village called Finglesham, close to Deal, and they started their excavations but concluded eventually that the actual spot where the engine was buried was now under concrete. Of course for my own part, the curiosity went on to know how I came to be in that predicament and so I thought well I'll get in touch with a chap who knows about German claims. There was a chap later on, a few decades after the war, who was putting claims and losses together, and sure enough up came a name called Balss, who said he got together with a German called Ring, who'd somehow collared all the German archives on this particular subject and between the two of them they made a lot of hay out of this but he said he asked Ring what the German claims were at that time of the morning on the date I was shot down. He said, 'Ah yes, there was only one claim that morning because there was no activity that morning. The only activity was the German weather *Schwarm* that was sent out daily on a recce of Kent and back to the airfields of France. On that morning a chap called Gustav 'Micky' Sprick claimed one Spitfire at about that time and it was he, and I was the only loss for that morning for the whole of the south-east because the weather was so bad and got worse after I had landed in the sea. It was cast iron. I was shot down by a chap who had twenty-eight victories and so he was in a senior position to say to his mates 'I've seen something. Leave it to me.' Afterwards I met a German who was in the same JG26 who was Sprick's flight commander who himself had collided with one of his own Me109 pilots over Britain and was a prisoner of war. After the war he got back into the records business again and I got put in touch with him and I corresponded with him for a while. Chaps in JG26 sent me photographs of this Sprick in his finery, his oak leaves and all that stuff but anyway poor old 'Micky' Sprick survived into the spring of 1941 and on the sweeps he got himself shot down and killed after he'd got thirty-two victories and he was thought, from what claims can make of it, to have been shot down by Sailor Malan, the South African of great repute.

Keith recovered and convalesced for more than a year before he was fit enough to rejoin 421 Flight, or 91 Squadron as it was now called. Early in 1942 he was posted to Malta where he initially flew as a flight commander, and later commanded, in 185 Squadron. Those few months in Malta were even more intense than those of the Battle of Britain and Keith found it very hard to even mention his time there. He was awarded the DFC for his service in Malta. Returning in the Autumn of 1942 Keith undertook various training and liaison roles until he returned to the front line in February 1945, joining 124 Squadron flying Spitfire IXs on bomber escort operations as well as ground attack sorties, many against V2 launching sites. By the end of the war he had completed three tours of operations.

Keith stayed with the squadron, converting to jets, flying Meteors until he returned to New Zealand in March 1946. He was an air traffic controller for the RNZAF before going back to the UK and eventually settling in Exeter.

Flight Lieutenant William Walker AE
24 August 1913-21 October 2012

William Walker was born in Hampstead, North London, and, after education at Brighton College, at the age of 18 he joined his father in the brewery trade. By 1933 he had moved to the Midlands centre of brewing, Burton upon Trent, and joined Ind Coope, a company he would rejoin after the war. However, like so many other young men in the 1930s William wanted to fly.

My first ever flight was at Croydon aerodrome when I was going past with a friend and saw a large notice up advertising flights for five shillings. We both went and had a flight and that was in 1933. I wanted to learn to fly after that but couldn't afford it until 1938 when I saw an advertisement in the local *Oxford Mail* where I happened to be working at the time. They were asking for volunteers to join the RAF Volunteer Reserve and so I joined on 1 September 1938. In those days you were supposed to be under 25 but in fact I was over 25 when I joined. Fortunately they accepted my application just before my birthday in August. I think they would have taken me anyway because at Kidlington they only had thirteen pilots when I joined and I was pilot number thirteen.

To an extent everybody was joining something, and having joined on 1 September 1938, on September 29 it was the day Chamberlain flew back waving his piece of paper saying it was going to be peace in our time, I thought perhaps my joining up had been a bit premature, but it didn't worry me because it was such fun learning to fly.

In September 1939 I was living in Romford and I remember hearing Chamberlain's announcement saying that he'd received no response to his appeal to Hitler and consequently this country was at war and I went outside and the people in my flats were building an air raid shelter. I said, 'Can I give you a hand?' They said, 'Oh no, you're in uniform.' One amusing incident was having been called up I was then sent home again to await further instructions and was walking down St James's Street in my brand new sergeant's uniform and two soldiers saluted me. I thought this was bizarre so I said, 'Why did you salute me?' and they said, 'We were told to salute anything in a collar and tie.' And that's how the war started. Everybody straight from civvy street knowing absolutely nothing.

On 15 November 1939 William was posted to 1 Initial Training Wing based around the colleges at Cambridge University. Three months later, on 17 February 1940, he went for officer training to 2 Service Flying Training School (SFTS) at Brize Norton.

I wanted to fly Spitfires and I was very lucky actually. I joined course number forty-five at Brize Norton and half went on bombers and half went on fighters. I asked for fighters thinking I'd be turned down because of my age, because by this time I was 26, but fortunately I got fighters and trained on Harvards. Having trained on Harvards and got my wings I was posted straight to a squadron. You had to learn the job while flying with other pilots. Later in the war you would have gone to an OTU, an Operational Training Unit, so that when you arrived at the squadron you were fully operational to join the other pilots. In my case I just picked it up as best I could.

William was posted to 616 Squadron at RAF Leconfield, about three miles from the Yorkshire town of Beverley. The squadron's role was defending Britain's northern industrial cities from Luftwaffe attack.

When I arrived at the squadron from flying school I was taken in to see the commanding officer (Squadron Leader Marcus Robinson) who asked me what I'd been flying. I said I'd flown a Magister, a Tiger Moth and a Harvard. So he said, 'Well I'm sorry I can't let you take up a Spitfire until you've flown some other operational plane.' The only thing they had on the aerodrome was a very old Fairey Battle bomber which was about three times the size of a Spitfire, very slow, and I had to do two circuits and landings in this enormous great single engined bomber before I was allowed to take up a Spitfire. Then I was entrusted with a Mk.1, which was the only Spitfire in which you had to pump the undercarriage up, and as everybody took off on their first flight, as soon as you were airborne you had to start pumping, and the tendency was to hold the stick and pump at the same time and you did this sort of zigzag take-off. It was a great thrill to be in a Mk.1. Anyway, I accomplished my first solo alright and then I was mostly entrusted with that Mk.1 whereas the squadron was being equipped mostly with Mk.IIs, but as an indication of how the country was armed with planes, my own squadron had only received Spitfires a month before I joined them in June.

As with so many fighter pilots at that time, William's main focus was on the squadron, the day to day routine, and in particular the characters who flew with him. At the beginning of the Battle of Britain, Fighter Command's squadrons were full of new, inexperienced pilots. Many would lose their lives in the coming months, but many would forge legends.

Hugh Dundas was in my flight. 'Cocky' Dundas was a great friend. He was a great chap. He was shot down the same time as I was and he never, rather like myself, never saw the enemy. Never knew what shot him down. That was the experience of so many of us.

Dundas would go on to fly with Douglas Bader's Tangmere Wing during 1941 and ended the war as a group captain with two DSOs and a DFC, having commanded a wing of five Spitfire squadrons in Malta and Italy until the end of the war. After retirement from the RAF he joined the world of television eventually becoming chairman of Thames TV. As chairman of British Electric Traction, Dundas received a knighthood in 1987. He died in 1995.

Teddy St Aubyn was a great friend. Teddy's story was interesting because he had been in the Guards and he married the daughter of a notorious night club Queen who kept the Spider's Web on the Watford bypass and because he had somebody who was the daughter of a notorious night club queen he had to resign his commission in the Guards so he joined the Auxiliary Air Force. He was great fun to be with.

Teddy St Aubyn's Spitfire crash landed after sustaining damage from an Me109 flown by Oberleutnant 'Pips' Priller of JG51. On recovery from his burns he joined 170 Squadron as squadron leader but his Mustang crashed into the sea on 27 May 1943 and he was never recovered.

Sergeant Ridley – I was very close to him because we did so many convoy patrols together. I felt his loss enormously. It was rather sad. It must be about ten years ago I had a letter from a chap asking whether I could give any information about his uncle, Sergeant Marmaduke Ridley. He said he had been onto his school and he'd been onto the RAF Museum and nobody could tell him anything at all. Fortunately I had taken a wonderful photograph of him up at Leconfield and because we had flown together there were several mentions of him in my logbook, and I gave him some background information which was all the information I had and he was so grateful to have this information, but what made it so desperately sad was here was a young chap who had given his life for his country yet nobody knew anything about him at all. I was the only person who could produce just a little information. Now he's just a name on a memorial wall on the Embankment and down at Capel Le Ferne. He's just a name but to me he was a very close friend and I missed him greatly.

The good fellowship between pilots in the squadron was something that was absolutely unique. Any one of us would have done anything for anybody else. They were probably the closest knit company of people I will ever find in all my life. It was the feeling between pilots that was something very special and something very precious.

William's regard was also heaped on the ground crews.

They were a remarkable lot really. They were completely dedicated to what they did. Their plane was most important, the one they looked after, and it must have been an awful shock when their plane didn't come back.

William had vivid memories of many aspects of the daily routine of a fighter pilot in 1940.

During the whole time one was at readiness you were tired. You were taken off readiness at about half past nine or ten at night and then you went to the mess and you had a beer or two in the mess and then it was bed so that you didn't probably get to bed until half past ten or eleven and at half past three you were woken up again. The one thing you remembered was you were always tired during those days. You were living for the moment. You sort of nodded off sitting in a chair. You never really went to sleep. That is the feeling of that time that is remembered more than anything else and everyone was the same. They always felt tired.

We used to practise dogfights. Two were killed while I was there and on both occasions I was flying with them. On one we were night flying in Spitfires which was the most hazardous thing I ever did. It was a terrifying experience, we were in complete blackout, no horizon whatsoever, the exhaust red hot and you spent all your time looking at instruments to keep the right way up. I was flying with one chap at night in our Spitfires and for some extraordinary reason he dived straight into the ground and was killed. They never knew why or how he did it, but on another occasion I was practice-dogfighting with a chap during the day and for some reason he did the same thing, simply crashed straight into the ground and was killed. Extraordinary. I had one very narrow escape when I was training. We used to take each other up in Harvards and I was a passenger with a chap called Woods. He was shooting up the house of a girlfriend, diving down and pulling out, and I was terrified as the passenger in the back. Anyway I survived, but the next day he was doing precisely the same thing with another pilot when he pulled out too quickly, the plane stalled and they both were killed. It could have been me the day before. About a year later I was given a night vision test which I failed. I had two crashes at night in Spitfires up at Leconfield.

I had only done about five hours on Spitfires and we were doing various exercises. We were on what my logbook said was a 'battle climb', which simply meant we climbed up to about 15,000 or 20,000 feet and then we would come down again. But while we were up there, at 15,000 feet, we received a message on the radio to say there was a bandit in the area. There was myself, another trainee and one operational pilot, and we were vectored onto this Hun. I had never been shown how to fire a gun and been told nothing about the gunsight and I was flying a Mark 1 with the other two in Mark IIs which were faster. We all haired off and I was left a long way behind. When I arrived at what turned out to be a Dornier, I realised that I'd never fired the guns so I thought I had better turn the switch to fire and closed in on the Dornier. I pressed the gun button and tracer bullets seemed to be flying all over the place, all hitting the Dornier, which caught fire and crashed in the North Sea and I watched it go down. If you could imagine one's feelings having done five hours on Spitfires I'd got my first Hun. The other two pilots, they were never seen when I was there. Anyway I went back and landed, and was being debriefed by the intelligence officer, and I'd just got to the bit where it caught fire, and the flight sergeant came in and said, 'Excuse me Sir, did you know your guns weren't loaded?' and of course apparently what had happened, they were using the plane for camera gun practice and hadn't rearmed it and the tracer bullets I saw was the German in fact firing at me but fortunately he didn't hit. I've dined out on that story many times. Because I'd been in action I was declared to be operational which was ridiculous really. I remember feeling a sort of nervousness. I remember my legs feeling slightly shaky as I was approaching the Germans. It was a feeling I'd never had before but my legs just felt weak, and once I saw the enemy I forgot all about it, but that short period catching up with the Dornier is remembered as an unusual experience.

William never did find out which of the other pilots had actually shot down the Dornier but the experience had provided him with his first taste of action.

After the first encounter I didn't have the feeling again, largely because I think you were so busy attending to what you had to do, fly the plane, looking around as best you could to see if there were any other planes in the area. The extraordinary thing was that when I was shot down I baled out. The sky had been full of planes, but during the whole time – it must have taken something like twenty minutes to actually land in the sea – I didn't see a single plane of any sort in the air at all.

We were at readiness every day waiting for something to happen. We did an enormous amount of convoy patrols. I spent hours flying around but mostly we practised and flew, waiting for the big raid that came on Goering's Eagle day.

FLIGHT LIEUTENANT WILLIAM WALKER AE

On 15 August the squadron was scrambled to intercept a large Luftwaffe raid from Norway and Denmark nearing the Yorkshire coast.

The squadron was mad keen to have a fight. The big raid came when we were all having lunch in the mess and suddenly the tannoy went absolutely mad: '616 Squadron scramble, 616 Squadron scramble!' We all dashed out from lunch, grabbed whatever transport we could get hold of and all took off in all sorts of directions, more or less formed up once we'd got airborne and we were vectored onto an enormous raid of about sixty or seventy German bombers, mostly Junkers. I had never seen so many aircraft in the air before. There were so many and, better still, they were unescorted because they'd come from Norway and the fighter escort had to turn back when they reached the British shores otherwise they wouldn't have enough fuel to get home, so they were completely unescorted, flying in very close formation and even I couldn't miss them. I managed to shoot at three in the short space of time before my ammo ran out. The only real damage they did was that they bombed Driffield and they hit a petrol dump which caused a blaze of fire, but the Whitley bombers were still able to operate that night so really it was a dead loss, but the important thing was that this was Goering's Eagle day and he was concentrating on the southern airfields and the south of England so he didn't expect to see any Spitfires. He thought they were all down south and didn't expect to see any Spitfires at all in the north. The extraordinary thing is there was never another raid on the north from Norway. It was enormous exhilaration. We were absolutely thrilled and we did rather well.

Just four days after this, on 19 August, the squadron was posted south to its new home at Kenley just south of Croydon in Surrey. Now they were right in the middle of the hottest period of the Battle of Britain.

Oh we were absolutely thrilled. I remember we had a terrific party in the mess before we left. We were drinking pints of Pimm's. We moved down south in August and things were very different to Leconfield. More than anything else, after the light area mess of Leconfield, Kenley really was the most dreary, dull, blacked-out place you ever saw. Some years later I was a guest at Kenley when they unveiled a memorial to all squadrons that had served there and it was precisely fifty years to the day they unveiled the memorial and it coincided with the day 616 Squadron landed at Kenley.

Being closer to the action meant that 616 Squadron was in the centre of the whole home defence network. Squadrons were scrambled and intercepts were made but still most of the pilots never knew how the information was gained.

The extraordinary thing is that radar is a complete mystery to me. All I knew was that we were controlled by the control centre who had a complete picture of all the planes that were flying. I didn't visit the control room at all until after the Battle of Britain; all I knew was that we were controlled. We received the messages on the radio as to where we had to go and the height we had to fly and we were vectored onto the area as required. What I didn't know, what I learned afterwards of course, was that Dowding started installing these radio stations all over the country and I certainly hadn't a clue as to what was involved and how farsighted it was to install these centres all over the South East in particular and all over England.

Every day the pilots would gather at dispersal waiting for the call to arms.

In those days we used to be called at three thirty in the morning, breakfast at four when you really don't feel like having breakfast, and then it was down to dispersal, and if you were still there at eight o'clock the second breakfast arrived. That was the breakfast I really enjoyed, in the open air, mostly in sunshine, eggs, bacon, sausages, mushrooms, coffee, everything.

It was a funny sort of time. You just sort of fooled around. I think we had a football we mucked around with. We looked forward to second breakfast and the tea when the NAAFI arrived. You were sitting there really dreading the telephone ringing. Sometimes it was just to tell you that the NAAFI had arrived, but more often than not it was a scramble.

We were at readiness each day and I survived until 26 August when yellow section was scrambled to patrol Dover–Dungeness at 'angels twenty', just three of us: myself, Teddy St. Aubyn who was leading us, and Sergeant Ridley. We hadn't been patrolling for very long when we were absolutely bounced by a whole squadron of 109s. As soon as you tried to turn to one there were about two on your tail. Teddy St. Aubyn was terribly badly burned but he survived although he would return to flying and was killed later in the war. Sergeant Ridley was killed and I got a bullet in my leg and my plane was shot to pieces. It wouldn't work. The propeller stopped turning and the only thing that saved me was that the bullet came underneath the armour plating at the back, came below the armour plating and went in through my ankle. I had to bale out. The only thing we did once while we were training was we had to pull our ripcords and open the parachute, and then it was stretched out on an enormous great table and we had to try and put it together again, but we never had a practice jump. I opened the hood and tried to jump, but I was still plugged into the radio so when I jumped it sort of pulled me back. I took my helmet off and then fell out. I wasn't taking any chances, I pulled the cord straight away, even at 20,000 feet, and it took ages and ages and ages to come down. I hadn't a clue where I was because it was ten tenths cloud and it was eventually, when I got through the clouds, that I realised I was over the sea, so I blew my Mae West up, and I thought I had better take my flying boots off as I was getting nearer the sea and so I reached down and took them off and dropped them in the sea – but it took ages and ages to land. I couldn't have realised how high I still was.

Anyway, I landed in the sea, and some distance away I could see the wreck of a ship sticking out of the water so I managed to swim to it. I reached it and climbed on but I kept falling off because the ship was at such an acute angle. After I'd been in the sea for about an hour or so a fishing boat came alongside and took me on and we set off. They gave me an enormous great mug of half tea and half whiskey and I can't tell you what it did to my tummy because I was suffering from hypothermia and when we got to within about a mile of the shore an RAF launch came out and I was transferred to that and set off for Ramsgate. Meanwhile, luckily, there was a loo on board to which I retired in absolute agony because you can imagine what the hot whiskey had done to my tummy. We eventually arrived at Ramsgate harbour and an airman kept knocking on the doors asking me if I was alright. I said 'yeeeesssss'. But I was eventually able to leave the loo and was carried up the steps of Ramsgate harbour. Meanwhile a crowd had collected and they all cheered and I really felt as if I was a hero. A dear old woman came forward and gave me a packet of cigarettes as I was landed into the ambulance and taken to Ramsgate, which would be very valuable.

They looked at my wound and saw it was way beyond anything they could do down there in view of the damage that had been done to the hospital and so I was put to bed under a lot of naked light bulbs and it took something like twelve hours before I began to feel any feeling at all in my body, but eventually I recovered and I was put to bed. The next day we set off about eight o'clock in the morning for Halton hospital, which is in Buckinghamshire, quite a long way, but first of all we had to pick up a shell shock case and then we set off, but the driver didn't know the way which wasn't helped by the fact that all the signposts had been taken down. Luckily I knew the area fairly well because when I was working at Romford I used to travel round that part of the world so I was able to direct him by leaning out and looking through the window and got to Kenley because I had to pick up my clothes. Having lost my boots all I had on was simply my trousers, shirt and Mae West so I collected my clothes and said to the driver, 'Go down to dispersal as I'd like to say goodbye to my chums.' When I went down, there was nobody there. The squadron had lost ten pilots in ten days, five killed, five wounded. We then set off again for Halton but that was a bit of a problem because of trying to find a street that was free from bomb damage or hidden bombs. Anyway I managed to direct him through and we were able to get out of London. We dropped the shell shock case off and we set off for Halton. I had still had nothing to eat since my second breakfast the day before and as we were going through Kings Langley I said to the driver I said stop at the next pub and get me a couple of pints of beer, which he did, and I gave him the money and said get one for yourself. I drank the beer and felt quite light headed when I got to Halton. The night nurse managed to produce some scrambled eggs which was rather a strange dish as they had been scrambled the day before and I was put to bed with painkillers and sleeping pills. The next morning I was awakened and the doctors were going round and looking at all the patients and nobody came near me. I was getting terribly worried. I had heard about gangrene in the First World War and so on and it was about midday when the head doctor, a group captain, came to my bed and said, 'Who are you?' I said, 'Walker Sir,' and he said, 'Why are you here?' I said, 'Well I've been wounded in my leg,' and he said, 'Oh yes, who's looking after you?' and I said, 'I haven't seen a doctor since I arrived last night,' and apparently what had happened was I'd arrived too late at night to be booked in, and he was absolutely furious, he blew up, he tore everybody off a strip and within literally ten minutes I was in the operating theatre.

When I came to after the operation, Squadron Leader Pocock, the doctor, was sitting by my bed and said as I came to, 'I think you'd like to have this. This is the bullet we got out of your leg. You won't believe it but as we prised your ankle open to get the bullet out it shot out and hit the ceiling of the operating theatre.' And I still have it as a cherished memento. The whole thing is completely vivid. I remember every second of it. It was a momentous moment. Certainly not something I could ever begin to forget.

After I had driven through London in the ambulance, obviously I saw a considerable amount of damage had been done to London and some of the suburbs too, but once we were out at Kenley there really wasn't. I can't remember an occasion when I saw any further damage. What I do remember was when I was in hospital at Halton was looking out of the hospital windows at night and seeing the whole of London as one big red fire covering enormous acres of London. There was this enormous great glowing fire.

FLIGHT LIEUTENANT WILLIAM WALKER AE

William took six months to recover from his wounds and it was 1941 before he could fly again. This time he was posted to an aircraft ferry unit, delivering new aircraft to squadrons round the country. Later he was posted to 116 Squadron which was an anti-aircraft calibration unit, this time flying both Spitfires and Hurricanes.

In 1945 William was demobilised and returned to civilian life. He rejoined Ind Coope in Burton upon Trent and rose to become the company chairman. However, William never lost his interest in the RAF and seldom lost an opportunity to promote its history.

I think the legend has grown since the war. I don't think at the time any of us realised that the Battle of Britain would be remembered in quite such a way. One considered oneself as just lucky to have joined Fighter Command. I had the greatest admiration for the 'Bomber Boys'. I think they deserve far more credit than they've been given and certainly more than the fighter boys. The idea of setting off on a flight to Berlin in a Lancaster, one pilot, because there was only one pilot, there was no dual control in a Lancaster, the long journey there for hours on end and arriving over Berlin having fought off enemy fighters on the way, arrive at Berlin to be shot by artillery and fighter aircraft and then drop your bombs and fly all the way home on a trip that lasted sometimes ten hours? That is bravery. Fighter pilots were up and down so quickly that you didn't have time to think. The longest time we spent in a Spitfire was in convoy patrols. We could just stay up for two hours on light mixture but normally we were never up for longer than an hour.

Remaining fit, William frequently travelled to the United States to talk to veterans' organisations, spreading the word and latterly reading his poetry which was based on his wartime adventures and experience.

William was a huge supporter of the Battle of Britain Memorial which is sited on the White Cliffs at Capel-le-Ferne. At the memorial is a wall listing all the names of those who flew during the battle. William wrote a poignant poem entitled Our Wall *which is now available, along with his other poetry, in an anthology published by, and available from, the Trust.*

Index

INDEX

RAF Stations

INDEX